# THE LIMITS OF SAFETY

PRINCETON STUDIES IN
INTERNATIONAL HISTORY AND POLITICS

Series Editors
John Lewis Gaddis
Jack L. Snyder
Richard H. Ullman

---

# THE LIMITS OF SAFETY

## ORGANIZATIONS, ACCIDENTS, AND NUCLEAR WEAPONS

*Scott D. Sagan*

PRINCETON UNIVERSITY PRESS    PRINCETON, NEW JERSEY

Copyright © 1993 by Princeton University Press
Published by Princeton University Press, 41 William Street,
Princeton, New Jersey 08540
In the United Kingdom: Princeton University Press, Chichester,
West Sussex
All Rights Reserved

Library of Congress Cataloging-in-Publication Data
Sagan, Scott Douglas.
The limits of safety : organizations, accidents, and nuclear
weapons / Scott D. Sagan.
p.    cm. — (Princeton studies in international history and
politics)
Includes index.
ISBN 0-691-03221-1
1. Nuclear weapons—United States—Safety measures.   2. Nuclear
weapons—United States—Accidents.   I. Title.   II. Series.
U264.3.S24   1993
363.17′9—dc20      93-12196   CIP

This book has been composed in Linotron Sabon

Princeton University Press books are printed on acid-free paper and
meet the guidelines for permanence and durability of the
Committee on Production Guidelines for Book Longevity of the
Council on Library Resources

Printed in the United States of America

1 3 5 7 9 10 8 6 4 2

_____ **For My Parents** _____

JOHN SAGAN AND MARGARET PICKETT SAGAN

Although observers of warfare have often noted the confusions of battle, the ideology of military decision-making emphasizes the imposition of order through organization and command and the importance of clarity, coherence and comprehensiveness. As a result, examining ambiguity in military decision-making is a little like examining the sexual habits of Victorian England. It requires a willingness to accept the possibility that things may not be exactly what they appear to be, or are supposed to be.

(James G. March and Roger Weissinger-Baylon
*Ambiguity and Command*, 1986)

# Contents

## Figures and Tables

### FIGURES

### TABLES

# Acknowledgments

AMONG the great joys of finishing a book is the pleasure of thanking those who made it possible. This project has taken more years than I originally anticipated. I have therefore been lucky to receive more than my fair share of assistance, advice, and encouragement along the way.

Financial support for the project was provided by the Carnegie Corporation of New York and the John D. and Catherine T. MacArthur Foundation. Frederic Mosher and David Hamburg of the Carnegie Corporation deserve special thanks for providing me with a discretionary grant, which enabled me to take time away from my teaching responsibilities to complete the first draft of the manuscript. The book would have taken much longer to complete without such generous support.

My research would not have been possible without good access to primary sources of information on the history of nuclear weapons safety. Archivists everywhere seem to be burdened with too much work and too little support; but many somehow overcome the difficulties to provide exemplary professional assistance to researchers. I especially want to thank George Culley at the Air Force Historical Research Center, Suzanne Forbes at the John F. Kennedy Library, David Humphrey at the Lyndon B. Johnson Library, and Edward Reese at the National Archives.

The book would also have been considerably less interesting without the willingness of so many retired U.S. military officers and government officials to be interviewed. Most of these individuals permitted me to identify them in the footnotes. A few preferred "not for attribution" interviews, and in such cases I have only identified their general position so as to permit readers to make at least some judgment as to the reliability of the source. I thank both groups of individuals.

A number of tireless undergraduates at Stanford University have served as my research assistants. They usually found most of what I asked them to find, and they often found important material that I did not realize existed. For all their hard work, I thank Mala Htun, Richard Lobel, John Louie, Trevor Macy, Marlene Rodriguez, Sarah Stevenson, Effie Toshav, and Benjamin Valentino.

Stanford's Center for International Security and Arms Control (CISAC) has been supportive of this project from its conception to its completion. CISAC not only provided an office and a stimulating academic environment, but also organized a special manuscript review meeting in February 1992 in which the following participants offered very helpful suggestions: Barton Bernstein, Lynn Eden, David Holloway, Kurt Gaubatz, John

Harvey, Stephen Krasner, and Richard Scott. The Program on International Political Economy and Security (PIPES) at the University of Chicago also hosted a meeting on the manuscript in April 1992, and I would like to thank all the participants, and especially John Padgett, Brad Thayer, and Stephen Walt for their written comments. In addition, the following friends and colleagues read all or parts of the manuscript in various drafts and saved me from committing many unnecessary errors: John Arquilla, Coit Blacker, James Blight, Kurt Campbell, Chris Demchack, Michael Desch, Daniel Ellsberg, Peter Feaver, John Gaddis, Robert Jervis, Peter Lavoy, Stefan Michalowski, Michael May, James Miller, Susan Okin, Barry O'Neill, Robert Powell, Edward Rhodes, Paul Stockton, Marc Trachtenberg, Stephen Van Evera, Dennis Ward, and Kimberly Zisk.

A number of people deserve very special recognition. Lynn Eden has been a wonderful source of ideas and an apparently inexhaustible reader of numerous drafts. Her enthusiasm for the project was critical at points when mine began to wane. Three scientists affiliated with CISAC—Sidney Drell, Gerald Johnson, and John Harvey—read draft chapters and guided me through many of the technical complexities of nuclear weapon systems, although I must absolve them from any remaining technical errors. I am also very grateful to Richard Scott for his neverending suggestions for further reading and for inviting me to try out some of my ideas at seminars sponsored by the Stanford Center for Organizations Research. In addition, a number of the organization theorists whose work I am building upon— scholars from both the normal accidents school and the high reliability camp—provided extremely valuable criticisms of earlier drafts of this work. I am especially grateful to Jonathan Bendor, Todd La Porte, Charles Perrow, Karlene Roberts, and Gene Rochlin for their ability to debate, their willingness to listen, and their high reliability as scholars.

Finally, I want to thank my wife, Bao Lamsam, and our son, Benjamin, for their love and support. It is good to know that some things in life are beyond the reach of accident.

| | |
|---|---|
| ADC | Air Defense Command |
| ADIZ | Air Defense Identification Zone |
| AFHRC | Air Force Historical Research Center |
| AFSC | Air Force Systems Command |
| ANMCC | Alternative National Military Command Center |
| BMEWS | Ballistic Missile Early Warning System |
| CC&DF | Command Control and Display Facility |
| CIA | Central Intelligence Agency |
| CINCEUR | Commander in Chief, Europe |
| CINCLANT | Commander in Chief, Atlantic Command |
| CINCPAC | Commander in Chief, Pacific Command |
| CINCSAC | Commander in Chief, Strategic Air Command |
| CINCUSAFE | Commander in Chief, United States Air Forces, Europe |
| CMEWS | Cuban Missile Early Warning System |
| DEFCON | Defense Condition |
| DEW LINE | Distant Early Warning Line |
| EAM | Emergency Action Message |
| ECC | Emergency Combat Capability |
| EMP | Electromagnetic Pulse |
| ESD | Environmental Sensing Device |
| EUCOM | European Command |
| FAA | Federal Aviation Administration |
| FDA | Food and Drug Administration |
| FOIA | Freedom of Information Act |
| GAO | General Accounting Office |
| GRU | Chief Intelligence Directorate for the Soviet General Staff |
| HASP | High Altitude Sampling Program |
| HF | High Frequency |
| ICBM | Intercontinental Ballistic Missile |
| IRBM | Intermediate Range Ballistic Missile |
| JCS | Joint Chiefs of Staff |
| KGB | Soviet Committee for State Security |
| LCC | Launch Control Center |
| NA | National Archives |
| NASA | National Aeronautics and Space Administration |
| NATO | North Atlantic Treaty Organization |
| NEACP | National Emergency Airborne Command Post |

| NMCC | National Military Command Center |
| NORAD | North American Air (or Aerospace) Defense Command |
| NSA-CMCC | National Security Archives–Cuban Missile Crisis Collection |
| NSAM | National Security Action Memorandum |
| PAL | Permissive Action Link |
| PARCS | Perimeter Acquisition Radar Attack Characterization System |
| PAVE PAWS | Precision Acquisition of Vehicle Entry New Phased-Array Radars |
| PCL | Positive Control Launch |
| PCTAP | Positive Control Turn-Around Point |
| PG&E | Pacific Gas and Electric |
| QRA | Quick Reaction Alert |
| RCA | Radio Corporation of America |
| ROE | Rules of Engagement |
| SAC | Strategic Air Command |
| SACEUR | Supreme Allied Commander, Europe |
| SAGE | Semi-Automatic Ground Environment |
| SEAGA | Selective Employment of Air and Ground Alert |
| SIOP | Single Integrated Operational Plan |
| SIS | Secret Intelligence Service (United Kingdom) |
| SLBM | Submarine Launched Ballistic Missile |
| SRF | Strategic Rocket Forces (USSR) |
| SWESS | Special Weapons Emergency Separation System |
| USAF | United States Air Force |

# THE LIMITS OF SAFETY

# Expecting the Unexpected

ON THE NIGHT of October 25, 1962, an air force sentry was patrolling the perimeter of a military base near Duluth, Minnesota. It was the height of the Cuban missile crisis, and nuclear-armed bombers and interceptor aircraft, parked on air base runways and at commercial airports throughout the United States, were alert and ready for war. The sentry spotted someone climbing the base fence, shot at the figure, and sounded the sabotage alarm. At airfields throughout the region, alarms went off, and armed guards rushed into the cold night to prevent Soviet agents from sabotaging U.S. nuclear forces.

At Volk Field in Wisconsin, however, the wrong alarm bell rang: the Klaxon signalling that nuclear war had begun went off. Pilots ran to their nuclear-armed interceptors and started the engines. These men had been told that there would be no practice alert drills during the tense crisis, and they fully believed that a nuclear war was starting as they headed down the runway. Fortunately, the base commander contacted Duluth before the planes took off and discovered what had happened. An officer in the command post immediately drove his car onto the runway, flashing his lights and signaling the interceptors. The pilots saw him and stopped their aircraft. The suspected Soviet saboteur that caused the whole incident was, ironically, a bear.

## Unlikely Events

When I began working on this book, I believed that the probability of a serious nuclear weapons accident in the United States was extremely low. I also believed that escalation from a single accident to an accidental nuclear war was even more unlikely. I still hold those beliefs. But new knowledge about bizarre and dangerous incidents within the U.S. nuclear weapons arsenal—like how a bear climbing a fence almost caused nuclear-armed aircraft to be launched—has led to a new appreciation of how often unlikely events occur. In the large and very complex organizations that control hazardous technologies in our society, one should expect that the unexpected will occur, that unimaginable interactions will develop, that accidents will happen.

The historical research presented in this book has discovered a large number of previously unknown "close calls" with U.S. nuclear weapons: serious incidents within the U.S. nuclear arsenal that could have produced an accidental or unauthorized detonation of a nuclear weapon, and potentially even an accidental war, had they occurred under different, though plausible, circumstances. The seriousness of some of these incidents was immediately recognized by the actors involved and the command system problems were properly reported and addressed at higher levels. My research has "discovered" these cases only in the most narrow sense of finding archival material or receiving declassified evidence through the Freedom of Information Act. Other cases, however, were not recognized as serious incidents or even as potential command system problems by the individuals or organizations involved. These incidents have been "discovered" in the more meaningful sense of identifying a real-world problem for the first time. Finally, a number of these events were recognized as being very dangerous by the individuals involved, but were not fully reported, either inadvertently or intentionally, to higher authorities. This research has "discovered" them in the sense that a detective can be said to have discovered hidden evidence about a criminal case, facts that were known to someone, but not to the judge.

## Motives and Methods

Why and how was this book written? It began, as most books do, with a puzzle. We live in a world full of hazardous technologies and some risk of catastrophic accidents is therefore ever present. We try to keep these risks as low as possible, yet in recent years, the names of many social and environmental tragedies have been etched into our memory: Chernobyl, the *Exxon Valdez*, Love Canal, the space shuttle *Challenger*, Bhopal. The safety record seems quite extraordinary, however, with the most hazardous technology of all: nuclear weapons. There has never been an accidental or unauthorized detonation of a nuclear weapon, much less escalation to an accidental nuclear war.

Why? How have imperfect humans, working in imperfect organizations and operating imperfect machines, been so successful? Have the military organizations that maintain custody and control over U.S. nuclear weapons done something extremely intelligent to avoid accidents? Have they been designed in such a way to produce reliable safety? Or have they merely been extremely lucky?

The first step toward solving this puzzle was to arm myself with the major scholarly theories that exist about the causes of safety and accidents in complex organizations. Two competing schools of thought—what I call normal accidents theory and high reliability theory—are analyzed in chapter 1. Such theories are always necessary to understand complex social phenomena; they are the conceptual tools we use to pull disparate events together and understand what caused them. The point is especially obvious for anyone who tries to do historical research with records kept in massive collections like the National Archives: theories are absolutely necessary to tell you where to look for evidence. (The final scene of the movie *Raiders of the Lost Ark*, in which the ark of the covenant is slowly wheeled into a mammoth government warehouse, conveys a sense how effectively historical objects are hidden in the recesses of the archives.) Using the theories discussed in chapter 1 as guides, I was able to explore the historical records of the U.S. military, searching for clues.

Let me give just one example of how the process worked. (See chapter 3 for the substantive details about this particular case study.) The literature on the Cuban missile crisis is immense, but no scholar has previously studied the emergency radar warning system, which the United States deployed on a crash basis in October 1962 after the Soviet missiles were discovered. A study of the activities at the three radars used in this Operation Falling Leaves appeared to me, however, to be a very useful way of comparing the strengths of the two theoretical perspectives outlined in chapter 1, since these theories provide contrasting expectations about this warning system's reliability. Normal accidents theory would predict that Falling Leaves would be a very accident-prone operation: the warning system displayed all the signs of high interactive complexity and tight coupling, the two structural factors that the theory suggests lead to dangerous accidents in other high technology systems. High reliability theory would predict that Falling Leaves would be a relatively safe operation, since the factors that the theory suggests produced safety in other hazardous systems also existed here: significant decentralized decision-making authority was given to operators in the field, redundant radars were used to provide more accurate warning information, and officers' caution was heightened by the crisis environment. I therefore visited the Air Force archives, found a number of relevant declassified documents, and then used the Freedom of Information Act to request that additional related documents be declassified and sent to me.

These historical records confirmed the more optimistic view of the high reliability theorists. They reported on no serious false warning incidents occurring during the crisis. Indeed, the Falling Leaves after-action reports recommended that the emergency radar system be set up again if there was ever another superpower crisis.

This success story was puzzling from a normal accidents perspective. That theory, however, also reminds us to be skeptical of documents that are written by organizational actors who are interested in promoting their cause. Operators do not want to get blamed for making serious errors and leaders of military organizations want to promote the reputation of their command. I therefore sent the documents to a large number of the retired Air Force officers and civilian contractors who had participated in the Falling Leaves operation, and asked that they comment on them. A number of these men recalled that there had been one or more serious false warning incidents during the crisis and expressed puzzlement as to why such events were not in the unit histories. I did not know whether to trust the documents (which could be faulty) or the memories (which obviously could be faulty too).

Fortunately, one retired officer said that he was sure that he had written something about a false warning incident in the command post log back at Air Defense Command Headquarters in 1962. I had not known that such records existed, but I immediately requested that the Air Force Space Command declassify these command post logs for the dates of October 26–29, 1962. These handwritten notes were like a smoking gun.

They revealed that a serious false warning incident occurred on October 27, 1962, at the height of the Cuban crisis. The radar operators at one site in Moorestown, New Jersey, informed the national command post that a missile had just been launched from Cuba and was about to detonate near Tampa, Florida. The command post officers immediately informed other U.S. military commands that a nuclear attack appeared to be under way. After the event, operators discovered that a software test tape, simulating a missile launch from Cuba, had been inserted into the radar operators' screen and that, simultaneously, a satellite came over the horizon. The operators "became confused," according to the command post log, and therefore reported "the test target as real." Who would have anticipated that a satellite would appear on the radar screen at the exact moment when a test tape was running and at the exact location where a missile launched from Cuba would have appeared? To make matters worse, the Falling Leaves system had been carefully designed to include overlapping redundant radars to provide more reliability, but the other radars were not turned on when the incident occurred. In addition, although the radars were supposed to get advance information on satellites passing overhead, the key facility involved had been taken off that mission, ironically, to help provide warning in the Falling Leaves operation. None of this was reported in the classified after-action reports on the operation.

The research strategy proved laborious, but it also proved necessary. This book thus attempts to show one way in which social science theories can illuminate, indeed even identify, important events in history. It also attempts to show how such historical case studies can be used to evaluate our theories, and thereby improve our broader understanding of how complex organizations manage and mismanage hazardous technologies.

## A Note on Sources

Nuclear weapons and military operations are obviously very sensitive sub-jects within the government. Getting information on nuclear weapons accidents and safety problems has therefore been an extremely difficult task. Four kinds of sources provide the primary evidence used in this book.

First, I made extensive use of the declassified government documents available to researchers at the National Archives, the presidential library system, and the operational archives of the U.S. Air Force and U.S. Navy. I had to visit a number of these archives many times, as new material became available or subsequent ideas suggested new areas of inquiry. Many important pieces of the puzzle were found, however, once I figured out where they might be hidden.

Second, I requested and received literally hundreds of formerly classified documents (some in their entirety and some in sanitized form) through the Freedom of Information Act and the Mandatory Declassification Review process. Responses were forthcoming in anywhere from three weeks to three years. Sometimes my requests were lost; sometimes the wrong documents were declassified. I appealed most decisions to withhold documents in their entirety and occasionally the agency involved released more information. Copies of these documents have been placed in the National Security Archives in Washington, D.C., so that other researchers can use them.

Third, I conducted dozens of interviews with individuals who were involved in these dangerous incidents. These interviews spanned the hierarchy from former senior civilian officials at the Pentagon and the White House, down to individual interceptor pilots and crewmen inside a Minuteman ICBM launch control center. Often I would send the available declassified documents to these individuals to get their views on the accuracy of the records. Evidence from such interviews obviously has to be treated with caution, given the inevitable vagaries of memory and the potential biases of the individuals involved.

Fourth, a great deal of useful information on the subject of nuclear weapons safety can be found in congressional hearings. One must also use the material from such hearings cautiously, however, since testimony given in such hearings may or may not be absolutely accurate. Moreover, critical material is often deleted from the transcript, to protect classified information necessary for national security, and what remains can therefore be misleading.[1]

---

[1] Difficult detective work is not always necessary to fill in the blanks. For example, I already knew that 30 percent of the U.S. bomber force was kept on day-to-day alert from the following sanitized testimony: "With regard to the bomber force, we keep approximately (*deleted*) *percent* of the bombers and supporting tankers—roughly (deleted) aircraft—on

Given the extreme sensitivity of the whole subject of nuclear weapons safety, many relevant documents remain classified even after thirty years. A special caveat is therefore in order. This is not, and could not be, the definitive story of accidents and near-accidents with U.S. nuclear weapons and command and control systems. Much more information would have to be declassified in order to provide a full glimpse into the heart of the problem. I have done the best I can with the limited material available, and try to provide enough detail so that each reader can develop his or her own judgment about the seriousness of each incident I discuss. I suspect that declassification of further documents may lead to reevaluation of some of my cases; I also suspect that such material will make some incidents seem more dangerous, and some less dangerous, than they appear in the light of the current evidence. And I strongly believe that more nuclear safety problems than are reported here will eventually surface from the recesses of the classified archives.

## Outline of the Book

The structure of this book is straightforward. Chapter 1 presents and develops two theoretical perspectives on the ability of complex organizations to manage hazardous technology. These two theories are lined up in a kind of comparative test to determine which provides better insights into the history of U.S. nuclear weapons safety. Chapter 2 and chapter 3 are a series of case studies of nuclear weapons operations during the Cuban missile crisis of October 1962. In chapter 2, I present what the logic of each theory would lead one to expect would happen when the United States put its nuclear forces on alert during the crisis, and then compare these expectations to the historical record. I follow the same approach, only this time looking at U.S. warning and intelligence operations, in chapter 3.

Chapter 4 moves forward to January 1968 and presents a detailed study of the causes and consequences (both real and potential) of the crash of a nuclear armed B-52 bomber near Thule, Greenland. The purpose of the chapter is to explore the consequences of a strategy for improved safety that attempts to produce high reliability by adding redundancy to the system. Chapter 5 focuses on the issue of organizational learning. It presents two case studies. The first is an examination of U.S. nuclear alert operations during the October 1973 Yom Kippur War, which examines the

---

constant alert. They are at the appropriate alert levels, so that they could escape prior to the impact of SLBM weapons. If we suffer a strike out of the blue, a surprise attack, we accept the probability that *the other 70 percent of the force* would be destroyed." Testimony of General Richard Ellis, Senate Armed Services Committee, *Hearings on DOD Appropriation for FY 1982*, part 7, p. 3799 (emphasis added).

degree to which the U.S. government and U.S. military commands learned from the experience with nuclear weapons operations during the Cuban crisis eleven years earlier. The second case study examines a series of false warning incidents that occurred within the North American Aerospace Defense Command in 1979 and 1980. Why did these incidents occur and what was learned from the experience?

Chapter 6 presents my conclusions. The implications of the study for organization theory, especially for our understanding of the causes of accidents involving hazardous technologies, are outlined first. Then the implications for deterrence theory and the study of nuclear weapons are presented. Finally, I conclude with a brief discussion of the policy implications of this book. What, if anything, can be done to reduce the dangers identified within?

### Beyond the Cold War

Like many books about international politics that have been published in recent years, this one was started during the Cold War and was completed in the post–Cold War era. Unlike some of these books, however, this one is, I believe, as relevant to the emerging new world as it was to the old. This is the case for two basic reasons.

First, while the end of the Cold War has clearly and dramatically reduced the risk of a deliberate conflict between the United States and the former Soviet Union, its impact on the likelihood of nuclear weapons accidents, and even accidental war, is less clear cut. A number of factors do appear to have reduced these risks. The likelihood of serious accidents is highest during a crisis, when nuclear forces are placed on a heightened state of alert readiness; and since the end of the Cold War reduces the likelihood of major crises, it thereby also lowers the likelihood of accidents. The major achievements in Russian and American arms control in 1991 and 1992— especially the U.S. decision to take Strategic Air Command bombers off day-to-day nuclear alert status and the Russian decision to take its largest ICBM, the SS-18, off alert—have further reduced the risks. Finally, it appears much less likely after the Cold War that Russian or American political or military authorities would react to a false warning of an attack against their country with rash orders to retaliate immediately.[2]

That is the positive side of the ledger. A number of important factors, however, appear on the negative side. The collapse of the Soviet Union has

[2] One should not, however, be too optimistic here. Imagine that a serious false warning that a nuclear attack was under way, like the events described in chapter 5, had occurred during the August 1991 coup attempt in Russia. Can we be certain that such a warning would have been treated with skepticism?

subjected its nuclear command and control system to unprecedented and unanticipated tensions. Short-range tactical nuclear weapons have reportedly all been successfully withdrawn, in great haste (and thus probably with considerable risk of accident), to Russia from other former Soviet republics. Yet, intercontinental-range strategic nuclear weapons are likely to continue to be deployed in Russia, Kazakhstan, and Ukraine for many years to come, and the safety of these weapons will likely be strained by emerging political, ethnic, and civil-military conflicts in the region. The elaborate system of nuclear weapons control there was simply not designed to cope with such events as a coup attempt or large-scale social unrest, and its ability to provide safety in such an environment is uncertain. In addition, for reasons spelled out in chapter 6, the danger of accidents with nuclear weapons, and the danger of accidental nuclear war, are more likely with new states that are developing their own nuclear arsenals in the post–Cold War world.

Finally, there is a serious problem of overconfidence here in the United States. If the theories and evidence presented in this book are correct, then there are likely to be a number of hidden bugs in the U.S. nuclear weapons system, latent technical and organizational safety problems that have not been recognized over time. To the degree that we become complacent, believing that the end of the Cold War has solved the problem of nuclear weapons safety, fewer of these problems will be identified and fixed. Some day, when we expect it least—during a military exercise, while transporting nuclear weapons to storage sites, during a missile flight test, or even during a routine missile maintenance operation—the unexpected will occur. That would indeed be an ironic and tragic consequence of the end of the Cold War rivalry.

The second basic reason that this book is relevant to the post–Cold War world is that the hidden history of nuclear weapons safety problems has many broader implications for other organizations that attempt to manage hazardous technologies. The U.S. military organizations studied here are widely considered to be models of discipline and reliability. Some of the problems they have experienced can therefore reasonably be expected to be repeated—in one form or another, and sometimes with a vengeance—in more "ordinary" civilian organizations, such as nuclear power plants, oil tankers, petrochemical factories, and biotechnology firms.

We will continue to live in a world filled with hazardous technologies and our understanding of how to control them is both terribly important and very incomplete. This book is an effort to identify some persistent problems that might be fixed, as well as some that probably cannot. It attempts to illuminate both the prospects for progress and the inherent limits of safety.

# CHAPTER 1

# The Origins of Accidents

An examination of page 752 of the reference
(Emergency Actions File) indicates that the President
is not included in the list of personnel to be notified
under declared conditions of an Air Defense Emergency
or a Defense Emergency or DEFCON 1.

*(Rear Admiral J. H. Wellings, Acting Director of
the Joint Staff, Memorandum, December 27, 1960)*

Accidents will happen.

*(Anon.)*

ACCIDENTAL nuclear war is a very difficult subject to study. The first reason for this difficulty is the most obvious, the most important, and the most fortunate one: there has never been a single accidental nuclear detonation, much less an accidental nuclear war. The traditional comparative methodology used by social scientists to explain complex political phenomena—comparing and contrasting cases in which the phenomena occurred against cases in which it did not—cannot be used here. There are, of course, many other difficulties involved in a thorough investigation of this subject. Many important pieces of evidence about past nuclear weapons incidents remain classified; some critical documents about sensitive military operations have been destroyed; faulty historical records have sometimes been created by military units; and inadequate social science theories exist to help us understand both the causes of war and the origins of accidents. But these difficulties pale next to the basic conceptual dilemma posed by the problem of accidental nuclear war. How does one even begin to study something that has never occurred?

One possibility is to assume that this central fact proves that the danger of nuclear weapons accidents and accidental nuclear war is minimal. Such an optimistic assessment is not unusual, in fact, since it can be argued that history has demonstrated that nuclear weapons can be maintained and operated in a safe and secure manner.[1] This assessment, however, is inade-

[1] See, for example, Kenneth N. Waltz, *The Spread of Nuclear Weapons: More May Be Better*, Adelphi Paper 171 (London: International Institute for Strategic Studies, 1981), p. 16.

quate for at least three reasons. First, things that have never happened before happen all the time in history. There must be a first time for every type of historical event that has occurred in the past, and the lack of earlier nuclear accidents is therefore insufficient evidence for making such a strong statement about future possibilities. Second, nuclear weapons have existed for less than fifty years and have been in the possession of only a small number of nations. This is a very limited pool of experience on which to base confident assessments of long-term nuclear weapons safety, especially under what could be quite different conditions during the next century. Third, an assessment of the risk of accidental nuclear war should examine close calls to catastrophe, and not be satisfied with the simple fact that accidental nuclear war has never occurred. For if we have had numerous "near-accidents" with nuclear weapons—incidents that could have resulted in an accidental nuclear war had they occurred under other plausible circumstances[2]—even an apparently perfect final safety record may not inspire extreme confidence.

A more thorough assessment therefore requires a deeper investigation into the hidden history of nuclear weapons. What has been the complete safety record, of accidents and near-accidents, with these weapons and their command and control systems? How have the military organizations that have custody over nuclear weapons been able to manage their complex operations with such apparent success? Have these organizations done something extremely intelligent to avoid accidents or have they merely been extremely lucky?

A useful place to start is to examine the causes of accidents and safety problems in other similar sociotechnical systems. For although there has never been an accidental nuclear weapons detonation or war, there have been numerous serious accidents in recent decades in other complex high-technology systems such as nuclear reactors, commercial and military aircraft, space programs, international shipping, and large petrochemical plants. Fortunately, a rich scholarly literature studying the causes of reliability and safety in these industries exists. What has caused serious accidents with these hazardous technologies? What organizational designs and strategies have been used to prevent accidents and enhance safety? A number of scholars have sought to explain successes and failures in organizational safety, and their ideas, if used very carefully, can help us understand the risks of serious accidents with nuclear weapons.

This chapter will examine the two most important schools of thought within the organization theory literature concerning the issue of safety and

[2] Here I am following the National Research Council's definition of a safety "incident." See National Research Council, Assembly of Engineering, *Improving Aircraft Safety: FAA Certification of Commercial Passenger Aircraft* (Washington, D.C.: National Academy of Sciences, 1980), p. 107.

reliability in complex technological systems. Subsequent chapters will then apply these theories to the military organizations that control U.S. nuclear weapons and test the theories competitively against one another by probing into the historical record of nuclear weapons accidents and "close calls" to accidental nuclear war. The goal is to provide a clearer understanding of the origins of accidents and the causes of safety.

## ORGANIZATION THEORY AND ACCIDENTS

Even a brief glance at the recent history of high-technology industries cautions against complacency. Why have such tragedies as Chernobyl, the *Exxon Valdez*, and Bhopal occurred? Are such accidents preventable? Or are they the inevitable consequence of the widespread use of hazardous technologies in the modern world?

The scholarly literature about complex organizations is large and diverse, but two general competing schools of thought on this specific issue exist. The first is the optimistic view of what I will call "high reliability theory," whose proponents argue that extremely safe operations are possible, even with extremely hazardous technologies, if appropriate organizational design and management techniques are followed. The second school, what I will call "normal accidents theory," presents a much more pessimistic prediction: serious accidents with complex high technology systems are inevitable.

The term *schools of thought* was used deliberately, since it is in many ways a better description of what exists in this literature on hazardous technologies than the term *theories*. The scholarship I will be analyzing is based on mixtures of abstract deductive logic and inductive empirical observation, and the authors within each school by no means agree on all details concerning organizational safety. Specific terms that appear often in this literature are not always used in a consistent manner. And perhaps most importantly the predictions of both schools are often imprecise. Nevertheless, proponents of each school do focus attention on a specific set of factors that they believe contributes to or decreases safety, and each school develops a set of general hypotheses that is meant to hold true in a variety of organizations across space and time. These ideas can therefore be viewed as nascent social science theories and can usefully be tested against one another.

These two schools of thought have intellectual roots in different traditions within the organization theory literature; they have different basic understandings of how organizations work and hold different views on how best to analyze complex organizations. The theories offer competing general explanations for the causes of accidents with hazardous technolog-

14 CHAPTER 1

ical systems and offer alternative prescriptions for improving safety in the future. At the broadest level, they have conflicting visions about what could be called the degree of perfectibility that is possible in complex organizations. Finally, and importantly for this book's purposes, high reliability theory and normal accidents theory lead to very different predictions about the causes and the likelihood of serious nuclear weapons and command and control accidents. Each will therefore be analyzed in some detail.

## HIGH RELIABILITY ORGANIZATION THEORY

How safe are nuclear power plants, commercial aircraft, oil tankers, petrochemical factories, and other potentially dangerous high-technology systems? Is it possible to design and manage such complex organizations so well that, even though they use inherently hazardous technologies, they are unlikely to produce serious accidents? One group of organization theory scholars—the high reliability theorists—are in essential agreement with the professional risk analysts and engineers who build these systems: serious accidents with hazardous technologies can been prevented through intelligent organizational design and management. Scholars in this school have studied a variety of high risk organizations and have reached quite optimistic conclusions about the prospects for safely managing hazardous technologies in modern society.

Three major scholarly efforts to understand safety problems in such hazardous high-technology organizations can best represent the high reliability school. First, Joseph Marone and Edward Woodhouse's *Averting Catastrophe: Strategies for Regulating Risky Technologies* is an innovative study of the management of toxic chemicals, nuclear power, recombinant DNA research, ozone layer depletion, and global warming problems in the United States. The authors maintain that "given the challenge posed by modern technologies, the record is surprisingly good: despite dire warnings, no catastrophes have occurred in the United States."[3] This positive historical record of safety was, according to Marone and Woodhouse, "a systematic product of human actions—the result of a deliberate process by which risks are monitored, evaluated, and reduced," and much of their research therefore focuses on identifying the specific organizational processes and strategies which produced this result.[4] Although they acknowledge that the strategies they discovered were not always fully developed or perfectly implemented, Marone and Woodhouse nevertheless believe that "taken together, the strategies we found in use suggest the elements of a

[3] Joseph G. Marone and Edward J. Woodhouse, *Averting Catastrophe: Strategies for Regulating Risky Technologies* (Berkeley: University of California Press, 1986), p. 5.
[4] *Ibid.*, p. 8.

*complete system for averting catastrophe.*"[5] Continued use of such wise management practices can therefore maintain and improve this safety record well into the future: "There is a good chance in areas of civilian technology that catastrophes will be prevented—even in new problem areas where society is not presently expecting trouble."[6]

The second example of high reliability theory is the work of a multidisciplinary group of scholars based at the University of California at Berkeley that has studied the "design and management of hazardous organizations that achieve extremely high levels of reliable and safe operations."[7] Their empirical research has focused on three hazardous organizations that they argue have achieved "nearly error free operations": the Federal Aviation Administration's (FAA) air-traffic control system, the Pacific Gas and Electric Company's electric power system (which includes the Diablo Canyon nuclear power plant), and the peacetime flight operations of two U.S. Navy aircraft carriers.[8] Their extensive field research into the daily operations of these specific organizations has identified a number of strategies and processes that are believed to have produced such impressive safety records. Although the Berkeley authors emphasize that further comparative research is needed to provide confident prescriptions for other hazardous organizations, they nonetheless maintain that "we have begun to discover the degree and character of effort necessary to overcome the inherent limitations to securing consistent, failure free operations in complex social organizations."[9] These successful organizations are therefore viewed as providing important lessons for the management of other risky

---

[5] *Ibid.* (emphasis added).

[6] *Ibid.*, p. 150.

[7] University of California, Berkeley, and other affiliated faculty members of the ongoing High-Reliability Organizations project include Geoffrey Gosling, Todd R. La Porte, Karlene H. Roberts, Gene I. Rochlin, Paul Shulman, and Karl Weick. The best descriptions of the project's overall findings are Todd R. La Porte and Paula M. Consolini, "Working in Practice but Not in Theory: Theoretical Challenges of 'High Reliability Organizations'," *Journal of Public Administration Research and Theory* 1, no. 1 (January 1991): 19–47; and Karlene H. Roberts, "New Challenges in Organization Research: High Reliability Organizations," *Industrial Crisis Quarterly* 3, no. 2 (1989): 111–125 (quotation at p. 111).

[8] Karlene H. Roberts, "Some Characteristics of One Type of High Reliability Organization," *Organization Science* 1, no. 2 (May 1990): 160. According to Roberts, "Within the set of hazardous organizations there is a subset which has enjoyed a record of high safety over long periods of time. One can identify this subset by answering the question, 'How many times could this organization have failed resulting in catastrophic consequences that it did not?' If the answer is on the order of tens of thousands of times the organization is 'high reliability'." Also see Todd R. La Porte, "On the Design and Management of Nearly Error-Free Organizational Control Systems," in David L. Sills, C. P. Wolf, and Vivien B. Shelanski, eds., *Accident at Three Mile Island: The Human Dimensions* (Boulder, Colo.: Westview Press, 1982), pp. 185–200.

[9] Todd R. La Porte, letter to author, September 29, 1991.

high-technology systems: "Most of the characteristics identified here should operate in most organizations that require advanced technologies and in which the cost of error is so great that it needs to be avoided altogether."[10]

The third work that will be used to represent the high reliability school is Aaron Wildavsky's *Searching for Safety*, a more deductive effort to develop "a theory accounting for the considerable degree of safety achieved in contemporary society."[11] The avowed purpose of the book is to alert readers to "the increases in safety due to entrepreneurial activity" in a variety of complex systems: "If this essay in persuasion achieves its purpose, the focus of the risk debate will shift from the passive prevention of harm to a more active search for safety."[12] Wildavsky's major focus is on examining the cost and benefits of what he calls two "universal strategies" for improving safety: "anticipation" (efforts to predict and prevent potential dangers from arising before they have ever occurred) and "resilience" (efforts to cope with dangers once they become manifest). The book then illustrates its central ideas by presenting evidence on the degree to which anticipation and resilience have improved safety in as diverse a set of systems as nuclear power plants, the human body's immune system, and the Food and Drug Administration's (FDA) drug approval process.

How can serious accidents be prevented, and how can safety be improved in organizations managing highly hazardous technology? These three groups of high reliability theorists have not focused entirely upon the same set of hazardous organizations, and they differ on a number of specific details of explanation and prescription. They share, however, one essential assumption about how such organizations function, and their analyses point to a common set of four major factors that are seen as contributing to high degrees of safety.

The common assumption of the high reliability theorists is not a naive belief in the ability of *human beings* to behave with perfect rationality; it is the much more plausible belief that *organizations*, properly designed and managed, can compensate for well-known human frailties and can therefore be significantly more rational and effective than can individuals. The high reliability theory can be best seen therefore as fitting into the tradition

[10] Roberts, "Some Characteristics of One Type of High Reliability Organization," p. 173. Roberts adds: "It is possible that all HROs (high reliability organizations) using hazardous technologies do not have all these strategies and processes. However, one that does not have most, if not all, of them is probably accident prone." Also see Karlene H. Roberts and Denise M. Rousseau, "Research in Nearly Failure-Free, High-Reliability Organizations: Having the Bubble," *IEEE Transactions on Engineering Management* 36, no. 2 (May 1989): 139.

[11] Aaron Wildavsky, *Searching for Safety* (New Brunswick, N.J.: Transaction Books, 1988), p. 1. Also see Mary Douglas and Aaron Wildavsky, *Risk and Culture* (Berkeley: University of California Press, 1982).

[12] Wildavsky, *Searching for Safety*, p. 2.

that W. Richard Scott has called the "closed rational systems" approach in organization theory. High reliability hazardous organizations are seen as "rational" in the sense that they have highly formalized structures and are oriented toward the achievement of clear and consistent goals (in this case, extremely reliable and safe operations). They are relatively "closed systems" in the sense that they go to great efforts to minimize the effects that actors and the environment outside the organization have on the achievement of such objectives.[13] As Todd La Porte and Paula Consolini have argued, high reliability organizations "are characterized by very clear, well-agreed-upon operational goals":

> Those in the organizations carry on intensive efforts to know the physical and dynamic properties of their production technologies, and they go to considerable pains to buffer the effects of environmental surprises. In most regards, the organizations come close to meeting the conditions of closed rational systems, i.e., a well-buffered, well-understood technical core requiring consistency and stability for effective, failure-free operations.[14]

The research of the different high reliability theorists has produced similar explanations for positive safety records within a wide variety of organizations. Four critical causal factors have been identified: the prioritization of safety and reliability as a goal by political elites and the organization's leadership; high levels of redundancy in personnel and technical safety measures; the development of a "high reliability culture" in decentralized and continually practiced operations; and sophisticated forms of trial and error organizational learning. These four factors constitute, according to this school of thought, a route to extremely reliable operations even with highly hazardous technologies.

## Leadership Safety Objectives

The first and most obvious requirement for high reliability organizations is that extreme reliability and safety must be held as a priority objective by both political leaders and by the heads of the organization. Such organizations maintain "the goal of avoiding altogether serious operational failures," according to La Porte and Consolini: "This has nurtured an organi-

[13] See W. Richard Scott, *Organizations: Rational, Natural and Open Systems* (Englewood Cliffs, N.J.: Prentice-Hall, 1987), pp. 20–22, 31–50 and 99–102. Also see James D. Thompson, *Organizations in Action* (New York: McGraw-Hill, 1967).

[14] La Porte and Consolini, "Working in Practice but Not in Theory," pp. 23–24. Although there will be consensus on goals in such an organization, La Porte and Consolini acknowledge that some disagreement about appropriate means may continue, which leads to a requirement for "*incremental* decision-making in the context of broadly rational planning." *Ibid.*, p. 26.

zational perspective in which short-term efficiency has taken a second seat to very high-reliability operations."[15] Consider the case, for example, of the U.S. air traffic control system for commercial airlines. La Porte argues that "the public (and especially its Congressional leaders) demands a system" in the United States that:

—Is always safe
—Carries anyone, anywhere, anytime (and is always safe)
—Enables private carriers to make a reasonable profit (while always being safe)[16]

Although political tensions and disagreements continue to exist over who should pay the costs of airline safety improvements, according to La Porte, "the twin pressures from the travelling public and elites for extraordinarily reliable and safe performance resulted in a system . . . (in which) the goal of failure-free performance is a central objective of everyone in the system."[17]

The literature postulates two central reasons why political and organizational leaders must place very high priority on safety if such a measure of high reliability is to be achieved. First, high reliability organizations require both significant levels of redundancy and constant operational training, and both of these factors cost a great deal of money. It should therefore be no surprise that, in Wildavsky's succinct phrase, "richer is safer," since wealth increases the "level of general resources upon which our safety mostly depends."[18] If political authorities and organizational leaders are not willing to devote considerable resources to safety, accidents will therefore become more likely. La Porte's study of airline safety, for example, emphasizes the fact that Congress has never reduced the budget requested by the FAA in support of air traffic control.[19] Similarly, in her review of safety in U.S. Navy aircraft carrier operations, Karlene Roberts argues that the navy has "gotten Congress to recognize the virtual impossibility of doing this job without enormous amounts of redundancy (in jobs, communication structures, parts, etc.) and training, both terrifically expensive. When hazardous organizations cut corners on either of these issues disaster is likely to occur."[20]

[15] *Ibid.*, pp. 21, 23. According to Roberts, "while the organizations of interest in this research focus on other outcomes, reliability is their number one concern." Roberts, "Some Characteristics of One Type of High Reliability Organization," p. 161.

[16] Todd R. La Porte, "The United States Air Traffic System: Increasing Reliability in the Midst of Rapid Growth," in Renate Mayntz and Thomas P. Hughes, eds., *The Development of Large Technical Systems* (Boulder, Colo.: Westview Press, 1988), p. 224.

[17] *Ibid.*, p. 225.

[18] Wildavsky, *Searching for Safety*, p. 58.

[19] La Porte, "The United States Air Traffic System," p. 224.

[20] Roberts, "Some Characteristics of One Type of High Reliability Organization," p. 173.

Second, if high reliability organizations require "very clear and well-agreed-upon operational goals," then organizational leaders must place high priority on safety in order to communicate this objective clearly and consistently to the rest of the organization. Over time, the organization will develop a "culture of reliability" as members are socialized into accepting the organizations's operational goals. Roberts notes, to give one example, that the commanding officer of the aircraft carrier she observed was constantly "laying down the culture of the organization" by briefing newly arriving crewmen on the importance of such safety procedures as the "buddy system" and training them never to break the ship's rules *unless* safety is at stake."[21] Such clear communication of the importance the leadership places on reliability and safety is considered necessary in order to "assure that there is agreement about organizational mission" by all members of the organization.[22]

## The Need for Redundancy

Numerous psychological studies have rigorously demonstrated what we all have suspected from our daily lives: human beings are not perfectly rational machines, but rather operate with limited and fallible cognitive capabilities.[23] Organization theorists, of course, have long been aware of the limits of human rationality and have therefore spent a great deal of effort seeking to solve a basic puzzle. Is it possible, in John von Neumann's phrase, to build "reliable systems from unreliable parts"?[24]

The answer, according to the high reliability organization theorists, is a resounding yes, and the key design feature of such organizations is redundancy.[25] Multiple and independent channels of communication, decision-making, and implementation can produce, in theory, a highly reliable overall system, even if each component of the organization is subject to error. Jonathan Bendor's sophisticated study of the effects of redundancy in

---

[21] *Ibid.*, p. 168.

[22] La Porte and Consolini, "Working in Practice but Not in Theory," p. 24.

[23] For important work on this matter see Daniel Kahneman, Paul Slovic, and Amos Tversky, eds., *Judgment under Uncertainty: Heuristics and Biases* (New York: Cambridge University Press, 1982), and Richard Nisbett and Lee Ross, *Human Inference: Strategies and Shortcomings of Social Judgment* (Englewood Cliffs, N.J.: Prentice-Hall, 1980).

[24] As quoted in Jonathan B. Bendor, *Parallel Systems: Redundancy in Government* (Berkeley: University of California Press, 1985), p. 295. Also see the seminal source, James G. March and Herbert A. Simon, *Organizations* (New York: John Wiley and Sons, 1958).

[25] For pioneering work on the use of redundancy in organizations, see Martin Landau, "Redundancy, Rationality, and the Problem of Duplication and Overlap," *Public Administration Review* 29, no. 4 (July–August 1969): 346–358. Also see Allan W. Lerner, "There Is More than One Way to Be Redundant," *Administration and Society* 18, no. 3 (November 1986): pp. 334–359.

U.S. government agencies provides a simple safety-related analogy to illustrate why "a system's reliability is *not* necessarily limited by its components' fallibility":

Suppose an automobile had dual breaking (sic) circuits: each circuit can stop the car, *and* the circuits operate independently so that if one malfunctions it does not impair the other. If the probability of either one failing is $^1/_{10}$, the probability of both failing simultaneously is $(^1/_{10})^2$, or $^1/_{100}$. Add a third independent circuit and the probability of the catastrophic failure of no brakes at all drops to $(^1/_{10})^3$, or $^1/_{1000}$.[26]

Although many politicians continue to call for eliminating government waste and bureaucratic overlap for the sake of efficiency, these theorists point to the important contribution made by such redundancy to a larger system's reliability. First, *duplication* (two different units that perform the same function) often exists. The Berkeley group's studies of U.S. aircraft carrier operations, for example, have stressed the critical importance of having both technical redundancy (such as backup computers, antennas, and safety devices specifically kept on board to take the place of any components that fail) and personnel redundancy (such different personnel given the same job of checking the carrier's arresting gear settings before each landing). The use of reserve units, to be brought into action only if the main unit is unavailable, is another obvious example of duplication. Second, *overlap* (two units with some functional areas in common) also often exists. Different communications systems are used for related purposes during day-to-day operations and therefore each can pick up the slack for another if necessary. Different officers are also given overlapping responsibilities, although their primary duties may differ, to ensure that they cross-check each others' work. Each time a plane lands on the carrier, for example, a continuous loop of orders and verifications is broadcast simultaneously over multiple channels: "This constant flow of information about each safety-critical activity, monitored by many different listeners on several different communications nets, is designed specifically to assure that any critical element that is out of place will be discovered or noticed by *someone* before it causes problems."[27]

Scholars in this school have found redundancy to be critical to the

---

[26] Bendor, *Parallel Systems*, pp. 26–27. Redundant proofreaders must not have been available.

[27] Gene I. Rochlin, Todd R. La Porte, and Karlene H. Roberts, "The Self-Designing High-Reliability Organization: Aircraft Carrier Flight Operations at Sea," *Naval War College Review* (Autumn 1987): 84–85. On the importance of redundancy, also see Jennifer J. Halpern, "Cognitive Factors Influencing Decision Making in a Highly Reliable Organization," *Industrial Crisis Quarterly* 3, no. 2 (1989): pp. 153–155, and Gene I. Rochlin, "Informal Organizational Networking as a Crisis-Avoidance Strategy: U.S. Naval Flight Operations as a Case Study," *Industrial Crisis Quarterly* 3, no. 2 (1989): 166–169.

success of virtually all the successful high-reliability organizations they have studied. La Porte notes, for example, that U.S. air traffic controllers continued to use a voice radio system as a redundant backup device to map the locations of aircraft, even after more accurate radar technology became available, and that the functional responsibilities of individual controllers often overlap in an effort to ensure that more than one set of eyes are monitoring each safety-critical event.[28] Marone and Woodhouse similarly emphasize the central role that redundancy plays in nuclear reactor "defense in depth" safety programs: for example, there must be at least two independent outside power sources for the plant, redundant instruments for measuring the reactor's operating parameters, and several coolant loops, so that if one system failed, others would be able to take over.[29] Roberts has noted the importance of both technical and personnel redundancy in Pacific Gas and Electric's distribution grid, in which reserve power sources compensate for any losses of regular sources and where multiple control centers monitor the output.[30] Finally, Dennis Coyle and Aaron Wildavsky's analysis of the human immune system also places considerable importance on the degree to which "the defense systems of the body are highly redundant": for example, several antibodies are capable of binding to a single antigen; two kidneys exist to eliminate harmful substances; and bone marrow can take over the job of producing red blood cells if one's spleen is removed.[31] The lessons of theory and evidence are clear for the high reliability school of organization theorists. Redundancy is absolutely essential if one is to produce safety and reliability inside complex and flawed organizations. In Bendor's terms, "duplication is a substitute for perfect parts."[32]

## Decentralization, Culture, and Continuity

Although high levels of redundancy in an organization's structure and operations can greatly enhance reliability, it is still beneficial to reduce the

[28] La Porte, "The United States Air Traffic System," p. 230. Also see La Porte and Consolini, "Working in Practice but Not in Theory," pp. 37–39.

[29] Marone and Woodhouse, Averting Catastrophe, pp. 44–45. Also see Joseph G. Marone and Edward J. Woodhouse, The Demise of Nuclear Energy? (New Haven, Conn.: Yale University Press, 1989), pp. 73, 77.

[30] Karlene H. Roberts, "Managing High Reliability Organizations," California Management Review 32, no. 4 (Summer 1990): 105.

[31] Wildavsky, Searching for Safety, p. 163. Wildavsky is an exception here in that his embrace of redundancy is less enthusiastic than the other high reliability theorists. Wildavsky's study of nuclear power plants, for example, argues that the addition of some redundant safety devices may add to safety, but that too many can decrease safety since "they get in each other's way" pp. 11, 125–147.

[32] Bendor, Parallel Systems, p. 291.

number and severity of individual component failures in order to avoid stressing the redundant systems beyond their capacity. The high reliability theorists have therefore focused considerable attention on operations and management strategies that can reduce the burden placed on redundancy. Three related characteristics of operations and management have been identified as contributing to organizational reliability and safety in this literature.

First, it is argued that considerable *decentralization* of decision-making authority must exist concerning safety issues in high reliability organizations in order to permit rapid and appropriate responses to dangers by the individuals closest to the problems at hand. The need for "decentralized anticipation" runs throughout Wildavsky's theoretical analysis emphasizing the superiority of entrepreneurial efforts to improve safety over centralized and restrictive government regulatory policies. He applies this idea at a more microlevel, for example, by explicitly calling for more discretion to be given to nuclear power plant operators concerning how best to run the plant in a safe manner.[33] Decentralized decision-making has also been found in other high-technology systems studied by these scholars. Although the U.S. Navy aircraft carriers and the U.S. air traffic control system may appear at first glance to be very hierarchical in their decision-making structure, for example, close observation has suggested that surprisingly collegial processes are at work and that considerable operational authority in fact rests at very low levels of the organization. During high-tempo carrier operations, higher ranking officers were found often deferring to the technical judgment of lower ranking personnel, and even the lowest ranking individual on the deck of the ship has the authority (and the obligation) to suspend immediately any takeoff or landing that he believes would result in an accident.[34] Similar patterns of nonhierarchical and decentralized decision-making have been observed in air traffic control centers, where supervisors and controllers may switch responsibilities when necessary and where informal teams are often formed to trade advice and manage dangerous operations at the radar screens.[35] Finally, it is considered important that commercial airline captains have the capability to delegate the task of flying the aircraft to subordinates during onboard crises; otherwise, the crisis can take everyone's attention away from the details of flying, resulting in a crash.[36]

This leads directly to the second operations management factor contrib-

---

[33] Wildavsky, *Searching for Safety*, pp. 125–147.

[34] La Porte and Consolini, "Working in Practice but Not in Theory," p. 32; and Rochlin, La Porte, and Roberts, "The Self-Designing High-Reliability Organization," pp. 83–84.

[35] La Porte and Consolini, "Working in Practice but Not in Theory," pp. 33–35.

[36] Karl E. Weick, "Organizational Culture as a Source of High Reliability," *California Management Review* 29, no. 2 (Winter 1987): 116.

uting to safety: the creation of a *"culture of reliability"* within the organization. Common organizational practices such as the promulgation of formal rules and standard operational procedures can contribute to reliability if the outside environment is stable, that is if the decisions required of operators all fall within a predictable set of contingencies.[37] The central problem for organizations operating with hazardous technologies, however, is that this is quite often not the case. They must cope with unexpected and unique environmental dangers in a very rapid fashion, which is precisely why a significant degree of decentralized authority is deemed necessary. Yet how can such an organization ensure that lower-level personnel will identify situations properly, behave responsibly, and take appropriate actions in crises?

The answer, according to the high reliability theorists, is to recruit, socialize, and train personnel to maintain a strong organizational culture emphasizing safety and reliability. This organizational culture will enable lower-level personnel, even when acting independently, to behave similarly and to make operational decisions that meet the approval of higher authorities. Karl Weick has described the concept extremely well:

> Before you can decentralize, you first have to centralize so that people are socialized to use similar decision premises and assumptions so that when they operate their own units, those decentralized operations are equivalent and coordinated. This is precisely what culture does. It creates a homogenous set of assumptions and decision premises which, when they are invoked on a local and decentralized basis, preserve coordination and centralization.[38]

Concerted efforts to socialize personnel into a "culture of reliability" have been observed within a variety of hazardous organizations. U.S. Navy aircraft carrier commanders use rituals, exercises, and punishments to train officers and enlisted men to follow established rules when it is appropriate, to improvise on their own authority when necessary, and to know which is which. According to Roberts, the navy has unusual advantages in this effort, even when compared to other high reliability organizations, since aircraft carriers are, borrowing Erving Goffman's phrase, a "total institution" in which members are isolated from a wider society and can therefore be more intensely socialized and trained.[39] Air traffic controllers

---

[37] See Jay Galbraith, *Designing Complex Organizations* (Reading, Mass.: Addison-Wesley, 1973), and Paul R. Lawrence and Jay W. Lorsch, *Organization and Environment* (Boston: Harvard Graduate School of Business Administration, 1967).

[38] Weick, "Organizational Culture as a Source of High Reliability," p. 124. Also see the classic work, Herbert Kaufman, *The Forest Ranger: A Study in Administrative Behavior* (Baltimore: Johns Hopkins Press, 1960).

[39] See Erving Goffman, *Asylums* (New York: Doubleday, 1961). Roberts argues that

and airplane crews must also be socialized into a set of shared missions and beliefs so that, when important authority is delegated to lower-level personnel, no one questions the action and everyone is confident that the correct operational decisions will be made on the spot. Such manifestations of a "culture of reliability" should promote reliability without hierarchy or extreme centralization. As La Porte and Consolini argue: "Such organizations invest a great deal in recruiting, socialization, and incentives to assure that there is agreement about organizational mission. At the operating levels, there is rarely any question at all. Consensus is unequivocal."[40]

The final element of intelligent operations management that has been identified in successful hazardous organizations is the maintenance of *continuous operations and training*. "One of the great enemies of high reliability," according to the Berkeley group, "is the usual 'civilian' combination of stability, routinization, and lack of challenge and variety that predispose an organization to relax vigilance and sink into a dangerous complacency that can lead to carelessness and error."[41] A constant process of on-the-job training improvements, frequent and realistic simulations of emergencies, and challenging operational work loads are therefore believed to contribute greatly to reduced error rates. Air traffic control accidents, for example, are reportedly more likely under light traffic conditions, when vigilance is low, than under heavy traffic conditions.[42] The Berkeley team similarly found that the constant flight training mode of aircraft carriers at sea has been critical to their ability to operate reliably: "It is in the real-world environment of workups and deployment, through the continual training and retraining of officers and crew, that the information needed for safe and efficient operation is developed, transmitted, and maintained. Without that continuity, and without sufficient operational time at sea, both effectiveness and safety would suffer."[43]

These three factors reenforce one another. Constant training, strong cultural norms, and decentralized decision authority can produce, according to Karlene Roberts, Denise Rousseau, and Todd La Porte, "a self regulating work unit where operators are empowered to directly address risks

---

carriers are "the most total of total institutions: That affords considerably more top down control than is possible in other organizations . . . that operate reliably over long periods of time." Roberts, "Some Characteristics of One Type of High Reliability Organization," p. 173.

[40] La Porte and Consolini, "Working in Practice but Not in Theory," p. 24.

[41] Rochlin, La Porte, and Roberts, "The Self-Designing High-Reliability Organization," pp. 82–83.

[42] Weick, "Organizational Culture as a Source of High Reliability, p. 118.

[43] Rochlin, La Porte, and Roberts, "The Self-Designing High-Reliability Organization," p. 80. Also see Roberts, "Some Characteristics of One Type of High Reliability Organization," p. 169.

and uncertainties."[44] In this sense, high reliability organizations are seen as being similar to modern industrial factories that have been designed according to "sociotechnical principles" in which multiskilled workers are organized into loosely supervised and semiautonomous production teams. According to Larry Hirschhorn, "the normal accident will become increasingly abnormal" in such settings since "workers are vigilant and committed to production quality and safety because of their desire to learn, their understanding of plant dynamics and policies, and their close relationships with teammates."[45] To the degree that organizations utilizing hazardous technologies can mimic such industrial practices, the high reliability theory would predict that their operations would become increasingly safe.

## Organizational Learning

The final factor necessary for high reliability in hazardous organizations, according to this school of thought, is a strong capability to learn. Two common modes of such organizational learning have been discussed in the theoretical and empirical literature. First, and most importantly, a high reliability organization, like other effective organizations, must adjust its procedures and routines over time, learning through a process of trial and error which activities promote safety and which do not. Such an incremental learning process need not be centrally controlled and will produce evolutionary progress as long as successful designs and standard operating procedures are maintained while unsuccessful ones are eliminated.[46]

A belief in the effectiveness of trial-and-error organizational learning lies at the heart of the high reliability theory. It can be most clearly witnessed in Wildavsky's argument against excessive government regulations on potentially hazardous technologies: "Without trials there can be no new errors; but without these errors, there is also less new learning."[47] According to Wildavsky:

[44] Karlene H. Roberts, Denise M. Rousseau, and Todd R. La Porte, "The Culture of High Reliability: Quantitative and Qualitative Assessment aboard Nuclear-Powered Aircraft Carriers" (unpublished manuscript, p. 8).

[45] Larry Hirschhorn, "On Technological Catastrophe," *Science* 228 (May 17, 1985) p. 847. Also see Hirschhorn, *Beyond Mechanization: Work and Technology in the Postindustrial Age* (Cambridge, Mass.: MIT Press, 1984), and Scott, *Organizations*, pp. 232–234.

[46] John D. Steinbruner, *The Cybernetic Theory of Decision* (Princeton, N.J.: Princeton University Press, 1974), pp. 78–79. Also see the discussion of "the complete cycle of choice" in James G. March and Johan P. Olsen, "The Uncertainty of the Past: Organizational Learning under Ambiguity," in James G. March, *Decisions and Organizations* (Oxford, U.K.: Basil Blackwell, 1988), pp. 337–345, and the analysis of "single loop learning" in Chris Argyris and Donald A. Schon, *Organizational Learning* (Reading, Mass.: Addison-Wesley, 1978).

[47] Wildavsky, *Searching for Safety*, p. 17.

26  CHAPTER 1

Trial and error is a device for courting small dangers in order to avoid or lessen the damage from big ones. . . . Because it is a discovery process that discloses latent errors so we can learn how to deal with them, trial and error also lowers risk by reducing the scope of unforeseen dangers. Trial and error samples the world of as yet unknown risks; by learning to cope with risks that become evident as the result of small-scale trial and error, we develop skills for dealing with whatever may come our way from the world of unknown risks.[48]

This perspective is echoed in the Marone and Woodhouse case studies of nuclear power safety (which note the changes in operational training, emergency procedures, and the design of reactor control panels after the incident at Three Mile Island) and toxic substance controls (which note how the government learned to conduct routine audits of testing laboratories after a series of fraudulent test results were exposed).[49] The Berkeley group's study of aircraft carrier operations similarly maintains that many of the safety-related innovations on U.S. carriers were implemented after aircraft incidents and deck fires in the past and therefore predicts that it will take many years and "some loss of lives in the learning process" before aircraft carriers in other nation's navies can equal the U.S. Navy's reliability and safety rates.[50]

Because the organizational and social costs of accidents with such hazardous technologies are so high, however, a second organizational learning strategy—improving procedures through *simulations* and *imagination* of trials and errors—is often used. Marone and Woodhouse have argued that such processes are an important part of a "sophisticated trial and error" strategy.[51] In the most dramatic case, the nuclear power industry deliberately boiled away the coolant under controlled circumstances in small experimental reactors, in an effort to gain understanding of the consequences of such incidents in regular operating nuclear power plants.[52] Less dramatic examples abound. In the mid-1970s, a set of biotechnology experiments were run in order to determine whether a genetically engineered organism could survive outside the laboratory. The FDA's elaborate drug testing process, using laboratory experiments and limited human tests as a simulation of what would happen if the drug was put on the marketplace, is another obvious example. Airplane pilots, air traffic controllers, aircraft

48 *Ibid.*, p. 37.

49 Marone and Woodhouse, *Avoiding Catastrophe*, pp. 132–133.

50 Rochlin, "Informal Organizational Networking as a Crisis-Avoidance Strategy," p. 164; and Rochlin, La Porte, and Roberts, "The Self-Designing High-Reliability Organization," p. 88.

51 See, especially, Edward J. Woodhouse, "Sophisticated Trial and Error in Decision Making about Risk," in Michael E. Kraft and Norman J. Vig, eds., *Technology and Politics* (Durham, N.C.: Duke University Press, 1988), p. 217.

52 Marone and Woodhouse, *Averting Catastrophe*, p. 132.

carrier crews, and nuclear power plant operators also undergo rigorous training in simulated crises in order to gain some of the experience of trials without large-scale errors. Finally, engineers and other consultants are hired by many hazardous organizations to provide risk analyses: to imagine potential operator and design errors, to draw fault tree diagrams to discover any hidden failure modes, and to identify technical solutions to the problems. In such cases, as Marone and Woodhouse put it, "Rather than wait to learn from experience whether their precautions were adequate, researchers and regulators chose to speed up the learning process."[53]

## High Reliability Summary

High reliability theorists believe that hazardous technologies can be safely controlled by complex organizations if wise design and management techniques are followed. This optimistic conclusion is based on the argument that effective organizations can meet the following four specific conditions, which are necessary to create and maintain adequate safety: (1) political elites and organization leaders place a high priority on safety and reliability; (2) significant levels of redundancy exist, permitting backup or overlapping units to compensate for failures; (3) error rates are reduced through decentralization of authority, strong organizational culture, and continuous operations and training; and 4) organizational learning takes place through a trial-and-error process, supplemented by anticipation and simulation. These conditions have been witnessed in an number of high reliability organizations, and if these conditions exist in other organizations, then the theory would predict that serious accidents and catastrophes can be prevented. As Marone and Woodhouse put it, "While the exact mix of strategies appropriate in a given case obviously depends on the nature of the particular problem, the catastrophe-aversion strategy outlined above should be applicable to virtually any risky technology."[54] The Berkeley group holds similar views: "We feel that most of the characteristics identified here should operate in most organizations that require advanced technologies and in which the cost of error is so great that it needs to be avoided altogether."[55]

[53] Marone and Woodhouse, *The Demise of Nuclear Energy?* p. 137. As La Porte and Consolini put it: "Analysis and search come before as well as after errors." "Working in Practice but Not in Theory," p. 29.

[54] Marone and Woodhouse, *Averting Catastrophe*, p. 136.

[55] Roberts, "Some Characteristics of One Type of High Reliability Organization," p. 173. She also notes that "we do not know yet which in the set of strategies and processes are most crucial to organizational success, but we suspect that continuous training and redundancy are at the top of the list."

Thus, while the high reliability theorists do not state what precise amounts and mixtures of these factors are necessary for operational success with hazardous technologies, their overall optimism is clear. Properly designed and well-managed organizations can safely operate even the most hazardous technologies. Although this literature does not explicitly address the issue of nuclear weapons and command and control safety, the logic of the theory would lead to a similar optimistic prediction: *if* nuclear weapons and command and control systems are designed and managed according to the factors outlined above, a high degree of safety and reliability will be maintained.

## NORMAL ACCIDENTS THEORY

A very different approach to understanding how complex organizations work, however, leads to a much more pessimistic conclusion about the risks of using hazardous technologies in modern society. A second group of scholars, the normal accidents theorists, have examined some of the same industries from a different theoretical perspective and have concluded that although such complex organizations may work hard to maintain safety and reliability, serious accidents are nonetheless a "normal" result or an integral characteristic of the system. Serious accidents in organizations managing hazardous technologies may be rare, but they are inevitable over time. The belief that intelligent design and management will result in complex organizations that are capable of safely operating hazardous technology is an illusion according to this perspective. What are the central assumptions and theoretical underpinnings of the normal accidents school that lead to this conclusion?

The high reliability theorists view successful hazardous organizations as reasonably rational actors: they have consistent and clear goals and can therefore learn how to maximize those objectives over time. If one relaxes those assumptions, however, a far more complicated and conflictual vision of organizational behavior emerges. James March has highlighted the profound changes in perspective that result from starting with a different set of assumptions:

> As long as we assume that organizations have goals and those goals have some classical properties of stability, precision and consistency, we can treat an organization as some kind of rational actor. But organizations do not have simple, consistent preference functions. They exhibit internal conflict over preferences. Once such conflict is noted, it is natural to shift from a metaphor of problem solving to a more political vision.[56]

[56] James G. March, "Decisions in Organizations and Theories of Choice," in Andrew H.

## Organized Anarchies and the Garbage Can Model

The resulting approach to understanding complex organizations fits more closely into the "natural open systems" tradition. Organizations are seen as "natural" in that they (as is natural with all social groups) actively pursue goals of narrow self-interest, such as their own security and survival, and not just their official goals, such as profit, production, or reliability. Organizations are also seen as "open" in that they are constantly interacting with the outside environment, both influencing and being influenced by broader social and political forces.[57]

March and his colleagues, Michael Cohen and Johan Olsen, developed an extremely important perspective on organizational behavior, with the infelicitous title of the "garbage can model," which seeks to explain how complex organizations make decisions under conditions that differ radically from those that reign under rational models.[58] According to the model, such "organized anarchies" exhibit three general properties. First, instead of having clear and consistent objectives, "the organization operates on the basis of a variety of inconsistent and ill-defined preferences." Different individuals at different levels of the organization may hold conflicting goals; the same individuals may hold different and incompatible goals at different times; organizations may not even know their preferences until after choices are made. Second, such organizations use extremely "unclear technology" in their operations: "Although the organization manages to survive and even produce, its own processes are not understood by its members." The organization's left hand does not know what the right hand is doing; what happened in the past and why it happened is not clear; and the connections between the organization's actions and the consequences of its actions are obscure. Third, there is extremely "fluid participation" in the organization's decision-making process. Participants come and go; some pay attention, while others do not; key meetings may be dominated by biased, uninformed, or even uninterested personnel.

This is a deliberately provocative theory of organizational behavior and Cohen, March, and Olsen acknowledge that such extreme properties will not be found at all times in all organizations. But they insist that the theory

---

Van de Ven and William F. Joyce, eds., *Perspectives on Organization Design and Behavior* (New York: John Wiley, 1981), p. 215, as quoted in Scott, *Organizations*, p. 107.

[57] See Scott, *Organizations*, pp. 51–116.

[58] Michael D. Cohen, James G. March, and Johan P. Olsen, "A Garbage Can Model of Organizational Choice," in March, *Decisions and Organizations*, pp. 294–334. (All quotations in the paragraph are from page 295.) Also see James G. March and Johan P. Olsen, "Garbage Can Models of Decision Making in Organizations," in James G. March and Roger Weissinger-Baylon, eds., *Ambiguity and Command: Organizational Perspectives on Military Decision Making* (Marshfield, Mass.: Pitman, 1986), pp. 11–35.

explains many of the actions of some organizations and some of the actions of almost any organization. This approach replaces the concept of rational organizations pursuing clear and consistent goals, with a more political vision in which "solutions" are actively looking for problems to attach themselves to, "problems" are ill-defined and often unrecognized, and "participants" have limited attention, shifting allegiances, and uncertain intentions. This complex mixture is often haphazardly dumped together at "choice opportunities"—such as budget conferences or hiring committee lunches, and board of directors meetings (such choice opportunities are the garbage cans in the title)—during which the "organization is expected to produce behavior that can be called a decision." The result is a very different way of conceptualizing organizational behavior:

> Such a view of organizational choice focuses attention on the way the meaning of choice changes over time. It calls attention to the strategic effects of timing, through the introduction of choices and problems, the time pattern of available energy, and the impact of organizational structure. . . . Such a theory of organizational decision-making must concern itself with a relatively complicated interplay among the generation of problems in an organization, the deployment of personnel, the production of solutions, and the opportunities for choice.[59]

The garbage can theory has become very influential since it was developed in the early 1970s. By not treating organizations as rational, problem-solving actors, the theory has illuminated the hidden and more capricious aspects of organizational life. It has encouraged scholars to examine how conflicting goals emerge and coexist, how organizational actors use power and information to promote their favored solutions to problems, how the rigid structure of an agenda can dominate the uncertain intent of a decision-maker, and how organizational leaders reinterpret the haphazard events of history to fit their preconceptions that the results must have been what they intended all along. Ideas borrowed from this somewhat "deconstructionist" approach to organization theory have been utilized to illuminate complex decision-making behavior in organizations as diverse as the Physics Department of the University of Oslo, the National Institute of Education; secretive Pentagon procurement agencies, the U.S. Congress, and a variety of New York state disaster relief agencies.[60] It has

---

[59] Cohen, March, and Olsen, "A Garbage Can Model of Organizational Choice," pp. 296–297.
[60] See, respectively, Johan P. Olsen, "Reorganization as a Garbage Can," in James G. March and Johan P. Olsen, *Ambiguity and Choice in Organizations* (Bergen, Norway: Universitetsforlaget, 1979), pp. 314–337; Lee Sproull, Stephen Weiner, and David Wolf, *Organizing an Anarchy: Belief, Bureaucracy, and Politics in the National Institute of Education* (Chicago: University of Chicago Press, 1978); John P. Crecine, "Defense Resource Alloca-

also strongly influenced the most important work of the normal accidents school studying how modern organizations manage and mismanage hazardous technologies.


## Structure, Politics, and Accidents


In an important 1977 essay, Charles Perrow argued that academic theorists often construct models of organizations whose behavior is far more rational and effective than that displayed by complex organizations in the real world. He therefore urged scholars to be more skeptical and conduct "revelatory" studies of "gross malfunctioning" organizations. Such studies, Perrow maintained, would be "more likely to reveal what most managers know but social scientists cannot afford to acknowledge, namely that complex social systems are greatly influenced by sheer chance, accident, and luck; that most decisions are very ambiguous, preference orderings are incoherent and unstable, efforts at communication and understanding are often ineffective, subsystems are very loosely connected, and most attempts at social control are clumsy and unpredictable."[61] In his influential 1984 book, *Normal Accidents: Living with High-Risk Technologies*, Perrow followed his own advice and used and modified many of the ideas found in the garbage can model in an effort to understand the safety risks in such hazardous systems as commercial airlines, nuclear power plants, international shipping, the petrochemical industry, and (in a very brief section) nuclear weapons.[62] His pessimistic conclusion—that "serious accidents are inevitable, no matter how hard we try to avoid them"[63]—sharply contrasts against the optimism displayed by the high reliability theorists.

---

tion: Garbage Can Analysis of C3 Procurement," in March and Weissinger-Baylon, eds., *Ambiguity and Command*, pp. 72–119; John W. Kingdon, *Agendas, Alternatives, and Public Policies* (Boston: Little, Brown and Company, 1984); and Lee Clarke, *Acceptable Risk?: Making Decisions in a Toxic Environment* (Berkeley: University of California Press, 1989). For an excellent review of the garbage can model, which places it in the context of deconstructionism, see Charles Perrow, *Complex Organizations: A Critical Essay*, 3d ed. (New York: Random House, 1986), pp. 135–140.

[61] Charles Perrow, "Three Types of Effectiveness Studies," in Paul S. Goodman, Johannes M. Pennings, and Associates, *New Perspectives on Organizational Effectiveness* (San Francisco: Jossey-Bass, 1977), p. 153.

[62] Charles Perrow, *Normal Accidents: Living with High-Risk Technologies* (New York: Basic Books, 1984). On the influence of the garbage can model on Perrow's theory, see Perrow, *Complex Organizations*, pp. 131–154, and his review of March and Olsen's *Ambiguity and Choice in Organizations* in *Contemporary Sociology* 6, no. 3 (May 1977): pp. 294–298.

[63] Charles Perrow, "Accidents in High Risk Systems," *Technology Studies* 1, no. 1, (forthcoming 1992), p. 1 (manuscript). Also see Perrow, *Normal Accidents*, p. 3.

What are the assumptions and arguments that lead to this conclusion? Compared to the high reliability approach, the normal accidents theory is both more structural and more political. It is more structural because Perrow identifies two specific structural characteristics of many organizations operating dangerous technologies—"interactive complexity" and "tight-coupling"—which make them highly accident prone regardless of the intent of their leaders or operators. The theory is also more political because it focuses attention on the interaction of conflicting interests both within these organizations and between the organizations and the broader political community. Such conflicting interests can exert a strong influence on the frequency of catastrophic accidents, on their interpretation and therefore who receives the blame for failures, and, finally, on the degree to which the organizational structures that make normal accidents inevitable are modified or abandoned.

## Complex and Linear Interactions

What does Perrow mean when he writes that an organization or technological system displays high degrees of interactive complexity and tight-coupling? Interactive complexity is a measure, not of a system's overall size or the number of subunits that exist in it, but rather of the way in which parts are connected and interact. According to Perrow, "*complex* interactions are those of unfamiliar sequences, unplanned and unexpected sequences, and either not visible or not immediately comprehensible." The opposite is a system with *linear* interactions, "those in expected and familiar production or maintenance sequence, and those that are quite visible even if unplanned."[64] An automobile assembly line is the prototypical linear system: it may be very large, but equipment is spread out; production steps are segregated and take place in a planned and familiar sequence; the assembly process is relatively well understood and if a broken conveyer belt stops the line, the problem is visible to operators and is, relatively speaking, easily comprehensible; and, finally, feedback and information on the what is happening on the plant floor is usually direct and simply verified.

None of these characteristics are found, however, in a nuclear power plant, the prototypical system with high interactive complexity. Critical components are kept, by necessity, in close proximity within a containment building, increasing the possibility of unplanned interactions. The nuclear energy production process is not a set of largely independent and serial steps, but rather requires many coordinated actions by numerous

[64] Perrow, *Normal Accidents*, p. 78.

mechanical components and operators. Despite years of operation, not all aspects of nuclear physics are completely understood. (Experts disagreed, for example, about whether the zirconium and water outside the fuel rods could interact under extreme heat and produce dangerous hydrogen bubbles until the accident at Three Mile Island proved that this was possible.) Finally, power plant operators cannot directly observe all the components involved in the production process. Many critical components and safety valves are inside the containment building or along the maze of pipes used for cooling purposes; control room operators must therefore rely on numerous (and fallible) warning devices, control panel lights that indicate whether components are functioning properly, and redundant monitoring systems to manage operations inside the plant.

Organizations and systems with high degrees of interactive complexity which include universities, biotech firms, and NASA space launch missions as well as nuclear power plants—will share a number of problems, according to Perrow. They are likely to experience unexpected and often baffling interactions among components, which designers did not anticipate and operators cannot recognize. They are highly vulnerable to *common-mode failures*: the sometimes deliberate, but usually inadvertent condition where critical components share a common feature, the failure of which causes them all to break down. Designers and operators in hazardous organizations may work hard to anticipate and fix all likely potential problems, but Perrow's case studies repeatedly discover that it is the unlikely problem, even the bizarre and often banal failure, that initiates a normal accident. A commercial airplane's coffee machine causes a fire that shorts out the wires controlling both the aircraft's warning lights and its landing flaps. A maintenance worker changing a light bulb at a nuclear power station accidently drops it onto some sensors and controls, causing a short circuit and the automatic scramming of the reactor. At Three Mile Island, a critical warning light properly indicated that the emergency feedwater valves were not open during the emergency, but the light could not be seen by control room operators because it was partially covered by a maintenance tag.[65] Such unanticipated and even freakish incidents are inevitable in organizations with high interactive complexity. As Perrow puts it:

> The argument is basically very simple. We start with a plant, airplane, ship, biology laboratory, or other setting with a lot of components (parts, procedures, operators). Then we need two or more failures among components that interact in some unexpected way. No one dreamed that when X failed, Y would also be out of order and the two failures would interact so as to both start a fire and silence the fire alarm. Furthermore, no one can figure out the

[65] *Ibid.*, pp. 134, 44, 19.

interaction at the time and thus know what to do. The problem is something that just never occurred to the designers.[66]

## Tight and Loose Coupling

Although interactive complexity will increase the likelihood of such bizarre and dangerous incidents, the second structural condition of tight coupling is necessary to produce escalation to a full-blown normal accident. Whether a system is tightly coupled or loosely coupled affects its ability to recover from small-scale failures before they cascade into larger problems. Perrow has identified a number of related characteristics that distinguish tightly from loosely coupled systems.[67] First, tightly coupled systems have more *time-dependent processes*: planned and unplanned interactions occur quickly; items must move continuously through the production process; delays, extensions, and storage of incomplete products are not possible. In contrast, in loosely coupled systems, production moves more slowly, it is possible to put the system on a stand-by mode, and delays are possible because unfinished products can sit for a while or can be stored without damage. Second, in tightly coupled systems the sequences and coordinated activities needed to produce the product are *invariant*: there is only one way to make the item and each step in the process must be taken in sequence. In loosely coupled systems, the products can be produced in a number of ways, items can be rerouted and schedules changed, and parts can be added later if delays or shortages occur. Third, tightly coupled systems have little *slack*: quantities used in production must be precise and the processes must be done right the first time or not at all. Such precision is not required for success in loosely coupled systems, and one part of the production process can always be repeated if necessary. Fourth, safety devices, redundancies, and buffers between parts of the production process in tightly coupled systems are largely limited to those that have been *planned and designed into the system*. Because of the time-dependent processes, invariant production sequences, and lack of slack in these systems, there is little opportunity to improvise when things go wrong, and fortuitous recovery aids rarely have time to emerge. Adequate mechanisms for safety and recovery must therefore be deliberately built into the system. In loosely coupled systems, one finds much more opportunity for unplanned, but nonetheless successful, responses to individual failures.

Organizations that display high interactive complexity can be either loosely or tightly coupled. An example of each combination can provide a better understanding of the general characteristics that have just been

[66] *Ibid.*, p. 4.
[67] *Ibid.*, pp. 93–96.

listed. A large university, on the one hand, shows all the signs of high interactive complexity, but is also a very loosely coupled system. Complex and unexpected interactions abound in the daily activities of students, staff, and faculty members living and working together on a campus. As college presidents undoubtedly know, no one can observe every activity that takes place on campus, much less plan or control them all, and the existence of bizarre, small-scale failures in the education process are commonplace. (It should be no surprise that universities have provided some of the best examples of the garbage can model.) No one thought that the professor who went to Los Angeles to give a talk to an alumni group would have her return flight canceled and therefore not show up for the semester's first lecture. No one anticipated that the secretary would forget to send a philosopher's course announcement sheet to either the department chairman or the course catalog office, leading to the course not being taught during the spring semester. Who would have guessed that the undergraduate entertainment committee would schedule a Grateful Dead concert on the afternoon of the Music Appreciation 101 midterm exam?

Such incidents do not lead to an accidental end of a student's education, however, because universities are loosely coupled systems. The learning process is not terribly time dependent, and the professor's lecture can be rescheduled for the next week without much damage to the class. The steps involved in getting a degree are usually very flexible, and it does not matter very much whether a student takes the philosophy course this semester or the next. There is a lot of slack in the system: the midterm could be offered the next morning; a good student might skip it altogether and rely on getting an A on the final in order to pass; a poor student could always take the class again next year. Finally, improvisation or fortuitous events could save the day: a smart undergraduate could run to the classroom and take the exam during the drum solo, or the whole concert might be canceled because of rain. In short, small failures happen all the time in universities, but they rarely escalate to the point where a student's education is irreparably harmed.

Contrast this situation, on the other hand, with a nuclear power plant, which has high degrees of *both* interactive complexity and tight coupling. If something goes seriously wrong due to a bizarre interaction—imagine that a forgetful maintenance worker accidently leaves a coolant pipe valve closed and that he also forgets to fix the broken warning light indicator for that valve in the control room—the tightly coupled system will not so easily recover. Nuclear energy production is a highly time-dependent and very precise process: there has to be continual and sufficient amounts of coolant moving through the reactor to avoid dangerous overheating. The process is invariant and operators cannot substitute air circulation for the water coolant or wait until tomorrow to extract the excess heat. The opportunity for successful improvisation during an emergency is also highly limited. This is precisely why there must be redundant coolant pipes, backup power sources, and multiple warning indicators carefully designed into nuclear power plants.

It is this particular mixture that produces Perrow's pessimism. If a system has many complex interactions, unanticipated and common-mode failures are inevitable; and if the system is also tightly coupled, it will be very difficult to prevent such failures from escalating into a major accident. Such accidents may not happen often; indeed, they may be rare. But this is of little consolation if one is talking about highly hazardous technologies such as nuclear reactors, toxic chemical plants, or recombinant DNA (gene-splicing) research. If significant degrees of interactive complexity and tight coupling are combined, according to the theory, the organization's structure will eventually lead to a serious accident.

## Four Factors Revisited

The high reliability theorists identified four factors that should produce extremely safe operations, even in organizations operating hazardous technologies. How are these specific safety factors viewed from the perspective of a normal accidents theorist? Can such conditions exist, and would they significantly reduce or even eliminate the dangers inherent in hazardous technologies?

In each case, the normal accidents approach provides reasons to suspect that significant improvements in safety will be much less forthcoming than the high reliability theorists suggest. Perrow's *Normal Accidents* directly addresses some of these factors, but in other cases I have been forced to deduce additional propositions, which are not explicitly raised by Perrow, from the general causal concepts present in the theory. In addition, research by other scholars who have been influenced by Perrow's ideas, has deepened and broadened the normal accidents theory by applying it to further case studies and new substantive areas.[68] This literature will therefore also be utilized to develop propositions and illustrate concepts.

[68] The important scholarship that has been influenced by this perspective includes: Clarke, *Acceptable Risk?*; James Reason, *Human Error* (Cambridge, U.K.: Cambridge University Press, 1990); Paul Shrivastava, *Bhopal: Anatomy of a Crisis* (Cambridge, Mass.: Ballinger, 1987); Michal Tamuz, "Monitoring Dangers in the Air: Studies in Ambiguity and Information" (doctoral dissertation, Department of Sociology, Stanford University, 1988); William H. Starbuck and Francis J. Milliken, "Challenger: Fine-Tuning the Odds until Something Breaks," *Journal of Management Studies* 25, no. 4 (July 1988): 319–340; and Diane Vaughan, "Autonomy, Interdependence, and Social Control: NASA and the Space Shuttle Challenger," *Administrative Science Quarterly* 35, no. 2, pp. 225–257.

## Conflicting Objectives

The first condition identified by the high reliability theorists was that safety is considered to be the priority objective by leaders of the organization. Normal accidents theorists do not disagree that it *can* be beneficial to have political elites and organizational leaders place higher priority on the objectives of safety and reliability. Error rates might be reduced if more money is spent in the right places and if clear operational safety goals are set. In fact, Perrow places considerable emphasis on the unnecessary risks caused by the leaders' and elites' lack of interest in improving safety in a number of high-risk technologies, arguing that "the nature of the victims in contact with the system should have *some effect* on the safety of that system":

> Elites fly on airplanes all the time, and airline pilots are in high demand, well paid, and in a position to have some, though not great, influence on the operation of the system. Captains and Admirals cannot escape naval vessels and a serious aircraft accident aboard a carrier will endanger their lives. But nobody of any great importance works directly in a nuclear power plant, travels aboard tankers and freighters loaded with explosive and toxic cargos, sits in the potato fields sprayed by genetically engineered microbes, or gets very close to a huge chemical plant.[69]

Yet, even though Perrow argues that increased leadership interests in safety can have *some* beneficial effects, the approach also leads one to expect that the goals of elites and organizations' leaders will only have a quite limited effect on the behavior of the entire organization. The structural factors of interactive complexity and tight coupling are seen as significantly increasing the likelihood of accidents in such organizations, regardless of the intent of the leaders. In addition, because complex organizations are conceived as having poorly defined and often inconsistent preferences, this perspective suggests that the pursuit of other objectives will continue, and conflict over organizational goals will remain, even if improved safety is recognized as the priority official goal by leaders.

This continued conflict over goals within high-risk organizations is significant in three major ways. First, significant pressure to maintain high production rates exist in most hazardous industries and may be only slightly moderated by increased interests in safety. The signs of such production pressures—hasty decision-making, violations of safety rules, and jerry-rigged procedures—are found during many normal accidents. Subtle and sometimes not so subtle reminders of the "need" to keep the ship on schedule, for example, often lead to captains and crews "cutting corners"

---

[69] Perrow, "Accidents in High Risk Systems," pp. 21–22, (emphasis added).

and hence to accidents at sea.[70] Diane Vaughan's study of the space shuttle *Challenger* incident similarly emphasizes the degree to which, despite the leadership's great concern about safety, NASA continued to provide strong pressures to its contractors and officials for immediate delivery of parts and strict maintenance of launch schedules.[71] Second, even if political leaders desire increased safety, differences in prioritization of goals between an organization and its ostensible political authority can continue. Organizations will seek to maintain their autonomy against outside pressures and numerous studies have noted the degree to which tensions exist between an industry and a regulatory agency created by the political authorities to monitor its behavior. Under such conditions, the normal accident approach focuses attention on the likelihood of government watchdogs being "captured" by the forces they are supposed to regulate.[72] Third, even if political elites and organizational leaders have consistent objectives favoring safety, they may be misinformed about the nature or frequency of dangerous operations by lower-level operators, whose interests include keeping their jobs and therefore not getting caught when rules are violated. Michal Tamuz's innovative research on the reporting of near-accidents in the U.S. airlines industry, for example, discovered that commercial pilots consistently underreported the number of safety violations they have witnessed.[73] Raymond Levitt's study of the California construction industry similarly showed how the incentives to withhold information about small accidents and near misses increase when concerned company officials offer rewards to employees with the best safety records.[74]

In short, although the normal accidents theory accepts that there can be "organizations with an avowed goal of safe operations," it treats the step from avowed goals to real organizational objectives as very problematic. The theory points to a number of reasons why safety and reliability may not increase even if political and organizational leaders claim to have placed increased priority on such goals. Even the serious intent by an organization's leadership to accord safety and reliability higher priority than other objectives is not seen as automatically leading to the acceptance of such goals by others within the organization. Inconsistent goals and conflicting interests remain and can increase the risks of accidents in important ways.

[70] See Perrow, *Normal Accidents*, pp. 179–189, and Reason, *Human Error*, p. 256.
[71] Vaughan, "Autonomy, Interdependence, and Social Control," p. 248.
[72] On this possibility see *Ibid.*; and Perrow's discussion of the FAA in *Normal Accidents*, pp. 162–167.
[73] Tamuz, "Monitoring Dangers in the Air."
[74] Raymond E. Levitt, "The Effect of Top Management on Safety in Construction," (doctoral dissertation, Department of Civil Engineering, Stanford University, 1975), pp. 40–44.

## The Perils of Redundancy

Given that individual parts of a complex technological system can always fail, the high reliability theorists place great emphasis on the need for redundancy—duplication and overlap in critical components and personnel—to produce improved safety. Accidents, of course, can still occur. It is always possible that more than one component can fail independently at the same time: during the 1984 Bhopal plant chemical disaster, for example, the deadly gasses escaped because three separate safety devices—a flare tower to burn off the gas, a scrubber to clean air emissions, and a water sprinkler system to neutralize remaining fumes—all failed simultaneously.[75] Such an event, however, does not directly contradict the high reliability theory. Indeed, it supports the theory, since simultaneous and independent failure of all critical components should be made less likely when more redundant backups are added to the system.

The normal accidents perspective, in contrast, focuses attention on the potential negative consequences of redundancy and, indeed, maintains that adding redundant parts to a complex technological system can *increase* the likelihood of accidents for three central reasons. First, while these authors do not disagree that redundant safety systems, *if* truly independent, can enhance system reliability in theory, they do suggest that, in reality, redundant systems are often less independent than their designers believe. Although redundant backups are supposed to be independent of one another, they also usually increase the interactive complexity of high-technology organizations and hence lead to unanticipated common-mode failures. A number of nuclear power plant accidents, for example, have been caused by recently added safety devices that interacted with other components in bizarre and unexpected ways to produce critical failures. The 1966 near meltdown of a power plant near Monroe, Michigan, was produced by a broken safety device that blocked the flow of coolant to the reactor, and the 1986 Chernobyl accident was caused by a test of backup safety power sources. (See chapter 4 for a more detailed discussion of these and other examples.) Second, adding redundancy often makes the system more opaque: individual component or human failures will often be less visible, since they have been compensated for by overlap or backup devices. If this occurs, such individual errors may remain unfixed, and latent problems will therefore accumulate over time, increasing the likelihood of both interactive common-mode failures and simultaneous failures of indepen-

[75] The flare tower was down for maintenance; the scrubber failed to operate; and the sprinklers did not throw water high enough to neutralize the escaping gas. Shrivastava, *Bhopal*, p. 55.

dent and redundant components.[76] Third, when redundancy makes the system appear more safe, operators often take advantage of such improvements to move to higher and more dangerous production levels. "Fixes, including safety devices," Perrow argues, "often merely allow those in charge to run the system faster, or in worse weather, or with bigger explosives."[77]

## Decentralization, Culture, and Continuity Revisited

From the perspective of a normal accidents theorist, doubts can also be raised about the three operational characteristics that high reliability theorists identified as being essential for safety. Decentralization of decision-making authority to individuals close to the operations may well be necessary to produce appropriate low-level responses to unanticipated events in systems that display high degrees of interactive complexity. Yet Perrow also argues that the characteristics of highly centralized decision-making—strict standard operating procedures, unquestioned individual obedience, and immediate responses—are equally necessary in tightly coupled systems. Because tightly coupled systems have invariant and time-dependent production processes with little built-in slack, there is no time for improvisation by operators in crises and little scope for recovery from faulty field-level decisions. When a system is *both* interactively complex and tightly coupled, therefore, the requirements for reliability are simply incompatible. Such systems are "organizational Pushmepullyous, straight out of the Dr. Doolittle stories, trying to go in opposite directions at once."[78] Neither strict centralization nor decentralization of authority can therefore ensure safety under such conditions.

High reliability theorists argue that a solution to this dilemma is a strong organizational culture, which creates a common set of decision-making premises and assumptions so that lower-level personnel, responding to surprises according to their own best judgement, nevertheless react in a uniform and appropriate manner. A normal accidents perspective, however, in accordance with garbage can model assumptions, would lead to doubts about whether organizational leaders know enough about their operations and technology to determine how lower-level authorities should respond in all contingencies. Uniformity of decentralized decisions

---

[76] Reason, *Human Error*, p. 179, citing Jens Rasmussen, "Interdisciplinary Workshops to Develop a Multi-Disciplinary Research Program Based on a Holistic System Approach to Safety and Management of Large-Scale Technological Operations" (unpublished paper, 1988).

[77] Perrow, *Normal Accidents*, p. 11.

[78] *Ibid.*, p. 10. Also see pp. 330–335.

may be helpful if the leadership has accurately identified how to prevent accidents; if it has not done so, however, then uniformity of lower-level responses will decrease safety and reliability. In addition, the intense organizational culture, which is viewed as necessary by the high reliability theorists, is seen as being simply impossible to achieve in an individualistic, democratic society. As Perrow argues:

> It calls for a wartime, military model in a peacetime civilian operation. A military model reflects strict discipline, unquestioning obedience, intense socialization, and isolation from normal civilian life styles. . . . Efforts to extend this model to industry in the nineteenth and early twentieth centuries failed; it was too incompatible with American social values and culture.[79]

In short, citizens in democratic societies are not willing to manage all hazardous organizations as if they were "total institutions," completely isolating their members from broader social life, socializing them into conformity, and controlling every aspect of their behavior.

Continuous training and operational experience helps develop and maintain the information necessary for maximum safety, according to the high reliability school. Analysts with a normal accidents perspective might agree in principle, but would also point out that an organization simply cannot develop operational experience with reactions to all the unanticipated and undesirable failure modes produced by high interactive complexity in hazardous technologies. Potential accident scenarios that have not been imagined obviously will not be practiced. Some dangerous operations cannot be practiced often, precisely because they are so dangerous. Finally, in the politicized environment of a conflicted organization, some highly unpalatable accident scenarios, especially those that clearly place blame on certain individuals or subunits, will not be addressed because to do so would require that those responsible implicitly acknowledge that such events are possible.

### Restrictions on Learning

In contrast to the belief that high-risk organizations will improve safety and reliability through trial-and-error learning and simulation, the normal accidents school suggests a number of reasons why effective learning will be very difficult, if not impossible. In the first place, the causes of accidents and near-accidents are often unclear, and in such situations even well-meaning organizational leaders are likely to reconstruct history to conform to their preconceptions, to attribute success to their own actions, and

[79] *Ibid.*, p. 335. On this issue also see Langdon Winner, "Do Artifacts Have Politics?" *Daedalus* 109, no. 1 (Winter 1980): 121–136.

to develop lessons to fit into their sense of mission. Unless the causes of an incident are relatively clear and cannot not be ignored, biased interpretations will therefore reign. Under severe conditions of ambiguity, instead of learning more effective behavior, March and Olsen have argued, "modern organizations develop myths, fictions, legends, folklore, and illusions."[80]

Second, analyses of real or potential accidents often take place in extremely politicized environments in which blame for failures and credit for successes must be assigned to someone within the organization. If this is the case, such analyses are likely to be designed to protect the parochial interests of the most powerful actors instead of promoting more objective learning.[81] These powerful interests help explain why, for example, internal investigations of industrial disasters almost always find that they were caused by "operator errors" and were rarely the result of mistaken design or faulty decisions by the senior management.[82] In such situations, organizational learning, in the sense of changing procedures to avoid repeating errors, would be expected to be highly constrained and severely limited in the types of lessons that can be accepted. Third, normal accidents theory highlights the possibility that faulty reporting will make it extremely difficult for organizations to assess their performance accurately. Unfortunately, the incentives to cover up serious errors and to fabricate positive records can be strong, especially if field-level operators or lower-level officials know that they will be blamed for the occurrence of any accidents or near-accidents. It therefore should not be surprising that faulty reporting has been witnessed in a variety of organizations in which it was not in the interests of lower-level individuals to acknowledge the truth. When the Federal Aviation Administration installed automatic flight path recording devices in air traffic control centers, the number of "near miss" collisions reported by pilots increased enormously. When U.S. Air Force pilots over North Vietnam bombed a Soviet naval vessel in error, the evidence was quickly covered up. After the December 1989 invasion of Panama, the secretary of defense inaccurately told the press that the new F-117A Stealth

[80] James G. March and Johan P. Olsen, "The Uncertainty of the Past: Organizational Learning under Ambiguity" in March, *Decisions and Organizations*, p. 349. Also see James G. March, Lee S. Sproull, and Michal Tamuz, "Learning from Samples of One or Fewer," *Organization Science* 2, no. 1 (February 1991): 1–13; and Starbuck and Milliken, "Challenger."

[81] For a fascinating study of how "killer drunks," rather than unforgiving automotive design or speed regulations, became seen as the primary cause of fatal car accidents, see Joseph R. Gusfield, *The Culture of Public Problems: Drinking-Driving and the Symbolic Order* (Chicago: University of Chicago Press, 1981).

[82] Charles Perrow, "The Organizational Context of Human Factors Engineering," *Administrative Science Quarterly* 28, no. 4 (December 1983): 521–541. Also see Leo Tasca, "The Social Construction of Human Error" (doctoral dissertation, Department of Sociology, State University of New York at Stony Brook, 1990).

fighter had delivered its weapons with "pinpoint accuracy," because the commander of the Tactical Air Force command failed to report that bombs had accidently been dropped away from the intended targets.[83]

In addition, organizational leaders who are informed of improper activities by subordinates often have an interest to cover up the mistakes so as to minimize outside criticisms of the organization's management. "Shielding members from external perception of their deviance also shields the organization from embarrassment," argues Jack Katz: when an official is fired, it is often represented as voluntary resignation; commanding military officers have been found to list AWOL soldiers as being on official leave; and corporation officials have been known to resist prosecution of discharged embezzlers in order to protect their image with stockholders.[84] While such shielding may enhance the organization's reputation with outsiders, it also decreases the incentives, which often stem from external pressures, to improve procedures after errors are discovered.

Finally, a fourth constraint on organizational learning is secrecy inside complex organizations and between organizations. Although compartmentalization of knowledge within an organization may be necessary to guard secrets from outsiders, it can also limit the overall organization's ability to learn and implement lessons from historical experience. It is not uncommon in such circumstances for one part of the organization to be unaware of what other subunits have learned from trials and errors.[85] Secrecy between organizations is also a common practice since it protects production methods or procedural innovations. This also has the negative effect, however, of limiting vicarious learning, that is, learning from the mistakes of others.

### Normal Accidents Summary

Normal accidents theorists take a natural open systems perspective in which organizations and members of organizations are self-interested ac-

---

[83] On commercial pilots see Michal Tamuz, "The Impact of Computer Surveillance on Air Safety Reporting," *Columbia Journal of World Business* 22 (1987): 69–77. On military pilots' reports in Vietnam, see Robert Jervis, *The Meaning of the Nuclear Revolution* (Ithaca, N.Y.: Cornell University Press, 1989), pp. 159–160, and Barry D. Watts, "Unreported History and Unit Effectiveness," *Journal of Strategic Studies* 12, no. 1 (March 1989): 88–98. On the F-117A reports see Michael R. Gordon, "New Report Says General Knew Stealth Failed," *New York Times*, July 2, 1990, p. 1.

[84] Jack Katz, "Cover-Up and Collective Integrity: On the Natural Antagonisms of Authority Internal and External to Organizations," *Social Problems* 25, no. 1 (October 1977): 6.

[85] See David R. Mares and Walter W. Powell, "Cooperative Security Regimes," in Robert L. Kahn and Meyer N. Zald, eds., *Organizations and Nation-States: New Perspectives on Conflict and Cooperation* (San Francisco: Jossey-Bass, 1990), p. 87.

tors with potentially conflicting interests, and in which organizations are strongly influenced by broader political and social forces in the environment. These theorists utilize a modified form of the garbage can model: they view organizations as often having inconsistent preferences, unclear technologies, and fluid participation. The theory predicts that serious accidents are inevitable if the organizations that control hazardous technologies display both high interactive complexity (which produces bizarre and unanticipated failures) and tight coupling (which causes the failures to escalate rapidly out of control). Each of the four factors previously identified as contributing to high reliability are seen from the normal accidents perspective as being ineffective, unlikely to be implemented, or even counterproductive. Even if leaders place a very high priority on safety and reliability, which is by no means a given, competing organizational and individual objectives will remain: the continuing desires to maximize production, maintain autonomy, and protect personal reputations, however, can severely impair efforts to improve safety. Adding redundancy does not necessarily enhance reliability because it also increases interactive complexity, encourages operators to run more risks, and makes the overall system more opaque. Decentralized decision-making does not necessarily enhance safety because tightly coupled systems require rapid responses and strict adherence to standard operating procedures. Intense socialization and a strong organizational culture are unlikely to be very productive in hazardous organizations both because their leaders cannot know how operators should respond in all contingencies and because democratic societies are unwilling to isolate and control all aspects of the lives of such organizations' members. Constant training and practice will not address accident scenarios that are unanticipated, excessively dangerous, or politically unpalatable. Finally, a number of factors will severely constrain the process of trial-and-error learning: uncertainty about the causes of accidents, the political interests and biases of organizational leaders and low-level operators, and compartmentalization within the organization and secrecy between organizations.

Although there has previously been no thorough study of nuclear weapons and command and control systems from the normal accidents perspective, the theory would not lead to optimistic predictions about safety with nuclear weapons systems.[86] A normal accidents theorist would look with alarm at the global command and control system that manages U.S. nuclear weapons operations, since it appears to be highly complex, by necessity, and appears to be tightly coupled, by design, so as to permit

[86] Although *Normal Accidents* does include a brief (twelve-page) discussion of nuclear command-and-control false warning problems, Perrow acknowledges that "the question of nuclear weapons cannot be sensibly discussed in a paragraph or even a chapter." Perrow, *Normal Accidents*, pp. 346–347.

prompt retaliation in a war. Indeed, from a normal accidents perspective, the fact that there has never been an accidental nuclear weapons detonation or an accidental war is surprising.

## THEORY TESTING AND NUCLEAR WEAPONS

These two theories explaining the origins of accidents in complex organizations are clearly competitive in a number of ways. At the most general level, they represent very different perspectives on how modern organizations function. Many of the specific conditions that the high reliability theorists argue will promote safety will actually reduce safety according to the normal accidents theorists. Other strategies that the first school argues are both necessary for safety and possible to implement in complex organizations are seen as simply impossible to achieve by the second school. Finally, the central conclusions reached by the two groups of scholars are very different from one another. One theory leads to the highly optimistic prediction that near-perfect reliability and safety are possible in complex organizations using hazardous technologies. The other theory leads to the more pessimistic prediction that serious accidents are inevitable. Table 1.1 outlines the contradictory assumptions, propositions, and conclusions drawn from both schools of thought. What lies at the heart of the disagreement between these two perspectives on safety in hazardous organizations? The opposing schools do *not* dispute the basic *logic* of Perrow's argument that the structural conditions of interactive complexity and tight coupling should, *in theory*, lead to accident-prone organizations. They do, however, hold very different visions of the degree to which the basic forces of human "agency"—the elements of culture, design, management, and choice—can counter or compensate for these dangerous structural pressures within hazardous organizations. Perrow's basic pessimism on this issue is unmistakable: "No matter how hard we try, no matter how much training, how many safety devices, planning, redundancies, buffers, alarms, bells and whistles we build into our systems, those that are complexly interactive will find an occasion where the unexpected interaction of two or more failures defeats the training, the planning, and the design of safety devices."[87] In direct contrast, the high reliability theorists argue that certain complex, tightly coupled "organizations have developed strategies for avoiding the negative effects of these (structural) characteristics."[88]

This position is most clearly laid out in the Berkeley group's studies of U.S. aircraft carriers. Weick and Roberts, for example, maintain that U.S. carriers "tend to be tightly coupled and interactively complex, a combina-

[87] Perrow, "Accidents in High Risk Systems," p. 4.
[88] Roberts, "Some Characteristics of One Type of High Reliability Organization," p. 173.

## TABLE 1.1
### Competing Perspectives on Safety with Hazardous Technologies

| High Reliability Theory | Normal Accidents Theory |
|---|---|
| Accidents can be prevented through good organizational design and management. | Accidents are inevitable in complex and tightly coupled systems. |
| Safety is the priority organizational objective. | Safety is one of a number competing objectives. |
| Redundancy enhances safety: duplication and overlap can make "a reliable system out of unreliable parts." | Redundancy often causes accidents: it increases interactive complexity and opaqueness and encourages risk-taking. |
| Decentralized decision-making is needed to permit prompt and flexible field-level responses to surprises. | Organizational contradiction: decentralization is needed for complexity, but centralization is needed for tightly coupled systems. |
| A "culture of reliability" will enhance safety by encouraging uniform and appropriate responses by field-level operators. | A military model of intense discipline, socialization, and isolation is incompatible with democratic values. |
| Continuous operations, training, and simulations can create and maintain high reliability operations. | Organizations cannot train for unimagined, highly dangerous, or politically unpalatable operations. |
| Trial and error learning from accidents can be effective, and can be supplemented by anticipation and simulations. | Denial of responsibility, faulty reporting, and reconstruction of history cripples learning efforts. |

tion which normally increases the tendency toward consequential failures, but in these organizations does not."[89] Rigorous exercises, continual training, and realistic simulations combat the negative effects of interactive complexity since such efforts are "directed to understanding the complexities of the technologies aboard the ships . . . in such a way that baffling interactions do not occur."[90] Redundant communication systems also play

[89] Karl E. Weick and Karlene H. Roberts, "Organizational Mind and Organizational Reliability: The Case of Flight Operations on an Aircraft Carrier Deck" (unpublished manuscript), p. 2.

[90] Roberts, "Some Characteristics of One Type of High Reliability Organization," p. 165. Also see Rochlin, "Informal Organizational Networking as a Crisis-Avoidance Strategy," pp. 163–168, and Rochlin, La Porte, and Roberts, "The Self-Designing High Reliability Organization," pp. 84–87.

a key role because "indirect sources of information that can lead to baffling perceptions are mediated against by many direct information sources"; indeed, "in one important decision making place aboard ship, 20 different phones are used by one person."[91] Personnel redundancy is similarly found to counter the negative effects of tight coupling. Roberts, for example, argues that having many officers responsible for checking the aircraft's landing gear can "decompose the tight time frames that are part of tight coupling" since "in a short time three pairs of eyes should be able to spot a problem that may take one pair of eyes longer to detect."[92] Finally, it is argued that continuous training and a strong "culture of responsibility" aboard U.S. aircraft carriers enables "simultaneous centralization and decentralization" to exist, which overcomes the contradictory organizational pressures caused by complexity and coupling. When such intense socialization occurs, according to Weick, "there are previously shared values concerning reliability which then allow for coordinated, decentralized action."[93] For the high reliability theorists, if these conditions are met, a highly optimistic prediction of near-perfect safety is warranted: "*Parts* of these systems do fail," Roberts concludes in a critique of Perrow's book, but "it is really *not* clear that all high-risk technologies will fail."[94]

### Evaluating the Theories

Which perspective on hazardous organizations is more accurate? It is not an easy task to evaluate these two theories. Both have relatively plausible assumptions and the propositions and conclusions of both theories appear to flow logically from those assumptions. Moreover, both the high reliability and the normal accidents theorists provide numerous hypothetical and empirical examples to illustrate and support their arguments. So how can one assess the general strength of the two theoretical approaches?

The most serious difficulty should be acknowledged from the start. Because neither theory provides a precise estimate of the likelihood of serious

---

[91] Roberts, "New Challenges in Organization Research," p. 117.

[92] Roberts, "Some Characteristics of One Type of High Reliability Organization," p. 168.

[93] Weick, "Organizational Culture as a Source of High Reliability," p. 124.

[94] Karlene H. Roberts, "The Significance of Perrow's *Normal Accidents*," *Academy of Management Review* 14, no. 2 (April 1989): 287–288 (emphasis added). La Porte objects to the "optimistic" label and argues that "we (the Berkeley High Reliability Organization project members) are more pessimistic than the other guys. We've seen what it takes to effect conditions of reliability, i.e. counter the 'natural' tendencies of social organizations (a la the garbage can caricature)! It's damn demanding, is very costly, and takes remarkable dedication and commits the future to assuring activities and social constriction on our best and brightest." La Porte, letter to author, September 29, 1991. I leave it to each reader to determine whether this view is best described as optimistic or pessimistic.

accidents with hazardous technologies, it is impossible to determine the precise number of accidents, which, if discovered over time, would support or weaken the theories. Members of the high reliability school are usually prudent enough to avoid the extreme claim that organizational perfection is possible.[95] Marone and Woodhouse therefore argue that "there is a *good chance* . . . that catastrophes will be prevented"; Roberts only states that there are "hazardous organizations that engage in *nearly error free* operations"; and La Porte and Consolini only claim that such organizations have "a *very low error rate* and *an almost total absence of catastrophic failure*."[96] Similarly, Perrow only claims that disastrous accidents will occur eventually: "*Accidents are inevitable* and happen all the time, serious ones are *inevitable though infrequent*; catastrophes are *inevitable but extremely rare*."[97] Such imprecise language suggests that the two theoretical schools have a common estimate about the probability of dangerous accidents despite the strong difference in the tone of their conclusions: Perrow may look at a glass of safety and find it 1 percent empty; high reliability theorists may see the same glass of safety as 99 percent full.

Yet, when one considers the causal mechanisms involved in the theories—the specific factors outlined in table 1.1 that each theory claims will lead to or prevent organizational accidents—the contradictions between them become more clear. This suggests that a more valuable test of the theories would involve detailed specific historical case studies in which a range of these factors existed, focusing on whether these factors had the predicted influence on safety and reliability.[98] For example, what effect did leaders placing a high priority on safety have on the beliefs and behavior of the rest of the complex organization? What was the impact of adding redundant safety devices? Did effective organizational learning take place, fixing the cause of safety problems, after serious incidents? Or did faulty reporting, denial of responsibility, and the reconstruction of history occur?

The following chapters attempt to evaluate these two theoretical ap-

---

[95] Occasionally exuberance overcomes such prudence. For example, Bendor writes that "duplication is a substitute for perfect parts" and Weick and Roberts state that "high reliability organizations such as nuclear powered supercarriers produce error-free performance." Bendor, *Parallel Systems*, p. 291 (also see, however, p. xiii); Weick and Roberts, "Organizational Mind and Organizational Reliability," p. 1 (abstract).

[96] Marone and Woodhouse, *Averting Catastrophe*, p. 150; Roberts, "Some Characteristics of One Type of High Reliability Organization," p. 160; and La Porte and Consolini, "Working in Practice but Not in Theory," p. 21 (emphasis added in all three quotes).

[97] Perrow, "Accidents in High Risk Systems," p. 26 (emphasis added).

[98] Here I am following the "process-tracing" approach to assessing cause-and-effect relationships as outlined in Alexander L. George and Timothy J. McKeown, "Case Studies and Theories of Organizational Decision Making," in Robert F. Coulam and Richard A. Smith, eds., *Advances in Information Processing in Organizations*, vol. 2 (Greenwich, Conn.: JAI Press, 1985), pp. 34–41.

proaches by applying them in a competitive manner to a new subject area. In these chapters I will deduce what each theory should predict about specific efforts to prevent the ultimate safety system failure—an accidental nuclear war—and will then compare these predictions to the historical experience of U.S. nuclear weapons command and control. Which theory provides better predictions of what happened and more compelling explanations of why it happened? Which theory leads to the discovery of more novel facts and new insights? Which one is therefore a better guide to understanding?

This is bound to be a very imperfect exercise in theory testing for a number of unfortunate, but unavoidable, reasons. The imprecision of each theory's predictions, the limited information available about the history of U.S. nuclear weapons safety and military operations, and the inability to control for the effect of perturbing variables all conspire to make this a less than fully satisfying test. I believe, however, that despite such imperfections, these theoretical perspectives will be made more credible to the degree that they lead to expectations that are found to be historically accurate. To the degree that empirical findings do not fit such predictions, the claims of the theory in question will be weakened.

## A Tough Test for Normal Accidents Theory

It is critical that social science theories be tested competitively against one another: since no theory is perfect, its relative strengths and weaknesses can only be measured in comparison to the best available alternative. It is also important, however, to subject theories to tough tests, "least-likely" cases in which the theory's applicability is not obvious or well-accepted. Under such conditions, as Kenneth Waltz notes, "if we observe outcomes that the theory leads us to expect even though strong forces work against them, the theory will begin to command belief."[99]

In this respect, a study of the command and control of U.S. nuclear weapons and the prevention of accidental nuclear war is a tough test for the normal accidents theory. At first glance, one would not expect that the normal accidents theory would provide a strong explanation for nuclear weapons safety. Indeed, there are four important reasons to suspect, at this initial point, that high reliability theory will prove a better tool for studying this subject.

The first reason should be obvious: there has never been an accidental nuclear war, nor even a single accidental detonation of a nuclear weapon.

---

[99] Kenneth N. Waltz, *Theory of International Politics* (New York: Random House, 1979), p. 125. Also see Arthur L. Stinchcombe, *Constructing Social Theories* (Chicago: University of Chicago Press, 1968), pp. 17–20.

This impressive safety record with nuclear weapons therefore appears to conform more closely to the optimistic predictions of the high reliability theorists. Indeed, even Perrow is optimistic about the possibility of high reliability with respect to at least one important aspect of nuclear weapons safety, the risk of an accidental war caused by false warnings. "There is much to fear from accidents with nuclear weapons such as dropping them or an accidental launch, but with regard to firing them after a false warning we reach a surprising conclusion, one I was not prepared for: because of the safety systems involved in a launch-on-warning scenario, *it is virtually impossible* for well-intentioned actions to bring about an accidental attack."[100] If this research discovers evidence that false warning problems have been more serious than Perrow recognized, his theory will thereby be given even more support than he provided for it.

The second reason why this subject is a tough test for normal accidents theory is that the prevention of an accidental nuclear war is undoubtedly a high priority objective of the senior leadership of the United States. Many hazardous systems, such as oil tankers, are far less safe than they could be simply because the individuals with the power to influence change are not potential victims of accidents and therefore do not place great importance on safety improvements. Nuclear weapons are not, however, discriminatory: political authorities, elites, and organizational leaders would suffer just as much as would local operators if there was an accidental nuclear war. As Perrow puts it, on the one hand, "elites do not sail on Liberian tankers"; on the other hand, "the nuclear weapons system is finally democratic."[101] Because the president would be a victim (indeed, potentially one of the first victims) in a nuclear war, even a normal accident theorist would expect that nuclear weapons safety would be a high priority of all American presidents.

Third, there is one aspect of the problem of safety about which Perrow and the high reliability theorists appear to agree: isolation away from society, intense socialization, and strict discipline of organization members, as in the ideal military model, can enhance reliability and safety. Where Perrow disagreed with the high reliability theorists is over the degree to which this military model can or should be applied to members of civilian hazardous organizations in a democracy. The military organizations that control U.S. nuclear weapons, however, have been designed to come as close as possible to that idealized military model. To the degree that the historical evidence suggests that such isolation, discipline, and socialization did not lead to enhanced safety, it will provide additional

---

[100] Perrow, *Normal Accidents*, p. 257 (emphasis added).
[101] *Ibid.*, p. 173; and Perrow, "Accidents in High Risk Systems," p. 21.

support for a pessimistic appraisal of the prospects for safety in other organizations.

Fourth, there is an unavoidable restriction in my selection of case studies to *United States* command and control problems because the secrecy surrounding this subject makes it virtually impossible to do the same kind of detailed historical study about the command and control of nuclear weapons in other countries. This practical necessity is a virtue for theory testing, however, since safety efforts cost a great deal of money, and one would therefore expect that the wealthiest nuclear power would also be the safest nuclear power. "Richer is safer," as Wildavsky states, all other things being equal. One would anticipate, for example, that just as U.S. nuclear power plants and commercial airlines are more reliable than their counterparts in the former Soviet Union, there should be better nuclear command and control safety in the United States.[102] If serious problems with the nuclear weapons system are found in the U.S., one would anticipate finding them to an even greater degree in Russia and in other nuclear powers.

In short, this study is a tough test for the normal accidents theory. It makes the theory compete on the home turf of high reliability theory. If the normal accidents theory does well here, it will be shown to be even stronger than previously estimated.

## The Catch 22 of Close Calls

The methodology used in this study is quite simple in conception, although it is often difficult in execution. To determine which theory provides a more useful tool for understanding nuclear weapons safety, I identify historical situations in which the theories would provide contradictory predictions. For the high reliability theory, I identify the extent to which the factors that the theory argues lead to safety were in fact present and then examine whether those factors, in fact, had the predicted effect. For the normal accidents theory, I deduce where and when accidents should have been likely if the theory is correct, and then check the historical record for evidence of safety problems occurring in those specific areas.

It is important to emphasize that the mere existence of near-accidents is inadequate evidence either to diminish the credibility of high reliability theory or to increase the credibility of normal accidents theory. Indeed, there is an irony here that could be called the catch 22 of close calls: the more near-accidents I discover, the more it could be argued that the system

---

[102] On safety and environmental problems in the former Soviet Union, see James E. Oberg, *Uncovering Soviet Disasters* (New York: Random House, 1988), and Murray Feshbach and Alfred Friendly, Jr., *Ecocide in the USSR* (New York: Basic Books, 1992).

worked, since the incidents did not in the end lead to an accidental nuclear war. The fact that individual errors will occur is, after all, the basic reason why redundancy and other safety measures are built into complex technological systems.

This is yet another reason why it is essential, in order to weigh the relative explanatory power of the two theories, to focus on their specific predictions that are in conflict. What were the causes of the incidents and the reasons why they did not escalate? For example, did adding more than one safety device prevent a serious accident, as would be suggested by high reliability theorists? Or was redundancy the cause of the problem, as predicted by normal accidents theory? And if redundancy caused the incident, what prevented it from escalating?

The following chapters attempt to answer such questions. The evidence will obviously illuminate the risks involved in relying on nuclear weapons for our national security. I believe that it will also, by evaluating the explanatory power of the two general theories of safety, have broader implications about our ability to manage the complex organizations using hazardous technologies in modern society.

# Nuclear Weapons Safety during the Cuban Missile Crisis

The explosion of a nuclear device by accident—
mechanical or human—could be a disaster for the
United States, for its allies, and for its enemies. If one
of these devices accidentally exploded, I would hope
that both sides had sufficient means of verification and
control to prevent the accident from triggering a
nuclear exchange. But we cannot be certain that this
would be the case.

*(John T. McNaughton, Assistant Secretary of
Defense, December 1962)*

A CURIOUS CONSENSUS has emerged in the literature on the Cuban missile crisis. Although "hawks" and "doves" continue to debate vigorously about such issues as Soviet motivations in placing the missiles in Cuba, the military significance of the missiles, and the effect of U.S. nuclear superiority on Soviet behavior, they appear to agree on one central issue: the likelihood of a nuclear war was actually remote during the crisis, much less likely than many participants and most of the public believed at the time. This consensus on the improbability of nuclear war in October 1962, however, is based on quite contrasting sets of assumptions.

Most hawkish participants in the crisis argue that Soviet Premier Nikita Khrushchev was so deterred by U.S. nuclear superiority that the Soviet Union would not have escalated the use of force elsewhere in the world, even if the United States had stopped Soviet ships on the quarantine line, launched an air strike against the missiles, or invaded Cuba. This belief in the deterrent effectiveness of U.S. nuclear superiority lay behind the arguments of the advocates of an air strike against the missiles during the crisis. Paul Nitze, for examples, argues that he "didn't think that the risk of the Russians responding in any way which would bring into action our undoubted strategic superiority was very great": "It seemed to me that we had both tactical superiority in the area of Cuba and we had overall strategic superiority; under those circumstances, we really were not running that great a risk."[1] Douglas Dillon likewise maintains that the Soviets were "more deterred by far than we were to start anything that would cause trouble": "The so-called hawks did not think that they were running any substantial risk of war with the Soviets, and certainly not of nuclear war."[2] Former U.S. military leaders hold similar perspectives. The chairman of the Joint Chiefs of Staff, General Maxwell Taylor, for example, has argued that there was "not the slightest" legitimacy for concern about nuclear war in the crisis since "I was so sure that we had 'em over a barrel," and the air force's operations deputy, Lieutenant General David Burchinal, later went as far as to assert that "we were never further from nuclear war than at the time of Cuba, never further."[3]

For many of the more dovish participants of the crisis, it was John F. Kennedy who was so deterred by even the significantly inferior Soviet nuclear arsenal that he would not have taken any risk of nuclear war by attacking Cuba. Thus, Abram Chayes asks why the United States didn't invade Cuba in October 1962: "It was because a small, ragtail nuclear deterrent on the other side was a powerful deterrent to us."[4] McGeorge Bundy and Robert McNamara also maintain that the United States was very unlikely to attack Cuba in October 1962 and would more likely have either tightened the blockade or publicly accepted a trade for the Jupiter missiles in Turkey, if Khrushchev had not backed down. These two senior U.S. officials have deflated traditional estimates about the likelihood of a nuclear war—such as Kennedy's oft-quoted statement that the chances were "somewhere between one out of three and even"[5]—during the crisis. McNamara now maintains that "at no time did I feel that strategic nuclear war was probable, even after a conventional clash" in Cuba: "I *knew* what I was going to do with the SIOP [the Single Integrated Operations Plan]. *None* of the options was going to be used at all."[6] Bundy similarly states that "the risk of nuclear war . . . was small, given the prudence and the

[1] Nitze interview in James G. Blight and David A. Welch, *On the Brink: Americans and Soviets Reexamine the Cuban Missile Crisis* (New York: Hill and Wang, 1989), pp. 147, 148.

[2] *Ibid.*, p. 100. Also see Ray S. Cline, "Nuclear War Seemed Remote," *Washington Post*, February 5, 1989, p. D7.

[3] Taylor interview in Blight and Welch, *On the Brink*, pp. 80–81. Burchinal interview in Richard H. Kohn and Joseph P. Harahan, eds., "U.S. Strategic Air Power, 1948–1962: Excerpts from an Interview with Generals Curtis E. LeMay, Leon W. Johnson, David A. Burchinal, and Jack J. Catton," *International Security* 12, no. 4 (Spring 1988): 95. Also see Marc Trachtenberg, "Commentary: New Light on the Cuban Missile Crisis," *Diplomatic History* 14, no. 2 (Spring 1990): 241–247.

[4] Blight and Welch, *On the Brink*, pp. 25–26.

[5] Theodore C. Sorensen, *Kennedy* (New York: Harper and Row, 1965), p. 705.

[6] McNamara is quoted in Blight and Welch, *On the Brink*, pp. 88, 69. Also see his statements on pp. 69, 89–90, 187, and 199. In addition see Arthur M. Schlesinger Jr., *Robert Kennedy and His Times* (New York: Ballantine, 1979), p. 570.

unchallenged final control of the two leaders": "The largest single factor that might have led to nuclear war—the readiness of one leader or the other to regard that outcome as remotely acceptable—simply did not exist in October 1962."[7]

## THE RISK OF ACCIDENTS

Both the hawkish and dovish positions reflect the belief that nuclear weapons had an intense inhibiting effect on the likelihood that either Nikita Khrushchev or John Kennedy would make a *premeditated decision to initiate a nuclear strike*. Neither view adequately considers the possibility that an *accidental nuclear war* could have occurred during the crisis. Given the horrendous consequences of a nuclear exchange, neither Khrushchev nor Kennedy was likely to decide to *jump* over the brink to war. Accidents, however, can happen. What was the probability that either power could have *stumbled* over the brink?

The following two chapters examine this question as a way of evaluating the competing organization theories about reliability accidents and safety that were described and developed in chapter 1. What would each of these theories predict about the risk of accidental war during the Cuban missile crisis? These predictions will then be checked against the existing evidence on nuclear weapons command and control operations in this chapter and about intelligence and warning system failures during the crisis in chapter 3.

### High Reliability Theory Applied

The high reliability theorists argue that specific management and design conditions can produce extremely reliable and safe organizations even when managing hazardous technologies. If they are right, one would expect to find very few nuclear accidents or near-accidents during the Cuban crisis, since the factors that they claim lead to high reliability appear to be present in this case. Five major propositions derived from the theory lead to a prediction that reliable safety would have existed in October 1962.

First, according to the theory, a high level of senior leadership interest and support for organizational reliability and safety is necessary in order both to ensure that adequate resources are available and to guarantee that priority goals are clearly communicated throughout the organization. Such high-level support for safety improvements was clearly evident during

[7] McGeorge Bundy, *Danger and Survival: Choices about the Bomb in the First Fifty Years* (New York: Random House, 1988), pp. 461, 453.

the Kennedy administration. Kennedy, in fact, emphasized precisely this need in his first defense budget message to Congress in March 1961:

> Our defense posture must be designed to reduce the danger of irrational or unpremeditated general war—the danger of an unnecessary escalation of a small war into a large one, or misinterpretation of an incident or enemy intention. . . . In addition our own military activities must be safeguarded against the possibility of inadvertent triggering incidents. But even more importantly, we must be certain that our retaliatory power does not rest on decisions made in ambiguous circumstances, or permit a catastrophic mistake.[8]

The considerable high-level attention paid to this issue in peacetime was heightened and focused during the crisis. Kennedy and McNamara—men of great intelligence, power, and energy—were determined to maintain control over the dangerous events of the crisis. "There was always the chance of error, of mistake, miscalculation, or misunderstanding," Robert Kennedy later wrote of the crisis, "and President Kennedy was committed to doing everything possible to lessen that chance on our side."[9] If the high reliability theory is right, such senior leadership concerns should have significantly enhanced the prospects for safety.

Second, redundancy in safety measures can produce, according to the optimist's perspective, high system reliability despite the existence of unreliable parts. Precisely because of the priority given by the Kennedy administration to the prevention of nuclear weapons accidents and inadvertent escalation, numerous types of redundant command and control measures—the new ballistic missile warning systems, electronic locking devices, and tightened safety-related operational procedures, which will be discussed in detail in this chapter—were integrated into U.S. military organizations in the early 1960s. In addition, special redundant warning systems were deployed, on an emergency basis, to increase the likelihood of the United States receiving accurate warning of a nuclear attack during the Cuban crisis (chapter 3). Because of these efforts, the high reliability theory would again predict, the likelihood of a serious nuclear command system accident during the Cuban missile crisis should have been remote.

Third, a high level of continuous operations and training is considered crucial to the success of high reliability organizations. U.S. military forces controlling nuclear weapons, especially the strategic forces of the Strategic Air Command (SAC), clearly met this condition during the early 1960s.

---

[8] *Public Papers of the President, John F. Kennedy, 1961* (Washington, D.C.: Government Printing Office, 1962), p. 99. The best study of the Kennedy administration's efforts to improve nuclear command and control is Peter Feaver, *Guarding the Guardians: Civilian Control of Nuclear Weapons in the United States* (Ithaca, N.Y.: Cornell University Press, 1992), pp. 172–198.

[9] Robert F. Kennedy, *Thirteen Days* (New York: W. W. Norton, 1969), p. 127.

Indeed, as Alfred Goldberg has put it, "SAC's training certainly became as demanding and realistic as was ever devised for a modern military force in peacetime."[10] Because of its prime responsibility for maintaining nuclear deterrence, beginning in the late 1950s, SAC was routinely kept at one higher level of Defense Condition (DEFCON) alert readiness, DEFCON 4 compared to DEFCON 5, than all other U.S. military commands. The command began keeping nuclear armed bombers on ground runway alert in 1957 and by 1961, a full 50 percent of its bombers and supporting tankers were on constant ground alert. In addition, through a rotating system of "airborne alert indoctrination training," SAC maintained at least twelve B-52 bombers in the air, twenty-four hours a day and 365 days a year, during the Kennedy administration.[11] Finally, throughout the command, a demanding program of major military exercises, "no-notice" practice bomber launches, and constant personnel training operations was instituted.

Fourth, all the signs of a strong "culture of reliability," which has been identified as crucial for high reliability in other settings, appear to be present in the major U.S. military commands involved in nuclear alert operations during the Cuban crisis. Compared to any civilian organization operating hazardous technologies, the military's ability to isolate and indoctrinate personnel, impose strict discipline and safety regulations, and encourage cultural conformity is extremely high. The U.S. military commands that controlled nuclear weapons had the particular challenge of training individuals to be able to fight in a nuclear war, while at the same time avoiding serious accidents with nuclear weapons. These commands therefore instilled a remarkable degree of discipline and responsibility in their officers and enlisted men to ensure that safety rules and routines were followed in peacetime and that wartime missions were accomplished. Williamson Murray has described the result in the Strategic Air Command very well:

> The turning over of nuclear bombs by the Atomic Energy Commission to direct air force control presented considerable problems in controlling those weapons. In response [General Curtis] LeMay and his subordinates created a highly structured, rigid force. . . . SAC lived (and still lives) by the book. Those who deviate are removed with dispatch. Given the implications of a nuclear incident, such an approach is understandable.[12]

[10] Alfred Goldberg, "Strategic Air Command," in Alfred Goldberg, ed., *A History of the U.S. Air Force* (New York: Arno Press, 1974), p. 126.

[11] See Henry M. Narducci, *Strategic Air Command and the Alert Program: A Brief History* (Omaha, Nebr.: Office of the Historian, Strategic Air Command, 1988), pp. ii, 5–8. The exact number of bombers on routine airborne alert during this period is given in the declassified Freedom of Information Act (henceforth FOIA) extract from SAC Study 90C, *SAC and the Cuban Crisis*, (hereinafter, *SAC and the Cuban Crisis*, FOIA extract), p. 3.

[12] Williamson Murray, "The United States Air Force: The Past as Prologue," in Michael

Fifth, and finally, high reliability theory leads an analyst to suspect that the likelihood of accidents would *decrease* in a military crisis because the seriousness of the international situation would heighten operators' attention to safety and therefore could counter what Todd La Porte has described as the "error-inducing conditions of routine, familiarity and continual success."[13] According to Karl Weick, accidents in other hazardous organizations decrease when performance pressures are high because "dynamic inputs create stable outcomes":

> A senior officer on a nuclear carrier: "When planes are missing the arresting wire, and can't find the tanker where they are to refuel, and the wind is at 40 knots and the ship is turning, there are not errors." This latter experience is confirmed in studies of air traffic controllers. There tend to be more errors in air traffic control under light traffic load than under heavy load because, under high load, controllers visually sweep the entire radar screen whereas in low load they don't.[14]

Following this logic, one would anticipate that crises would result in safer and more reliable nuclear operations than exist in the routine of day-to-day alert in peacetime.

These five factors would lead a high reliability theorist to predict that a nuclear alert during the Cuban missile crisis would be an extremely safe military operation. High-level leadership interest, significant redundancy, continual alert and training operations, a strong culture of reliability, and enhanced attention and care in crises would all contribute to high reliability. From this perspective, it would be surprising if a set of serious accidents occurred in October 1962, given that all these signs were pointing toward safety.

### Normal Accidents Theory Applied

The normal accidents theory, however, would predict exactly the opposite outcome: nuclear alert operations during the Cuban missile crisis should have been extremely dangerous. Consider first, the structural conditions—

Mandelbaum, ed., *America's Defense* (New York: Holmes and Meier, 1989), pp. 254–255. As Goldberg put it, Curtis LeMay's "insistence on the highest standards of readiness and performance eventually gave the command the *elan* and the pride of service that have always distinguished the great military forces of history." Goldberg, "Strategic Air Command," p. 122.

[13] Todd R. La Porte, "On the Design and Management of Nearly Error-Free Organizational Control Systems," in David L. Sills, C. P. Wolf, and Vivian B. Shelanski, eds., *Accident at Three Mile Island: The Human Dimensions* (Boulder, Colo.: Westview Press, 1982), p. 194.

[14] Karl E. Weick, "Organizational Culture as a Source of High Reliability," *California Management Review* 29, no. 2 (Winter 1987): 118.

high degrees of interactive complexity and tight coupling—which Charles Perrow identifies as leading to inevitable accidents in other high-technology organizations.[15] From a systems perspective, the U.S. nuclear arsenal in the early 1960s displayed all the conditions of high interactive complexity. Hundreds of thousands of military personnel controlled over twenty-five thousand nuclear weapons, which were deployed on military bases around the globe.[16] These weapons and their command and control systems were often maintained in close proximity to one another, increasing the risk of unplanned interactions and common-mode failures. For example, the weapons on alert bombers were kept, by necessity, nearby one another; this was also the case with the weapons on board U.S. submarines. On military bases, nonalert weapons were maintained, for security purposes, in restricted bunkers and command centers; warning systems, and nuclear forces were often located in the same area. Peacetime logistics and training were extremely complicated operations, involving numerous commands and many coordinated procedures. Critical information sources, both warning of an enemy attack and monitoring the status of U.S. weapons systems, were indirect and usually dependent upon distant communication systems. Finally, a significant degree of opaqueness was *deliberately* built into the command and control system for nuclear weapons: the need to hide potential vulnerabilities from foreign intelligence agencies meant that secret information was kept highly compartmentalized and that no single individual could know the full details of the whole system.

Such signs of interactive complexity coexisted with signs of significant tight coupling. Because the U.S. nuclear command organizations and their war plans were designed to provide the options of preemption (if a Soviet attack appeared imminent and unavoidable) and prompt retaliation (if the U.S. suffered a surprise attack), a high degree of tight coupling was deliberately built into the system.[17] The U.S. nuclear war operations therefore consisted of very rapid warning and response time-lines; invariant bomber, tanker, and missile launch sequences; and intricate coordination between various commands. Even the name of the U.S. nuclear war plan itself, the *Single Integrated* Operational Plan (SIOP), is indicative of strong tight coupling.

A normal accidents theorist, examining the nuclear alert operations that

---

[15] Charles Perrow, *Normal Accidents: Living with High-Risk Technologies* (New York: Basic Books, 1984).

[16] The weapons stockpile estimate is from Thomas B. Cochran, William M. Arkin, and Milton M. Hoenig, *Nuclear Weapons Databook* (Cambridge, Mass.: Ballinger, 1984), p. 15, vol. 1, *U.S. Nuclear Forces and Capabilities*, p. 15.

[17] On the continued existence of U.S. preemptive options in 1962 and operational exercises emphasizing launching on tactical warning during the Kennedy Administration, see Scott D. Sagan, *Moving Targets: Nuclear Strategy and National Security* (Princeton, N.J.: Princeton University Press, 1989), pp. 26–32, 70–72.

were planned for a military crisis, would predict that the likelihood of an accident would increase because both interactive complexity and tight coupling would increase. Not only would a larger number of nuclear forces be on alert in a crisis, but the U.S. alerting system required that numerous complex operations take place in a coordinated manner between commands across the globe. A declassified 1959 North American Air Defense Command (NORAD) DEFCON alert checklist, for example, is thirty-eight pages long, and outlines almost three hundred individual military actions to be implemented by air defense commanders, unless ordered otherwise, at the five major DEFCONs and various intermediate posture levels.[18] Since such increases in force readiness taken by one U.S. command influenced the capabilities of another command, DEFCON alert operations lists also presented guidelines for significant supplementary actions that must be taken or at least considered by the Joint Chiefs of Staff and other unified and specified commanders.[19] The alert activities and anticipated wartime operations of many U.S. commands were also interlocked with those of allied militaries—such as the European members of the North Atlantic Treaty Organization (NATO) and Canada, the other member of NORAD—which further complicated both war planning and alert operations.

In addition, a major consequence of a nuclear alert was to raise the *readiness* of bombers, interceptor aircraft, and nuclear-armed missiles to be able to respond more rapidly to the receipt of orders. Aircraft could be placed at the end of the runway, for example, fully prepared for an immediate launch. Sleeping ICBM launch control officers would wake up and could initiate last minute missile readiness checks, to shorten reaction time. Such crisis alert actions inevitably increased the tight coupling of the system; indeed, that was their central purpose.

In addition to these structural considerations, a number of factors at the operational level would also lead a normal accidents theorist to suspect that serious problems with nuclear safety would emerge during the Cuban missile crisis. First, the theory focuses attention on the degree to which conflicting objectives and unclear preferences exist within complex organizations. This perspective would raise concerns that even if leaders placed the highest priority on developing effective safety rules, such rules might not be followed in many cases. When alerting nuclear forces for a potential war, military officers would also face severe "production pressures" to maintain maximum military effectiveness. Under such conditions, impro-

---

[18] North American Air Defense Command, DEFCON checklist, CCS 3180, Emergency Readiness Plans (April 20, 1959), (Group 2), Records of the Joint Chiefs of Staff 1959, Modern Military Branch, National Archives, Washington, D.C., (hereinafter JCS followed by records year).

[19] *Ibid.*, and *Alert System of the Joint Chiefs of Staff*, March 1, 1981, FOIA, Part I, p. 1–3.

vised readiness procedures, work-around solutions to restrictive rules, and even direct safety violations are likely to occur. Thus, although senior political and military authorities might well attempt to maximize safety in a crisis, centralized control over such complex and dispersed nuclear operations would be fundamentally elusive.

Second, the theory predicts that adding redundancy to complex systems often backfires because the effort can inadvertently increase the complexity of the system and thus produce unanticipated and incomprehensible failure modes. This perspective would therefore lead one to anticipate that many Defense Department attempts to enhance safety and reliability during the crisis might have had the opposite effect. Any effort to impose additional safety measures on officers or to add new redundant warning systems might, according to this perspective, inadvertently reduce safety, and a normal accidents theorist would therefore look for safety problems in such systems.

Third, in contrast to the earlier emphasis on the positive effects of constant training and exercises, normal accidents theory suggests that there will be many crisis operations that will not have been thoroughly practiced ahead of time. No one will have practiced fixing problems that have not been imagined. Full training for particularly dangerous operations may not occur simply because the training itself is so dangerous. Bugs would exist in a variety of new weapons systems, unique command and control procedures, and politically sensitive operations that have not been fully tested in peacetime. Safety problems would therefore be likely to occur during such unanticipated operations.

Finally, the theory's perspective on organizational learning would lead an analyst to suspect that if an accident or near-accident occurred, the organizations involved might not fully understand what had just happened, would try to cover up organizational failures when possible, and would place the blame for accidents on operator errors when necessary. Since it would often not be in the operators' interests to report on safety violations, nor in the organizations' interest to report to higher authorities on accidents, an accurate account of crisis safety would be difficult to construct. Under extreme conditions, the senior Washington officials interested in maximizing reliability and safety might not even be aware of any serious problems that developed.

### Evaluating the Theories

Which of these theories on high-risk organizations is best supported by the experience of the Cuban missile crisis? A detailed look at U.S. nuclear operations in October 1962 can reveal the strengths and weaknesses of these contrasting approaches to the management of hazardous technologies. This chapter will start the process by examining the complex history of the nuclear alert operations of U.S. and NATO strategic and tactical nuclear forces during the crisis. Chapter 3 continues the effort by examining warning and intelligence operations in October 1962, and will then provide conclusions.

## THE CUBAN CRISIS ALERT

The system by which U.S. military forces are placed on a higher state of alert is called the Defense Condition (DEFCON) system. (See table 2.1 for a description.) Although U.S. nuclear forces have been placed on a higher state of readiness in a number of instances since the DEFCON system was created in 1959, the nuclear alert during the Cuban missile crisis represents both the highest state of readiness for nuclear war that U.S. military forces have ever attained and the longest period of time (thirty days) that they have maintained an alert.[20] Global U.S. military forces were placed on DEFCON 3 when President Kennedy publicly announced a plan to impose a U.S. naval quarantine on Cuba on October 22. The Strategic Air Command moved, for the first and only time in its history, to DEFCON 2 on October 24, as the quarantine came into effect.

The resulting increase in the size of the U.S. nuclear alert force during the crisis was massive. At its highest readiness level on November 4, SAC had more than doubled its nuclear capability from its precrisis alert level: alert bombers increased from 652 to 1,479; ICBMs on alert went from 112 to 182; and total SAC-alerted nuclear weapons peaked at 2,952, compared to 1,433 before the crisis.[21] The number of Polaris SLBMs on alert increased from the regular peacetime level of 48 to the full force of 112 missiles by October 24.[22] Increased numbers of forward-based U.S. aircraft were also readied for SIOP and theater nuclear missions. In the Pacific Command, available Quick Reaction Alert (QRA) aircraft were loaded with nuclear weapons and readied for immediate launch on October 22 and remained at

[20] See Scott D. Sagan, "Nuclear Alerts and Crisis Management," *International Security* 9, no. 4 (Spring 1985): 102–106.

[21] USAF Historical Division Liaison Office, *The Air Force Response to the Cuban Crisis* (FOIA, declassified with deletions), p. 18.

[22] The normal 1962 DEFCON 5 Polaris alert level is given in Cyrus Vance, Memorandum for the President, October 3, 1964, "Military Strength Increases since Fiscal Year 1961." Department of Defense, 11–63, vol. 1, tab G, Agency Files, National Security Files, Lyndon Baines Johnson Library (henceforth, LBJ Library), Austin, Texas. The DEFCON 3 alert Polaris figure is from JCS message No. 6968 to the Secretary of State, October 25, 1962 (henceforth JCS message 6968). National Security Files, Cuba Cables, October 25, 1962, box 41, John F. Kennedy Library (henceforth JFK Library), Boston.

that alert status until November 1.[23] Numerous nuclear alerting activities also took place in U.S. forces in Europe: the commander of U.S. air forces in Europe (CINCUSAFE) alerted additional nuclear-armed QRA aircraft at the height of the crisis, and SAC sent approximately thirty B-47 bombers to forward bases in Great Britain and Spain, where they assumed SIOP "Reflex" alert status.[24]

### The SAC Bomber Alert: A First Cut

How safe and well managed were these nuclear weapons operations? The best place to start an investigation of this subject is with the most dramatic and most dangerous alert operation of the crisis: the Strategic Air Command's bomber alert. When DEFCON 3 was declared on the evening of October 22, SAC immediately increased the numbers of bombers on ground alert by almost 50 percent (from 652 to 912) and dispersed 183 B-47 bombers to thirty-three civilian and military airfields.[25] Personnel leaves, training programs, and exercises throughout SAC were immediately canceled. In addition, SAC evacuated its nonalert and alert tankers and bombers from bases in Florida, which were now needed for forces preparing for a possible invasion of Cuba, and placed them on alert in Georgia, Texas, and Michigan.[26]

Most dramatically, timing the action to begin precisely at the moment when Kennedy's television address began, SAC increased the size of the B-52 airborne alert operation—coded named Chrome Dome—from its peacetime "training" level of twelve sorties a day to sixty-six sorties daily.[27] These aircraft flew along three basic routes in October 1962. Bombers on the southern route crossed the Atlantic Ocean, were refueled over Spain, and maintained orbits over the Mediterranean Sea.[28] A northern route

[23] Headquarters Pacific Air Force, Cuban Crisis Chronology, FOIA, pp. 2, 5. On October 25, after the alert, the Pacific Command had eleven B-57s, fifty F-100s, sixteen A-4s and sixteen Mace surface-to-surface missiles, and four Regulus cruise missiles, on alert, JCS message 6968.

[24] On USAFE see Air Force Response, p. 11, and History of the 353rd Tactical Fighter Squadron, 1 July–31 December, 1962, p. 5, Tactical Air Command, FOIA. On SAC see SAC and the Cuban Crisis, FOIA extract, p. 6; Special Annex to the History of the 96th Strategic Aerospace Wing, 20–29 October 1962, pp. 1, 5, K-WG-96-HI, Air Force Historical Research Center (henceforth AFHRC), Maxwell Air Force Base, AL; and History of the 100th Bombardment Wing, 1–31 October 1962, pp. 23, 26, K-WG-100-HI, AFHRC.

[25] Air Force Response, pp. 8, 18; Department of Defense Annual Report for FY 1963, p. 5.

[26] SAC and the Cuban Crisis, FOIA extract, pp. 1–2.

[27] Ibid., FOIA extract, p. 3.

[28] History of the 4239th Strategic Wing, 1 August–31 October 1962, K-WG-4239-HI, AFHRC, p. 9.

## TABLE 2.1
### The United States DEFCON System

**DEFCON 5** (Exercise term: Fade Out): A normal readiness posture that can be sustained indefinitely and that represents an optimum balance between the requirements of readiness and the routine training and equipping of forces for their primary mission.

**DEFCON 4** (Exercise term: Double Take): A readiness posture requiring increased intelligence watch and a continuing analysis of the political/military situation in the area of tension. Review contingency plans for the area concerned, and based on the above analysis make modifications or formulate new plans as required. Take actions to increase security and antisabotage measures, etc., if considered necessary; keep appropriate commanders informed of the developing situation. During this condition, no measures will be taken that could be considered provocative or that might disclose operational plans. Readiness actions should be accomplished without public notice, if possible.

**DEFCON 3** (Exercise term: Round House): A readiness posture that requires certain portions of the assigned forces to assume an increased readiness posture above that of normal readiness. Generally, in this condition, all forces and resources will come from within the command. Plans of the next higher condition are readied and reviewed. During this condition, no measures will be taken that could be considered provocative or that might disclose operational plans. Readiness actions should be accomplished without public notice, if possible.

**DEFCON 2** (Exercise term: Fast Pace): A readiness posture requiring a further increase in military force readiness that is less than maximum readiness; certain military deployments and selected civil actions may be made available from outside the command; preliminary measures are taken to permit the most rapid transition to maximum readiness, if necessary.

**DEFCON 1** (Exercise term: Cocked Pistol): A maximum readiness posture requiring the highest state of preparedness to execute war plans. Situation: International relations have deteriorated to such a degree that measures must be taken to achieve readiness. Significant strategic and/or tactical indications of hostilities against U.S. forces overseas, U.S. allies, and/or the continental U.S. or its possessions. War is imminent and may occur momentarily.

**Defense Emergency** (Exercise term: Hot Box): A major attack upon U.S. forces overseas, on allied forces in any theater, or a covert attack of any type upon the United States and confirmed by a unified or specified commander or higher authority.

**Air Defense Emergency** (Exercise term: Big Noise):

    **Warning Red** (Exercise term: Apple Jack): Attack by hostile aircraft/ missiles upon the continental United States, Alaska, Canada, or Greenland is imminent or taking place.

TABLE 2.1

(*Continued*)

Warning Yellow (Exercise term: Lemon Juice) Attack by hostile aircraft/missiles is probable.

Warning White (Exercise term: Snow Man): Attack by hostile aircraft/missiles is not considered immediately probable or imminent.

*Sources:* Appendix II to annex B to 6595 ATW OPLAN 1-63, 6 Sept. 1962, FOIA; Alert System of the Joint Chiefs of Staff, 29 Jan. 1981, part 1 Concept, FOIA, p. 31-1 and p. 3-7; Emergency Conference Procedures, Papers of Robert S. McNamara, Organization Files, RG 200, National Archives.

circumnavigated the North American continent: dozens of B-52s flew daily around the Newfoundland coast, across Greenland, across the Arctic Ocean north of Canadian territory, and then crossed Alaska before heading along the Pacific coast to their bases in the western United States.[29] A third bomber route, code named Hard Head, crossed Ontario to the Hudson Bay and orbited near Thule, Greenland.[30] (See chapter 4 for an explanation of the purpose of this Thule B-52 orbit). Each airborne B-52 carried three or four thermonuclear weapons assigned to SIOP targets.[31]

On October 24, at the direction of Secretary of Defense Robert McNamara and the Joint Chiefs, SAC went to DEFCON 2, which further increased the alert bomber force to 1,436 aircraft capable of responding to tactical warning.[32] According to the official Strategic Air Command history, "SAC squeezed every possible resource to increase its alert capability."[33] Available B-47, B-52, and B-58 bombers, from nonready reserves forces and ongoing modification programs, were rushed onto advanced ground alert status.[34] The command maintained its DEFCON 2 alert with this large scale force generation, dispersal of bombers and the massive airborne alert—approximately seventy-five B-52 sorties with 150 tanker refueling missions were flown daily along Arctic and Mediterranean routes by the beginning of November—for the entire month of the crisis alert.[35]

[29] History of the 4170th Strategic Wing, 1–30 November 1962, K-WG-4170-HI, AFHRC, p. 26.

[30] History of the 8th Air Force, K-520.01 July–December 1962, vol.2, exhibit 49, AFHRC (declassified by AFHRC, June 19, 1990), and History of the 379th Bombardment Wing, April–June 1964, K-WG-379-HI, p. 12.

[31] Cuba Fact Sheet, Cuba General Folder, October 26–27, 1962, National Security Files, box 36A, JFK Library.

[32] *Air Force Response*, p. 8.

[33] *SAC and the Cuban Crisis*, FOIA extract, p. 6.

[34] *Ibid.*, and History of the 4133rd Strategic Wing, 20 October–27 November 1962, pp. iii, 2, K-WG-4133-HI, AFHRC.

[35] *SAC and the Cuban Crisis*, FOIA extract, p. 3.

## Purpose and Consequences

Why were the SAC nuclear armed bombers placed on such a high state of alert? The answer is suggested by the fact that senior political authorities discussed the possibility of alerting SAC's nuclear forces as early as October 16, during the first day of meetings of the Executive Committee (Ex-Comm) of the National Security Council. The central political objective of the alert, as described by Secretary McNamara, was to deter Soviet military countermoves—what today would be called horizontal escalation—in response to a potential U.S. air strike, blockade, or invasion of Cuba. As McNamara argued during the crisis: "It seems almost certain to me that any one of these forms of direct military action (blockade, air strike or invasion) will lead to a Soviet military response of some type some place in the world. . . . We must recognize it by trying to deter it which means we probably should alert SAC, probably put on an airborne alert."[36] General Thomas S. Power, the SAC commander, was slightly more blunt in his description of the purpose of the alert: "This action by the nation's primary war deterrent force gave added meaning to the President's declaration that the U.S. would react to any nuclear missile launched from Cuba with a full retaliatory response upon the Soviet Union itself."[37]

Did the dramatic SAC bomber alert serve that purpose? Any assessment of the effect of the SAC nuclear alert on Soviet behavior in October 1962 must remain speculative, until more detailed information is made available on decision-making in Moscow during the crisis. Although it is clear that Soviet leaders were aware of the U.S. nuclear alert during the crisis, whether the alert influenced Khrushchev's calculations about the likelihood and consequences of war is not currently known.[38]

---

[36] Off the Record Meeting on Cuba, October 16, 1962, 6:30–7:55 P.M., pp. 9–10, JFK Library. When the JCS issued recommendations to the secretary of defense for the major increases in SAC's DEFCON status, McNamara therefore rapidly approved the augmented airborne alert and DEFCON 2. *Chronology of JCS Decisions Concerning the Cuban Missile Crisis*, Historical Division, JCS, December 21, 1962, pp. 30, 34, 36, 39, National Security Archives, Cuban Missile Crisis Collection (henceforth NSA-CMCC).

[37] Thomas S. Power letter to Robert S. McNamara, November 7, 1962, attachment 1, proposed public release on SAC Airborne Alert, p. 1, Papers of General Curtis LeMay, SAC 1962 file, Box 143, Manuscript Division, Library of Congress, Washington, D.C. McNamara revealingly refused to grant permission for SAC to release this information on the alert.

[38] Khrushchev noted in his December 12, 1962, speech to the Supreme Soviet that "about 20 percent of all U.S. Strategic Air Command planes, carrying atomic and hydrogen bombs, were kept aloft around the clock" during the crisis. Reprinted in Ronald R. Pope, *Soviet Views on the Cuban Missile Crisis* (Washington, D.C.: University Press of America, 1982), p. 86. For important analyses of the role of the nuclear balance during the Cuban crisis, see Richard K. Betts, *Nuclear Blackmail and Nuclear Balance* (Washington D.C.: Brookings Institution, 1987), pp. 109–123; Bundy, *Danger and Survival*, pp. 445–453; and Marc Trachtenberg,

It is noteworthy, however, that U.S. leaders in 1962 believed that the alert was critical in signaling U.S. resolve and contributing to deterrence. SAC alert activities, including particularly the B-52 airborne operation, were perceived by a number of key officials in 1962 as a major factor in deterring Soviet military escalation. At the October 20 meeting of the ExComm, for example, when U.S. leaders discussed possible Soviet reactions to a U.S. air strike against the missiles in Cuba, according to one declassified account of the discussion, "it was held unlikely that the Soviets would retaliate, *especially since the Strategic Air Command would be in a full alert condition.*"[39] Similarly, Robert McNamara refused to permit SAC to go *off* alert late in the crisis, arguing at the November 12 ExComm meeting that "this could not be done without giving a signal to the Russians": "the Russians would know immediately if our state of alert was reduced" and "any reduction in the state of readiness of U.S. forces would be a sign to the Soviet Union."[40] Finally, President Kennedy himself emphasized the importance of the SAC alert after the crisis: "There is no doubt that it contributed greatly to the maintenance of peace and the security of the United States. . . . The airborne alert provided a strategic posture under which every United States force could operate with relative freedom of action."[41]

## Reliability Revisited

The safety statistics of the Chrome Dome airborne alert were truly impressive: SAC B-52s flew over 2,088 missions—flying 47,000 hours and 20

---

"The Influence of Nuclear Weapons in The Cuban Missile Crisis," *International Security* 10, no.1 (Summer 1985), pp. 137–163.

[39] Frank Sieverts, *The Cuban Crisis, 1962*, National Security Files, box 49, JFK Library, p. 75 (emphasis added). Although the once top-secret Sieverts' report was based on a range of government documents, Paul Nitze's ExComm meeting notes, and personal interviews, its discussion of the White House meetings cannot be taken as representing verbatim ExComm conversations. It is likely that this particular statement represents the recollection of one or more of Sievert's sources who attended the ExComm meeting.

[40] Summary Record of NSC Executive Meeting no. 24, November 12, 1962, Declassified Documents Reference Collection, Carrolton Press, 1985, no. 001205, p. 1. Therefore, on November 15, when SAC adjusted its existing DEFCON 2 posture to permit "minimum essential training" sorties for bomber crews and essential aircraft maintenance, the special airborne alert continued and "there was to be retention of the *maximum force posture image* to include utilization of all dispersed bases." History of the 509th Bombardment Wing, November 1962, p. 9 (emphasis added), K-WG-509-HI, AFHRC.

[41] The quotations are from the safety award plaque given to SAC on December 7, 1962, and from Kennedy's speech during the ceremony. See Thomas S. Power, "Dynamic Deterrence Pays Off," *Combat Crew* 13, no. 8 (February 1963): 5, and *SAC and the Cuban Crisis*, FOIA extract, p. 3. Also see *Department of Defense Operations during the Cuban Crisis*, February 13, 1963, reprinted in *The Naval War College Review* 32, no. 4 (July–August 1979): 98.

million miles with 4,076 aerial refuelings—during the crisis without a single plane crash or known weapons safety incident.[42] How was such an outstanding record of safety achieved? A high reliability theorist examining the historical record would find evidence suggesting that four of the factors identified as leading to safety in other hazardous organizations could also have been critical in SAC's alert.

First, there are two important indications in the historical record of the degree to which the senior leadership in the United States placed high priority on safety and reliability and gave direct attention to ensure that the nuclear alert operation would not produce an accident. Declassified documents show that civilian officials not only made the final decision to implement the SAC airborne alert, but that they also required that the individual SAC bomber routes be approved by political authorities in order to ensure that flights would not accidently fly into or approach Soviet airspace: the secretary of defense approved the annual alert program and had to be informed of any significant changes in SAC bomber routes; these routes also had to be reviewed and approved by the State Department; and even President Kennedy himself was apparently kept appraised of the routes prior to the crisis.[43]

In addition, it is revealing that on October 24, shortly after DEFCON 2 was declared, General Power also sent the following special message to all SAC wings, in a clear (uncoded) voice transmission, emphasizing the need for safety and caution in the dangerous operation:

This is General Power speaking. I am addressing you for the purpose of re-emphasizing the seriousness of the situation the nation faces. We are in an advanced state of readiness to meet any emergencies and I feel that we are well prepared. I expect each of you to maintain strict security and *use calm judgment during this tense period.* Our plans are well prepared and are being executed smoothly. If there are any questions concerning instructions which by the nature of the situation deviates from the normal, *use the telephone for clarification.* Review your plans for further action to *insure that there will be no mistakes or confusion.* I expect you to cut out all nonessentials and put

[42] *SAC and the Cuban Crisis,* FOIA extracts, p. 3; and "Strategic Air Command," *Air Force and Space Digest* 46, no. 9 (September 1963): 66.
[43] Memorandum, Secretary of Defense to Chairman JCS, July 21, 1959, CCS 3340 (June 8, 1959), (sec. 1), JCS 1959; Memorandum AFXPD to JCS, August 16, 1961, and McNamara Memorandum to Secretary of the Air Force, August 10, 1961, CCS 4615 (April 3, 1961), (Sec. 2), JCS 1961. Kennedy received a chart of the airborne alert routes from the Defense Department in June 1962. See Cyrus Vance, Memorandum for the President, May 16, 1966, National Security Files, memos to the President, Walt Rostow, vol. 7, box 8, LBJ Library.

yourself in a maximum readiness condition. *If you are not sure what you should do in any situation, and if time permits, get in touch with us here.*[44]

Although Power has been widely criticized for revealing the readiness status of U.S. strategic forces in an uncoded transmission (which was reportedly picked up by Soviet intelligence services), the message's major purpose appears to have been to encourage subordinate SAC officers to place priority on "calm judgement" and the prevention of mistakes in the crisis.[45] Such signs of leaders' concerns for safety should have had a positive impact in reducing the risks of accidents.

Second, while a large-scale SAC bomber alert was an inherently dangerous operation, constant training and exercises were designed to reduce risks. SAC alert and force generation had been thoroughly practiced prior to the crisis, in JCS sponsored exercises in May and September 1962, and civilian officials had received detailed briefings on such activities.[46] The B-52 airborne alert indoctrination program had been in operation since at least 1960, making the Chrome Dome alert system a relatively smooth running machine by October 1962.[47] The Cuban crisis alert simply increased the numbers of bomber missions involved in what had become a permanently functioning bomber alert system. Finally, the high day-to-day SAC alert status also was considered to have contributed to safety in the

[44] Fourteenth Strategic Aerospace Division, Cuban Crisis Annex, October History 1962, vol. 2, pp. 3–4 (emphasis added), NSA-CMCC.

[45] Earlier assessments, my own included, were critical of Power's decision to send this message in the clear. See Raymond L. Garthoff, *Reflections on the Cuban Missile Crisis*, revised ed. (Washington, D.C.: Brookings Institution, 1989), p. 62; Bundy, *Danger and Survival*, p. 610; and Sagan, "Nuclear Alerts and Crisis Management," p. 108. My earlier views on this matter were based on the recollections of a SAC officer involved in the incident. They changed after I saw the full declassified message printed above. It is also important to note here that DEFCON increases apparently were routinely transmitted in unclassified messages in the clear to federal agencies until 1972, when the Nixon administration mandated that only classified messages could be used. It is likely therefore that the Soviet Union would have immediately picked up DEFCON alert increases, even without Power's actions. See Office of Emergency Preparedness, Memorandum for Emergency Coordinator National Security Council, September 15, 1972, Papers of Richard Nixon, White House Central Files, ND box 3, Ex ND Civil-Defense July 1, 1971–December 31, 1972, file. The author would like to thank Robert Glasser for providing him with this document.

[46] SAC Final Report, Exercise WHIP LASH, June 12, 1962, CCS 3510 (February 6, 1962), (S.2A) JCS 1962 and CM-981–62, Memorandum for the President, Subject: Joint Chiefs of Staff-Sponsored Exercise HIGH HEELS II, September 25, 1962, FOIA. This second document notes that McNamara met with the JCS three times on September 20 and 21 to participate in the decision-making process in the crisis alert and SIOP execution exercise.

[47] Narducci, *Strategic Air Command and the Alert Program*, p. 6. See Chapter 4 for more details on the origins of the SAC airborne alert operation.

alert. Indeed, General Power's explanation for the alert's success resonates with the tenets of high reliability theory:

We could not have placed a sizable portion of our heavy bomber fleet on airborne alert and not only sustained it but also achieved a perfect safety record if we had not prepared ourselves for precisely such a contingency for years. And we could not have attained a full readiness posture at a moment's notice if we had not maintained the Command in a continuous state of combat-readiness, seven days a week and 365 days a year.[48]

Third, the culture of reliability, as exemplified in the strict discipline and strong sense of mission found in SAC crews and officers alike, appears to have been beneficial in producing safe operations. In contrast to the perfect safety record of SAC airborne alert bomber force, for example, the Air Defense Command, which did not have the same reputation for discipline nor elite status within the air force, had at least five accidents with its interceptor aircraft during the crisis.[49] Indeed, President Kennedy emphasized precisely such characteristics of SAC personnel, after the crisis, when he presented the command with a special flight safety plaque honoring its perfect safety record: this was "a unique accomplishment in the history of airpower," which "was possible only because of the extraordinary dedication and professional skill demonstrated by the combat crews and support personnel of the Strategic Air Command."[50]

Fourth, the available evidence from the official Air Force safety records shows that SAC aircraft accident rates significantly *decreased* during October and November 1962. For example, there were five major accidents among all SAC aircraft (tankers and reconnaissance aircraft, as well as bombers) from October 1 through December 31, 1962 (1.48 accidents per 100,000 flying hours), in contrast to twenty-three major accidents (2.99 accidents per 100,000 flying hours) for the SAC force during the combined preceding and subsequent three-month periods.[51] The B-52 bomber records appear even more impressive in this regard: a complete absence of major or minor accidents despite accumulating over 109,000 flying hours from October through December 1962, compared to seventeen accidents (8.62 major and minor accidents per 100,000 flying hours) in the B-52

[48] Power, "Dynamic Deterrence Pays Off," p. 5.

[49] *The Air Defense Command in the Cuban Crisis*, Air Defense Command Historical Study 15, FOIA, pp. 59, 201, 215; and NORAD Combat Operations Center Logs, October 29, 1962, FOIA. SAC did, however, suffer one serious accident with a RB-47 reconnaissance aircraft, during the crisis. See Sagan, "Nuclear Alerts and Crisis Management," p. 110, fn. 27.

[50] Power, "Dynamic Deterrence Pays Off," p. 5.

[51] *United States Air Force Statistical Digest, FY 1963*, K-134.11–6, AFHRC, p. 31. A "major accident" is one in which "the aircraft is destroyed or has received substantial damage," p. 29.

force during the combined preceding and subsequent three-month time periods.[52] It is highly unlikely that such decreases in accident rates were purely coincidental.[53] This evidence thus appears to be strong conformation of the expectation about crisis performance derived from the high reliability theory.[54]

In short, many of the factors that contribute to reliability according to the theory do indeed appear to have played an important role here. A senior leadership interested in safety, a robust training program, a strong sense of mission and discipline, and improved performance under pressure are exactly the conditions that the high reliability theorists would anticipate finding in a well-managed system. The SAC ground and airborne bomber alert operation thus appears to provide significant support for the belief that it is possible to create "high reliability organizations" even with inherently hazardous technologies and tightly coupled operations.

## The SAC Bomber Alert: A Second Cut

Organization theorists who emphasize that "normal accidents" cannot be avoided in complex and tightly coupled systems would be skeptical, however, and would not be satisfied with the evidence given thus far. From this perspective, one should be especially sensitive to the fact that the impressive history has been largely written by the organization itself and contains only what it wanted its civilian leaders to know. A closer look would try to get behind the veil of SAC's public image of safety.

If one looks carefully through the declassified record one finds, in fact, two possible exceptions to the "perfect" record of safety during the SAC bomber alert operation. Neither of the two events produced a serious accident or an international incident. Both of them had the potential to do so, however, and both provide important insights into organizational behavior during crises.

---

[52] Ibid., pp. 33–36.

[53] A test for the statistical significance of these decreases in accident rates shows that the likelihood of the overall SAC aircraft accident rates being pure coincidence is .063. The likelihood of the "perfect" B-52 safety record being due to pure chance is less than 1 in 10,000. I would like to thank Barry O'Neill for making these calculations, applying standard accident analysis methodology with a Poisson distribution, to the air force data.

[54] An alternative explanation for these decreases in aircraft accident rates could be that SAC aircraft (especially B-52s) flew longer missions, on average, during the crisis. Since commercial aircraft have many fewer accidents while cruising at high altitudes, compared to their take-offs and landings, one can deduce that B-52s on airborne alert missions would on average have fewer accidents than B-52s on shorter training or dispersal flights. See Richard W. Taylor, Twin-Engine Transports (Seattle, Wash.: Boeing Company, publication D6–55631, 1990), p. 21.

## A Safety Rule Dispute

The first safety problem was the cause of a dispute between civilian and military authorities over nuclear weapons' safety standards in the Strategic Air Command. In October 1962, as continues to be the case today, detailed safety rules had to be approved by high-level civilian authorities for each new type of nuclear weapon and delivery vehicle that entered into the U.S. arsenal. In 1962, the assistant to the secretary of defense for atomic energy, Dr. Gerald Johnson, had primary responsibility for this matter in the Pentagon, and concurrence on all safety rules had to be received from the Atomic Energy Commission before final approval could be made. The final set of weapon safety rules would then be sent to President Kennedy for final approval.[55] Only after such an approval could specific weapons be placed on day-to-day alert.

In an emergency, however, if operational considerations required an immediate decision on safety rules, the time-consuming process could be *temporarily* bypassed, and an "interim approval" for safety rules could be granted by Defense Department officials alone.[56] October 1962 was such an emergency. When SAC went to DEFCON 2, it discovered that safety rules had *not* been approved for the B-53 gravity bomb, a massive nine megaton thermonuclear weapon, which was just entering the U.S. nuclear stockpile.[57] These bombs had been scheduled to be placed on a wing of B-58 bombers at Bunker Hill Air Force Base in Indiana and had already been incorporated into the SIOP war plan by SAC. But Johnson had denied approval of the required safety rules because there was a deficiency in the weapon's arming and fusing circuitry that increased the likelihood of an accidental detonation; the bomb could not therefore be placed on alert aircraft until the safety deficiency was corrected and certified.[58]

For SAC, however, given the crisis conditions, accepting a safety deficiency was apparently considered a better alternative than accepting a shortfall in the ability to execute the war plan.[59] The command therefore

[55] This procedure was changed in November 1963, giving the secretary of defense the formal approval function, while notification would be provided to the president: "The President feels that this will expedite your putting the safety rules into action without waiting for staff action here." Major General C. V. Clifton, Memorandum for the Deputy Secretary of Defense, "Revised Format for Safety Rules," November 19, 1963, NSAM 272 file, box 342, National Security Files, JFK Library.

[56] Roswell Gilpatric, Memorandum for the Chairman of the Joint Chiefs of Staff, "Safety Rules for the B-47 and B-52/MK 28 FI Weapon Systems," November 16, 1962, CCS 4615 (July 12, 1962), Sec. 1, JCS 1962.

[57] For details on the MK 53 (B53 bomb) see Chuck Hansen, *U.S. Nuclear Weapons: The Secret History* (Arlington, Tex.: Aerofax, 1988), pp. 162–164.

[58] Gerald W. Johnson, Assistant to the Secretary of Defense for Atomic Energy, interview with author, April 7, 1989.

[59] This trade-off was not unique. To give one example from the declassified record, it was

requested that an immediate "interim approval" be granted to enable it to load the noncertified B53 bomb onto the bombers at Bunker Hill, because the "lack of safety rules is preventing SAC from attaining SIOP planned figures."[60] Johnson refused to approve this emergency action, however, and despite a direct phone call from General Power himself and subsequent pressure from Air Force Chief of Staff Curtis LeMay (who called Johnson immediately to urge that SAC be permitted to load up the bomb), Johnson did not budge.

What should one conclude from this event? This incident is, on the one hand, a good example of how senior level civilians' concerns for safety can reduce the likelihood of accidents. It is also an important sign, on the other hand, that the Strategic Air Command did not place safety first in October 1962. The degree to which SAC placed priority on maximizing its SIOP war fighting ability in this case can perhaps be best understood when one considers how little the unsafe weapon would have added to its arsenal: after the crisis, Johnson discovered that there had been less than a dozen B53 weapons available for potential alert at Bunker Hill during the crisis.[61]

Finally, it should be noted that Johnson could never determine whether SAC actually accepted his ruling on this matter: "At the civilian level we had no way of knowing whether LeMay loaded the unsafe bomb or not."[62] Unfortunately, the available record still does not provide an answer. The declassified wing history states only that SAC doubled the number of B-58 bombers on alert at Bunker Hill during the crisis; it does not state which bombs were placed in these aircraft.[63] We may therefore never know who really won the dispute over the B53 gravity bomb.

### The Lost Bomber Incident

The second exception to the perfect record of safety is more alarming since it concerns a close call to an accident along the arctic B-52 airborne alert

---

determined in 1961 that the use of a particular capsule in the arming mechanism of the MK-7 atomic gravity bomb on NATO F-84 aircraft increased the danger of an accidental nuclear explosion. It was therefore ruled that the capsule could not be inserted into the weapon system *in peacetime*. Although the Joint Chiefs of Staff recognized "that there is an increased risk of a nuclear yield in the event of an accidental one-point detonation of the MK-7 weapon with the 210 capsule" they nonetheless agreed that *in a crisis*, "the degree of risk is acceptable, in view of the overriding operational requirement in a DEFCON 2 situation for all commanders to take all practicable measures to improve the posture and effectiveness of their alert force." History of the Directorate of Plans, Deputy Chief of Staff, Plans and Programs, Headquarters U.S. Air Force, vol. 22, July 1–December 31 1961, pp. 107–108, NSA-CMCC.

[60] Message AF IN 57920, SAC to RUEAHQ/JCS, October 25, 1962, NSA-CMCC.

[61] Gerald W. Johnson, Assistant to the Secretary of Defense for Atomic Energy, interview with author, April 7, 1989.

[62] Gerald W. Johnson, letter to author, October 31, 1990.

[63] History of the 305th Bomb Wing, September 1–October 31, 1962, pp. 2–3, FOIA.

routes used by SAC Chrome Dome bombers during the crisis. These routes were supposed to be safe, and direct orders from the secretary of defense stated that airborne alert bombers "will not approach or fly toward Soviet territory or the territory of Communist China."[64] The Chrome Dome alert routes were reviewed by the Defense and State Department officials, and approved by the president, in large part precisely to ensure compliance with the strong political desire to avoid such incidents.

Despite these efforts, however, the routes used during the Cuban crisis were *not* safe. Although there is no record of an accidental B-52 penetration of the Soviet Union's territory during the crisis, the risk of such an accident was higher than was believed by civilian leaders in October 1962. Declassified documents now demonstrate that these officials had reviewed and approved an increased Chrome Dome operation using an unsafe airborne alert route in the Arctic, but were apparently never informed of the danger.

On August 23, 1962, a serious incident occurred during a Chrome Dome mission. The crew of a B-52 committed a navigational error, which caused the bomber to fly off course, flying over 1,300 miles along a nonapproved route over the Arctic Ocean. The lost bomber was heading directly toward the Soviet Union, and was only about three hundred miles away from Soviet airspace when it was picked up by a ground control intercept (GCI) contact in Alaska and ordered to change its course immediately. (See figure 2.1.)

The seriousness of this incident should not be underestimated. The Soviet Union had invested significant resources into air defense interceptors in the late 1950s and early 1960s, and by 1962 hundreds of MIG-19 and MIG-21 aircraft, with combat radii of four hundred miles and two hundred miles respectively, were deployed with the PVO Strany air defense command.[65] Although the precise location of Soviet airfields and deployment patterns of Soviet interceptor aircraft are not available, it is known that in 1962 the U.S. government believed that an interceptor base existed near Wrangel Island, just off the Chukotski peninsula.[66] A careful plotting of distances on the map therefore reveals that the lost B-52 was almost certainly *within* the combat radius of the longest range Soviet interceptor during the incident. Although there is no evidence that the U.S. bomber encountered a Soviet interceptor during the incident, the risk of such a dangerous encounter was not negligible.

[64] Secretary of Defense Memorandum for the Chairman, Joint Chiefs of Staff, July 21, 1959, "Strategic Air Command Exercises," CCS 3340 (June 8, 1959) sec. 1, JCS 1959.

[65] Robert P. Berman, *Soviet Air Power in Transition* (Washington, D.C.: Brookings Institution, 1978), pp. 32, 15.

[66] NSC Executive Committee Record of Action, October 27, 1962, 4 P.M. meeting, no. 8, JFK Library.

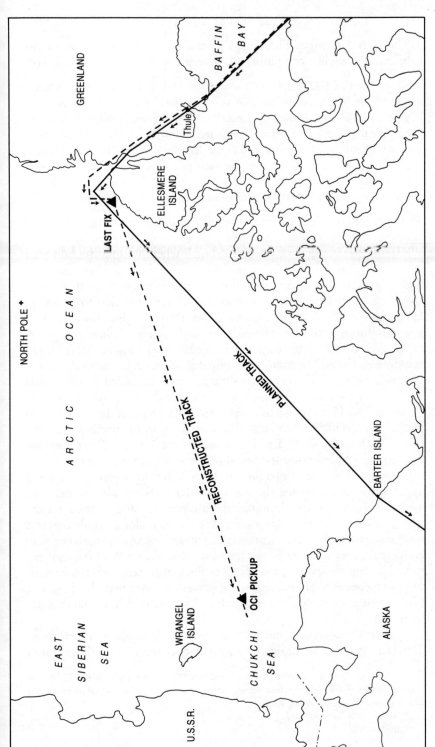

2.1 The Lost B–52 Incident (History of the 15th Air Force, July–December 1962, vol. 1, p. 59, FOIA.)

The 15th Air Force's history of the incident presents the Strategic Air Command's serious, but parochial, perception of the dangers involved:

> While flying a CHROME DOME mission on 23 August, a crew of the 92nd BW (Bomb Wing) committed a gross navigational error in the Arctic region. . . . The error carried the aircraft some 470 nautical miles off course heading toward Soviet Siberia before being returned to its correct course by GCI (Ground Control Intercept). The incident demonstrated the seriousness of celestial computation errors in the polar region. *An extension of the aircraft's track could have carried it into Soviet territory and would have lead (sic) to a grave international incident with serious implications for SAC.*[67]

The 15th Air Force immediately ordered an "informal investigation" of the incident, which concluded that the B-52's onboard navigator had repeatedly used the wrong "convergence factor" when plotting the bomber's position during the flight. (Celestial navigation could not help since the flight was in twilight.) Although the investigation concluded that "crew error" caused the incident, it did note that the airborne alert route was so far north that B-52 bomber crews could not easily double-check their position through radar contacts with ground objects: "Reliable radar fixing could preclude such navigational errors if the Greenland-Alaska leg of the CHROME DOME route were moved southward, closer to the Canadian archipelago." The investigation report recommended therefore that SAC modify the arctic airborne alert route to reduce the risk of a similar incident. The 15th Air Force agreed with this proposal and "gave wide publicity to the incident among navigators" in order to "preclude a repetition of such an error."[68] This is evidence of the 15th Air Force's serious concern about preventing accidental penetrations of Soviet airspace.

Unfortunately, it took *two months* for SAC headquarters to study and approve this proposal for the use of a safer airborne alert route. SAC approval was finally forthcoming on November 1, 1962.[69] Thus, for the first ten days of the crisis, dozens of SAC B-52s flew along a route that was recognized by a subordinate command as presenting an unnecessary risk of accidental penetration of Soviet territory. Had such a B-52 incident occurred during this period, the height of the Cuban crisis when Soviet air defense forces were alerted and when nerves were strained, the danger of inadvertent escalation or even accidental war would have significantly increased.

In the final analysis, therefore, this incident also provides a mixed lesson. The fact that the Strategic Air Command changed its airborne alert

---

[67] History of the 15th Air Force, August 1962, pp. 59–60 (emphasis added), FOIA. The 470 miles figure refers to the distance between the planned route and the actual route, not the distance flown along the wrong route.

[68] Both quotes are from *Ibid.*, p. 61.

[69] *Ibid.*, p. 61.

bomber routes to minimize an accidental escalation problem is reassuring and so is the fact that a redundant safety unit, the ground control radar in Alaska, stopped the bomber from penetrating the USSR. Yet, the mere existence of this close call and the fact that SAC did not adjust its routes to enhance safety until the second week of the Cuban missile crisis is far less reassuring. Finally, there is no evidence currently available that suggests that SAC reported the incident to the senior civilian authorities in Washington. That may indeed be the most disturbing aspect of the stray B-52 incident.

## Normal Near-Accidents

These two incidents provide only limited support for the more pessimistic view that accidents may be inevitable in any complex and tightly coupled organization. A normal accidents theorist would suspect, however, that this complex global nuclear alert operation simply could not have been run as smoothly as was suggested in the public record and would anticipate that, if an analyst dug deeper into the evidence, many more safety problems could be found that were hidden from the sight of senior Washington officials. For if there were such problems with SAC bomber operations, which were constantly practiced by the command and closely monitored by civilian authorities, then there should have been other near-accidents and command and control problems during more complex and less thoroughly practiced operations, especially those that reflected the existence of conflicting priorities about safety and combat readiness.

The most serious nuclear incidents should not have occurred, if the normal accidents theory is correct, in the most obvious place. The bomber alert, precisely because it was believed to be so dangerous, received considerable attention and was managed with considerable skill. That is not where a normal accidents analyst would look for problems. A closer examination of Air Force nuclear alert operations in October 1962 should focus on what were considered by political authorities to be less important nuclear operations: alert activities that were not considered to be as dangerous or were not fully anticipated, and that were therefore subject to less focused attention. Bizarre interactions and serious safety problems were likely to have developed in a number of these "minor" alert operations.

## EMERGENCY ICBM ALERT OPERATIONS

One logical change in priorities that could take place when a military organization shifts from peacetime conditions to a war footing is that weapons systems normally used for peacetime training and test purposes, or those still undergoing the prolonged and complex initial deployment procedures, could be rushed into operational condition. In May 1961, an agreement to implement precisely such emergency actions was signed by the commanders of the Strategic Air Command and the Air Force Systems Command (AFSC), which is responsible for the development, testing, and deployment of Air Force weapons systems. Under this Emergency Combat Capability (ECC) agreement, all AFSC controlled missiles that were technically capable of being launched "under strategic warning" were to be turned over to SAC's operational control upon declaration of DEFCON 2 or any higher state of alert.[70] This emergency agreement therefore went into effect on October 24, 1962, and the AFSC temporarily turned over thirty-six ICBMs to SAC. SAC took immediate control of these Atlas, Titan, and Minuteman I missiles, located at a number SAC combat bases as well as Air Force testing facilities, and was able to put twenty on immediate operational alert, adding approximately seventy-one megatons to the SIOP force.[71]

Although the existence of this plan was known to civilian authorities, it was not the subject of high-level scrutiny.[72] The number of weapons involved was small, the alerting process was believed to be well understood, and the existing safety rules were considered adequate. The following investigation of the emergency ICBM operation in October 1962, however, reveals that in fact at least two serious unanticipated command system and nuclear weapons safety problems did emerge during the crisis.

### The Vandenberg Missile Launch

The first potentially dangerous incident involving these emergency alert ICBMs took place at Vandenberg Air Force Base in southern California. In 1962, Vandenberg housed, as it still does today, both the missile test facilities launching ICBMs into the Pacific Kwajalein test range and the SAC

[70] SAC/AFSC Agreement for Emergency Combat Capability of Ballistic Missile Launch Complexes, May 4, 1961, from *SAC Operations in the Cuban Crisis of 1962*, vol. 4, annex document 2, AFHRC (declassified July 14, 1988).

[71] *Air Force Response*, p. 33, and *History of the Air Force Systems Command*, July 1–December 31, 1962, vol. 1 (declassified extract Freedom of Information Act), p. II-74 both place the number of AFSC missiles put on emergency alert as twenty. CINCSAC General Thomas Power, however, reported during the crisis that "of the 36 available AFSC missiles, 25 were generated within 10 days." Power to HQ USAF, November 20, 1962, in Curtis LeMay Papers, SAC 1962 File, box 143, Library of Congress, Washington, D.C. At SAC's request the AFSC agreed also to turn over one B-58 and five B-52 bombers to SAC on October 26, but these bombers were determined to be unsuitable for immediate use in a nuclear delivery role, and the transfer request was withdrawn, *History of the Air Force Systems Command*, July 1–December 31, 1962, pp. II-79, II-83.

[72] *Department of Defense Appropriations for 1962*, Hearings before the Subcommittee of the Committee on Appropriations, U.S. Senate, 87th Congress, 1st sess., p. 297.

operational test and evaluation facilities. On October 22, 1962, when DEFCON 3 was ordered, some of the test silos and gantries contained research and development missiles, and others were in various states of repair, but immediately AFSC and contractor personnel began to prepare the sites for Emergency Combat Capability status. Operational Atlas, Titan, and Minuteman test flight missiles were quickly prepared to permit launches against "the Sino-Soviet Bloc": SIOP war plan targets were assigned and programmed into the systems, and munitions maintenance personnel replaced the test reentry vehicles with nuclear warheads. The first missile, an Atlas F ICBM, was placed on full alert on October 23 and the AFSC and civilian contractor personnel working in the launch control facility were replaced by a SAC combat crew. By October 30, crews had placed nuclear warheads onto nine missiles at Vandenberg.[73]

This emergency operation continued until November 2, when all the missiles and launch facilities were returned to Air Force Systems Command control. From SAC's perspective, the Vandenberg operation was a major success: nine extra weapons had been added to the SIOP force.[74] From a broader safety perspective, however, the emergency action should raise concerns. Although the Vandenberg facilities were placed on combat alert status without any reported lapse in nuclear weapons safety, one totally unanticipated problem did emerge.

When DEFCON 3 was declared at the beginning of the crisis, one Atlas ICBM was ready for a test launch that had been previously scheduled for later that week. Although nuclear warheads were being placed on the ICBMs in surrounding launch facilities, the test reentry vehicle was maintained on this single missile. Despite the severity of the crisis and the emergency alert operations taking place, *this Atlas ICBM was actually launched, without further orders from the Washington political authorities, at 4:00 A.M. on October 26.*[75] Ironically, while senior leaders in

[73] The paragraph is based on History of the 6595th Aerospace Test Wing 22 October 1962–20 November 1962, FOIA, pp. 2–9. Although the ECC agreement did not come into effect until DEFCON 2 was declared on October 24, the Vandenberg officers "jumped the gun" by putting the first missile on full alert a day earlier, according to the Wing history, "in anticipation of an assumption of DEFCON 2." *Ibid.*, pp. 1, 5.

[74] See, for example, Thomas S. Power memorandum to HQ USAF, "Missile Items," November 20, 1962, p. 1, Curtis LeMay Papers, SAC 1962 file, box 143, Library of Congress, Washington, D.C.

[75] History of the 6595th Aerospace Test Wing, 22 October–20 November 1962, FOIA, p. 7. The AFSC history states only that the regular missile test schedule was continued "with SAC concurrence." *History of the Air Force System Command,* 1 July–31 December 1962, vol. 1, p. II-102. The author has found no record in the JCS archives suggesting that the launch schedule was reviewed at the Joint Staff level during the crisis. Furthermore, none of the civilian officials interviewed by the author recall having any awareness of these specific ECC activities or the ICBM launch at Vandenberg during the crisis.

Washington were carefully monitoring the operational alert status of the Soviet missiles in Cuba, a U.S. missile was actually being launched, without their knowledge, in California.

## False Warning Dangers

It is difficult to assess how dangerous this Atlas ICBM launch was in the middle of the crisis. Since the Soviet Union did not yet have reconnaissance satellites providing tactical intelligence on U.S. missile launches, and its line-of-site warning radar system was extremely primitive in 1962, the KGB and the GRU (the Chief Intelligence Directorate of the Soviet General Staff) maintained a network of covert base-watchers to provide warning of any impending nuclear attack.[76] If such agents were present near Vandenberg, they might have witnessed activities suggesting that nuclear warheads were being placed on the test ICBMs and would then see, in the middle of the night, a missile being launched. Moreover, if Soviet naval ships in the Pacific were providing strategic warning information during the Cuban crisis, they too might have picked up the test ICBM launch from Vandenberg.[77]

Whether *Soviet* intelligence sources picked up the U.S. ICBM launch is not known. What does appear certain, however, is that none of the senior civilians in the *U.S. government* had any awareness of the possible dangers involved. Although the Air Force System Command's senior officer at Vandenberg did make a local press announcement that a missile test was about to take place to reduce the risks of "alarm among the civilian populace of the surrounding communities," there is no evidence that the problem of potential false warnings or the possibility of communications with the Soviet Union were ever considered.[78] No one in Washington apparently imagined the possibility that Soviet intelligence might learn of the launch just as it was taking place, and then misinterpret it as part of an actual attack. Failure to anticipate potential problems in this area was a serious lapse in U.S. government planning for safe crisis management.

[76] See Stephen M. Meyer, "Soviet Nuclear Operations," in Ashton B. Carter, John D. Steinbruner, and Charles A. Zraket, eds., *Managing Nuclear Operations* (Washington, D.C.: Brookings Institution, 1987), p. 488, fn. 41.

[77] There is evidence that Soviet trawlers in the Atlantic were involved in electronic intelligence operations during the crisis, and it is possible that similar Soviet intelligence activities were taking place in the Pacific. *CINCLANT Historical Account of the Cuban Missile Crisis*, April 29, 1963 (declassified 1986), Operational Archives, Naval Historical Center, Washington, D.C., p. 123.

[78] History of the 6595th Aerospace Test Wing, 22 October 1962–20 November 1962, pp. 6–7.

## Minuteman Problems at Malmstrom

A second safety incident concerning ICBMs alerted under the Emergency Combat Capability plan during the crisis occurred at Malmstrom Air Force Base in Montana, where the first squadron of solid-fuel Minuteman I missiles was about to be deployed when the crisis broke out. The first Minuteman missiles arrived at Malmstrom in September 1962 and began their lengthy process of systems testing and certification by the Air Force System Command, to ensure reliability and safety prior to their scheduled turnover to SAC.[79] The Emergency Combat Capability agreement between SAC and the AFSC came into effect immediately when DEFCON 2 was declared on October 24, and officers at the base began to improvise emergency alert procedures under crisis conditions, which had never been thoroughly exercised. SAC, AFSC, and contractor personnel worked literally twenty-four hours a day in order to rush the nation's first Minuteman missiles onto alert. The first ICBM was placed on alert on the morning of October 26, and by October 30, a total of five Minuteman missiles had reached operational alert status.[80]

To achieve this rapid surge in readiness, however, many routine safety procedures used at other bases had to be adjusted. Throughout the ICBM complex, Air Force and contractor personnel jerry-rigged the missile systems with available material: according to the declassified history of the 341st Strategic Missile Wing's activities, "lack of equipment, both standard and test, required many work-arounds."[81] Individual missiles were therefore repeatedly taken on and off alert as maintenance crews discovered problems and improvised fixes to permit maximum emergency readiness.[82] Numerous unanticipated operational difficulties had to be surmounted under the tense pressure of the crisis alert. Officers quickly discovered, for example, that these Minuteman missiles might be inadvertently armed through miswiring, wire shorts, or burn-throughs, and each missile at Malmstrom was therefore tested for such faults when it was removed from alert status.[83] Emergency communications and launch crew

---

[79] Jim Kristl, "Missiles of October," *Combat Crew*, October 1987, pp. 16–17.

[80] History of the 341st Strategic Missile Wing, October 1–31, 1962, vol. 2, Cuban Missile Annex, K-WG-341-HI, AFHRC, pp. 5–6.

[81] *Ibid.*, p. 5.

[82] Indeed, all ten Minuteman missiles of Flight A at Malmstrom were capable of staying on alert for only part of one day of the crisis, with one missile undergoing five "restarts and shutdowns," when its guidance and control devices repeatedly failed, during the month. History of the 341st Strategic Missile Wing, November 1–30, 1962, Cuban Crisis Annex, p. 1, K-WG-341-HI, AFHRC.

[83] Arming the missile connects the ignition and ordnance circuits and enables a launch to take place if proper launch commands are subsequently entered into the system. During the

certification procedures also had to be improvised. It was discovered that the land lines to the Malmstrom Launch Control Center (LCC) intermittently failed, and because there was no time to test and fix the communication system as designed, a special "walkie-talkie" system of transceiver radios was installed at the site.[84] There was also insufficient time for regular launch crew certification procedures to be followed as the ICBMs were rushed onto alert status, and the crews taking control of the first operational Minuteman missiles therefore were *not* fully evaluated or certified when they accepted this awesome responsibility.[85]

## Minuteman Safety Rules and Launch Procedures

Most important, in the confusion of the emergency alert, a seriously flawed procedure was initially used when the Minuteman missiles were placed on full alert. A detailed explanation of the complex command and control procedures and safety rules for the Minuteman ICBM (rules that were in the process of being approved in October 1962) is necessary here to understand what happened at Malmstrom Air Force Base. Although some of the details of these nuclear command and control mechanisms remain classified, the Proposed Minuteman Safety Rules from October 1962 have been declassified, with only a few paragraphs deleted,[86] and sufficient information from the records at Malmstrom is available to provide at least a preliminary assessment of the effectiveness of these safety rules during the crisis.

The safety rules for the Minuteman ICBM force were designed to prevent both inadvertent and unauthorized arming or launching of the mis-

---

crisis it was determined that "certain shorted conditions could arm these devices upon removal of the safing pins without indication of an armed status, that is, a no-go shut down would not result. This condition is a safety hazard." Undated message, December 1962, Ballistic Systems Division, Norton to SATAF, Malmstrom, Subject: Personnel Safety Hazard, NSA-CMCC.

[84] History of the 341st Strategic Missile Wing, October 1–31 1962, pp. 2, 5.

[85] Crew certification tests began *after* the first missiles were placed on alert, but were completed during the first week of the crisis. *Ibid.*, pp. 3–5, and History of the 3901st Missile Evaluation Squadron, November 1962–January 1963, p. 5, K-SQ-EVAL-3901, AFHRC. Similar waivers of a peacetime missile crew training were granted at other bases involved in the crisis alert. See, for example, History of the 47th Strategic Aerospace Division, October 1–31, 1962, p. 4, K-DIV-47-HI, AFHRC.

[86] Unless otherwise stated, the following information and direct quotes concerning Minuteman launch procedures and safety rules are from this document. Maxwell Taylor, Memorandum for the Secretary of Defense, "Proposed Safety Rules for the HSM-80A (Minuteman)/MK 5 RV Weapon System," October 18, 1962 (henceforth "Minuteman Safety Rules"), CCS 4615 (October 2, 1962), JCS 1962.

siles. A complex set of personnel regulations, operational rules, and redundant mechanical safety devices designed to achieve these objectives was prescribed. In each of the two-man underground launch control centers (LCCs) for the ICBMs, a set of ten switches (the Launch Enable System switches) had to be activated in order *to arm* the missiles, which connected the missiles' ignition circuits. The two LCC officers had to turn two separate key switches on opposite sides of the room (the Launch Control Switch and the Cooperative Launch Control Switch) within two seconds of one another in order *to launch* the missiles. A status panel existed in the LCC, which provided both a light and an audible alarm to inform the officers on whether a missile under their control was on alert, was armed, was not functioning properly, was in the middle of a launch countdown, or had been fired. Each Minuteman missile was also equipped with a safety control switch on its motor ignition system, which could be manually locked in safe position during routine maintenance. All electrical circuits between the missile and the LCC were required to have electrical surge arrestors and to be checked prior to deployment to ensure that they could not be inadvertently activated by electrical tests or monitoring equipment. All personnel directly involved with nuclear warheads or launch control equipment were required to hold secret clearances. Finally, the Air Force's "two-man rule" was to be followed at all times, with one important exception: one of the two crewmen in the LCC was permitted to sleep as long as the other remained awake and alert.[87]

It is important to note that no coded locking devices existed on U.S. ICBMs in 1962, and the officers inside Minuteman Launch Control Centers held the physical *capability*, though not the *authority*, to launch the missiles under their control. The Minuteman command and control system was therefore designed so that a number of LCCs were to have overlapping responsibilities in order both to permit authorized launches under all conditions of war initiation and to prevent an unauthorized launch under any circumstances. The resulting system of checks and balances is de-

---

[87] "During any operation affording access to a War Reserve Warhead, a Re-Entry Vehicle with a War Reserve Warhead installed, and/or to control equipment which could cause arming, launching, or detonation of the warhead, a minimum of two authorized persons, each capable of detecting incorrect or unauthorized procedures with respect to the task to be performed and familiar with pertinent safety and security requirements, will be present." "Minuteman Safety Rules," p. 18. According to a declassified 1973 air force document: "With the first Minuteman system deployed, Minuteman I, SAC was allowed to authorize one crew member at a time to sleep. However, with the deployment of Minuteman II, and later Minuteman III, more stringent safety requirements were identified. These requirements forced SAC to increase its crew manpower authorizations in order to keep two crew members awake at all times." HQ USAF Required Operational Capability no. 3-73, April 3, 1973, in History of the Strategic Air Command FY 1975, vol. 12, exhibit 128, p. 1, K146.01–153, AFHRC.

scribed below and is displayed in figures 2.2 and 2.3. Each launch control center had primary responsibility for one flight of ten missiles out of a squadron of fifty Minuteman ICBMs. (See figure 2.2.) If an emergency action message (EAM) to launch the force was received by the two officers in a LCC, they were to authenticate and validate it through their code books; if the message was authentic, the crewmen were supposed to take out their launch keys, insert them into the proper switches, and turn them simultaneously. Three different things could happen next. (See figure 2.3.)

First, officers in the other four LCCs could stop the launch immediately. An Inhibit Launch Switch existed in each LCC in the squadron, and the officers were instructed to turn it immediately if they had not received a valid EAM and indications on their status panels showed that another LCC had just issued a launch order to the missiles. This Inhibit Launch Switch was therefore the system's protection against an unauthorized launch attempt from one LCC: if the switch was turned by a single LCC officer in the squadron, the thirty-second missile launch countdown would be terminated, unless a third LCC also issued a "second vote" launch command to the missiles.

Second, the ICBMs could be launched *immediately* through coordinated action by four officers in two different LCCs. Even if one or more "inhibit commands" had been issued, a "second vote" launch command issued from any one of the other four LCCs in the squadron would fire all enabled missiles in the squadron in an immediate salvo after the thirty-second countdown or in rapid ripple fire (depending on the SIOP war plan option chosen). This procedure was designed to ensure that a properly authorized launch would still take place, even if one LCC had failed to receive the EAM or for any other reason turned the Inhibit Launch Switch.

Third, the ICBMs could be launched in a *delayed* manner by a single Launch Control Center. Each missile in a Minuteman squadron was equipped with a "delay timer" in its electronic system, which would be activated by the first launch command. This timer could be set by SAC SIOP planners for any time between one and six hours, and if neither an "inhibit vote" nor a second "launch vote" was received, the ICBMs would automatically fire once the delay timer expired. This delayed launch procedure was designed to permit the ICBMs to be launched by the crew members in the sole surviving LCC in the event that all others were destroyed by a Soviet first strike.[88]

[88] "Minuteman Safety Rules." In 1967, as a response to concerns about Soviet targeting of the Minuteman LCCs, the U.S. developed the Airborne Launch Control System, by which a SAC command post aircraft can itself launch the missiles if all the LCCs are destroyed in a Soviet first strike. For discussion of these procedures, see *Fiscal Year 1978 Authorization for Military Procurement, Research and Development, and Active Duty, Selected Reserve, and Civilian Personnel Strengths*, Hearings before the Committee on Armed Services, U.S. Senate,

## Safety First?

This complex system of checks and balances was designed for normal peacetime conditions in which five Launch Control Centers were operating in each missile squadron. At a *minimum*, it would be necessary to have *two* LCCs in operation for the system to provide some protection against an unauthorized delayed launch by one or two individuals in a single LCC. Under routine conditions, therefore, at least *two* flights of Minuteman ICBMs, with their *two* operating LCCs, were usually brought onto alert status at the same time during initial deployments of Minuteman ICBMs at new bases in the 1960s.[89]

When DEFCON 2 was declared on October 24, 1962, however, the situation was not routine. There was in fact only *one* Launch Control Center close enough to completion at Malmstrom Air Force Base to be used in the crisis operation. How could the Malmstrom missiles therefore be placed on alert without a having a serious compromise in nuclear weapons safety?

The Minuteman Safety Rules were so thorough that they also addressed this possibility. If only one LCC was operational in any squadron during an international crisis, the missiles could still be placed on alert, as long as the following *additional* Emergency Combat Capability safety procedures were implemented. The only available LCC was *not* to be equipped with all the necessary devices to permit a missile to be fired. Specifically, the launch panel operational encoders, needed to execute a missile launch, were required to be "retained in a target materials vault" at a support base until "directed by CINCSAC in preparation for a possible Emergency Combat Launch." These operational encoders were supposed to be carried by a launch team "accompanied by an armed escort" to the LCC if so ordered.[90]

These special precautionary measures added significantly to the time it would take to launch the ICBMs in an authorized manner. They therefore represent a deliberate decision to sacrifice some degree of SIOP readiness to increase the margin of safety. A high reliability theorist would be comforted: thorough analysis, redundant safeguards, personnel reliability programs, and prioritization of safety led to what was considered to be a foolproof system. As General Maxwell Taylor explained, in the official

---

95th Congress, 1st sess., part 10, pp. 6845–6846, and Bruce G. Blair, *Strategic Command and Control* (Washington, D.C.: Brookings Institution, 1985), pp. 165–166.

[89] See, for example, Hopkins and Goldberg, *The Development of the Strategic Air Command, 1946–1986*, p. 113.

[90] "Minuteman Safety Rules," p. 21. It is important to note, however, that a further precaution to be taken under ECC status has been deleted from this declassified document.

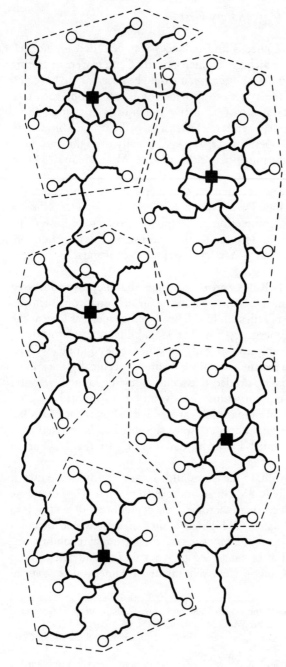

TYPICAL SQUADRON LAYOUT

• Five Flights per Squadron each containing ten ICBM's and one Launch Control Center

• Minimum distance between sites – four nautical miles

■ Launch Control Center
○ Launch Facility (ICBM)
- - - Flight Location
—— Hardened Cable Route

2.2 Minuteman Deployment (Clyde R. Littlefield, *The Site Program*, Air Force Systems Command, History of DCAS, 1961, vol. 3, p. 74, K243.012–8, AFHRC.)

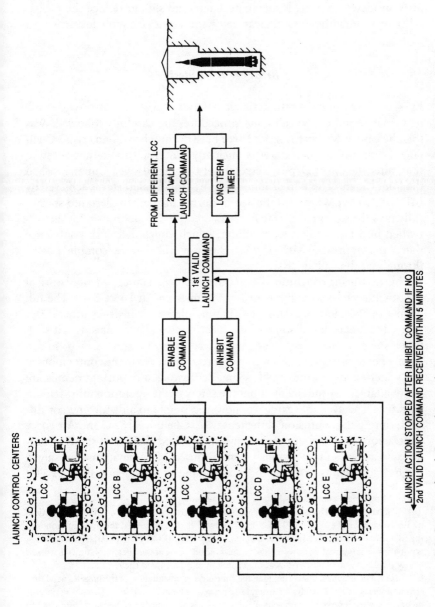

LAUNCH CONTROL CENTERS

FROM DIFFERENT LCC

LCC A
LCC B
LCC C
LCC D
LCC E

ENABLE COMMAND

INHIBIT COMMAND

1st VALID LAUNCH COMMAND

2nd VALID LAUNCH COMMAND

LONG TERM TIMER

LAUNCH ACTION STOPPED AFTER INHIBIT COMMAND IF NO 2nd VALID LAUNCH COMMAND RECEIVED WITHIN 5 MINUTES

2.3  Command and Control Launch Sequences (FY 1978 Authorization for Military Procurement . . . Committee on Armed Services hearings, 95th Congress, 1st sess., part 10, p. 6845.)

cover letter that accompanied the Proposed Minuteman Safety Rules, to Pentagon civilian authorities: "The safety rules and procedures attached are considered to provide adequate safety and should reduce the probability of an unauthorized nuclear detonation to a negligible factor."[91]

## Breaking the Rules?

Even the most intelligently designed safety system will not provide adequate safety unless the rules and procedures are carefully followed. Was this the case at Malmstrom Air Force Base during the Cuban crisis? Civilian officials in Washington were sufficiently concerned about that question that, after the crisis, Deputy Secretary of Defense Roswell Gilpatric asked the Joint Chiefs of Staff to produce a report "on the alert status achieved by MINUTEMAN Wing I (Malmstrom) during the Cuban alert and specifically how the safety rules were implemented."[92] On December 15, the JCS replied in a two-page memorandum, which concluded with confidence that "the approved MINUTEMAN safety rules were complied with throughout the Cuban crisis."[93]

This reassuring conclusion is *not* borne out by an independent historical investigation into what happened at Malmstrom Air Force Base. The full details of the alert operation are impossible to reconstruct after thirty years: the memories of some of the individuals involved have faded with time; some of the relevant documents continue to be classified; and a number of important details were never recorded even in the contemporary top secret history of the missile wing. Because such important details are not available, any judgment about the safety of the operation must remain tentative. The available evidence, however, points to a disturbing conclusion: during the confusion of the tense crisis, field-level SAC and Air Force contractor personnel appear to have improvised their own safety procedures in a manner that seriously compromised Minuteman nuclear safety.

This judgment is based on three central pieces of evidence. First, careful

[91] "Minuteman Safety Rules," cover memorandum, p. 2.

[92] JCSM-982–62, December 15, 1962, Subject: Alert Status of Minuteman Wing I, CCS 4730 (November 10, 1962), p. 1, JCS 1962. Why Gilpatric requested the investigation into the ECC alert activities at Malmstrom, but *not* at any of the ECC Titan or Atlas missile bases, is not known. It is possible, however, that rumors about some of the safety violations discussed below reached civilian authorities at the Pentagon and prompted the request.

[93] *Ibid.* The Boeing engineering manager in charge of installation of the missiles at Malmstrom in October 1962, Melvyn Paisley, later proved to be quite capable of breaking government rules when it served his interests. Paisley, the assistant secretary of the navy from 1981 to 1987, later pleaded guilty to conspiracy and bribery charges stemming from efforts to rig a large number of military procurement contracts. See Neil A. Lewis, "Ex-Naval Official Makes Guilty Plea in Bid-Rigging Case," *New York Times*, June 15, 1991, p. 1.

comparison of declassified messages and the Malmstrom operational history suggests that the first ICBM actually went on alert *prior* to the approval and dissemination of the Minuteman safety rules. Emergency efforts to prepare the Malmstrom ICBMs for a potential war started immediately when DEFCON 2 was declared October 24, and SAC officers and contract personnel in the launch control center rapidly wired the circuitry to permit a SIOP launch. According to the wing's operational history, the first missile was placed on full alert, capable of being launched, at 11:16 a.m. (local time) on October 26.[94] The approved Minuteman safety rules, however, apparently did not reach Malmstrom until sometime after that first missile reached complete alert status.[95] This suggests, in short, that as the first U.S. Minuteman missile was being alerted, critical technical decisions concerning nuclear weapons safety were being made by individuals located at Malmstrom, who were both figuratively and literally at very low levels in the Strategic Air Command.

Second, the available evidence raises doubts about whether the critical parts of the launch panel, which were needed for a missile launch, were in fact kept in a secure vault away from the LCC, in accordance with the Minuteman Safety Rules. Although the declassified 341 Wing history from October 1962 states that "the lack of security . . . has dictated that the launch panels and alternate crews remain at the Strategic Support Base," the declassified November wing history states that at the end of the crisis, when DEFCON 2 was canceled, the "Launch Panels and Positive Control materials (were) *returned* to the vault."[96] Close attention to the estimated timing for an authorized SIOP launch of these missiles reenforces concerns about whether the safety rules were followed. The Air Force reported to the JCS after the crisis that the Malmstrom Minuteman force could have been launched *90 minutes* after receiving a valid execution order, which is approximately how long it would take if the full safety precautions had been

[94] History of the 341st Ballistic Missile Wing, October 1–31, 1962, Cuban Crisis Annex, p. 5. It is important to note here that the official *Air Force Response to the Cuban Crisis* and the JCS report on the incident both state that the first missile went on alert on October 27.

[95] A SAC message, sent to Malmstrom on the *afternoon* of October 26, requested a technical evaluation of the "possibility of (an) accidental launch" and noted that the SAC safety rules issued on October 3 were "being re-evaluated by this headquarters." SAC to BSD, 15 AF, and 341 SMW (Malmstrom), 1630/October 26, 1962, in *SAC Operations in the Cuban Missile Crisis of 1962*, vol. 4, chapter 3, tab 23 (declassified July 14, 1988), AFHRC. This message did *not* make any reference to the official "proposed Minuteman safety rules," which had not been sent to the secretary of defense for approval until October 18. Although full details remain classified, it appears likely that even an interim civilian approval of the Minuteman rules was not transmitted to SAC until November 5, 1962. JCS case file cover sheet, CCS 4615 (October 2, 1962), JCS 1962.

[96] History of the 341st Strategic Missile Wing, October 1–31, 1962, Cuban Crisis Annex, p. 3; History of the 341st Strategic Missile Wing, November 1–30, 1962, Cuban Crisis Annex, p. 3 (emphasis added).

implemented; the 341st Strategic Missile Wing history explicitly states, in contrast, that "*45 minutes or less* will be required to effect a successful launch," which suggests that less stringent safety procedures were in fact used during the crisis.[97]

Third, two of the individuals who worked inside the Malmstrom launch control center during the crisis stated, in not-for-attribution interviews with the author, that the official safety rules were not fully implemented during the crisis and that less than adequate measures preventing unauthorized launch existed. Both men suggested that the personnel in the single launch control center held the capability to fire the missiles in an unauthorized manner. According to one of these individuals: "We didn't literally 'hot wire' the launch command system—that would be the wrong analogy—but we did have a second key. . . . I could have launched it on my own, if I had wanted to."[98]

### How Serious a Problem?

Although the Minuteman alert at Malmstrom did not cause a nuclear accident or an unauthorized launch in October 1962, the potential appears to have been greater than realized by senior officials in Washington, who were inevitably unaware of all the details of the operation. The risk of an *accidental* launch did not go entirely unnoticed in Air Force safety inspections after the crisis. As an Air Force Ballistic Missile Office document noted: "As the first Minuteman operational flights were completed and turned over to the Strategic Air Command electronic problems—inevitably—emerged which required 'fixes.' These centered on correcting possible malfunctions of automated equipment *that posed serious hazards; accidental launch*, explosive dangers, communications failures, etc."[99] The equally serious nuclear safety problems concerning the risk of *unauthorized launch* that appear to have existed because of the improvised command and control procedures during the crisis, however, were not reported and therefore not fully recognized by higher authorities in 1962.

There is a large gap, of course, between lower-level individuals having the *capability* to launch missiles in an unauthorized manner and the *actual*

---

[97] Memorandum AFXPD-JS to Secretary JCS, subject JCS Paper 2304/116, December 11, 1962, CCS 4730 (10 November 1962) JCS 1962; History of the 341st Strategic Missile Wing, October 1–31 1962, pp. 3–4 (emphasis added).

[98] "Not-for-attribution" interviews with personnel involved in the Malmstrom alert operation. It should be noted, however, that these statements were explicitly denied in the author's interviews with other Malmstrom officers and contractors.

[99] Minuteman Chronology, 1955–1967, 31 December 1962, Ballistic Missile Office, p. 57 (emphasis added).

*occurrence* of such a launch. The command and control safety system had been designed, however, so that such responsibility did not fall on one or two crewmen in a single Minuteman launch control center, as it apparently did during the crisis. In this limited sense, it can be said that the safety system failed.

It is certainly *possible* that senior Pentagon or White House officials would have nonetheless approved of some of the critical aspects of these emergency ICBM operations during the crisis if they had been aware of them. The fact that senior Pentagon civilian officials refused to permit SAC to place nonsafety certified weapons on the B-58 bombers during the crisis, however, strongly supports the opposite conclusion. Given how marginal the increase was in the U.S. nuclear arsenal produced by the SAC/AFSC Emergency Combat Capability plan—the ECC agreement contributed only approximately twenty missiles out of the SIOP crisis alert force of almost thirty-three hundred nuclear weapons or seventy-one megatons out of an alerted force with approximately seven thousand megatons of explosive power[100]—it is much more probable that central political authorities would *not* have authorized these particular ICBM alert operations had they been even minimally aware of the dangers at the time of the crisis. In short, it is highly unlikely that a 1 percent increase in nuclear strength would have been judged to be worth even a small decrease in nuclear weapons safety by responsible civilian officials in October 1962.

### NUCLEAR WEAPONS AND AIR DEFENSE OPERATIONS

SAC was the most highly disciplined and frequently exercised command in the U.S. military. How were nuclear alert operations run in a less elite command? Normal accidents theory argues that complexity and tight coupling lead to unanticipated and often bizarre interactions between units and rapid escalation to serious accidents once things go wrong. There is always a tension therefore in organizations that are both interactively complex and tightly coupled. Decentralization is needed to cope with complexity, increasing the ability of field operators to respond appropriately to unexpected events. And yet, centralization—in the form of high-level policy decisions, strict rules for implementation, and unquestioned and prompt obedience—is needed to cope with tight coupling, reducing the risk of faulty improvisation and low-level paralysis. How can an organization cope with such contradictory pressures?

[100] The extra nuclear capability produced by the ECC procedures is given in *Air Force Response*, p. 33. The total 1962 crisis-generated SIOP estimate is based on p. 11 and on Cyrus Vance Memorandum, "Military Strength Increases Since Fiscal Year 1961."

A detailed examination of the October 1962 nuclear alert in the Air Defense Command (ADC) can illuminate this issue, since a deep tension existed in the system between the need to ensure that air defense nuclear weapons could be utilized effectively if the United States faced a surprise attack from the Soviet Union and the need to prevent accidental or unauthorized use. The central wartime mission of ADC interceptor aircraft was to destroy Soviet bombers before they could drop nuclear weapons on U.S. cities. There was a risk, however, that a Soviet first-strike missile attack would disrupt communications, or even destroy Washington, and thereby prevent air defense forces from receiving presidential authority to use their surface-to-air and air-to-air nuclear missiles against incoming Soviet bombers. To cope with this risk, President Eisenhower delegated authority to U.S. military commanders in the mid-1950s to use such *defensive* nuclear weapons immediately in the event of an attack.[101] As one U.S. Army Air Defense Command 1958 memorandum on "Authority to Employ Atomic Weapons" states: "A thorough indoctrination concerning authority to employ atomic weapons in air defense is mandatory *for commanders at all operational echelons . . .* (because) *autonomous operations are necessary when all communication with NORAD commanders is lost.*"[102]

In October 1962, this decentralized system of control authorized U.S. air defense commanders *at regional levels* to order the use of nuclear weapons on their own authority, if there was "unambiguous" evidence that the United States was under attack and further communication with higher authorities was either not possible or was considered inappropriate because of the need for prompt reaction. This authority was further delegated by regional NORAD (North American Air Defense) and Air Defense Command (ADC) commanders to subordinates in their chain of command in the event that they were absent or otherwise unavailable to make such critical decisions. During the Cuban missile crisis, therefore, the authority to order the use of nuclear weapons against "objects determined to be

---

[101] See Jack Raymond, "Swift Reprisal Set for Arctic Attack," New York Times, May 17, 1958, p. 1; the 1957 interview with General Earle Partridge is reprinted in U.S. News and World Report, October 5, 1964, p. 49; and David Alan Rosenberg, "The Origins of Overkill: Nuclear Weapons and American Strategy, 1945–1960," International Security 7, no. 4, (Spring 1983): 43.

[102] HQ U.S. Army Air Defense Command, ADGCC 471.6, "Authority to Employ Atomic Weapons," December 8, 1958, p. 358 enclosure, CCS 4615, Use of Custody (25 February 1959), 1959 JCS (emphasis added). Also see JCS Memorandum for the Secretary of Defense, March 14, 1955, Subject: Report of the Continental Defense Panel of the Joint Congressional Committee on Atomic Energy, Appendix, p. 2, Carrolton Press, Declassified Document Reference System, 1985, no. 000889, and CINCLANT letter 00049/54, 5 August 1957, Subject: Implementing Instructions for the Expenditure of Nuclear Weapons, Carrolton Press, Declassified Documents Reference System, 1980, no.273A.

hostile" was delegated down to the deputy for operations, usually a colonel, in NORAD regional divisions.[103]

## Coping with Decentralization

Under this decentralized system, a complex system of procedural checks and mechanical safety devices evolved to reduce the risk of unauthorized nuclear use or inappropriate lower-level decisions. Beginning in the mid-1950s, for example, rules of engagement (ROE) for interceptor aircraft provided guidance to U.S. air defense commanders on when incoming aircraft could be reasonably considered to be displaying hostile intent and therefore attacked:

> Aircraft may be considered "manifestly hostile in intent" when:
> (a) The pattern or actions of incoming unidentified aircraft indicate beyond a reasonable doubt that a hostile raid is in progress.
> (b) Aircraft not properly cleared and not obviously in distress are observed in a Coastal ADIZ (Air Defense Identification Zone) and it is ascertained beyond a reasonable doubt that they have hostile intentions against the United States . . .
> (c) Current evaluated intelligence is available which indicates that aircraft are airborne and enroute toward the United States with the obvious intention of attacking targets within the United States.[104]

It is important to note that such rules of engagement were written in a flexible manner to encourage commanders to use their best professional judgment in any ambiguous situation, and that officers were explicitly reminded that "nothing in these instructions shall be construed as preventing any responsible commander from taking such action as may be necessary to defend his command."[105]

Safety in the Air Defense Command was further complicated by that fact that the majority of the ADC nuclear-armed interceptors in the early 1960s were single seat aircraft, so that, prior to the deployment of Permissive Action Links (PALs) locking devices, an important violation of the "two-

---

[103] John Dennison, *26th Air Division (SAGE) Participation in the Cuban Crisis*, vol. 1, pp. 5–8, K-DIV-26-HI, AFHRC.

[104] Intercept and Engagement Instructions, November 23, 1954, pp. 2–3, 373.24 U.S. (September 8, 1949), S.6, Geographic File, 1954–1957, JCS. Although minor changes in the air defense ROE were made in the late 1950s, these 1954 rules reflect the essence of the ROE in the early 1960s.

[105] *Ibid.*, p. 1. For a discussion of the evolution of U.S. rules of engagement see Scott D. Sagan, "Rules of Engagement," in Alexander L. George, ed., *Avoiding War: Problems of Crisis Management* (Boulder, Colo.: Westview Press, 1991), pp. 443–470.

man rule" was inevitable in air defense operations.[106] The ADC and NORAD alert procedures were therefore designed to reduce the resulting risk of unauthorized use. In normal peacetime conditions, only conventionally armed air interceptors were placed on maximum five-minute alert readiness, capable of being flushed immediately on tactical warning of a missile attack. In contrast, to ensure extra nuclear safety, nuclear-armed interceptors were normally maintained at a lower thirty-minute state of readiness. Only at DEFCON 3 could nuclear-equipped interceptors be fully armed and placed on higher fifteen-minute alert at their home base and not unless a DEFCON 1 or Defense Emergency alert was declared were nuclear-armed interceptors planned to be launched into the air on defense missions.[107] Mechanical devices also were essential to prevent nuclear weapons accidents and unauthorized use. For example, special rocket ignition and warhead enabling devices were attached to nuclear-armed air-to-air missiles when they were loaded onto the aircraft. These were to be used to render the missile and warhead inoperable whenever the interceptor was dispersed to alternate bases or flown on any "tactical ferry" mission, taking the weapons to new locations.[108] Hence, a significant violation of the "two-man rule" would occur only under the most extreme conditions: if interceptors were launched in the belief that an attack was imminent.

This delegation of authority and ability to use defensive nuclear weapons inevitably produced a situation of "*ambiguous command.*"[109] Air Defense Command interceptor pilots were trained to request authority to use their nuclear weapons and to receive orders from ground control command posts. But these interceptor pilots were also fully aware that there was some possibility that ground control centers would be destroyed in an initial attack and that they would be forced to use their individual judgment on appropriate action under such grave circumstances. The Air

[106] The Air Defense Command used three interceptor aircraft on nuclear-armed defense missions in 1962. The Convair F-106A "Delta Dart" and the Convair F-102A "Delta Dagger" were single-seat interceptors. The McDonnell F-101B "Voodoo" was, however, a two-seat interceptor. See *Jane's All the World's Aircraft 1960–1961* (New York: McGraw Hill, 1960), pp. 286–287, 347. The primary nuclear armament for air defense interceptors in 1962 was the MB-1 "Genie" air-to-air missile and the GAR-11 "Falcon" air-to-air missile. For descriptions of the missiles and their "low kiloton" yield warheads, see Chuck Hansen, *U.S. Nuclear Weapons* (Arlington, Tex.: Aerofax, 1988) pp. 177–178.

[107] North American Air Defense Command, DEFCON "Check List," CCS 3180, Emergency Readiness Plans (April 20, 1959) (Group 2), JCS 1959.

[108] *The Air Defense Command in the Cuban Crisis, October-December 1962*, ADC Historical Study 15, FOIA, p. 44; Weapons Mechanic/Weapons Maintenance Supervisor (AFSCs 46250 and 46270), vol. 2, Air Munitions and Aircraft Weapons, Extension Course Institute, Air University, pp. 43, 72–76.

[109] On the concept of ambiguous command, see Paul Bracken, *The Command and Control of Nuclear Forces* (New Haven, Conn.: Yale University Press, 1983), pp. 224–232.

Defense Command post officers, who held authority for declaring forces "manifestly hostile in intent" and for ordering nuclear use if necessary, were also fully cognizant of the grave responsibility that could descend upon them in a nuclear war. All possible scenarios had not been, and could not be, thoroughly thought through in advance, and in the event of a nuclear attack, individual officers would have to use their own personal judgment to determine appropriate action.[110]

These delegations of authority were considered necessary by senior political and military authorities in 1962 in order to ensure that a Soviet ICBM strike would not eliminate the ability of the United States to destroy incoming Soviet nuclear-armed bombers. The resulting set of organizational procedures and safety devices had been subjected to high level review, under both the Eisenhower and the early Kennedy administrations. The system was considered to be a highly reliable and safe system under peacetime conditions. It was, however, subjected to a severe and not fully reassuring test during the Cuban missile crisis.

## The Crisis Interceptor Alert

On the afternoon of October 22, five and a half hours *before* President Kennedy's public address, Air Defense Command Headquarters ordered all nuclear air defense weapons to be alerted and, ninety minutes later, ordered the immediate dispersal of nuclear-equipped interceptors to alternate bases.[111] This action was not only unprecedented, it was also contrary to existing Air Defense Command DEFCON safety regulations, since the ADC was still at DEFCON 5 and dispersal of nuclear-armed interceptors was not permitted until DEFCON 1 was declared.[112] A number of local commanders were therefore concerned that the dispersal order was a communications error or a procedural mistake by higher authorities. Indeed, more than one regional air defense commander, operating without any

[110] Although no similar evidence exists in Air Defense Command records, it is worth noting that senior officers of the Air Force Systems Command were explicitly reminded of this grim possibility, during the Cuban crisis, when General Bernard A. Shriever sent a message stating: "It is my desire that every commander personally see to the readiness of his command, and be prepared to exercise his capability to the utmost if the eventuality occurs that he must proceed on his own." *History of the Air Force Systems Command*, July 1–December 31, 1962, vol. 1, p. II-78.

[111] *The Air Defense Command in the Cuban Crisis*, pp. 37–38.

[112] The air force had announced plans to change the safety rules to permit dispersal of nuclear-armed aircraft at DEFCON 3, but the new rules had not yet been issued in October 1962. See Message Commander 28th Air Division to CINCNORAD, 182200Z December 1962, in Cuban Crisis 28th Air Division (SAGE), October–December 1962, exhibit 7, K410.041–15, AFHRC; and History of the 15th Fighter Interceptor Squadron, October–December 1962, K-SQ-FI-15-HI, AFHRC.

knowledge of the impending crisis over the missiles in Cuba and still officially at DEFCON 5, demanded confirmation of the order before he was willing to disperse the aircraft.[113] DEFCON 3 was officially declared when President Kennedy announced the quarantine that evening. By the next morning, 161 nuclear-armed interceptors (66 F-101Bs, 64 F-106As, and 31 F-102As) were on alert at sixteen dispersal bases scattered across the northern United States. Air defense nuclear-armed interceptors remained on DEFCON 3 alert at these dispersal bases until November 17, when they finally returned to their home bases.[114]

## Safety Problems Again

These air defense operations in October 1962 produced a number of nuclear weapons safety and command and control incidents. None of them, obviously, led to an accidental nuclear detonation or an accidental war. They are nonetheless alarming since each had at least some potential to produce such dangers.

An immediate breach of safety procedures occurred during the initial interceptor dispersal. In almost all cases, the nuclear-equipped planes that dispersed on October 22 apparently followed the approved "tactical ferry" safety procedures: the rocket ignitor and ejection devices were disconnected, the warhead's strike enabling plug was placed in a safe position, and interceptors flew over sparsely populated areas whenever possible. After receiving the surprise order to disperse, however, at least one fighter squadron under the control of the 28th Air Division in California did *not* fully follow the safety procedures. According to the division's declassified history: "Aircraft were dispersed with very little warning, *fully armed and with all safety devices removed. Only the pilot stood between the complete weapon system and a full scale nuclear detonation.*"[115] The complex set of

---

[113] At the 25th ADC region headquarters the Director of Operations "felt that CONAD had made a mistake in directing dispersement with primary weapons because, up to this time, such flights were allowed only under higher conditions of readiness." *The Air Defense Command in the Cuban Crisis*, p. 38. Also see p. 115.

[114] *Ibid.*, p. 30, n. 24, and p. 136. For further details see Richard F. McMullen, *The Fighter Interceptor Force 1962–1964*, ADC Historical Study no. 27, pp. 9–12, K410.041–27, AFHRC. The "alert posture" of the interceptor force was adjusted on November 3 permitting a smaller number of aircraft to be kept on fifteen-minute alert within the DEFCON 3 status. Memorandum for the JCS, Supplemental Situation Report, no. 24, November 3, 1962, CCS 9123/9108 (G2), 1962 JCS.

[115] History of the 28th Air Division (SAGE), January–December 1962, vol. 1, p. 118, K-DIV-28-HI, AFHRC (emphasis added). This was apparently not the only case during the crisis in which air defense interceptors were launched with fully armed nuclear air-to-air

mechanical and organizational inhibitions on nuclear weapons use was therefore rendered temporarily ineffective. Inadvertent or unauthorized use by the pilot was not impossible and, had an interceptor crash occurred, the possibility of an accidental detonation was heightened with the weapons carried in this configuration. Fortunately, these particular interceptors landed without incident and maintained a high alert status at their dispersal bases, where proper safety procedures and the "two-man rule" could be followed.

At the home bases, ADC units apparently experienced relatively few command and control or safety problems during the prolonged alert. One problem that was reported, fortunately, was in a relatively low-level unit and did not affect interceptor operations. On October 22, when a nuclear munitions maintenance group at K. I. Sawyer Air Force Base in northern Michigan, received the alert notification, the message was garbled. This maintenance group reacted by assuming that DEFCON 1 was in effect: "Notification of alert status was CINCONAD [Commander in Chief Continental Air Defense] DELTA—no definite DEFCON was given. Since it was an actual alert, the decision was made to implement our plans in support of DEFCON 1."[116]

At the interceptor dispersal bases, however, more serious operational and safety problems quickly emerged, which were exacerbated by four factors. First, the Air Defense Command dispersal plan was still in the process of being developed when the crisis broke out and many of the special dispersal bases were not yet fully equipped at the time. Second, ADC dispersal plans had been built on the assumption that interceptor dispersal would take place only if a Soviet attack was imminent. Refueling, maintenance, and weapons safety facilities were therefore designed, even in the more well-equipped bases, for the aircraft to be stationed there for only a few hours, and not for what ended up being four weeks.[117] Third, the plan had assumed the full participation of Canada in an allied NORAD alert, and interceptor squadrons were scheduled to disperse from the U.S. to bases in Alberta, British Columbia, Saskatoon, Manitoba, New Brunswick, and Quebec. These dispersal sites were also not fully equipped

---

missiles on board. One former F-106A pilot states that he was specifically ordered *not* to place the appropriate safety mechanisms on the Genie missiles on his interceptor aircraft when he flew from Selfridge Air Force Base in Michigan to the dispersal base at Terre Haute, Indiana, on October 22. The reason given for this violation of "tactical ferry" safety rules was that there were no nuclear weapons maintenance personnel at the dispersal base and therefore no certified individuals would be available to place the nuclear weapons back on full combat alert status. Dan Barry, interview with author, December 10, 1992.

[116] 56MME-W Air Defense Readiness Resume, in 30th Air Division (SAGE)—30th NORAD Region and the Cuban Missile Crisis, vol. 9, K410.041–15, AFHRC.

[117] *The Air Defense Command in the Cuban Missile Crisis*, p. 204.

for nuclear-armed interceptors, however, and in Ottawa, Prime Minister John Diefenbaker refused to permit a full NORAD alert on October 22.[118] Although some "unauthorized" Royal Canadian Air Force alerting activities did take place nonetheless, large-scale use of Canadian dispersal bases for nuclear-armed interceptors was impossible.[119] Fourth, the Air Defense Command also planned to disperse some nuclear-armed interceptors to U.S. Navy air fields, but final navy approval of the plan had also not been given when the crisis alert was called, effectively ruling out this option as well.[120]

The nuclear-equipped ADC interceptors, therefore, dispersed in the crisis to both inadequately equipped planned bases and a number of "interim" bases, which were even more poorly prepared for the alert. At the sixteen austere dispersal sites, local ADC commanders struggled to maintain full readiness without unduly compromising nuclear safety. Some unanticipated work-arounds did receive official attention and proper authorization: for example, a temporary waiver of the "quantity-distance" safety rules governing the placement and handling of nuclear weapons in dispersal storage areas was granted by higher authorities.[121] Other *unauthorized* safety deficiencies were also documented: dispersal bases did not have safety-approved nuclear weapons storage and maintenance facilities, proper security fences and armed guards were often lacking, and the refueling and fire-prevention procedures for the nuclear-armed interceptors were determined to be inadequate.[122]

### False Warning Problems

Despite such safety deficiencies, the Cuban crisis alert continued uneventfully at most Air Defense Command bases. Two low-level false warn-

[118] McMullen, *The Fighter Interceptor Force*, p. 10.

[119] Canadian Defense Minister Douglas Harkness in fact ordered, on his own authority, the Royal Canadian Air Force (RCAF) to alert its forces "in as quiet and unobtrusive way as possible" on October 22, but deliberately did not tell the prime minister and misled the House of Commons on the issue. Official authorization for a limited RCAF alert did not come until October 24. It has been claimed that a U.S. request to disperse interceptors to Canadian bases was turned down, but there is nothing in the declassified record to confirm this report. See J. L. Granatstein, "When Push Came to Shove: Canada and the United States," in Thomas G. Patterson, ed., *Kennedy's Quest for Victory* (New York: Oxford University Press, 1989), p. 16; and "How Canada Rubs NORAD," *The Financial Post* (Toronto), November 3, 1962, p. 1; Jocelyn Maynard Ghent, "Canada, the United States, and the Cuban Missile Crisis," *Pacific Historical Review* 48, no. 2 (May 1979): 159–184; and Jon B. McLin, *Canada's Changing Defense Policy, 1957–1963* (Baltimore: Johns Hopkins University Press, 1967), pp. 156–158.

[120] McMullen, *The Fighter Interceptor Force*, pp. 10–11.

[121] *Air Force Response*, p. 25.

[122] *The Air Defense Command in the Cuban Missile Crisis*, pp. 121, 124, 129, 214.

ings, however, did occur during the crisis. The officers involved believed that war had begun, but, fortunately, in neither case were irreversible steps taken.

One minor false warning incident occurred at a set of U.S. Air Force control and warning centers in Ontario. On October 31, the radar warning system at these bases reported that two unidentified planes had penetrated across the Mid-Canada Line of NORAD radars. In response: "Full base defense plans were implemented, and *all personnel notified to expect impending attack*. All personnel off-shift were directed to report to their duty stations and stand by to assist as required."[123] The two "tracks" did not materialize, fortunately, and the two air force bases affected by the warning returned to regular DEFCON 3 readiness after forty minutes.[124] Whether the false warning was due to an equipment failure or misidentification of commercial or SAC aircraft, however, was never determined.

A more serious and bizarre incident occurred at bases in Minnesota and Wisconsin. In 1962, Joint Chiefs of Staff war planners anticipated that a Soviet decision to launch a nuclear first-strike might be preceded by sabotage operations against U.S. military units and command and control facilities. Such precursor special "spetznaz" unit attacks were therefore included in U.S. military exercises, and officers were trained to expect serious sabotage efforts at the brink of war.[125]

Around midnight on the night of October 25, an air force guard at the Duluth Sector Direction Center saw what appeared to be a saboteur climbing the base security fence. He immediately shot at the figure and set off a sabotage alarm, which was tied into the alarm systems at nearby bases. Immediately, throughout the area, dozens of armed sabotage alert squads were sent into the night to patrol the base perimeters.

At Volk Field in Wisconsin, however, the alarm system was faulty: according to the ADC history, the Klaxon went off instead of the sabotage alarm, ordering an immediate launch of the aircraft. Pilots of the nuclear-equipped F-106A interceptors rushed to their aircraft and started the engines. These pilots had been told that there would be no practice alert drills, because of the DEFCON 3 status, and as they began to taxi down the runway, they fully believed that a nuclear war had just started. Just before takeoff, a car, flashing its lights, raced from the command post to the tarmac, and an officer signaled the aircraft to stop. The ADC declassified

---

[123] 913th Aircraft Control and Warning Squadron, Historical Resume 22 October 1962 through 27 November 1962 and 639th Aircraft Control and Warning Squadron, Chronological Resume of Events Occurring during the Cuban Crisis, in 30th Air Division (SAGE) 30th NORAD Region and the Cuban Crisis, vol. 2, exhibits 29 and 47, K410.041–15, AFHRC (emphasis added).

[124] *Ibid.*

[125] See, for example, "Instructions for Exercise High Heels," CCS 3510, (3 May, 1961) JCS 1961.

history reports that further communications to Duluth had revealed that no nuclear attack was under way and that "the incident led to changes in the alert Klaxon system . . . to prevent a recurrence." The "Russian spetz-naz saboteur" that caused the incident was, ironically, a bear.[126]

## Escalation Potential

This bizarre incident would be almost comical had it not fit into an disturb-ing picture of potential air defense accidents during the crisis. One dan-gerous possibility under these circumstances would be an accidental shoot-down of a Strategic Air Command bomber by an ADC interceptor. The likelihood that a SAC B-47 or B-52 bomber moving to a dispersal base would have been misidentified by interceptor pilots, had they been launched in the fog of crisis believing that a war had begun, was not negligible.[127] Indeed, prior to the crisis, SAC had neglected to provide the ADC with full information concerning bomber dispersal plans. Thus, when SAC bombers were dispersed to a number of bases on which ADC interceptors were also based, there was "little or no warning" to these interceptor squadrons, a development that "came as a complete surprise and something of a shock to the air defense system."[128] U.S. bombers returning from airborne alert missions were also in some danger of being misidentified by interceptors, because the ADC units were not given the classified information on B-52 airborne alert routes, a condition which, according to the ADC history, "vastly complicated the identification and safe passage of SAC aircraft."[129]

Even if U.S. interceptor pilots did not *deliberately*, though mistakenly, attack a B-52 through some mixture of confusion and stress, there was also an increased risk of an *accidental* nuclear air-to-air missile launch if the interceptors were scrambled due to *a false alarm* during the crisis. Intercep-tor pilots were well-trained and firing procedures were well-designed to reduce the likelihood of accidental launches of air-to-air missiles, but such accidents did occur prior to the Cuban crisis. Indeed, as recently as April 1961, an Air Defense Command F-100 interceptor had accidentally shot

[126] *Air Defense Command in the Cuban Crisis*, pp. 212, 229. Dan Barry (F106-A pilot), interview with author, December 10, 1992.

[127] "Accidental" shootdowns of one's own forces, due to misidentification and misunder-standing of orders, are not an uncommon experience in air defense operations. In 1987, for example, a navy F-14 inadvertently shot down an air force RF-4C reconnaissance plane in an exercise, when the navy pilot misunderstood a radio order. Mark Thompson, "Downing of U.S. Jet Exposes War Games' Danger," *Chicago Tribune*, April 19, 1988, p. 1. Also see W. Hays Parks, "Righting the Rules of Engagement," *United States Naval Institute Proceed-ings*, vol. 115/5/1035, May 1989, pp. 83–93.

[128] *The Air Defense Command in the Cuban Crisis*, pp. 215, 132–133.

[129] *Ibid.*, p. 232.

down a SAC B-52, killing three crew members, when the electrical connector plug of a *conventional* sidewinder missile malfunctioned and automatically fired the missile during a mock intercept exercise.[130]

There was also at least some risk that the accidental detonation of one nuclear weapon might lead, through some mixture of unanticipated events, to further accidents. The Joint Chiefs specifically addressed the question of rules of engagement for U.S. interceptors during the crisis and ordered that conventional armaments only were to be used against any Soviet or Cuban aircraft entering airspace over the southeastern United States in response to a U.S. invasion of Cuba. The JCS reminded NORAD and the ADC on October 28, however, that the usual authority and rules of engagement for all other U.S. interceptor forces were still in effect: "If the pattern of actions elsewhere in the NORAD . . . system indicated the existence of a Cuban and Sino-Soviet attack, nuclear weapons could be used to destroy hostile aircraft."[131]

The following hypothetical scenario is not implausible in this highly complex and tightly coupled system. Imagine an accidental nuclear detonation inside the United States: it could be produced by a SAC bomber crash, mishandling of a weapon at an air force base, or an inadvertent use of an interceptor's nuclear air-to-air missile. Under such conditions, communications might be impaired by electromagnetic pulse (EMP) or other nuclear weapon's effects, and any lower-level commander in the vicinity of the detonation might see this as unambiguous evidence that a Soviet attack was under way. If the deputy for operations in the regional command post held this belief, he could, *acting fully within his proper authority*, order interceptors to use nuclear weapons against any suspected incoming hostile aircraft. The danger of "ambiguous command" could also become severe under these circumstances: if an airborne interceptor pilot witnessed a nuclear burst in the distance, could not establish radio contact with base command posts, and believed a hostile aircraft was approaching in range, what would be the appropriate response? The possibility that one accidental or unauthorized use of a nuclear weapon could lead to further accidental escalation cannot therefore be entirely ruled out.

Such a bizarre combination of events was *unlikely*, in my judgment. The bizarre incidents that actually did occur during the crisis should serve as a reminder, however, that unlikely events, even highly improbable events, do

---

[130] On this incident see *Department of Defense Appropriations for 1962*, Hearings before the Subcommittee of the Committee on Appropriations, U.S. Senate, 87th Congress, 1st sess., pp. 372–375; and Frederic Philips, "Aerospace World," *Air Force Magazine*, May 1961, pp. 26–27. Such incidents still occur. In March 1990 an Alaskan Air Command pilot accidentally shot down another F-15 in an exercise intercept operation when he inadvertently launched a live sidewinder missile instead of the inert exercise missile mounted on his plane. See John Ginovsky, "Lapses in Communication," *Air Force Times*, July 30, 1990, p. 12.

[131] *Chronology of JCS Decisions Concerning the Cuban Crisis*, p. 50.

happen. Once one unlikely event occurs, moreover, the likelihood of another one increases, since the incidents would not be independent. The fact that the Air Defense Command dispersal did not produce an accidental or unauthorized use of a nuclear weapon is therefore far less comforting when one fully recognizes the degree to which nuclear safety was reduced in unanticipated ways during the tense days of October and November 1962.

## MANAGING ALERT ACTIVITIES IN EUROPE

The history of the SAC emergency ICBM operations and the ADC interceptor dispersal demonstrates that safety can be seriously compromised in both elite and nonelite commands if senior political and military leaders do not focus attention on safety in complex nuclear alert operations. A high reliability theorist might be tempted to argue, nonetheless, that had central authorities anticipated or known about such problems during the crisis, they could have eliminated them. From the normal accidents perspective, however, this assumption is highly problematic. Complex organizations are viewed as having conflicting goals: critical actors may not have consistent objectives and different decision makers may maintain very different priorities. If this is the case, specific safety problems and risky behaviors can continue to exist even if high-level leaders have recognized the dangerous behavior and have explicitly ordered it to stop. "Production pressures" on lower-level personnel can be particularly intense in crises and lead to unauthorized or unapproved activities. The following examination of nuclear alert activities in the North Atlantic Treaty Organization (NATO) during the missile crisis illustrates this possibility.

In October 1962, General Lauris Norstad had been commander of the U.S. European Command (CINCEUR) and NATO's Supreme Allied Commander, Europe (SACEUR) for six years. Having served through the successive Berlin crises, he was highly sensitive to allied concerns that any NATO military activities that might be provocative to the Warsaw Pact must be avoided. When the Cuban crisis began, he therefore met with British Prime Minister Harold Macmillan and agreed that NATO forces should *not* be placed on DEFCON 3 alert and so advised the Joint Chiefs of Staff. Macmillan's fear of a repetition of the uncontrolled mobilization plans in July 1914 is evident in his diary entry for October 22: "I told him (Norstad) that we would *not* repeat *not* agree (to a NATO alert) at this stage. N. (Norstad) agreed with this, and said he thought NATO powers would take the same view. I said that 'mobilization' had sometimes caused war."[132]

[132] Harold Macmillan, *At the End of the Day* (London: Macmillan, 1973), p. 190. Also see Bruce G. Blair, "Alerting in Crisis and Conventional War," in Carter, et. al., eds., *Managing Nuclear Operations*, p. 117, fn. 97.

When the JCS ordered a global DEFCON 3 on October 22, Norstad therefore was explicitly authorized "to use his discretion in complying with (the) directive."[133] In response, Norstad informed the JCS and the State Department on October 23 that the forces of the United States European Command (EUCOM) would *not* be placed on DEFCON 3 and that, instead, he had sent the following message to all U.S. subordinate commanders and allied military commanders:

> In view of the actions proposed by the United States in connection with Cuba, you are of course aware that a period of international sensitivity can be expected. I therefore recommend that *appropriate precautionary military measures* be taken by all addressees. Those might include:
> A. Intensification of intelligence collection.
> B. Increased security and anti-sabotage measures
> C. *Review* of alert procedures and emergency plans.
> D. Manning of operational centers at reduced strength.
> E. Checks of equipment and supplies.
> *No measures will be taken which could be considered provocative or which might disclose operational plans.* Actions should be taken without public notice if possible.[134]

This message was Norstad's effort to dampen the potentially provocative effect of an alert in Europe. Although the full details of subsequent decisions and nuclear alerting activities are not available, sufficient information exists to demonstrate that U.S. Air Force and British Royal Air Force nuclear operations in the field did not meet this central political objective as seen in Washington, in London, and at NATO Headquarters in Paris.[135] Norstad initially could not even coordinate alerting orders and activities among his subordinate commanders. Considerable confusion emerged on October 22 because some U.S. commanders in Europe had been directed *through individual service channels* to go immediately to DEFCON 3, despite Norstad's decision against an alert in Europe. Norstad therefore quickly requested that the Chairman of the Joint Chiefs intervene to "direct the respective services to refrain from issuing any further DEFCON implementing directives to USCINCEUR's component commanders."[136]

---

[133] *Chronology of JCS Decisions Concerning the Cuban Crisis*, p. 32.

[134] Message 230009Z October, USCINCEUR to Secretary of State, October 23, 1962 (emphasis added), National Security Files, Countries, Cuba Cables, part 1, box 40, JFK Library.

[135] A thorough analysis of the USAFE and NATO alert operation would require full declassification of the Norstad-Kennedy correspondence and USAFE records during the crisis.

[136] Message 222255Z USCINCEUR to CJCS, October 22, 1962, File Folder Cuba (3), Subject Series, box 99, Lauris Norstad Papers, Dwight David Eisenhower Library (hereinafter DDE Library), Abilene, Kansas.

Even after Norstad's complaint, satisfactory control of alert operations was not achieved. The problem was most severe with respect to the nuclear operations of the United States Air Forces Europe (USAFE). On October 22, 1962, USAFE had its routine peacetime contingent of thirty-seven fighter-bombers (F-100s, F-101s, F-104s, and F-105s) on nuclear Quick Reaction Alert (QRA) at military bases in NATO countries including West Germany, Italy, Turkey, and the United Kingdom.[137] These so-called "Victor alert" aircraft covered thirty-seven high-priority targets (twenty-two targets in East Germany, three in Czechoslovakia, four in Hungary, and eight inside the Soviet Union), and represented approximately 10 percent of SACEUR's total nuclear strike force.[138] The QRA aircraft were kept fully armed on a fifteen-minute alert and SACEUR had the authority, like CINCSAC, to launch his alert aircraft under positive control launch ("failsafe") procedures in the event that tactical warning of an attack was received.[139]

General Truman Landon, as commander of U.S. Air Forces Europe (CINCUSAFE), had primary responsibility for the readiness of U.S. air forces to meet their wartime missions in Europe. The evidence suggests that Landon's primary concern was to maximize his war fighting capability and that he was therefore less sensitive than Norstad to political concerns about dangerous mobilization activities. Landon clearly pushed his individual authority for alerting his forces to its limit. For example, when Norstad ordered that the series of low-level precautionary readiness measures be implemented on October 22, CINCUSAFE had already instituted nearly all of them, beginning on October 17, in anticipation of a serious crisis over Cuba.[140] Landon also interpreted Norstad's directive that "no measures would be taken that could be considered provocative" in light of his strong desire for increased combat readiness. Therefore, although CINCEUR's message had merely recommended that component commands *review* alert procedures, on October 23, CINCUSAFE ordered a "discrete increase in the overall capability of his forces in a gradual and unobtrusive

---

[137] JCSM-808–62 (October 23, 1962), CCS 4614, JCS 1962 (declassified May 19, 1989), and *Air Force Response*, p. 27. The locations of USAFE QRA aircraft are given in the following documents: TACOP Final Report, FOXABLE 133, in History of the 474th Tactical Fighter Wing, July 1–December 31, 1962, K-WG-474-HI, AFHRC; History of the 36th Tactical Fighter Wing, July–December 1962, K-WG-36-HI, AFHRC; History of the 20th Tactical Fighter Wing, July 1–December 31, 1962, K-WG-20-HI, AFHRC; and History of the 353rd Tactical Fighter Squadron, 1 July–31 December 1962, FOIA.

[138] JCSM-808–62.

[139] *Ibid.*, and DD Form 173, OSD to USNMR, September 1958, Kaplan Papers, National Security Archives.

[140] *The Cuban Crisis, 1962: Impact in the USAFE Area* (declassified extract), p. 28, NSA-CMCC. The single exception was the intensification of intelligence collection, which USAFE began only after receiving SACEUR's October 22 directive.

manner to avoid exacerbating tensions in Europe."[141] Despite the Norstad prohibition against a formal DEFCON 3, numerous operational activities fully commensurate with such an alert status were instituted by this USAFE order.[142] Most dramatically, Landon ordered an increase in the number of nuclear QRA aircraft on alert throughout his command, on October 24 or 25.[143] Some of these extra nuclear QRA aircraft were alerted in Great Britain, to compensate for U.S. aircraft in West Germany, which were taken *off* nuclear "Victor alert" on October 24 and placed on conventional QRA status in anticipation of a potential Soviet attack on Berlin.[144] Other increases in the "Victor alert" force, however, were designed to enhance Landon's capability to attack Warsaw Pact targets promptly in the event that general war broke out.

## Leadership Involvement

In direct contrast with the management of SAC's DEFCON 2 and airborne alert, operations that were reviewed and approved by senior authorities, there is no evidence that this increase in the size of the QRA strike force in Europe was the subject of high-level review.[145] White House and Pentagon officials were fully engaged in monitoring other operations during the crisis, and USAFE's alert was apparently never discussed at the senior level in Washington.[146] There was little reason for them to be concerned. Au-

[141] *Air Force Response*, p. 26.

[142] A large-scale stand-down of tactical training flights throughout the command significantly increased the operational readiness of USAFE forces; ninety-four aircraft on training missions in Libya were transferred to bases in Europe; and a further squadron of F-104s in Spain was moved to military bases in West Germany. *Ibid.*. A USAFE message to the Air Staff complained after the crisis that "USAFE capability was restricted because of the prohibition against a declaration of formal alert" and objected to Norstad's refusal to permit USAFE to disperse aircraft to forward bases in Germany, pp. 26–27.

[143] The date is derived from the following sources: the peak readiness dates given in the USAFE Alert Status chart in *USAFE Chronology of the Cuban Crisis*, NSA-CMCC, p. 31; History of the 20th Tactical Fighter Wing, p. 5; and History of the 353rd Tactical Fighter Squadron, Tactical Air Command (TAC), July 1–December 31, 1962, p. 5, FOIA. This latter TAC squadron was on a rotational tour based at Aviano Air Base in Italy when it reached its peak "Victor alert" level on October 25.

[144] *Air Force Response*, p. 26, and History of the 36th Tactical Fighter Wing, July 1–December 1, 1962, K-WG-36-HI, AFHRC.

[145] It is noteworthy that the Cuba Fact Sheet given to President Kennedy on October 24 presented detailed SAC and NORAD alert information, but did not mention the ongoing USAFE alert operation. Cuba Fact Sheet, Cuba General File, October 16–27, 1962, box 36A, NSF, JFK Library.

[146] This statement is based on the following interviews: Vice-Admiral William Houser, (USN-retired), military assistant to Deputy Secretary of Defense Roswell Gilpatric, interview with author, February 14, 1990; General W. Y. Smith (USAF-retired), military assistant to the

thorities in Washington had just been informed, after all, that U.S. forces in Europe were *not* being placed on a higher state of alert in the crisis, and General Norstad had explicitly informed the press in Paris on October 25 that "the present phase of the Cuban situation did *not* call for readiness or alert, in their military connotations" in Europe.[147] Norstad may not have been fully aware of USAFE's activities: a Norstad memorandum written on October 25 incorrectly states that "U.S. forces (in Europe) are on the same basis as those of other countries."[148] In short, the currently available evidence strongly suggests that General Landon independently decided to alert more nuclear-armed aircraft.

## Civil-Military Conflict?

In placing extra aircraft on QRA alert, Landon was certainly acting within the bounds of his authority as U.S. Air Force commander in Europe. He did not, however, have authority to institute a major additional increase in his military capability, which he strongly desired: loading up larger yield thermonuclear weapons, rather than the lower yield atomic bombs that were on the QRA aircraft when the crisis began. President Kennedy had become extremely concerned about the danger of unauthorized use of nuclear weapons on QRA aircraft in Europe after having been informed that the only thing preventing a QRA pilot from taking off with a fully armed weapon was a lone U.S. sentry armed with a carbine of standing at the end of the runway.[149] In June 1962, he therefore ordered that all U.S. and NATO QRA aircraft be equipped with electronic PAL locking devices. Two months earlier (in National Security Action Memorandum 143 on April 10), Kennedy had ordered that all thermonuclear weapons be taken off USAFE and NATO QRA aircraft due to these concerns about the lack of security and safety measures at bases throughout Europe.[150] Only lower

---

chairman of the Joint Chiefs of Staff, interview with the author, July 7, 1989; U. Alexis Johnson, deputy under secretary of state, interview with author, February 20, 1990; Gerald Johnson, assistant to the secretary of defense for atomic energy, interview with the author, April 7, 1989; and McGeorge Bundy, special assistant for national security affairs, interview with author, October 10, 1989.

[147] "NATO Units' State of 'Awareness,'" *The Times* (London), October 26, 1962, p. 9 (emphasis added).

[148] Memorandum, October 25, 1962, Lauris Norstad papers, File Folder Cuba (2), Subject series, box 99, DDE Library.

[149] See Peter Stein and Peter Feaver, *Assuring Control of Nuclear Weapons: The Evolution of Permissive Action Links* (Lanham, Md.: University Press of America, 1987), p. 30.

[150] JCSM-808–62, and Roswell Gilpatric Memorandum for the President, October 24, 1962 (henceforth Gilpatric QRA memorandum), NSAM 199 File, box 339, NSF, JFK Library. Forces in Great Britain were exempted from this restriction.

yield weapons were permitted. The further increases in USAFE's alert force desired by General Landon therefore required a reversal of this highest-level political directive.

These restrictions had been opposed by the U.S. military, which had repeatedly (though unsuccessfully) appealed the decision. On October 23, taking advantage of the pressure of the crisis, the Joint Chiefs of Staff requested "as a matter of urgency" that the Secretary of Defense "approach the President for the third time on the two stage [thermonuclear] weapon authorization."[151] This time the appeal worked.

The JCS request contained two central arguments. First, although antic-ipated collateral damage had been reduced by the president's decision, they claimed that the probability of creating severe damage against the entire Warsaw Pact QRA target set had also decreased (from 90 percent to 50 percent). This was unacceptable to the JCS, especially since the U.S. nu-clear war plan had been built with the larger weapons included.[152] Second, there was an apparent shortage of single-stage weapons in the USAFE stockpile: the secretary of defense was informed that "of critical sig-nificance is the problem that will confront USCINCEUR *in the event that he is required to generate additional alert aircraft.*"[153] The JCS there-fore concluded: "In view of the gravity of the present world situation, USCINCEUR has requested, and the Joint Chiefs concur, that restoration of two-stage nuclear weapons on Quick Reaction Alert aircraft is an over-riding consideration to those considerations which influenced the Presi-dent's policy decision on this matter."[154]

Deputy Secretary of Defense Roswell Gilpatric immediately drafted a top-secret memorandum for the president, in which he repeated the JCS military rationale. Gilpatric was aware of Kennedy's great concern about unauthorized use of nuclear weapons, but downplayed the risk:

> There is always, of course, some theoretical possibility of unauthorized use of a nuclear weapon, and this is probably greater when a weapon is in a QRA aircraft. . . . However, the difference between (deleted) would not seem to be of great significance. It is questionable, therefore, whether we should be pre-pared to pay a significant political or military price to guard against the unauthorized detonation of a higher yield weapon than of a lower yield weapon. In addition, top priority has been given to the installation of permis-

[151] The quotes are from JCSM-808–62 and Extracts from The Cuban Crisis, 1962: Impact in the USAFE Area, p. 31, CMCC–NSA.

[152] JCSM-808-62.

[153] *Ibid.* (emphasis added). Here, it is worth noting that although Landon's orders to increase the number of QRA on alert with atomic weapons had not been issued when the JCS memorandum was written, the increased QRA alert had started by the time the White House decided to permit the loading of thermonuclear weapons.

[154] *Ibid.*

sive action link (PAL) mechanisms in dispersed weapons. Proposed schedules for installation of appropriate devices will be submitted for your approval at an early date.[155]

These military and political arguments apparently were persuasive. The Defense Department received rapid concurrence from the secretary of state, and on October 25 the White House issued National Security Action Memorandum (NSAM) 199 permitting thermonuclear weapons to be placed on the U.S. European-based QRA aircraft.[156] On October 27, Landon was informed by the Joint Chiefs that he could proceed immediately with its plans to upload thermonuclear weapons onto its QRA aircraft in Europe.[157]

## Central Control and Provocations

It is difficult to assess the significance of these events for safety management and the prevention of accidental nuclear war. The record is mixed and the proper lessons to draw are uncertain. The record is mixed because high-level authorities were aware that there was a risk of dangerous military actions in Europe and sought to prevent it; yet only well into the crisis did they exert even a modicum of direct control over important alerting measures. On the one hand, central authorities were properly involved in the decision to place thermonuclear weapons on the U.S. QRA aircraft in Europe, even if it was made under the pressure that the requirements of the war plan could not otherwise be met. On the other hand, they were *not* involved in, and were apparently unaware of, the decision to increase the number of USAFE aircraft on QRA alert with lower yield nuclear weapons. The lesson to draw from this experience is inevitably uncertain, however, since it cannot be determined that either of the USAFE alert actions—the increase in QRA aircraft or the loading of higher yield thermonuclear weapons—in fact undermined the intent of the October 22 orders to avoid measures "which could be considered provocative." Until the archives in the former Soviet Union are opened, one cannot know whether such QRA actions had a deterrent effect, or increased the likelihood of a Soviet preemptive attack, or, indeed, whether they were even picked up by Soviet intelligence at all.

Despite these uncertainties, a strong argument can be made that the military commanders' priorities to maximize combat potential under-

[155] Gilpatric QRA memorandum, p. 3.

[156] Dean Rusk, *Memorandum for the President*, October 24, 1962, National Security Files, M&M, NSAM 199, box 339, JFK Library; and Index to the National Security Files, JFK Library.

[157] *Chronology of JCS Decisions Concerning the Cuban Crisis*, p. 38.

mined political interests in preventing accidents and potential provocations. Central authorities cannot be aware of all the details of the complex activities they set into motion with their decisions and inevitably rely upon the judgment of lower-level commanders to implement their orders effectively. Yet in this case, it was precisely the operational "details" of the QRA alert activities, which were not focused upon by senior Washington authorities, that contradicted their central political and strategic objectives.

The point is best made by noting that one of USAFE's QRA bases was at Incirlik Air Force Base, in Turkey, where the 523rd and 613th Tactical Fighter Squadrons doubled their QRA commitment during the crisis, peaking with sixteen F-100s on fifteen-minute Victor nuclear alert after USAFE had received permission to load up thermonuclear bombs on the QRA forces.[158] While this QRA activity was taking place at Incirlik, the ExComm, meeting at the White House, was focusing its attention on the possibility that the Soviet Union would attack Turkey in response to an American air strike and invasion of Cuba. At this October 27 meeting, Secretary of Defense McNamara sought to convince the rest of the Ex-Comm of the need to reduce the likelihood of a retaliatory attack on the Jupiter missiles in Turkey, and therefore repeatedly proposed that the United States "defuse" the Jupiters prior to any military action against Cuba.[159] McNamara was especially concerned that the Jupiter missiles might be fired without presidential orders, if Turkey was attacked. There were no PAL locks on the Jupiter forces in October 1962, and McNamara was justifiably concerned that Turkish officers, if they seized the warheads from the American custodians, might independently retaliate against the Soviet Union.[160] Responding to this concern, the JCS had explicitly instructed General Norstad on October 22 to inform U.S. commanders in Turkey to "destroy or make inoperable Jupiters if any attempt is made to fire them without [the] specific authorization of [the] president.[161]

[158] United States Forces in Europe: Chronology of the Cuban Crisis, p. 31, NSA-CMCC; History of the 401st Tactical Fighter Wing, p. 36, K-WG-401-HI, AFHRC; and 27th Tactical Fighter Wing History, July-December 1962, pp. 25–26, FOIA.

[159] Cuban Missile Crisis ExComm Transcript, October 27, 1962, pp. 23, 26, 43–44, 50–53.

[160] A crash effort to retrofit PALs onto the Jupiter warheads started soon after Kennedy's June 1962 decision, but had not been completed when the crisis broke out in October. The installation schedule for the PALs on the Jupiters was not issued until November. See withdraw sheet, CCS 4615 (January 11, 1961), JCS 1961. Also see Robert McNamara's statements in Blight and Welch, eds., On the Brink, pp. 56, 52. Although Turkish officers controlled the missiles, U.S. officers maintained control over the warheads. See Headquarters TUSLOG (USAFE) Historical Data Record, July 1–December 31, 1962, vol. 1, p. 3, K-DIV-7217-HI, AFHRC; History of TUSLOG Detachment 116, July 1–December 31, 1962, p. 1, K-GP-SUP-7231-HI, AFHRC; and SAC Missile Chronology 1939–1988, p. 35.

[161] Chronology of JCS Decisions Concerning the Cuban Crisis, p. 34.

McNamara's recommendation at the ExComm meeting to take further steps—defusing the missiles to render them completely inoperable—reflected his continuing concern about unauthorized use and the potential provocative nature of the Jupiters in Turkey.

This extensive ExComm discussion about "defusing" the missiles in Turkey contrasts sharply with the *complete* lack of discussion about the alert of QRA aircraft there. Indeed, throughout this critical meeting, the ExComm members, including McNamara, displayed absolutely no awareness that nuclear QRA aircraft were being alerted in Turkey.[162] The risk that USAFE QRA activities at Incirlik might provoke the Soviets into an attack on Turkey was simply never considered by senior U.S. decision makers. This possibility of provoking a preemptive attack should not be taken lightly: it can be *roughly* compared to the dangers that would have existed if the United States had learned, while bargaining over the withdrawal of the Soviet missiles, that a significant number of Soviet IL-28 bombers in Cuba were being armed with thermonuclear weapons and placed on advanced alert.

In addition, placing extra nuclear-armed fighter-bombers on alert in the crisis increased the probability of an accidental or unauthorized use of a thermonuclear weapon at a time when the consequences of such a use would have been most severe. The QRA forces at Incirlik had also not yet been equipped with PALs, and the pilots at maximum alert, sitting in their cockpits by day and sleeping under the planes at night, were subject to considerable stress. The picture of the Incirlik alert in the memory of commander of the 613th QRA squadron stationed there in the crisis is not reassuring: "It [nuclear safety] was so loose, it jars your imagination. . . . We loaded up everything, laid down on a blanket on the pad for two weeks, planes were breaking down, crews were exhausted. . . . We had no idea that a pilot—being a true American—would do such a thing [use weapons in an unauthorized manner]. In retrospect, there were some guys you wouldn't trust with a .22 rifle, much less a thermonuclear bomb."[163]

This was, undoubtedly, not the picture of the alert in the minds of senior authorities, for whom the operation, if they had any awareness of it at all, would have appeared as a few more F-100s listed on the daily status reports of the number of U.S. aircraft on alert.[164] There is no indication in the available records that senior Washington authorities ever focused on such

[162] See especially McNamara's discussion of possible *future* increases in U.S. QRA aircraft. Cuban Missile Crisis ExComm Transcript, October 27, 1962, pp. 43, 51.

[163] Lt. Col. Robert Melgard, interview with author, July 26, 1990.

[164] The JCS situation reports given to civilian authorities during the crisis listed the numbers and kinds of aircraft on alert and did not state either the type of nuclear weapons on alert or the location of forces. See JCS Message 6968, October 25, 1962, National Security Files, Cuba Cables, box 41, JFK Library.

nuclear safety and provocation problems with the QRA aircraft in Turkey. These dangerous operations were the result of CINCUSAFE's devotion to his war plan; senior civilian decision makers, although highly concerned about safety, failed even to address the potential trade-offs involved in nuclear aircraft alerts in Turkey.

## British Alerting Actions

A second case of European nuclear alert activities that were not integrated with higher political objectives in the crisis concerns British, not American, nuclear forces. In October 1962, there was a sizable land-based nuclear force in the United Kingdom. Although the United States maintained operational control over SAC's dispersed B-47s in England and USAFE's fighter-bombers, the United Kingdom's Bomber Command maintained its own nuclear force of sixty Thor missiles and approximately 140 medium-range V-bombers.[165] Under normal peacetime conditions, only a small portion of the British force was maintained on alert status. As was the case with American military commanders, the commander in chief of the Bomber Command, Air Marshal Kenneth Cross, had full authority, however, to raise the readiness level in an emergency.[166]

When the U.S. naval quarantine of Cuba went into effect on October 24, and SAC went to its DEFCON 2 alert, the Bomber Command was in the middle of a previously scheduled readiness exercise, completely unrelated to the crisis in the Caribbean. On October 26, Air Marshall Cross, *on his own authority*, decided to prolong the exercise to maximize Bomber Command capabilities in the event of war. As the crisis continued to deteriorate that week, Cross decided, as commander in chief of the Bomber Command, to increase the British nuclear forces' alert even further. According to Air Vice-Marshal Stewart Menaul:

> In the early hours of Saturday morning, 27th October, the Commander-in-Chief (Air Marshal Cross) went to the operations room to discuss the exercise with his senior staff members and to hear the latest news from America, in particular President Kennedy's statements on the gravity of the situation and Russian reactions to American warnings. *The C-in-C decided to increase the readiness of the force, purely as part of the training exercise.* The necessary instructions were given over the broadcast telephone system; within seconds

165 Andrew Brookes, V-*Force: The History of Britain's Airborne Deterrent* (London: Janes, 1982), pp. 92, 102. The warheads for the Thor missiles were controlled by the United States Air Force; the V-bombers carried the independent British nuclear deterrent.
166 Air Vice-Marshal Stewart Menaul, *Countdown: Britain's Strategic Nuclear Forces* (London: Robert Hale, 1980), pp. 164–165.

orders were being flashed simultaneously to all stations and were just as promptly obeyed.[167]

All British nuclear forces were at that point on "full operational capability," and able to be launched within fifteen minutes or less, against 230 targets in the Soviet Union and the Warsaw Pact.[168]

This increase in Bomber Command alert status was the result of a decision taken by Air Marshal Cross and was not ordered by British civilian authorities. F. W. Mottershead, deputy secretary for the Ministry of Defense in October 1962, has written: "Nothing in my own recollection nor in that available in the Ministry of Defense without much more study than they feel able to undertake is at variance with the indication in Air Vice Marshall Menaul's book that higher authority was not sought for the measures taken by the bomber command."[169] Although full evidence on this issue is lacking, the record suggests that the senior civilian officials in London—Prime Minister Harold Macmillan (who had just warned General Norstad that " 'mobilization' had sometimes caused war"), Defense Minister Peter Thorneycroft, and Foreign Secretary Alec Douglas-Home— were not fully cognizant of these increased alert activities at the time and were only informed about them after the fact.[170]

[167] *Ibid.*, pp. 114–115 (emphasis added). Menaul was serving as the Senior Air Staff officer at Headquarters Bomber Command in October 1962.

[168] The British alert is described in *Ibid.*, pp. 114–116.

[169] F. W. Mottershead, letter to author, November 21, 1989. Other senior British officials agree. According to Lord Solly Zuckerman, the chief scientific advisor to the Ministry of Defense in 1962, "so far as the Ministry of Defense is concerned, although I was at the centre of things, I do not recall that the Prime Minister, the Secretary of State or Lord Mountbatten, the Chief of the Defense Staff, were directly concerned with what the Bomber Command would do. . . . to the best of my knowledge, the Ministry of Defense did not order him (Air Marshal Cross) to increase the readiness state of his force." Lord Solly Zuckerman, letter to author, April 26, 1989. Sir Arthur Hockaday, principle private secretary to the Minister of Defense during the crisis adds: "I have no recollection of any involvement of Ministry of Defense headquarters, or specifically of Defense Minister Thorneycroft . . . in any heightening of the state of alert of RAF Bomber Command during the crisis." Sir Arthur Hockaday, letter to author, September 13, 1989.

[170] During the crisis, the Ministry of Defense explicitly told the British press that increased alert measures were *not* being taken. When allegations of Bomber Command actions were leaked in early 1963, Macmillan reported to Parliament only that "certain additional steps were taken, but they are of a kind which is merely intended as normal and no more than normal." See *Parliamentary Debates* (Hansard), 5th series, vol. 672, House of Commons, Session 1962–1963, February 28, 1963, pp. 1439–1442, and Macmillan, *At the End of the Day*, p. 190. In an interview conducted in 1969, Thorneycroft did recall that a "modified" alert was ordered but suggested that he only learned about the alert on Sunday, *after* it had been ordered by Cross and was, even then, very unclear about the full extent of the British nuclear alert operation involved: "I don't think that the bomber command were put under full alert . . . and really the things that could be done were so limited and the alerts required in a field which was so alert anyway that we don't have to do a lot." Lord Thorneycroft, Oral

There is also no indication in the available records that high-level *American* political or military authorities in Washington were aware that Britain's nuclear forces were being put on a higher state of alert.[171] Soviet intelligence was likely to pick up evidence of any special alert activity, however, and political authorities in Moscow may have been more aware of the Bomber Command's actions than were the U.S. civilian officials in Washington. Although this incident did not apparently play a significant role in the crisis, Air Marshall Cross's actions are another example of how the military commanders' interests in combat readiness can cut against civilian authorities' interests in safety.

### Perceptions and Provocation

How dangerous were these decentralized nuclear alert activities in Europe in October 1962? No conclusive answer is possible. It is, however, worth speculating on how the Moscow leadership might have perceived these NATO nuclear operations if they were informed of them during the crisis. It is certainly *possible* that Soviet military and civilian leaders would perceive these nuclear alert activities accurately, as the result of uncoordinated actions by individual U.S. and British military commanders and *not* reflecting a top-level NATO political decision to go to a high level of alert. Strong political and psychological arguments exist, however, which suggest that Soviet leaders would be *much more likely* to perceive these nuclear alert operations as part of a coordinated NATO plan. In 1962 the Moscow leadership presided over a very centralized military command system and dominated the alliance decision-making process in the Warsaw pact. To the degree that Soviet leaders practiced "mirror imaging of their adversary," therefore, it is likely that they would have seen the nuclear operations taking place in NATO countries as being more coordinated than they, in fact, were. This specific characteristic of a totalitarian government, moreover, is reinforced by a more general tendency for individuals and states to see adversaries' behavior as more coordinated than it really is. This common cognitive bias enables individuals to gather together and make sense

---

History, JFK Library, p. 10. On Douglas-Home see Len Scott, "Close to the Brink? Britain and the Cuban Missile Crisis," *Contemporary Record* 5, no. 3 (Winter 1991): 510.

[171] There is no evidence in the available National Military Command Center's (NMCC) situation reports that U.S. military intelligence was aware of the activity. In contrast, for example, American political authorities were immediately informed when the Japanese Air Defense force was placed on alert on October 24. NMCC Situation Report, October 24, 1962, NSA-CMCC. It is likely, however, that SAC Headquarters knew about the British operation. See Stevenson Pugh, "When Britain Went to the Brink," *Daily Mail* (London), February 18, 1963, p. 1.

of numerous activities in the outside world. It also, however, produces a strong propensity to see unrelated acts of independent organizations as part of a coherent plan.[172]

In the final analysis, it must be noted that such a belief, if it existed within the Soviet leadership, could have cut both ways—for and against escalation—in the October 1962 crisis. On the one hand, a perception in Moscow that the NATO leadership had decided to alert nuclear forces on the periphery of the Soviet Union could have been interpreted as a warning indicator that war was imminent and unavoidable, thereby increasing the likelihood of a desperate decision to preempt an attack. On the other hand, these alert operations could have been interpreted in a more defensive light, as signaling NATO's military strength and political resolve, thereby enhancing deterrence.

It is not currently known whether Soviet leaders knew of these NATO alerting activities, much less how they may have interpreted them. The nuclear command and control system can be said to have failed in an important sense, however, despite this basic uncertainty. It is the central political authorities, not the head of the Bomber Command or the USAFE commander, who should make the critical decisions about whether or not to take potentially provocative nuclear alert actions. Civilian leaders in both countries, as well as General Norstad in Paris, strongly desired that no alert activities take place that might be provocative to the Soviet Union. Such actions were nonetheless taken. Military priorities reigned over political objectives.

## CONCLUSIONS

How reliable and safe were U.S. military alert operations in October 1962? According to the declassified top-secret Defense Department report on military operations during the crisis, the answer was clear: "The military establishment responded to a threat to our national security promptly, with imagination, vigor, and an exemplary degree of professional competence and skill."[173] The U.S. Air Force's official study of these operations agreed that "the Air Force response to the Cuban crisis was outstanding."[174]

---

[172] For a thorough discussion of this psychological phenomenon, see Robert Jervis, *Perception and Misperception in International Politics* (Princeton, N.J.: Princeton University Press, 1976), pp. 117–202, and Robert Jervis, *The Meaning of the Nuclear Revolution: Statecraft and the Prospect of Armageddon* (Ithaca, N.Y.: Cornell University Press, 1989) pp. 155–156.

[173] *Department of Defense Operations during the Cuban Crisis*, p. 98.

[174] *Air Force Response*, p. 14.

High reliability theorists would not be surprised by such assessments, since many of the specific factors that they have identified as contributing to safety and reliability in other complex organizations appeared to be present in this case. Indeed, the analyses of the organizations themselves appear to echo the themes found in the high reliability theory literature. Constant training and continuous operations are critical according to the theory; the Air Force similarly argued that "the Cuban crisis validated the measures taken by SAC over the years to maintain its units in a high state of readiness" and "reaffirmed the value of conducting exercises."[175] Images of a strong culture of reliability are seen in General Power's description of SAC bomber, tanker, and missile crews who displayed "both the highest degree of professionalism and unlimited dedication to their mission . . . in order to make the accidental or inadvertent firing of a nuclear weapon all but impossible."[176] An appreciation of the importance of top leadership support for high reliability may even be found in the Defense Department report's concluding admonition that the crisis proved that "control [must] be held firmly in the hands of the man preeminently responsible for national security; that is, in the hands of the President."[177]

## Unchallenged Final Control?

From the perspective of normal accidents theory, these Air Force statements appear to be self-promotion, and the conclusion of the Defense Department report comes close to pandering to presidential vanity. For this investigation of the October 1962 nuclear alert has discovered numerous instances of safety violations, unanticipated operational problems, bizarre and dangerous interactions, and unordered risk-taking by both senior and junior military commanders. There were clearly no nuclear accidents on the brink. But there were more close calls than were ever acknowledged.

How should this new evidence influence our assessments of the likelihood of war during the Cuban missile crisis? A thorough answer cannot be given until the conclusion of the next chapter's examination of warning and reconnaissance operations in October 1962. Let it suffice here to note that the widespread belief that nuclear war was unlikely is based on the belief that Nikita Khrushchev and John F. Kennedy really had the power to ensure that the crisis would not escalate to an "unwinnable" war or even an "unthinkable" use of nuclear weapons. To quote McGeorge Bundy again,

---

[175] *Air Force Response*, pp. 19, 28.

[176] Thomas S. Power, *Design for Survival* (New York: Coward-McCann, 1964), p. 150.

[177] *Department of Defense Operations During the Cuban Crisis*, p. 99.

"the risk (of nuclear war) was small, given the prudence and unchallenged final control of the two leaders."[178]

It is this faith in the efficacy of nuclear deterrence that is challenged by the evidence that many serious safety problems, which could have resulted in an accidental or unauthorized detonation or a serious provocation to the Soviet government, occurred during the crisis. None of these incidents led to inadvertent escalation or an accidental war. All of them, however, had the potential to do so. President Kennedy may well have been prudent. He did *not*, however, have unchallenged final control over U.S. nuclear weapons.

[178] Bundy, *Danger and Survival*, p. 461.

# CHAPTER 3

# Intelligence and Warning during the Cuban Missile Crisis

There is always some son-of-a-bitch who doesn't
get the word.
*(John F. Kennedy*
*October 27, 1962)*

AN ACCIDENTAL NUCLEAR WAR could begin, in theory, in three different ways: an unauthorized use of nuclear weapons, an accidental launch or detonation of a weapon, or a false warning that an enemy attack was imminent or actually under way. The frightening specter of all three scenarios appeared in the U.S. nuclear alert operations during the Cuban missile crisis discussed in chapter 2. A number of nuclear safety incidents occurred that directly raised the risk of an unauthorized or accidental use of a weapon. Minuteman ICBM officers jerry-rigged an independent launch capability with inadequate safeguards. Interceptor pilots were dispersed with nuclear air-to-air missiles without mechanical safety devices. A bear climbing a fence at a base in Minnesota almost caused the launch of nuclear-armed interceptors in Wisconsin. Other incidents were discovered that occurred during the U.S. nuclear alert that increased the danger that a false warning would be issued *in Moscow* declaring that an American attack was imminent or under way. A lost B-52 bomber flew into the Soviet air defense warning net just prior to the crisis. A test ICBM was launched from Vandenberg during the emergency missile alert. Offensive nuclear forces near the periphery of the Soviet Union were readied for war without full awareness by U.S. political leaders.

What about the other side of the equation? How great was the risk that *American officials* might have received a false warning that a Soviet nuclear attack was imminent or under way during the crisis? This chapter focuses on that question in order to assess the reliability of U.S. strategic and tactical warning systems in October 1962. These warning systems were carefully designed to minimize such false warning dangers, and a number of the specific design and operational characteristics recommended by the high reliability organization theorists were present, making this issue an interesting test for that theory.

The chapter will therefore first describe the redundant warning systems and the safety procedures that existed at the start of the crisis and then outline the contrasting predictions about crisis warning activities that can be derived from the high reliability and normal accidents theories. The main section of the chapter examines how well the U.S. intelligence and warning system actually performed during the Cuban crisis. The chapter concludes with a broader assessment of the significance of these nuclear command and control incidents on the brink.

## WARNING, REDUNDANCY, AND RELIABILITY

The official mission of the North American Air Defense Command (NORAD) is to provide "timely, reliable, unambiguous warning" of an attack on the United States and Canada.[1] This command faced a severe challenge after the October 1957 Sputnik launch, as the Soviet Union demonstrated a capability to deploy intercontinental range ballistic missiles (ICBMS). Even a brief description of the U.S. missile warning systems built in response and the operational procedures in place in 1962 suggests that three major components of high reliability organizations— prioritization of reliability, high levels of redundancy, and decentralized "flexible" decision making—were critical to NORAD's effort to achieve its mission.

The priority Washington officials placed on getting reliable warning of a Soviet missile attack can be seen in their immediate willingness to spend unprecedented sums of money on the BMEWS (Ballistic Missile Early Warning System) radars and supporting programs. Congress acted quickly after Sputnik, adding funds for the first BMEWS site in an emergency supplement to Defense Department appropriations, and eventually authorizing almost a billion dollars for the system.[2] Because of the importance of reliable warning to national survival, these expensive defense programs received strong bipartisan political support.

Redundancy, both in terms of personnel procedures and mechanical systems, was a critical component of reliability designed into the system. Personnel redundancy existed at every level of the command system, so that individuals always shared overlapping responsibilities. A "two-man rule" came into existence in the Air Force in the late 1950s, for example, requir-

---

[1] As quoted in John C. Toomay, "Warning and Assessment Sensors," in Ashton B. Carter, John Steinbruner, and Charles A. Zraket, eds., *Managing Nuclear Operations* (Washington, D.C.: The Brookings Institution, 1987), p. 286.

[2] Richard F. McMullen, *Air Defense and National Policy, 1958–1964*, p. 2, Air Defense Command Historical Study 26, K410.041–26, Air Force Historical Research Center (hereinafter AFHRC), Maxwell AFB, Ala.

ing that at least two individuals be involved in all nuclear weapons and related command and control operations.[3] A similar principle of redundancy apparently continues to be followed even at the highest levels: for example, the NORAD commander and the senior NMCC (National Military Command Center) officers reportedly share responsibility for determining whether a warning is a real or a false alarm, and the official Pentagon definition of the "national command authority" (the body authorized to order the use of nuclear weapons) is "the President *and* the Secretary of Defense."[4]

A significant degree of mechanical redundancy was also built into the national warning system. The three-station BMEWS system, for example, was designed to provide overlapping coverage so that if one radar failed, another could compensate for the error: with any two of the radars in operation, a missile attack from virtually anywhere in the Soviet Union would be detected.[5] The communication systems connecting the radars to NORAD headquarters were also redundant: the Thule, Greenland, site was connected to the United States via a submarine cable as well as a tropospheric radio relay system, for example, and each of the numerous microwave radio towers linking the Clear, Alaska, site to NORAD used three different sources of power just to be certain that one was always operating.[6] Redundant aircraft warning radars lines of defense—including the Distant Early Warning (DEW) line, Mid-Canada Line, U.S. Air Force ground radars, and U.S. Navy picket ships radars—provided layers of supplementary information on whether Soviet bombers were also attacking the United States. In addition, almost three hundred ground-based nuclear bomb alarm sensors—small signaling devices mounted on telephone poles near cities and military bases, which were automatically triggered by the thermal flash of a nuclear explosion—were deployed at ninety-nine sites. This bomb alarm system was designed primarily to assess the

[3] See Jack Raymond, "U.S. Tightens Screening Rules for Handlers of Atom Bombs," *New York Times*, November 29, 1962, p. 1 and Joel Larus, *Nuclear Weapons Safety and the Common Defense* (Columbus: Ohio State University Press, 1967), pp. 74–80.

[4] Kurt Gottfried and Bruce G. Blair, eds., *Crisis Stability and Nuclear War* (New York: Oxford University Press, 1988), pp. 64–65; and Paul Bracken, "Delegation of Nuclear Command Authority," in Carter et al., eds., *Managing Nuclear Operations*, p. 363 (emphasis added).

[5] A valuable account of the creation of the BMEWS appears in Stanley L. Englebardt, *Strategic Defenses* (New York: Thomas Y. Crowell, 1966), pp. 105–131. For details on BMEWS' overlapping coverage of the Soviet ICBM threat see: Major General J. B. Knapp, Memo for Record on BMEWS Monitor Procedures, in History of the Strategic Air Command, January–June 1968, vol. 8, exhibit 1, AFHRC.

[6] Air Defense Command Study no. 32, *History of BMEWS, 1957–1964* (declassified extract, HQ Air Force Space Command), Freedom of Information Act (hereinafter FOIA), pp. 15–16, and Englebardt, *Strategic Defenses*, p. 129.

damage to the U.S. in a nuclear war, but it also would give final evidence on whether an attack had occurred.[7] Finally, U.S. intelligence agencies also maintained a complex set of programs—covert agents inside the Soviet Union, reconnaissance aircraft flying near or across Soviet borders, and electronic communications intercepting equipment on the periphery—which could provide additional strategic or tactical warning of an attack.[8]

A third characteristic of the U.S. warning system that conforms to the high reliability theory is the degree of decentralization and flexibility exhibited in organizational decision-making. Because every possible contingency could not be anticipated in such a complex technological system, formal decision rules about how to behave in all situations could not be created and followed. Operators at various levels within the organization were encouraged to use their personal judgment about appropriate action when faced with surprises and to devise "work-around" procedures to make the system operate effectively. "Given the complexity of air defense," Paul Bracken later argued, "it is not surprising that informal understandings would evolve to fix problems unanticipated by the system's planners."[9] In addition, although computers were obviously needed to process information in the system, it was recognized that computer program designers could not anticipate all the errors that could occur. The warning system therefore always had a "man in the loop" to make decisions based on human judgment; computers could not commit the nation to war.

These design characteristics would lead high reliability theorists to hold optimistic expectations about the performance of U.S. warning systems during the Cuban crisis. Indeed, signs of all three factors identified by the theory can be seen in a paper written by Assistant Secretary of Defense John T. McNaughton in late 1962:

> The ambiguous evidence of attack with which the United States might be confronted poses an additional challenge, which can be met only by a command and control system possessing *great flexibility* and the ability to assemble, evaluate, and utilize accurate and complex information. . . . In military

---

[7] *Department of Defense Appropriations for 1974*, Hearings before the Subcommittee of the Committee on Appropriations, House of Representatives, 93rd Congress, 1st sess., part 7, p. 1057.

[8] See Paul Bracken, *The Command and Control of Nuclear Forces* (New Haven, Conn.: Yale University Press, 1983), pp. 10–16. In addition, the Midas satellite system was launched in 1960 to provide initial detection of a Soviet missile launch. The satellites proved unable to detect ICBM launches with high probability in initial tests, however, and the system was therefore *not* operational in October 1962. See McMullen, *Air Defense and National Policy*, p. 48, and Curtis Peebles, *Guardians: Strategic Reconnaissance Satellites* (Novato, Calif.: Presidio Press, 1987), pp. 306–312.

[9] Bracken is describing the SAGE aircraft warning and defense system, but the same point holds for BMEWS. Bracken, *The Command and Control of Nuclear Forces*, p. 12.

jargon, *it must have great "redundancy."* What this means is that the system requires multiple "brains" and multiple "nervous systems" in case one or another set of facilities is lost. . . . The Defense Department and the rest of the government have been giving *top priority* to meeting these requirements.[10]

These reliability features designed into the peacetime system could also be supplemented during a crisis. Even more resources could be devoted to intelligence and warning, and better and more alert personnel could be assigned to positions throughout the national network of military command posts. From the perspective of high reliability theory, there would be little reason to worry about safety in the U.S. warning systems in October 1962.

## Normal False Warnings?

From a normal accidents theory perspective, such confidence would not be warranted. As discussed in the two previous chapters, this more pessimistic perspective on organizations points to a number of reasons to suspect that the risk of accidents will always be significant in highly complex and tightly coupled systems. Senior decision makers may genuinely desire high reliability and safety, but others within the organization may have other priorities. Redundancies may be added to the system, but this can inadvertently reduce safety by making the system more complex and therefore more prone to hidden interactions and mysterious failures. All potential problems cannot be anticipated and cannot therefore be fixed ahead of time. Flexibility in decision-making authority and "man-in-the-loop" rules can reduce the danger of excessive reliance on fallible machines, but can also produce higher level human failures.

Did such problems occur in the U.S. warning system during the Cuban missile crisis? Clearly there was no false warning that produced a mistaken "retaliation" against the Soviet Union. Yet the following three case studies of incidents in U.S. warning and intelligence systems in October 1962 demonstrate that a number of serious command and control problems did develop during the crisis. The first case is a study of a series of false warnings emanating from the emergency ballistic missile warning systems that were activated in October 1962 to detect missile launches from Cuba. The second case study focuses on the potential for dangerous interactions that developed during an accidental U.S. Air Force U-2 overflight of the Soviet Union on October 27, perhaps the most tense day of the crisis. The third

[10] John T. McNaughton, "Arms Restraint in Military Decisions," *Journal of Conflict Resolution* 7, no. 3 (September 1963): 231 (emphasis added).

case concerns a bizarre false warning incident that occurred in Moscow, after Colonel Oleg Penkovsky, a Soviet military officer who was a spy for the United States, was arrested during the crisis. None of these false warning incidents led to further escalation; each of them had the potential to do so.

## THE CUBAN MISSILE EARLY WARNING SYSTEM

How reliable was the U.S. missile warning system during the Cuban missile crisis? In October 1962, two of the three scheduled BMEWS stations (at Thule and Clear) were in operation, and Secretary of Defense Robert McNamara testified to Congress in early 1963 that "it is reasonable to assume that the BMEWS would be able to provide adequate warning."[11] Yet, when the Soviet missiles in Cuba were discovered by the United States, a serious deficiency became immediately obvious: despite the enormous sums spent on the BMEWS radars facing north, the United States had absolutely no capability in place to detect a missile launched from the south, from Cuba. Washington policymakers had simply never anticipated that the Soviets would outflank the BMEWS radars in this manner. The seriousness of this gap in missile warning coverage was immediately recognized by the Strategic Air Command, which required warning in order to launch vulnerable bombers into the air to avoid destruction, and by the Executive Committee (ExComm) of the National Security Council, which was also informed of the problem.[12] In response, the air force quickly initiated an emergency Cuban Missile Early Warning System (CMEWS) program, code-named Operation Falling Leaves, to provide tactical warning in the event that the Soviet missiles in Cuba were launched.[13] Three radars in the United States were utilized in the Falling Leaves emergency warning program (see figure 3.1).

---

[11] *Department of Defense Appropriations for 1964*, Hearings before a Subcommittee of the Committee on Appropriations, House of Representatives, 88th Congress, 1st sess., part 1, p. 124.

[12] According to CINCSAC General Power, the missiles in Cuba "could for example, knockout all the command and control, Washington and SAC Headquarters, and time that with a missile attack over BMEWS, and maybe catch the whole thing (SAC strategic forces) on the ground," *Thomas Power Interview*, Strategic Air Command, FOIA, p. 4. Also see Raymond Garthoff's October 27, 1962, memorandum for the ExComm, reprinted in Raymond L. Garthoff, *Reflections on the Cuban Missile Crisis*, 2d ed. (Washington, Brookings Institution, 1989), pp. 202–203.

[13] Unless otherwise noted, this section is based on Headquarters 9th Aerospace Division, Memorandum for the Record, Subject: Falling Leaves, January 11, 1963 (henceforth Falling Leaves Memorandum) NSA-CMCC.

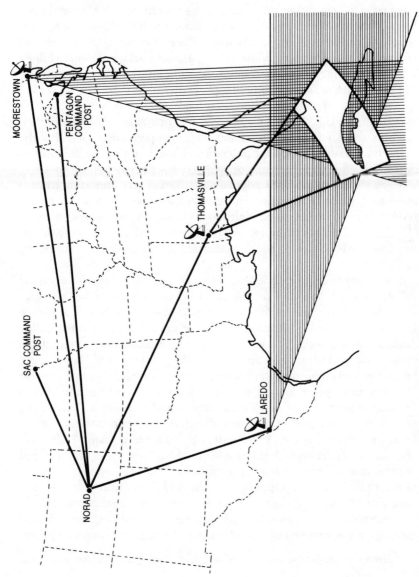

MOORESTOWN

PENTAGON COMMAND POST

THOMASVILE

SAC COMMAND POST

LAREDO

NORAD

3.1  Falling Leaves (32nd Air Division in Cuban Crisis, October–December 1962, p. 81, FOIA.)

## The Quest for Reliability

The first and most important Falling Leaves operation took place at the Air Force Systems Command FPS-49 radar installation at Moorestown, New Jersey. At the time of crisis, this RCA (Radio Corporation of America) radar was utilized for eight hours a day as a space tracking system to follow satellites and other material in space and eight hours a day as a prototype BMEWS radar, testing the computer program for the real BMEWS station then under construction in Fylingdales, England.[14] RCA personnel, under contract to the U.S. Air Force, ran all regular operations. On October 24, however, the Air Defense Command assumed operational control of the radar, immediately turned the antenna south to face Cuba, and began to operate it, with the assistance of RCA contract personnel, as an active warning system twenty-four hours a day.[15] It was very important to continue to provide information on satellites and debris in space to the BMEWS radars to prevent possible false warnings of missile attacks, and a U.S. Air Force radar in Trinidad was therefore tasked to serve as the substitute for the Moorestown radar's space tracking responsibilities during the crisis.[16]

Emergency telephone "hot lines" were immediately set up between the Falling Leaves radars and the NORAD Command Center in Colorado, with a second "hot line" going from NORAD directly to the U.S. Air Force Command Post in the Pentagon.[17] These open telephone lines, called "squawk boxes," permitted immediate communications in the event that a missile launched from Cuba appeared on the radar screens. They had not been subjected to thorough tests, however, since there had been no time for such peacetime procedures in middle of a crisis. The air force officers at Moorestown, moreover, were using improvised warning and reporting procedures in the first days of the emergency, since operational instructions for the system had not yet been drafted by higher-level staffs.[18] The final after-action report also identified a series of problem areas that required changes in any future emergency operations: "major equipment failures" in the radar's antenna support structure and "intermittent transmitter failure caused by overloading circuit breakers" caused several outages in the system during the crisis; the radar operators had inadequate technical guidance for operations and maintenance of components of the system;

[14] *Electronic Systems Division Historical Report on "Cracker Jack,"* December 1962, vol. 1, FOIA, p. 20.

[15] *Ibid.*

[16] *Ibid.*, vol. 1, p. 20, and supporting documents 62 and 63.

[17] Operations Report, Falling Leaves, Task Force Able, 9th Aerospace Division (Thomasville, Ala.), December 1962, p. 17, NSA-CMCC.

[18] Falling Leaves Memorandum, p. 3.

and perhaps most importantly air force duty officers in the control room did not receive "a complete indoctrination and system orientation prior to engaging in the operation."[19] Despite these difficulties, the final report on Moorestown radar operations informed air force headquarters that the "facility did provide an acceptable detection capability against the Cuban missile threat."[20]

What about the other sites? To provide independent and redundant sensors, the Air Defense Command also immediately proceeded to alter two other radars and turned them to face Cuba. At Laredo, Texas, an air force MPS-14 space-tracking radar was shifted to the ballistic missile warning mission after real-time radar display equipment was sent from the Sheyma, Alaska, sensor site. The Laredo radar became operational on the night of October 28–29, and was considered to be a backup system for the more capable Moorestown radar. It too had to overcome significant operational problems. Several outages were caused by lack of spare parts and a failure to send the maintenance instructions for the display equipment sent from Sheyma. Inadequately trained contractor crews manned the radar control center throughout the crisis. Most importantly, there was no capability for a rapid and accurate test of the Laredo system. After the crisis it was therefore acknowledged by the commanding officers that, "system degradation could have been present without [the] knowledge of the operating crew." Nevertheless, the after-action report noted that "the Laredo sensor site performed its 'Falling Leaves' mission in a satisfactory manner."[21]

The third Falling Leaves site was in Thomasville, Alabama, where an Air Defense Command Semi-Automatic Ground Environment (SAGE) system FPS-35 radar (a radar normally used for aircraft detection and identification) was modified to provide a backup ballistic missile warning capability. Numerous outages occurred at Thomasville, however, due to lack of spare parts and maintenance instructions for the modification equipment, and the radar was therefore not operating for over 16 percent of the emergency period. Inadequate secure communications capability between Thomasville and higher headquarters also existed for the first days of operation. Although the telephone "hotline" between the site and the NORAD Command Control and Display Facility (CC&DF) enabled instantaneous verbal reports, all classified messages had to be sent over a jerry-rigged network, which took over two hours to deliver messages between Air Defense Command Headquarters and Thomasville.[22]

19 *Ibid.*, pp. 6–7.
20 NORAD's 9th Aerospace Division's after-action report added, however, that such statements "present an over optimistic evaluation of the system capability." *Ibid.*, pp. 5, 7.
21 All information and direct quotes are from *Ibid.*, pp. 3, 8–9.
22 The paragraph is based on *Ibid.*, pp. 10–11, and Operations Report Falling Leaves,

## Hidden False Warning Problems

The existence of these operational problems in the individual CMEWS radars does not, however, contradict the central message of the high reliability theorists. Indeed, it is precisely because individual components can fail that redundancy is considered to be so critical to success. The high reliability theorists would also not be surprised by finding these types of minor problems emerging in a newly deployed system; that is precisely why incremental organizational learning is so important.

What would cut against the predictions of the high reliability theory would be evidence that serious false warnings occurred despite or even because of the redundancy designed into the warning system and that the organizations failed to learn from the experience. In this respect, it is very important to note that the formerly classified evaluations of the operation do *not* report on the existence of any serious false warning incidents during the crisis, leading senior civilian and air force officers to view the improvised CMEWS operations in a quite positive light in 1962. The military and civilian operators of the radars were specifically commended for "superior performance" during the crisis, and each of the three radar sites was deemed to have "satisfactorily performed its assigned mission."[23] The Falling Leaves after-action reports, the Defense Department's internal evaluation of U.S. military operations during the crisis, and the air force's report on its operations, all paint a clear picture of a reliable warning system, free of serious false warning problems.[24]

This is puzzling from a normal accidents perspective. How did the CMEWS system avoid having the kinds of bizarre failures modes and unanticipated interactions that plague other complex high technology organizations? The answer is that it did *not* avoid having such problems.

This judgment is based on evidence obtained from the records of the NORAD Combat Operations Center, which had primary responsibility for operations and assessment in the U.S. national warning system in October 1962. Portions of the handwritten daily log books kept by officers at the Combat Operations Center have been declassified at the author's

---

Task Force Able, 9th Aerospace Division (Thomasville, Ala.), December 1962, pp. 17–19, NSA-CMCC.

[23] Falling Leaves Memorandum, pp. 6, 8, 10.

[24] *Ibid.*; *Department of Defense Operations during the Cuban Crisis*, February 13, 1963, sanitized version (Dan Caldwell, ed.) published in *The Naval War College Review* 32, no. 4 (July–August 1979): 91; and *The Air Force Response to the Cuban Crisis* (hereinafter *Air Force Response*), USAF Historical Division Liaison Office, HQ USAF, NSA-CMCC, pp. 9, 33. The one exception is the following hint in the Moorestown after-action report: "Friendly launch information and count down was not available on a timely basis." Falling Leaves Memorandum, p. 6.

request. These log book entries, supplemented by air force unit histories and interviews with the key participants in the Falling Leaves operations, paint a much more alarming picture of the CMEWS project than that which exists in the official after-action reports.[25] Indeed, these documents demonstrate that at least three false warning incidents occurred during the Cuban crisis.

## Spoofing Ourselves

The first incident was a relatively minor "scare" at the Moorestown radar site, the cause of which was quickly discovered and soon fixed. In 1962, the U.S. Air Force and the U.S. Navy regularly flight-tested ICBMs, IRBMs (intermediate range ballistic missiles), and SLBMs (submarine launched ballistic missiles) into the Atlantic Ocean out of Patrick Air Force Base on Cape Canaveral and adjacent ocean areas off Florida. NASA also regularly launched space vehicles and satellites from Cape Canaveral.

A small number of these launches went directly over the island of Cuba and officials at the Department of Defense quickly recognized the potential for such missile launches to be misinterpreted by the Cubans or Russians in Cuba. It was possible, for example, that Soviet or Cuban warning systems might misidentify a test missile as an attack. An errant or malfunctioning rocket could be particularly provocative if it hit Cuba during the crisis. In fact, as recently as November 1960, portions of a Thor missile that malfunctioned in flight during a satellite launch, had impacted in Cuba, reportedly killing a cow and causing strong diplomatic protests from the Castro government.[26] The Pentagon therefore ordered that any missile

[25] NORAD Combat Operations Center logs, October 26–29, 1962, FOIA (hereinafter NORAD-COC logs, followed by date and time of entry). The author confirmed the reports and filled in the details of these incidents through interviews with the following former U.S. Air Force officers and RCA employees: Theodore Cannon (USAF), June 14, 1990; John Ciccolella (USAF), November 17, 1989; Roy Donegon (USAF), November 17, 1989; Robert Lund (RCA), December 5, 1989; George S. Fulghum (USAF), September 10, 1989; Jack Gabus (USAF), October 25, 1989; Kirby Nunn (USAF), December 21, 1989; Douglas Shipes (USAF), January 31, 1990; Norman Some (RCA), June 15, 1990; Bernard Szczutkowski (USAF), June 25, 1990; David Tudor (USAF), November 9, 1989; William C. Watts (USAF), September 8, 1989; and Ronald Winkleman (RCA), November 28, 1989, and June 14, 1990.

[26] R. Hart Phillips, "Rocket Fragments Fell on Cuba: 'Yankee Aggression' is Charged," *New York Times*, December 2, 1960, p. 1, and "Reconstructed Rocket" (caption) *Miami Herald*, January 4, 1961, p. 7-C. Portions of this Thor rocket (the verniar chamber of the propulsion system) were sold by the Castro government to the government of the People's Republic of China, which used the pieces to design the second stage of its DF-5 (NATO designation CSS-4) ICBM. *Chronology of the First Academy of Ministry of Astronautics, 1957–1987* (Beijing, 1988), p. 89. (I would like to thank Hua Di for providing the last document).

launches whose trajectory went over Cuba should be postponed, a decision that fortunately stopped a scheduled Thor missile launch that would have passed over the island on October 24.[27]

The postponement of this potentially provocative missile launch demonstrates that Pentagon officials were cognizant of the danger that these missile launch operations in Florida might create a false warning for Soviet and Cuban forces in Cuba. They treated the danger seriously and took immediate action to solve the problem. In the haste to deploy an emergency U.S. missile warning system against the Soviet missiles in Cuba, however, no one apparently thought about the possibility that a U.S. missile launch might be misidentified by the *U.S. Falling Leaves radars*. No one had arranged for the CMEWS radars to receive timely advanced notification of all U.S. missile launches from Florida, most of which (like the ICBM tests at Vandenberg Air Force Base in California discussed in chapter 2) continued according to schedule during the crisis.[28]

The danger of a false warning was greater than was anticipated during the first days of the Cuban crisis because the redundant sensors, which had been designed into the system to provide overlap and confirmation capabilities, did not become operational simultaneously. It was considered critical to get at least some warning systems in place as soon as possible. The Moorestown radar was the first of the Falling Leaves sites to become operational, achieving initial capability against Cuba on October 24.[29] The second sensor site, at Laredo, did not become operational until October 28.[30] On the afternoon of October 26, however, before the second sensor site was available to provide redundant warning information, a Titan II ICBM was fired on a test launch toward the south Atlantic.[31] The Moorestown radar operators had *not* been anticipating this missile launch when, suddenly, it appeared on their display screens. Because of the extremely close range of the Soviet missiles in Cuba to the United States, the Falling Leaves operators expected to receive only five minutes of warning, and perhaps less, between detection of a medium-range ballistic missile in

[27] History of the Air Force Missile Test Center, Development and Operation of the Atlantic Missile Range, 1962, vol. 2, p. 190, K241.01, AFHRC.

[28] According to the Air Force Missile Test Center history, with the exception of the Thor cancellation on October 24, "it was business as usual on the Atlantic Missile Range during the period of the Cuban Crisis." Fourteen missile and space rocket launches were therefore conducted between October 22 and November 28, 1962, p. 190.

[29] The Moorestown radar's capability appears to have been intermittent over the first few days of its alert operation, going on and off alert as the new software program was being refined and the tracker was being realigned. See Falling Leaves Memorandum, p. 2, and NORAD COC logs, October 25, 1962 (2355z).

[30] NORAD COC logs, October 29, 1962 (0140z).

[31] History of the 6555th Aerospace Test Wing, July 1–December 31, 1962 (WS-107C Weapons Division report), chapter 3, p. 2, K-WG-6555 HI, AFHRC.

flight and its impact in the southern United States.[32] The radar operators recall in interviews that they were, quite naturally, shocked when a missile suddenly appeared on their radar screens. It took a few tense minutes, in the crisis control room at Moorestown, for air force duty officers and contract civilian personnel to recognize, as the radar began to show the missile heading southeast, that this was "a friendly" missile with no impact point predicted inside the United States.

The Air Defense Command immediately acknowledged the potential for serious false warnings here. Colonel William Watts, of the 9th Aerospace Division, flew down to Patrick Air Force Base to explain the problem to officials there and to ensure that advance notification of U.S. missile launches would be sent to the CMEWS radar sites.[33] On October 27, the commander of the Air Force Missile Test Center further informed higher headquarters that "the test schedule would continue, with the prelaunch announcement policy changed so as to avoid international misunderstanding or 'inadvertent action.'"[34] After that procedural change, there were apparently no further alarms caused by U.S. ICBM launches. The Moorestown operators were sufficiently concerned to recommend that in the future "a procedure be established to allow an immediate 'on call' reaction for launch and final count-down information, (to) be provided (to) all sensors."[35]

There is both good news and bad news in the history of this brief incident. The good news is that the system worked even without redundancy: the Moorestown radar by itself was able to discriminate between a hostile missile launch toward the U.S. and a friendly launch toward the Eastern Test Range impact area. Moreover, rapid organizational learning took place: a potential for false warning problems was recognized and the operational procedures for integrating U.S. missile launches with the Falling Leaves sites were adjusted immediately. Imagination also helped; all missile test launches over Cuba were canceled.

---

[32] Message BMEWS ESD to RCA Moorestown, n.d., supporting document 61, *Electronic Systems Division Historical Report on "Cracker Jack."* The five-minute estimate is given for a hypothetical attack from Cuba against Savannah, Georgia, and warning time for any target south of that area could be even less. Also see James Daniel and John G. Hubbell, *Strike in the West: The Complete Story of the Cuban Crisis* (New York: Holt, Rinehart and Winston, 1963), p. 118.

[33] William C. Watts, interview with author, September 8, 1989.

[34] History of the Air Force Systems Command, July 1–December 31, 1962, vol. 1, p. II-82, FOIA.

[35] Falling Leaves Memorandum, pp. 6–7. The AFSC history states that after November 1, "to avoid misleading the missile warning network covering Cuba, the Center also arranged to notify the North American Air Defense Command of any planned Cape Canaveral test launches which would rise above 70,000 feet." History of the Air Force Systems Command, July 1–December 31, 1962, vol. 1, p. II-87.

The bad news from the incident, however, is that it could have been worse: had the missile launched on October 26 been a satellite booster rather than a test ICBM launch, for example, it would have been more difficult for the Moorestown radar operators to identify it correctly, since these satellite booster shots were often launched along a significantly less southeastern trajectory. This was not a remote possibility. A DELTA rocket was, in fact, launched from Cape Canaveral on October 27, placing a U.S. satellite into orbit.[36] The risk of CMEWS misidentifying a satellite booster rocket, fortunately, had already been reduced by that date, through the launch schedule announcement procedures.

## Software and Satellites

The second false warning incident in the Falling Leaves operation during the crisis proved far more serious. The NORAD command post log for that date provides the only available evidence of a very serious incident that occurred on the morning of October 28, the final tense Sunday of the crisis. Just before 9 A.M. (local time), the Moorestown radar picked up what appeared to be a missile launch from Cuba against the United States and immediately reported it over the voice hot line to the NORAD command center in Colorado. According to the command post log data, the missile appeared over Florida and the Moorestown radar predicted an impact point eighteen miles west of Tampa at 9:02 A.M. The rest of NORAD was alerted that a missile attack might be under way and the ballistic missile warning operators were asked to recheck the data immediately. The radar information appeared to be unambiguous: a missile was coming. The NORAD officers immediately passed on the warning information to the Strategic Air Command in Omaha.

Since the missile impact was expected momentarily there was little the NORAD command post duty officers could now do. They therefore checked within the NORAD control center for information from the bomb alarm system, the network of nuclear detonation devices placed on telephone poles around cities and military bases in the United States,[37] but were told that no detonation had been reported. A nuclear-armed missile had apparently not hit Florida, or if it had, at least the warhead had not detonated.

[36] History of the 6555th Aerospace Test Wing, July 1–December 31, 1962 (SLV II/IV Division report), chapter 3, p. 2.

[37] Portions of the bomb alarm system became operational in September 1962. Department of Defense Appropriations for 1964, Hearing before a Subcommittee of the Committee on Appropriations, House of Representatives, 88th Congress, 1st sess., part 1, p. 124, and "Bomb Alarm System," *Military Review* 45, no. 9 (September 1965): 103. See chapter 4 for more details about the bomb alarm system.

A few minutes *after* the expected detonation failed to occur, the NORAD command center was finally told what had happened: "Moorestown now informs [us] that a test tape had been inserted in the equipment and that at the same time Moorestown had a pick-up in the Gulf Coast area and became confused. Called the Central Control and Display Facility [and reported] the test target as real."[38]

Any missile warning system requires occasional use of software test tapes, simulating attacks, to test the software programs and radar display facilities. No one had anticipated, however, that the Moorestown radar would "pick up" a satellite, right at the time when the tape was inserted and right in the location where a missile launched from Cuba would appear, thereby confusing the operators.[39] Who would have expected such a bizarre and dangerous coincidence? The inability of operators and designers to anticipate and recognize such strange interactions within a highly complex system should not come as a surprise from the normal accidents perspective.[40] Perhaps it should also not be surprising that the Falling Leaves after-action reports do not mention this event at all. Yet, whether surprising or not, this organizational reporting failure had very unfortunate consequences. It ensured that higher authorities would fail to learn from the incident, increasing the likelihood of a later repetition of this particular failure mode in nuclear command and control systems.[41]

### Confusion and Redundancy

A third, admittedly less dangerous, false warning incident occurred later on Sunday, October 28. The need for *immediate* warning of any missile

[38] NORAD COC logs, October 28, 1962 (1608z).

[39] The identity of the object in space that caused the incident is not given in the logs. A satellite is the most likely possibility. Another possibility, however, is that a fragment of a destroyed Soviet Mars probe caused the problem. (See the discussion in footnote 47 below.) It also is possible that the unidentified object "picked-up" by Moorestown was a weather or space research rocket. A number of the RCA and air force personnel interviewed by the author recalled that a NASA research rocket launched from Wallops Island, Virginia caused a false warning incident during the crisis. There was, in fact, an Aerobee sounding rocket launched for Wallops Island during the crisis, but NASA records state that the launch was on October 29, the day after the incident reported above. See *Astronautical and Aeronautical Events of 1962*, Report of the National Aeronautics and Space Administration to the Committee on Science and Astronautics, U.S. House of Representatives, 88th Congress, 1st sess., p. 223.

[40] The Trinidad radar, which had taken over the Moorestown radar's space tracking mission, might have been able to provide some assistance, but unfortunately it was not up and operating until after October 31. See Message ADC to CSAF, October 312140z, Supporting document 62, in Electronic Systems Division, *Historical Report on Operation "Cracker Jack."*

[41] See chapter 5 for a discussion of a similar, though not identical, NORAD "training tape" incident in November 1979.

launched from Cuba was considered so pressing that a live telephone voice link, a so-called "squawk line," was created between the three Falling Leaves sensors and the NORAD Command Center. At 5:26 P.M., a verbal report came over the "squawk line" warning that two unidentified objects, potential missiles appearing one minute apart, were in the air. The objects were apparently somewhere over Georgia, exactly where a missile launch from Cuba might have been picked up. The operators were unable to discern, however, whether these objects were moving toward or away from the United States.[42]

Although the information on what happened next is incomplete, the NORAD command post logs clearly state that the report was "understood to be from Moorestown" and therefore was taken more seriously than otherwise would have been the case.[43] They immediately tried to contact the commanding officer on duty at NORAD that afternoon to get a determination of what to do next, "but through an error" according to the logs, the commander in chief of NORAD was called at his home. The command post officers told General Gerhart, however, that the objects had "*low* credence as a threat," most likely because no missile impact points had been registered in the warning system.[44]

There was, again, no detonation reported through the bomb alarm system. The officers at NORAD once again were only able to figure out what happened, in the evocative phrase of the command post logs, "after the smoke cleared."[45] The *Laredo* tracker—a much less capable radar than Moorestown—had just become operational when it picked up what was later determined to be a single satellite orbiting the earth and moving away from the United States. Compound errors had then occurred. The operators at the new Falling Leaves Laredo site could neither accurately count the number of objects detected nor identify the direction of their movement. (The existing documents do not report on whether this inability was due to the radar's limited capacity or an operator's error, or a mixture of both.)[46] In addition, there were apparently inadequate procedures for identification of who was speaking on the live telephone "squawk line," since the NORAD controllers all believed the verbal warnings were ema-

[42] NORAD COC logs, October 29, 1962, (0140z).

[43] *Ibid.* According to the Falling Leaves report, "Based upon known capability of the [Laredo] site, 'small game' sightings which were not tracked required verification by Moorestown, since Laredo's sightings alone afforded a low credence value to the over-all system." Falling Leaves Memorandum, p. 8.

[44] NORAD COC logs, October 29, 1962.

[45] *Ibid.*

[46] The Falling Leaves report acknowledged: "Due to the normal mission of Laredo, contractor experience in the area of ballistic missiles was very limited. There was considerable doubt as to the adequacy of scope interpretation during periods of real-time display (RTD) degradation." Falling Leaves Memorandum, p. 8.

nating from the more capable radar at Moorestown, not from Laredo. Finally, the fact that the Moorestown operators did not immediately intervene in the warning process, to provide disconfirming evidence, suggests that the "hot line" communication system did not provide for the operators at the sensor sites to speak with or listen to one another (see figure 3.1).

Adding a redundant warning site therefore *decreased* system reliability in this strange incident. Indeed, the addition of the jerry-rigged Laredo warning radar actually *produced* a false warning problem during the height of a serious superpower crisis. Although there were no further military actions taken in response to this false warning, the risk would have been significantly greater under other plausible circumstances. Indeed, it is fortunate that there was only one satellite on the horizon and that it was moving away from the United States when it was picked up by the CMEWS radar. Had more than one satellite appeared and had objects been moving toward the United States, it is more likely that the Laredo radar would have reported a set of false nuclear warhead impact points as well. That report would have been treated even more seriously. This incident could have had a more frightening ending.

## On the Blink

What should be the lesson of this experience with emergency warning radars during the Cuban crisis? An optimistic argument could be that this proved that the system worked. Despite a series of false warning incidents, component redundancy, organizational flexibility, and "man-in-the-loop" decision-making prevented escalation from taking place.

This is a narrow vision, however, because what prevented further escalation was *not* primarily the designed features of redundancy nor the requirements for having a human decision maker determine appropriate responses. The only sense in which redundancy helped was that the bomb alarm system did not report confirming evidence that detonations had occurred. But these nuclear explosion detection devices in the U.S. were designed *primarily* for attack assessment purposes, and not to provide the extra warning necessary to launch the bombers or order prompt retaliation. The system was considered reliable because it was *designed* to have redundant components in the additional radar sites. Yet, two of the incidents occurred when only one radar was operating. Furthermore, the third incident was caused *by* the additional radar and "resolved" only by the inability of the commands to do anything during the brief moments when an attack seemed to be under way. The men in the decision-making loop also did not prevent false warnings through superior human interpretation skills: in the test tape incident, the operators themselves became confused and issued false reports that the United States was under attack.

These false warnings therefore provide stronger support for the more pessimistic perspective on complex systems found in normal accidents theory. Had the incidents occurred under slightly different conditions—if a satellite booster instead of a test ICBM had been launched from Cape Canaveral or if more than one satellite had passed overhead—the danger of some sort of escalation would have been significantly greater.[47] At a minimum, a failsafe launch of SAC and ADC nuclear armed aircraft would have been likely. Such actions, while not committing the United States to war, would have increased the risk of further accidents. A final cause for pessimism should be noted. Learning from these incidents was limited: there is no evidence that the existence of these particular false warning problems ever entered the organizational memory of the U.S. Air Force after the Cuban crisis. Indeed, not only did the Air Force, Air Defense Command, and Department of Defense studies of Cuban crisis operations fail to record these incidents, but the Moorestown radar operators were so enthusiastic about the Falling Leaves contribution to national security that they proposed that the Moorestown radar be used in future crises, if there was an emergency need for warning against potential submarine launched ballistic missiles (SLBMs) off the U.S. East Coast.[48] This proposal was eventually accepted: the Moorestown radar was therefore maintained in a "standby mode" to provide emergency missile warning capabilities if needed.[49] The U.S. nuclear command system was thus primed to repeat the Falling Leaves experience in future crises.

[47] It is worth noting here that there may have been another serious false warning incident during the crisis. According to Sir Bernard Lovell, director of the Jodrell Bank Observatory, "the explosion of a Russian spacecraft in orbit during the Cuban missile crisis of October 1962 led the U.S. to believe that the USSR was launching a massive ICBM attack." Letter SMLS/Capt. Flynn to Chairman IRMFSG Secretariat, March 27, 1968, Air Force Space Division Archives. Secondary sources do report on the launch and subsequent explosion of a Soviet Mars probe, after it entered its temporary parking orbit on October 24 or sometime soon thereafter; and U.S. space tracking stations were explicitly directed on October 31 to sort "the debris resulting from breakup of 62 BETA IOTA thereby lessening effect of this debris when observed by BMEWs." This event is shrouded in mystery, and, unfortunately, the NORAD command post logs covering possible dates for the launch remain classified. See Nicholas Johnson, *Handbook of Soviet Lunar and Planetary Exploration*, vol. 47 (San Diego, Calif.: Univelt Inc., 1979), p. 183; James E. Oberg, *Uncovering Soviet Disasters* (New York: Random House, 1988), pp. 151–152; and Message ADC to CSAF, October 312140z, Supporting document 62, in Electronic Systems Division, *Historical Report on Operation "Cracker Jack."*

[48] Falling Leaves Memorandum, p. 7.

[49] Barbara Spector, "Space Sentinel," *Newark Sunday News*, July 18, 1965, pp. 6–8, and *Fiscal Year 1975 Authorization for Military Procurement, Research and Development, and Active Duty, Selected Reserve and Civilian Personnel Strength*, Hearings Before the Committee on Armed Services, U.S. Senate, 93rd Congress, 2d sess., part 1, p. 75.

## THE ALASKAN U-2 INCIDENT

A different kind of incident, which could have produced a dangerous false warning of an attack, occurred when a Strategic Air Command U-2 spy plane accidently flew into Soviet airspace in the Arctic on October 27, 1962. This stray U-2 incident was made public soon after the event and has become perhaps the most commonly cited example of a serious organizational mistake in the literature on the Cuban missile crisis.[50] New information reveals, however, that the incident was even more dangerous than was previously believed. To understand the risks involved one has to examine, in some detail, the military operations of the air defense interceptors of the U.S. Alaskan Air Command, reconnaissance aircraft of the Strategic Air Command, and the strategic defensive and offensive forces of the Soviet Union. These forces became entwined in a bizarre set of unanticipated interactions at the height of the Cuban crisis.

The Alaskan Air Command was still at DEFCON 5 on October 22, 1962, when it was ordered to deploy twelve F-102A interceptors armed with Falcon (GAR 11) nuclear air-to-air missiles to forward operational bases. The message, sent eighty minutes before the formal declaration of DEFCON 3, carefully specified the safety procedures to be followed during the dispersal: "Deploy six aircraft with primary armament to Galena. Six aircraft with primary armament to Eielson. GAR 11 ignitor plugs will be disconnected—repeat disconnected."[51] These nuclear-armed, single-seat interceptors reached their dispersal bases safely and successfully maintained an advanced alert posture there. There was no indication of unusual Soviet military activity in the region, however, and with the exception of a brief report of "a bright flash" on a mountain peak near Eielson Air Force Base, south of Fairbanks, the first days of the crisis were uneventful.[52]

One unit that remained very active during the crisis was the U-2 detachment of the Strategic Air Command's 4080th Strategic Wing, deployed at Eielson. The main mission of this detachment was to fly High Altitude Sampling Program (HASP) missions, testing the Arctic atmosphere for radioactive debris from the Soviet Union's nuclear weapons test sites. The

[50] See, for example, Graham T. Allison, *Essence of Decision: Explaining the Cuban Missile Crisis* (Boston: Little Brown, 1971), p. 141, and McGeorge Bundy, *Danger and Survival: Decisions about the Bomb in the First Fifty Years* (New York: Random House, 1988), p. 455.

[51] Extracts from the Alaskan Air Command central command post log, October 22, 1962, in Alaskan Air Command, Chronology of the Cuban Crisis, 31 July–27 November 1962, K484.052–1, AFHRC. The igniter plugs controlled the motor of the Falcon missile and were to be disconnected under tactical ferry conditions. Air Force regulation 122–23, Safety Rules for the TF/F-102A/AIM-26A/MK54 Weapons Systems, November 22, 1968, FOIA, p. 3.

[52] Extracts from the Alaskan Air Command's command post log. NORAD Region Historical Report, 1 July-31 December 1962, K-484-011-1, AFHRC.

Soviet nuclear test program, like U.S. nuclear tests, continued according to their prearranged schedules throughout the crisis.[53] The Eielson U-2 detachment flew at least one HASP sortie each day, following normal routes during the first week of the crisis.[54] These U-2 pilots had orders not to fly closer than one hundred miles from Soviet airspace[55] and because neither civilian nor military authorities apparently considered these operations to be particularly dangerous, no effort was made to postpone or terminate them.

On the night of October 26, however, U-2 pilot Major Charles Maultsby took off from Eielson flying a HASP mission along a *new* route over the North Pole. The air force believed that Soviet radioactive debris had recently been carried by atmospheric conditions farther north than usual. It was therefore decided that a more northerly route, which had only been flown twice before by other SAC pilots, had to be used. Since this extreme polar route did not permit accurate compass use, celestial navigation with a primitive sextant was necessary. Maultsby strayed off course, unfortunately, when the aurora borealis prevented accurate star-sighting, and he flew well into Soviet airspace above the Chukotski Peninsula.[56]

Soviet MIG-interceptors, based near Wrangel Island, were scrambled in an attempt to shoot down the U-2.[57] Maultsby immediately established radio contact, in the clear, with a U.S. command post in Alaska and was told to turn due east and return to U.S. airspace as quickly as possible. The U-2 then ran out of fuel and flamed out over Siberia. The plane was losing altitude as it glided toward Alaska. Maultsby was not sure he would make it back safely.

In response to Maultsby's SOS signal, U.S. F-102A interceptors were

[53] The Soviet Union conducted five above-ground nuclear tests between October 15 and October 30: two tests (one at Novaya Zemlya and one at Kazakhstan) on October 22; one test (Novaya Zemlya) on October 27; and two tests (both at Kazakhstan) on October 28. Thomas B. Cochran, William M. Arkin, Robert S. Norris, and Jeffrey I. Sands, *Nuclear Weapons Data Book* (New York: Harper and Row, 1989), vol. 4, *Soviet Nuclear Weapons*, p. 353. The U.S. also detonated five test weapons during that two week period. See Chuck Hanson, *U.S. Nuclear Weapons: The Secret History* (Arlington, Tex.: Aerofax, 1988), p. 84.

[54] History of the 4080th Strategic Wing (SAC), 1–30 October 1962, K-WG-4080-HI, p. 17, AFHRC.

[55] Draft letter, John F. Kennedy to Nikita Khrushchev, October 28, 1962, NSA-CMCC.

[56] Unless otherwise noted, the information on this incident is based on the author's following interviews: Charles Maultsby (U-2 pilot), September 15, 1988; Donald Webster (U-2 pilot), October 31, 1988; Dean Rands (F-102A interceptor pilot), November 18, 1988; Joseph W. Rogers (F-102A interceptor pilot), September 8, 1989; Squire O'Connor (F-102A interceptor pilot), September 8, 1989; and Leon Schmutz (F-102A interceptor pilot), September 21, 1989. A very useful history of the U-2 program is Chris Pocock, *Dragon Lady—The History of the U-2 Spyplane* (Shrewsbury, U.K.: Air Life Publishing, 1989).

[57] NSC Executive Committee Record of Action, October 27, 1962, 4:00 P.M. meeting no. 8, JFK Library.

immediately launched from Galena Air Force Base, in western Alaska, in an effort to rescue the lost U-2 and to prevent the Soviet MIGs from freely entering U.S. airspace. Under normal peacetime conditions, conventionally armed interceptors would have been used. But because the Alaskan command was at DEFCON 3, the interceptors at Galena were armed with the nuclear Falcon air-to-air missiles and, under existing safety rules, were authorized to carry the weapons in full readiness condition in any "active air defense" mission.[58] Disconnecting the rocket ignitor plugs, as was required during tactical ferry flights, would have forced the interceptors to scramble with less than full armament into a potential combat situation. The F-102A interceptors were therefore launched fully armed with nuclear Falcon missiles, and the only nuclear weapons control mechanism remaining was the discipline of the individual pilots in the single-seat interceptors.[59] The critical decision about whether to use a nuclear weapon was now effectively in the hands of a pilot flying over Alaska.[60]

Somewhere over the Bering Straits, Maultsby established visual contact with one of the U.S. interceptors from Galena and the U-2 was escorted to a remote landing site on the coast. He was immediately taken back to Eielson and then flown down to SAC Headquarters in Omaha, where he briefed General Power and the SAC staff on the incident. According to Maultsby, Power did not reprimand him and said that he only wished the U-2 had not been on a HASP mission, since if it had been equipped with photographic or electronic intelligence devices, SAC would have learned even more about Soviet military forces as their air defense system reacted to the overflight.[61]

---

[58] Air Force Regulation 122–23, p. 3.

[59] Three safety switches, each of which had to be turned by the pilot, existed inside the aircraft. The final "safety seal" on the weapon's switch was not supposed to be opened until "the launching of an armed nuclear missile has been authorized by the commander declaring or designating an object HOSTILE in accordance with the applicable rules of engagement." There were, however, no physical constraints against unauthorized launch. *Ibid.*, p. 3. In a series of interviews with the author, former Alaskan interceptor pilots acknowledged that nuclear armed air defense missions were relatively rare during the crisis, but may have occurred in other cases as well.

[60] It is worth noting here that the rules permitting the launch the nuclear-armed interceptors at DEFCON 3 in 1962 were apparently not in place for U.S. tactical bombers in 1968, as witnessed in USS *Pueblo* incident. The only U.S. aircraft based close enough to have rescued the *Pueblo* were standing on nuclear-armed alert and could not be downloaded and re-equipped with conventional munitions in time to be sent on a conventional attack against the North Korean gunboats and their potential MIG support. U.S. military commanders decided, therefore, not to send the QRA aircraft on a rescue mission. On this incident see: William Beecher, "Tie-up of U.S. Jets Laid to Atomic Role," *New York Times*, January 25, 1968, p. 15; and *Inquiry into the U.S.S. Pueblo and EC-121 Plane Incidents*, Report of the Special Subcommittee on the USS *Pueblo* of the Committee on Armed Services, House of Representatives, 91st Congress, 1st sess., July 28, 1969, p. 1669.

[61] Charles Maultsby, interview with author, September 15, 1988.

Immediately after the incident, Secretary of Defense McNamara ordered that these U-2 air sampling flights be suspended until adequate means were developed to prevent another accidental overflight.[62] Fortunately, this order apparently reached Alaska quickly enough to prevent the possibility of another accidental overflight. SAC had continued to follow its routine HASP schedule, despite the incident: another U-2 on a HASP mission had already taken off from Eielson and had to be recalled.[63]

U-2s on HASP missions had accidentally flown into the Soviet Union before—indeed, as recently as August 30, 1962[64]—yet no one had apparently focused on the potential danger during the crisis. No one therefore turned off the mission. The failure to review these operations during the crisis was thus a serious oversight in the management of military operations. The cause of the incident was *not* an operator's error, the failure of communications, which is suggested in John Kennedy's famous comment when he heard about the overflight: "There is always some son-of-a-bitch who doesn't get the word." The problem was that no word had been given.

### "Accidental" Use Scenarios

How dangerous was this incident? The stray U-2 flying over Siberia did not, obviously, prevent a peaceful conclusion of the Cuban missile crisis. Yet the risk that this incident could have led to further escalation was not trivial. Indeed, there are a number of potential paths by which this incident could have led to further escalation.

First, the possibility of an accidental, unauthorized, or mistaken use of a U.S. nuclear weapon during this incident was not remote. As noted in Chapter 2, the rules of engagement (ROE) for nuclear-armed interceptor forces during this period authorized pilots to use their nuclear weapons if two conditions were met: first, when an enemy aircraft either had committed a "hostile act" or was declared "manifestly hostile in intent" by regional or higher commanders; and second, if regional commanders subsequently authorized pilots to use their nuclear air-to-air missiles to destroy the intruding aircraft. These rules of engagement were deliberately written with some flexibility to permit air defense commanders and pilots to take into account the unpredictable wartime or crisis conditions at the time of the incident. For example, an aircraft could be considered "manifestly hostile in intent" if "the pattern or actions of incoming unidentified air-

---

[62] NSC Executive Committee Record of Action, October 30, 1962, 10:00 A.M., Declassified Documents Reference Collection, Carrollton Press, 1980, No. 64C.

[63] History of the 4080th Strategic Wing (SAC), October 1–30, 1962, p. 18.

[64] See Jay Miller, *Lockheed U-2* (Austin, Tex.: Aerofax, 1983), p. 39, and "Tass Statement on Aid to Cuba and U.S. Provocation," *Pravda*, September 12, 1962, pp. 1–2 in *Current Digest of the Soviet Press* 14, no. 37, p. 15.

craft indicate beyond a reasonable doubt that a hostile raid is in progress" or "current evaluated intelligence is available which indicates that aircraft are airborne and en route toward the United States with the obvious intention of attacking targets within the United States."[65] A "hostile act" included an enemy aircraft's use of any weapons against U.S. ground, air, or naval forces; the laying of mines; or any other acts "openly committed with obvious intent to injure the United States."[66] Although the central command posts at NORAD and the Alaskan Air Command headquarters were to provide overall direction if possible, decision-making authority was decentralized in order to permit nuclear use if a prompt response was needed or if full communications were not available:

> Nothing in these instructions shall be construed as preventing any responsible commander from taking such action as may be necessary to defend his command. . . . When the force composition and behavior indicates with reasonable certainty that an attack on the continental United States is intended, any military commander possessing forces with an air defense capability may direct his forces to engage recognized Soviet military aircraft when outside the tactical direction limits of the continental air defense system.[67]

Individual U.S. interceptor pilots lacked this contingent *authority* to use nuclear weapons, but they did maintain the *capability* to launch their missiles. Although these officers were well briefed on rules of engagement and delegations of authority, they understood that under some conditions they would be forced to decide for themselves whether to use the weapons under their physical control. These pilots were well aware of the gravity of any such decision and would be unlikely to take matters into their own hands unless they were thoroughly convinced the United States was under attack and emergency communication with higher authorities was not possible.

Given these rules of engagement and command and control procedures, at least five plausible pathways to "accidental" use of nuclear weapons can

---

[65] Intercept and Engagement Instructions, November 23, 1954, pp. 2–3. CCS 373.24 U.S. (September 8, 1949), s.6, Geographic File, 1954–1957 JCS. The U.S. interceptor pilots confirmed that, although some details had changed, the essential components of the ROE were unaltered in October 1962.

[66] According to the 1954 rules of engagement for U.S. air defense, "hostile act" was defined as follows: "Any act by an aircraft openly committed with obvious intent to injure the United States shall be considered hostile. Further, any action by aircraft such as, *but not limited to those examples listed below*, committed within an area of air defense concern shall be considered hostile unless previous notification is received that such actions are scheduled for operations or training within the specific area for the time at which they occur and clearance has been granted by appropriate authority. (1) Aircraft releases bombs or fires guns, rockets or other weapons at any air, ground, or water target other than recognized weapons ranges. (2) Aircraft conducts mine-laying operations." *Ibid.*, p. 3 (emphasis added.)

[67] *Ibid.*, pp. 1, 4.

be identified if Soviet MIGs had crossed the border in hostile pursuit of the U-2 intruder (or if U.S. interceptors strayed into Soviet or international airspace). First, if a U.S. interceptor pilot was unable to contact ground control, he might assume that a precursor Soviet strike had been launched and that he should immediately attack any hostile aircraft entering what he believed to be Alaskan territory. Although such an attack would be technically unauthorized, it is conceivable that pilots would believe such actions to be in the national interests under these conditions. Second, it is possible that an interceptor pilot might panic if confronted with hostile MIGs and fire his most effective weapon regardless of what his orders were from the command post. Third, if a regional Air Defense commander incorrectly believed that Soviet interceptors entering U.S. airspace constituted a hostile act and signaled that war was imminent, he could have ordered, acting fully within his authority, the use of the Falcon nuclear-armed missiles. Fourth, there is some possibility that Soviet MIGs, entering Alaskan airspace in a crisis, could be misidentified by officers in the regional command post as Soviet bombers attacking the United States, again producing an authorized, but mistaken, order to fire the Falcon missiles. Finally, it is possible that a Falcon missile could be accidently launched by the pilot in the tense moments of the confrontation.

The risk of escalation after any initial use would not be negligible. It is conceivable, for example, that a detonation of a nuclear air defense weapon would be misinterpreted by other interceptor pilots or command post operators and thereby provide false evidence that a Soviet nuclear attack was under way. Under such conditions, should a regional command post director order all interceptor aircraft to launch and destroy Soviet aircraft? If a pilot saw a nuclear detonation in the distance, and could not reach the command center by radio, how should he respond? The answer was by no means clearly defined in the U.S. rules of engagement.[68]

### Soviet False Warning Problems

A second set of problems concerns Soviet false warnings. The U-2 incident could have produced an accidental war if it led the Soviet Union to launch a

---

[68] Although this "ambiguous command" scenario was not raised in air defense rules of engagement, SAC officers had apparently discussed the issue with respect to airborne alert bombers. According to Marvin Stern, the Defense Department's assistant director of Defense Research and Engineering, Strategic Systems in 1960, when General Thomas Power, the SAC commander, was asked whether airborne crews would proceed toward the USSR if they saw a mushroom cloud in the distance and contact with SAC was broken, he answered: "The captain of the plane is an American; he will know what to do." Quoted in Peter Stein and Peter Feaver, *Assuring Control of Nuclear Weapons: The Evolution of Permissive Action Links*, Center for Science and international Affairs Occasional Paper no.2 (Lanham, Md.: University Press of America, 1987), p. 34.

preemptive strike in the belief that a U.S. nuclear attack was under way.[69] A number of possible scenarios are worth considering here.

First, Soviet warning and intelligence officers might have believed that the U-2 was on a last minute reconnaissance mission—to locate mobile targets—prior to a U.S. nuclear attack. Such a belief would not have been unreasonable in October 1962. In fact, this was precisely the concern of President Kennedy on October 27, when he learned of the U-2 incident: according to Theodore Sorenson, Kennedy "wondered if Khrushchev would speculate that we were surveying targets for a pre-emptive nuclear strike."[70] The U.S. nuclear war plan at the time, SIOP-63, did in fact include "pre-strike reconnaissance" missions, which Kennedy should have been informed about when he received his SIOP briefing in September 1962.[71] These final prewar reconnaissance missions were apparently scheduled to take place just prior to actual SIOP execution, but *after* the orders to attack or retaliate were delivered.[72] The penetration of Soviet airspace by an American reconnaissance plane in a crisis, therefore, might plausibly have appeared to Soviet intelligence and radar system operators as a most serious warning indicator that a U.S. nuclear attack was imminent and unavoidable.

The likelihood that the Soviet government would make such a desperate decision to preempt an American attack would be significantly heightened if the reconnaissance mission was followed by confirming evidence that a U.S. nuclear attack was imminent. Unfortunately, during the U-2 incident, a potential piece of false confirming evidence *was* present. There was at least some possibility that the F-102A interceptors, flying west into the

---

[69] On the preemptive emphasis in Soviet nuclear doctrine at this time see Stephen M. Meyer, "Soviet Nuclear Operations," in Carter et al., eds., *Managing Nuclear Operations*, pp. 487–490, and David Holloway, *The Soviet Union and the Arms Race* (New Haven, Conn.: Yale University Press, 1983), pp. 39–43.

[70] Theodore C. Sorensen, *Kennedy* (New York: Harper and Row, 1965), p. 713. Also see John Steinbruner, "An Assessment of Nuclear Crises," in Franklyn Griffiths and John C. Polanyi, eds., *The Dangers of Nuclear War* (Toronto: University of Toronto Press, 1979), p. 39, for a similar speculation.

[71] Joint Strategic Target Planning Staff Memorandum, March 29, 1962, General Format for SIOP-63, p. 2, CCS 3105 (Joint Planning) (March 8, 1961), (3) Section 2, JCS 1961. Kennedy's SIOP-63 briefing was held on September 14, 1962, exactly one month before the crisis began. See JCSM 467-62, June 20, 1962, Memorandum for the Secretary of Defense, CCS 3105 (Joint Planning), (March 8, 1961), (3), Section 4, JCS 1961; President's Appointment Book, September 14, 1962, JFK Library.

[72] SAC reconnaissance plans are not currently declassified. It is likely, however, that SAC war plans were based on similar planning assumptions as the Pacific Command's nuclear strike plans. These stated: "After declaration of E-hour, pre-strike reconnaissance of non-SIOP nuclear targets and target complexes . . . may be conducted to assure confirmation of intelligence and effective targeting." CINCPAC Operations Plan no. 1-61, Pacific Command General War Plan, Annex H Reconnaissance, CCS 3146 (January 26, 1961) Section 1, JCS 1961.

Bering Straits to rescue Maultsby, could have then been picked up by Soviet radar and misidentified as incoming bombers in the panic of the moment. A related scenario leading to an accidental war is that the Soviet warning system might have misidentified the stray U-2 as a Strategic Air Command bomber. This was, in fact, Nikita Khrushchev's specific complaint when he protested to Kennedy about the incident on October 28:

> The question is, Mr. President: How should we regard this? What is this, a provocation? One of your planes violates our frontier during this anxious time we are both experiencing, when everything has been put into combat readiness. Is it not a fact that an intruding American plane could be easily taken for a nuclear bomber, which might push us to a fateful step . . . ?[73]

It is unlikely that Khrushchev's expression of alarm was disingenuous. After all, as the Soviets apparently knew, nuclear armed airborne alert B-52s were flying their routes across the Arctic Ocean above Alaska. Indeed, it is worth recalling again that a lost SAC B-52 flew some fourteen hundred miles along the wrong route, entering the Soviet air defense perimeter in this area in August 1962. (See figure 2.1 for a map of this incident.) Had a B-52 bomber on this particular airborne alert route been ordered to attack the Soviet Union, it would therefore have entered Soviet territorial airspace in the same general vicinity as did the lost U-2 on October 27. In addition, on at least one occasion in the 1950s U.S. bombers had apparently penetrated the Soviet warning net by accident, triggering Soviet air defense preparations.[74] Nikita Khrushchev's concern over such an incident somehow causing "a fateful step" in escalation was therefore justified.

## Soviet Accidents

It is valuable to consider one more potential path by which this incident could have led to further escalation. What if Soviet military reactions to the U-2 overflight, such as emergency nuclear alerting activities, had produced a nuclear weapons accident in the USSR? A decision by the Soviet government to launch a preemptive attack based on the ambiguous warning that

[73] Reprinted in Robert F. Kennedy, *Thirteen Days: A Memoir of the Cuban Missile Crisis* (New York: W. W. Norton, 1969), p. 210.

[74] According to a May 1958 JCS report on the Positive Control (Failsafe) Launch procedures used for SAC bombers, "for ten years we have been conducting exercises of a similar nature and the only time we have ever had a Soviet reaction was when our airplanes inadvertently penetrated the Soviet early warning net." Report by the Joint Strategic Plans Committee to the JCS on "Positive Control" Presentation to NSC, JCS 1899/402, May 1, 1958, p. 2619, CCS 381-U.S. (May 23, 1946) Section 97, JCS 1958. (See chapter 4 for further discussion.)

an aircraft had penetrated Soviet territory would clearly be an extremely desperate decision. A less rash and therefore more likely response to such ambiguous evidence of an attack would be to place all available nuclear forces on a higher state of alert, purely as a precautionary measure. As has been seen with U.S. nuclear weapons operations in the crisis, however, the danger of an accident occurring would have been heightened if Soviet nuclear forces were alerted.

What nuclear alert actions were implemented by Soviet nuclear forces in the crisis? Did the Soviet government order any emergency alert measures in response to this U-2 incident, and was there an increased risk of an accident as a result? Any answer to these questions must be very speculative in nature, given the continued lack of firm evidence on the details of Soviet nuclear forces operations during the Cuban crisis. The limited information that does exist is nevertheless quite interesting.

Numerous scholarly analyses of the Cuban crisis have assumed, based on the little evidence available at the time, that the nuclear forces of the Soviet Union did *not* go onto any higher state of alert in October 1962.[75] The currently available evidence strongly suggests, however, that this traditional view needs revision. Although Soviet General Staff records have not been declassified, two retired General Staff officers (both participants in the nuclear alert operations in October 1962) have discussed Soviet nuclear weapons activities in "not-for-attribution" interviews with the author. Such interviews, conducted almost thirty years after the crisis, cannot be given as much evidentiary weight as would be given declassified Soviet documents from 1962. A number of U.S. intelligence reports from 1962, however, provide supporting evidence for some of the critical points made in these interviews.

The first officer was a captain in the Strategic Rocket Forces (SRF) in October 1962, assigned to an SS-7 ICBM launch control center. According to this officer, the Soviet ICBM force had a three-stage alert system in 1962: routine peacetime alert; an intermediate alert level; and full combat readiness. When the U.S. placed the blockade around Cuba, the SS-7 force was immediately placed on the mid-level alert status, which it maintained throughout the months of October and November.[76]

---

[75] See, for example, the following works: Richard K. Betts, *Nuclear Blackmail and Nuclear Balance* (Washington, D.C.: Brookings Institution, 1978), p. 120; Bracken, *The Command and Control of Nuclear Forces*, p. 223; Richard Ned Lebow, *Nuclear Crisis Management: A Dangerous Illusion* (Ithaca, N.Y.: Cornell University Press, 1987), p. 67; Raymond L. Garthoff, *Reflections on the Cuban Missile Crisis*, revised ed. (Washington, D.C.: Brookings Institution, 1989), p. 65; and Marc Trachtenberg, *History and Strategy* (Princeton, N.J.: Princeton University Press, 1991), pp. 253–258.

[76] Not-for-attribution interview with retired Soviet General Staff colonel, Moscow, July 9, 1992.

Declassified U.S. documents from 1962 confirm that Soviet military forces were believed to be on a higher, intermediate condition of alert during the crisis. The Defense Department's post-mortem on the crisis, for example, suggests that some mid-level of military alert was implemented in the USSR: "When the quarantine became effective on October 24, our intelligence reported that Soviet forces were not releasing individuals whose normal term of service had been completed; and within the Soviet and European satellite forces, an advanced state of alert was established. We could find no conclusive evidence, however, that the USSR was preparing to initiate general war."[77] SAC intelligence specifically maintained on November 3 that the "strategic forces of the Soviet Union are estimated to remain on partial alert with (the) capability to advance to maximum state of readiness swiftly, and by reason of strict security measure, achieve a force-cocked position without warning."[78] Finally, SAC intelligence reported on November 16 that "Soviet strategic, air defense and tactical forces are believed retained in an alert status" and the Executive Committee of the National Security Council was explicitly informed on November 29 that "Soviet/Warsaw Pact forces have resumed routine activity."[79]

This evidence indicates only that Soviet nuclear forces were put on a higher state of alert on October 24, 1962; it does not provide any evidence on whether there were any specific emergency alerting actions taken in response to the SAC U-2 incident on October 27. The interview with the second retired General Staff officer, however, provided some information that may be relevant here. Under routine conditions in the early 1960s, all Soviet nuclear warheads were kept in special storage facilities, separated from their delivery vehicles, for safety and security reasons.[80] This retired general, who was a lieutenant colonel in the Operations Department at the Strategic Rocket Forces' Headquarters in October 1962, stated that sometime in the middle of the crisis, the SRF received an emergency order from the highest authorities to go to maximum combat readiness, which appar-

---

[77] *Department of Defense Operations during the Cuban Crisis*, p. 92.

[78] History of the 15th Air Force 1962, Annex: Special Study on the Cuban Crisis, vol. 2, exhibit 48A, Message 15 AF to Zulu Two, November 3, 1962, FOIA. The term "force-cocked position" suggests that the Soviet alert was seen as the equivalent of a U.S. DEFCON 2 condition since "cocked pistol" was the exercise term in the U.S. for moving up to a DEFCON 1 alert status. See the exercise terms listed in table 2.1.

[79] History of the 15th Air Force 1962, Annex: Special Study of the Cuban Crisis, exhibit 66, Message 15 AF to Zulu Two, November 16, 1962, FOIA; Alan Evans Memorandum for Roger Hilsman, Subject Debriefing re Executive Committee meeting, November 29, 1962, Cuban Missile Crisis Collection, no. 2630, p. 1.

[80] Gottfried and Blair, eds., *Crisis Stability and Nuclear War*, pp. 128–129, and Draft Memorandum for the President, Recommended FY 1967–71 Strategic Offensive and Defensive Forces, November 1, 1965, p. 20, FOIA.

ently entailed mating the nuclear warheads with the missiles. This order, however, was rescinded after a matter of hours.[81]

The placement of nuclear warheads on Soviet ICBM forces was an extremely dangerous activity for two different reasons. First, such an emergency alert action might be picked up and perceived by U.S. intelligence as evidence that "the USSR was preparing to initiate general war," which would have significantly increased pressures for a preemptive U.S. attack. Second, such actions would have significantly increased the risk of a nuclear accident at the missile site.

Any link between these dangerous Soviet alert activities and the U-2 incident is speculative. The officer involved did not recall the specific date on which these orders were given; nor was he informed in October 1962 about the cause of the emergency order. In addition, no evidence currently exists in declassified U.S. records to know whether such activities, if they really occurred, were in response to the U-2 penetration.[82] It is at least plausible, however, that the U-2 overflight produced such missile-alert actions. It would not be surprising for final preparations for combat to occur in response to a serious (though false) warning: U.S. ICBMs in 1962 were supposed to be placed on a "minimum hold" posture, for example, if there was a warning from the BMEWS system.[83] Similar procedures may have existed in the USSR. Until the relevant documents are declassified in Moscow, however, the existence of this particularly frightening example of unintended interactions between U.S. forces and Soviet forces cannot be confirmed.

## Unlikely Scenarios?

All of the scenarios by which a spy plane straying over Siberia could have led to further escalation, are obviously counterfactual. The U-2 incident became a minor footnote to history, rather than the cause of nuclear war. Yet, history could have taken a different, unexpected, course, much as Charles Maultsby did when returning from the North Pole in his U-2.

[81] Not-for-attribution interview with retired Soviet General Staff general, Moscow, July 9, 1992. I would like to thank David Holloway for his assistance in setting up and conducting these interviews.

[82] John Prados asserts that the Soviets placed their "ICBM forces on a maximum state of alert" in response to the U-2 overflight, but provides no evidence to support the statement. Prados, The Soviet Estimate: U.S. Intelligence Analysis and Soviet Strategic Forces, 2d ed. (Princeton, N.J.: Princeton University Press, 1986), p. 144.

[83] History of the Directorate Of Plans, Deputy Chief of Staff, Plans and Programs, HQ USAF, July 1–December 31, 1961, p. 114, NSA-CMCC. Also see the analysis of the June 1980 NORAD "computer chip" incident in Chapter 5.

Given the available evidence, it is impossible to make a confident estimate of the likelihood that one of these dangerous scenarios could have happened. It is by no means clear, however, that the event that actually occurred—Maultsby's return to Alaska without triggering further escalation—was the most probable one. And it should not be forgotten that the likelihood that a U-2 would accidently fly into Soviet airspace at the height of the Cuban crisis was itself extremely low. The recognition that unexpected, and even unimaginable, events can occur in complex warning and intelligence systems is further underscored by one more false warning incident that happened during the tense days of October 1962.

## THE PENKOVSKY FALSE WARNING

In the fall of 1962, Moscow's counterintelligence services suspected that a Soviet Military Intelligence officer, Colonel Oleg Penkovsky, was serving as a spy, passing highly classified government information to the American Central Intelligence Agency (CIA) and the British Secret Intelligence Service (SIS). They were right. Rather than arresting Penkovsky immediately, however, Soviet counterintelligence agents continued to monitor his activities closely, apparently in an attempt to learn more about other potential agents and Western intelligence networks in Moscow. The need to know precisely what information Penkovsky had given to the CIA and SIS became far more pressing after President Kennedy publicly announced the discovery of the missiles in Cuba and the imposition of an American naval quarantine on October 22. Penkovsky was immediately arrested in Moscow and placed under intense interrogation. He was eventually tried for espionage and was executed in early 1963.

Two valuable accounts of the circumstances surrounding Penkovsky's arrest exist. The first is by Raymond Garthoff, based on the information given to him by CIA sources in 1962, when he was the special assistant for the Soviet Bloc in the State Department's Office of Politico-Military Affairs.[84] The second, written by Jerrold Schecter, a journalist and former associate White House press secretary, and Peter Deriabin, a former KGB officer, revises some important details based on the release of further evidence.[85] Both accounts report on an incident that presented a false warning to the U.S. that a Soviet attack might be imminent during the crisis.

American and British intelligence officials wanted to make sure that Penkovsky was able to provide them with emergency intelligence in the

[84] This account appears in Garthoff, *Reflections on the Cuban Missile Crisis*, pp. 63–65.
[85] Jerrold L. Schecter and Peter S. Deriabin, *The Spy Who Saved the World* (New York: Charles Scribner's Sons, 1992), pp. 262–263, 337–349.

event that the Soviet Union had decided to launch a nuclear attack. An elaborate warning system, code named DISTANT, was therefore created. Penkovsky was given two telephone numbers in Moscow and was told to call one of them, blow three times into the mouth piece, wait one minute, and then repeat the procedure, if he had emergency warning information. Penkovsky was not to speak over the phone, which was presumably bugged by the KGB; but, if possible, he was supposed to leave more detailed information in a secret "dead drop" location. The telephone signal alone, however, was to be considered a warning message of the utmost importance:

> Penkovsky had been told he must appreciate fully the significance of the early-warning communications system. *His signal alone, whether or not the dead drop was serviced, would result in prompt action at a high level in the United States and Great Britain.* . . . [He] must give such a signal only if he had learned for a fact that the Soviet Union had decided to attack, or that the Soviets had decided to attack should the West take specific action, or that the Soviet Union had decided to attack should the West fail to undertake specific actions.[86]

## The Warning Message

The CIA and SIS did not hear from Penkovsky during the first two weeks of the crisis. On November 2, 1962, however, the DISTANT emergency warning signal was given. The two phone calls came, one minute apart, and someone blew three times into the mouthpiece each time. When a CIA agent went to check the dead drop (a book shop on Puskinskaya Street) for further information, KGB officers were there. The CIA officer was immediately taken away for interrogation.[87]

Unbeknownst to the CIA, Penkovsky had been arrested on October 22.[88] During his subsequent interrogations, he apparently told the KGB how to activate the DISTANT warning message procedures. The KGB had then activated the warning system, giving the signal that a Soviet attack was imminent.

Why did the KGB activate the DISTANT warning system? Two alternative explanations exist. It is possible that Penkovsky had told his KGB interrogators all the details about this special telephone signal system, including that it was only to be used if he had positive information that a

---

[86] *Ibid.*, pp. 262–263 (emphasis added).
[87] *Ibid.*, pp. 337–341.
[88] *Ibid.*, p. 353.

Soviet attack was imminent. The KGB nevertheless could have decided to use the system since the most intense period of the crisis was clearly over by November 2, and using DISTANT was the only way the KGB had to learn the identity of Penkovsky's contacts with the CIA and SIS.[89] It is at least as plausible, however, that Penkovsky deliberately informed the KGB only about *how* to use the DISTANT procedures, but *not* about *what* the telephone signal alone was supposed to mean. Penkovsky, knowing that he was going to be placed on trial and executed, could have decided to let the KGB unknowingly initiate a false warning message that an attack was imminent, in the hope that an American military response would be forthcoming. That would be his final revenge on the Soviet system.[90]

### *Escalation Potential?*

This incident did not result in any further action, since the message was sent on November 2, after the crisis had begun to wind down, and because the KGB presence at the book store dead drop had indicated to the CIA that Penkovsky had been arrested. John McCone, the CIA director, met with President Kennedy on the morning after the incident. He reported that Penkovsky "in all probability had been compromised and in an effort to save himself he had exposed this prearranged plan of the transmission of information."[91]

Imagine what could have happened if the message had been received at the height of the crisis? If American political leaders or senior military commanders had been informed then that Penkovsky had just sent a signal that a Soviet nuclear attack was imminent, how would they have reacted?

Any answer to such a hypothetical question must obviously also be highly speculative in nature. A reasonable conjecture is that Kennedy and his advisers would have been highly skeptical and, in the absence of other intelligence, would not have placed great credence on such a dubious source of warning information. Yet, there are at least four legitimate reasons for concern. First, it should be noted that SIOP-63, the U.S. nuclear war plan in October 1962, contained nuclear attack options specifically designed for preemptive use in the event that a Soviet attack appeared

---

[89] This is the interpretation offered by Schecter and Deriabin, *Ibid.*, p. 347.

[90] Garthoff, writing before he knew that the KGB, not Penkovsky, had actually placed the signaling calls, made a similar speculation: Penkovsky "evidently decided to play Samson and bring the temple down on everyone else as well." Garthoff, *Reflections on the Cuban Missile Crisis*, p. 65.

[91] Schecter and Deriabin, *The Spy Who Saved the World*, p. 346, quoting the CIA director's memorandum of November 5, 1962.

imminent and unavoidable.[92] Second, declassified documents suggest that President Kennedy did have considerable interest in maintaining an ability to order a prompt, preemptive nuclear attack if he received intelligence that a Soviet strike was imminent. In January 1962, Kennedy explicitly asked his senior military advisers, "What would I say to the Joint War Room to launch an immediate nuclear strike?": "Assuming that information from a closely guarded source causes me to conclude that the U.S. should launch an immediate nuclear strike against the Communist Bloc, does the JCS Emergency Actions File permit me to initiate such an attack without first consulting with the Secretary of Defense and/or the Joint Chiefs of Staff?"[93] The existence of SIOP options designed for certain contingencies or a president's apparent interest in having such capabilities does *not* demonstrate that such options actually would be used, even if "information from a closely guarded source" *falsely or accurately* reported that a Soviet attack was imminent or under way. There is an immense and important difference between promoting the existence of an option and actually having the intention to use it. But this evidence does suggest that one should not completely dismiss the idea that the U.S. might have reacted to the initial DISTANT warning message.

The third reason for concern over this incident is that, while the likelihood that a political leader would order a preemptive response to such a single source of warning was probably extremely low, other sources could have provided false confirmation. It is possible that unrelated events could have occurred—such as weapons accidents, alerting actions, false warnings in the BMEWS radars—which might have reenforced the Penkovsky message. Under such conditions, it is less clear that skepticism about a desperate spy's warning would remain strong.

Fourth, a final, and most dangerous, scenario must confronted here: one cannot entirely rule out the possibility that senior American military commanders would have taken matters into their own hands in October 1962 if they had been faced with what they believed to be unambiguous intelligence that a Soviet nuclear strike was imminent or under way. Full documentation about whether or not President Kennedy ever granted senior American military commanders "predeligated authority" to order nuclear

[92] See Scott D. Sagan, *Moving Targets: Nuclear Strategy and National Security* (Princeton, N.J.: Princeton University Press, 1989), pp. 26–31.

[93] Alert Procedures and JCS Emergency Actions File (questions for Norstad meeting), National Security Files, Departments and Agencies, JCS, January–December 1962, box 281, JFK Library. The answers to Kennedy's questions are not available, but McGeorge Bundy's summary memorandum of the meeting states that "it was apparent from the meeting that the President expects to be able to initiate, as well as participate in, an emergency conference with the Secretary of Defense and the Joint Chiefs of Staff." Bundy Memorandum for the Secretary of Defense, January 17, 1962, National Security Files, Departments and Agencies, JCS, January–December 1962, box 281, JFK Library.

strikes on their own authority, under emergency conditions, is not available. The very few pieces of information that have been declassified about this sensitive subject, however, are not comforting.

It is known, for example, that senior military officers, including the chief of staff of the air force, believed during the Eisenhower administration that "authority to order retaliatory attack may be exercised by CINCSAC if time or circumstances would not permit a decision by the President."[94] It is also known that President Kennedy was explicitly warned by his national security adviser in January 1961 that "a subordinate commander faced with a substantial Russian military action could start the thermonuclear holocaust on his own initiative if he could not reach you (by failure of communication at either end of the line)."[95] In light of this information, it is frightening to read the following comment about General Thomas Power, the SAC commander in October 1962, made by someone who knew him well, General Horace Wade, Power's subordinate commander of SAC's 8th Air Force:

> General Power . . . was demanding; he was mean; he was cruel, unforgiving, and he didn't have the time of day to pass with anyone. A hard, cruel individual. . . . I would like to say this. I used to worry about General Power. I used to worry that General Power was not stable. I used to worry about the fact that he had control over so many weapons and weapon systems and could, under certain conditions, launch the force. Back in the days before we had real positive control, SAC had the power to do a lot of things, and it was in his hands, and he knew it.[96]

## Uncertainty and Danger

In the final analysis, the whole Penkovsky incident is shrouded in mystery and conjecture. It is therefore difficult to access the degree of danger involved. This incident should, at a minimum, serve as yet another reminder of the potential for bizarre incidents that could conceivably lead to escalation in a crisis. The possibility that a highly placed secret agent in an adversary's government would, either deliberately or inadvertently, arrange for a false warning of an impending attack to be issued, sounds like a story from a particularly unbelievable spy novel. But this, and even less likely things, happened during October 1962.

[94] Thomas D. White letter to Thomas Power, November 22, 1957, Thomas D. White Papers, box 41, 1957, Top Secret General File, Library of Congress.

[95] McGeorge Bundy memorandum for the President, January 30, 1961, box 313, National Security Files, JFK Library.

[96] U.S. Air Force, Oral History of General Horace M. Wade, October 10–12, 1978, pp. 307–308, K239.0512-1105, AFHRC.

## CONCLUSIONS: SAFETY ON THE BRINK

The overall lessons to be drawn from this analysis of nuclear weapons and command system operations during the Cuban crisis are inevitably contradictory. On the one hand, the system appears to have worked: major alerting actions took place without producing inadvertent escalation or an accidental war. On the other hand, the system failed. Although there was no *catastrophic* failure in the nuclear command system during the crisis, numerous lower-level "close call" incidents occurred, incidents that could have produced serious accidents under other conceivable circumstances.

Thus, while an optimist might be heartened by the final outcome of the crisis, a pessimist could note that the command system failed in its central goal of keeping the danger of accidental war remote. John F. Kennedy told Congress in March 1961 that "we must make *certain* that our retaliatory power does not rest on decisions made in ambiguous circumstances, or permit a catastrophic mistake."[97] In the test of a real crisis, however, that certainty was not available. The U.S. nuclear command system clearly did not provide the certainty in safety that senior American leaders wanted and believed existed at the time.

Both high reliability theory and normal accidents theory have provided useful lenses with which to reexamine the events of October 1962. As a test of the relative strengths of the two schools of thought, however, the history of the Cuban crisis gives considerably more support for the normal accidents approach. Although some of the design and operations characteristics identified by the high reliability theorists did have a positive impact on safety, their total contribution was limited. A brief synopsis of the impact of these factors can underscore the point.

Senior political leaders placed high priority on maintaining nuclear safety and avoiding false warnings or provocations during the crisis, but in a number of instances the contrary priorities of subordinate officials resulted in precisely such dangerous nuclear operations. Strict safety rules for U.S. nuclear-armed interceptors and Minuteman ICBMs were drafted; but operators in the field, seeking to maximize alert levels, did not always follow them thoroughly. Civilian leaders wanted to avoid sending false warnings of an attack against the Soviet Union and Cuba; but officers at Vandenberg, needing to keep to their testing schedules, nevertheless launched an ICBM in the middle of the crisis. Political authorities in Washington and London, as well as General Norstad in Paris, sought to prevent any activities that might be considered provocative in Europe; but senior

---

[97] *Public Papers of the President, John F. Kennedy, 1961* (Washington, D.C.: Government Printing Office, 1962), p. 232 (emphasis added).

British and American military commanders, hoping to improve their readiness for war, alerted nuclear forces on their own authority.

Redundancy sometimes did help prevent accidents when one part of the system failed. Special ground control radars were able to provide backup flight information to the lost B-52 bomber, for example, and the bomb alarm sensors did provide disconfirming evidence about the missile attack out of Cuba. Yet designing a redundant Falling Leaves radar system facing Cuba did not prevent false warnings. Some incidents occurred before the extra warning radars became operational; another occurred because the new Laredo radar issued a false warning and the NORAD command post operators falsely believed that the information was coming from the more reliable Moorestown radar.

Decentralized decision-making capabilities may have helped prevent further escalation in some cases: for example, the NORAD officers correctly assessed the October 28 warning from Laredo as having "low credence as a threat." The capability of lower-level officers to determine their own readiness levels, however, also enabled the dangerous alert activities at Malmstrom Air Force Base and in Europe to occur. Constant training and exercise operations contributed to the safety and reliability of the SAC airborne alert. But many of the most important and dangerous military operations during the crisis had not been anticipated and therefore had never been practiced before. A demanding organizational culture, emphasizing reliability and discipline, may have contributed to safety during SAC alert operations and when air defense aircraft were launched without safety devices installed. Yet the strong culture and discipline of SAC also appears to have enhanced the tendency to place increased nuclear readiness as a top priority and may have encouraged organizational cover-ups when official safety rules were violated.

## Complexity and Tight-Coupling Revisited

Normal accidents theory emphasizes how the interactive complexity of an organization using hazardous technologies will confound the efforts of system designers and operators to produce adequate safety and reliability. The hidden history of the Cuban crisis provides considerable evidence to support this view. Despite the attention given to safety by political and military leaders and despite the enormous sums of money spent on redundant warning and safety devices, numerous failure modes were not anticipated and never fixed.

The set of bizarre interactions, and their banal causes, that occurred during the crisis resonates strongly with the kinds of unpredictable events that have produced accidents in nuclear power reactors, petrochemical plants, and commercial aircraft. Who could have imagined ahead of time that initiating a sabotage alarm in Duluth would ring the war Klaxon, ordering nuclear-armed aircraft into the air in Wisconsin? What warning system designer would have dreamed that a satellite would pass over the Moorestown radar just as the software simulation of an attack was on the screens? Could Pentagon officers have planned for the possibility that a U-2 would accidently stray into Soviet airspace and that Alaskan Air Command interceptors would then be launched with nuclear weapons on a rescue mission? These types of dangerous interactions between components of a complex organizational system could not be fully anticipated, and numerous potential failure modes remained hidden in the command system. During the crisis, these latent problems became real.

When one moves from the history of these "normal near-accidents" to the realm of counterfactuals, an additional disturbing aspect about nuclear weapons safety becomes more clear. The lower-level incidents that could have led to escalation were not independent of one another. Thus, although the likelihood of any single failure of the system may be relatively low, once a nuclear command accident does occur, the probability of further accidents is significantly increased.

Many of the "close calls" during the Cuban missile crisis can be used to illustrate this point. If a U.S. nuclear weapon had been accidentally detonated, or used in an unauthorized manner, during the U.S. interceptor alert, for example, both the likelihood of a false warning (through a misidentification at NORAD of the cause of the detonation) and the probability of a second "accidental" detonation (by a second interceptor pilot panicking in the belief that a war had started) would be increased. Similarly, if a false warning of a missile attack on the United States produced a full-scale positive control launch of the SAC bomber and ADC interceptor force, both the probability of a purely accidental nuclear detonation (through a crash of a B-52) and an inadvertent use of a nuclear air-to-air missile (by an airborne interceptor pilot misidentifying a SAC plane in the pressure of the crisis) would be heightened. Either one of these accidental nuclear detonations, especially if it occurred near a U.S. military base, might furthermore be treated as confirming evidence that a *Soviet* nuclear attack was under way. A false warning caused by a computer software glitch could thus produce its own falsely confirming evidence. In short, the danger of *cascading accidents*—one accident leading to a second leading to a third—was not negligible in this serious crisis.

## Design and Good Fortune

The sheer number and drama of the "close calls" that did occur in the crisis should not obscure one central fact: there may have been many safety violations, false warnings, and bizarre interactions, but nonetheless no accidental or unauthorized use of a nuclear weapon took place. In the light of the evidence presented here on everything that did go wrong during the crisis operations, it may be that basic piece of good news that needs further explanation. Why did escalation to a nuclear war not occur?

It is always much more difficult to explain why possible twists in history did *not* happen than it is to explain the actual outcome of events. The normal accidents theory, however, provides a final set of useful ideas here. Two related factors appear to have been crucial in avoiding accidental war in October 1962.

First, tight coupling is a matter of degree, and it appears that the U.S. nuclear command system was not *so* tightly coupled so as to prevent recovery from the serious nuclear weapons incidents that did develop during the crisis.[98] Even more tightly coupled systems, as is often seen in nuclear power plant accidents, have such highly time-dependent and invariant production processes that recovery is not possible. When one problem occurs, therefore, others often follow, and there is inadequate time to learn what is happening and to plan or improvise solutions.

There was time to react properly in most of the U.S. nuclear command system incidents in 1962. The false warnings that did occur did not immediately or automatically produce a reaction that could not be terminated prior to war. These false warnings—at the Air Defense Command bases and with the emergency Falling Leaves CMEWS network—took place at relatively low levels in the system and were not all passed up to the highest levels of the chain of command. The reactions to the warnings that did take place, such as preparing to launch nuclear-armed interceptors or preparing air bases for imminent attack, were by no means irreversible. While such actions may have increased the likelihood of other accidents occurring, they did not automatically produce further escalation.

The irony here is that the nuclear command system was designed to be more tightly coupled than it turned out to be. For example, the Strategic Air Command was supposed to launch the bombers, under failsafe procedures, before nuclear weapons were predicted to detonate on U.S. soil. SAC, however, failed to do this during the October 28 "test tape" warning incident. There was clearly some slack in this system; but a large part of it was not there by design.

The second important factor should therefore be acknowledged: there was an element of *good luck* involved in avoiding accidental war in October 1962. If the Soviet early warning system had misidentified Maultsby's stray U-2 as a bomber, as Khrushchev suggested was possible, *then* the

---

[98] It is obviously problematic to determine the degree of tight coupling present in a system by the frequency of or outcomes of accidents, instead of through a rigorous assessment of the system's internal characteristics. I have tried to base my judgment on these internal properties, but recognize that future work will be necessary to develop better measurements.

danger of a decision in Moscow to "retaliate" would have been greater. *If* the Delta satellite booster, which was launched almost vertically, rather than a Titan test missile, which was launched down range, had been picked up by the Moorestown radar, *then* the chance of a positive control launch of SAC bombers would have been greater. *If* the U.S. interceptor pilots who were launched with fully armed nuclear weapons aboard had crashed or "accidentally" launched their weapons, *then* the dangers of escalation caused by a misidentified nuclear detonation inside U.S. territory would have been heightened.

These dangers are, like all counterfactual scenarios, a mixture of logic and imagination. None of the "ifs" occurred; but had they, all of the "thens" might well have come next. Good luck held, but the knowledge of the numerous nuclear command system incidents that did occur during the crisis should reinforce Winston Churchill's observation that in history, "the terrible ifs accumulate."

I do not want to push this point about good fortune to an extreme. There was also plenty of bad luck—garbled messages, the bear climbing the fence, the bright aura borealis coming out—at the heart of these incidents. It would be to going too far, therefore, to argue that the successful outcome of the Cuban missile crisis was, to borrow Dean Acheson's phrase, "a homage to plain dumb luck." It is nonetheless frightening to recognize fully the degree of caprice upon which nuclear safety insecurely stood in October 1962.

# CHAPTER 4

# Redundancy and Reliability: The 1968 Thule Bomber Accident

I don't mind ground alert because I know it's necessary.
But I like our air alert so much better. Instead of sitting
around and waiting for something to happen, I do
what I know and like best—flying. . . . If General
Power could invite that guy Khrushchev to fly a Head
Start mission [airborne alert] . . . [it] would keep him
peaceful for a while. Gee, and just think of the money
we could save because we could do away with the
Army, the Navy, and the rest of the Air Force!

*(Strategic Air Command*
*B-52 Bomber Crew Members*
*Spring 1959)*

ON THE AFTERNOON of January 21, 1968, a Strategic Air Command B-52 bomber on an airborne alert mission was orbiting thirty-three thousand feet above the Ballistic Missile Early Warning System (BMEWS) radar at Thule, Greenland. At around 3:30 P.M., the copilot turned the cabin heater dial to its maximum heat in order to combat the arctic cold. A few minutes later, one crew member reported that he could detect the smell of burning rubber. The crew searched the aircraft and discovered a small fire in the rear of the lower cabin. The flames quickly grew out of control, dense smoke rendered the flight instruments unreadable, and, seven minutes later, all electrical power was lost. The pilot immediately gave orders to evacuate the plane. Six of the crew members successfully ejected and landed safely in the snow. The seventh was killed.

The B-52 also had four 1.1 megaton thermonuclear bombs on board. The pilotless aircraft continued descending, passed directly above the Thule base, and then crashed into the ice seven miles away. The speed of the plane at impact was in excess of five hundred miles per hour, and 225,000 pounds of jet fuel immediately exploded. The conventional high explosives in all four of the nuclear bombs went off. No nuclear detonation occurred, but radioactive debris was dispersed over a wide expanse of ice.[1]

[1] The description of accident is based on the following sources: *USAF Nuclear Safety,*

The B-52 crash produced a number of international protests against American nuclear weapons policy and eventually resulted in the termination of nuclear-armed airborne alert flights. Why was a nuclear-armed SAC bomber flying above the U.S. warning radar? How dangerous was the accident? How did the Strategic Air Command interpret the causes of the accident and what did the organization learn from the experience?

## FACTS AND THEORIES

The official "facts" can be quickly presented. Why was there an armed B-52 flying over the arctic under routine peacetime circumstances? A small number of SAC B-52s had been kept on constant airborne alert since 1960, as part of the redundant triad of U.S. strategic bombers, submarine launched ballistic missiles (SLBMs) and intercontinental ballistic missiles (ICBMs), to ensure that retaliation would be possible under any conceivable circumstances in which the United States might be attacked. Why was one of these bombers orbiting near the Thule radar? The B-52 was on what was called the Thule Monitor Mission, a secret SAC airborne alert operation specifically designed to provide redundant confirmation on whether Thule had been destroyed in a Soviet nuclear attack. Did the crash raise the risk of an accidental detonation or an accidental war? According to the anonymous "responsible officials" who spoke to reporters after the Thule accident, there was no "substantial hazard" when the bomber crashed, since "safety devices and precautions provide 'virtually 100 percent' certainty that there will be no nuclear explosion if a plane crashes with its load of bombs."[2] "Our nuclear weapons can be activated only after a prescribed sequence of actions is followed," the SAC officer responsible for the clean-up operation confidently explained: "there was, of course, no nuclear explosion since the design of the weapons precluded any nuclear reaction."[3] As the official State Department announcement maintained: "Our policies and practices designed to meet this nuclear threat have only been adopted after the most careful assessment of security requirements and after provisions of necessary safeguards."[4]

---

Special Edition on Project Crested Ice, vol. 65, no. 1, part 2 (January/February/March 1970), (henceforth *Project Crested Ice*), Freedom of Information Act (henceforth FOIA); Supplemental Report no. 1 of Nuclear Accident (Broken Arrow), January 23, 1968, Mandatory declassification review no, 88-122, Lyndon Baines Johnson Library (henceforth LBJ Library), Austin, Texas; and USAF Incident/Accident Report File, Thule, Greenland accident, January 25, 1968, p. 5 and tab S, FOIA.

[2] As quoted in Richard Dudman, "B-52 H-Bomb Flights Expected," *St. Louis Post Dispatch*, April 30, 1968, p. 10.

[3] Richard O. Hunziker, "Foreword," *Project Crested Ice*, p. 1.

[4] As quoted in John W. Finney, "U.S. Reviews Need for H-Bomb Alert," *New York Times*, February 28, 1968, p. 6.

This chapter examines the causes and consequences of the Thule B-52 accident as a case study exploring the effects of redundancy on organizational reliability. As noted in chapter 1, the high reliability theorists and the normal accidents theorists hold quite contrasting views on the likely effects of adding redundancy in efforts to prevent accidents in complex organizations. This chapter will therefore review the arguments for and against redundancy and then will examine the history of the Thule B-52 bomber accident as a test of the strengths and weaknesses of the two competing theories.

## Conflicting Visions of Redundancy

Accidents will happen. In the real world, individuals and machines cannot be perfect. That is precisely why organizations that use highly hazardous technologies must, according to the high reliability theorists, take full advantage of the benefits of redundancy. "The most basic argument for redundancy rests on the practicality of increasing a system's reliability without increasing the reliability of its constituent elements," Jonathan Bendor notes: "uncertainty, that is, the possibility of failure, is redundancy's raison d'être."[5]

Empirical studies of high reliability organizations often argue that overlap and duplication, of both mechanical devices and responsible personnel, are a key to their success. PG&E has multiple monitors controlling the flow of energy into San Francisco and maintains reserve electrical power sources to compensate for any individual units that fail. U.S. air traffic controllers are assigned to radars in groups of two in order to check one another, and older equipment is kept in reserve in case the primary radars fail. "One of the first things one is struck with on the (U.S. Navy's nuclear aircraft) carriers is the vast amount of redundancy that occurs," notes Karlene Roberts.[6] Backup computers are available to substitute for on-line systems, deck personnel have overlapping responsibilities to ensure that safety-sensitive jobs get done, and the central control tower has more than twenty communication devices, ranging from radios to sound powered phones, to keep in contact with other parts of the ship.

Redundancy is also a defining characteristic of the U.S. nuclear weapons and command and control system. It has been argued, for example, that

---

[5] Jonathan B. Bendor, *Parallel Systems: Redundancy in Government* (Berkeley: University of California Press, 1985), pp. 291, 67.

[6] Karlene H. Roberts, "Some Characteristics of One Type of High Reliability Organization," *Organization Science* 1, no. 2 (May 1990): 165–170, quote at p. 168. The other examples appear in Karlene H. Roberts, "Managing High Reliability Organizations," *California Management Review* 32, no. 4 (Summer 1990): 104–105.

the size and diversity of the nuclear forces that were built during the Cold War appear to be clear cases of "unnecessary overkill," until one recognizes that "both the United States and the Soviet Union have deliberately built some redundancy into their nuclear arsenals."[7] Communications lines, safety devices, and warning systems likewise proliferated in an effort to ensure that individual component failures would not produce a systems failure. Given the needs for credibility and safety in this area, it should not be surprising that statements can be found in which high-ranking military officers echo the themes raised by the high reliability organization theorists. To give one example, Lieutenant General William Hilsman, the director of the U.S. Defense Communications Agency, argued in 1983: "My answer to the issue you gave me to address—failures—is redundancy. Have enough of it going in so many different directions that if one thing doesn't work, the other one will. . . . Tell me what you want. I will deliver it for you reliably, and it will be there."[8]

This perspective is not uncommon. The imperfection of men, machines, and organizations is the problem. Redundancy is the answer.

The normal accidents theory offers a quite different perspective on both the probable causes and the likely consequences of redundancy in complex organizations. Why are redundant systems constructed at such great expense? Instead of assuming that redundancy was the solution chosen by leaders to enhance overall system reliability, a more "garbage can" conception of decision-making would highlight the possibility that each redundant unit has its own interests, which can influence the choices made within the organization. As Michael Cohen, James March, and Johan Olsen put it, "an organization is a collection of choices looking for problems . . . (and) solutions looking for issues to which they might be the answer": "A solution is somebody's product. A computer is not just a solution to a problem in payroll management, discovered when needed. It is an answer actively looking for a question."[9]

This perspective leads to a more political, less managerial vision of the origins of redundancy within large organizations. It focuses attention on the political process of choice. In whose interests are specific redundant systems? Who has the information necessary for effective analysis? Who

[7] Albert Carnesale, Paul Doty, Stanley Hoffmann, Samuel P. Huntington, Joseph S. Nye, Jr., and Scott D. Sagan, *Living with Nuclear Weapons* (Cambridge, Mass.: Harvard University Press, 1983), p. 108. Also see Barry R. Posen, *Inadvertent Escalation: Conventional War and Nuclear Risks* (Ithaca, N.Y.: Cornell University Press, 1991), p. 209.

[8] William Hilsman, "Communications Failures," in Hilliard Roderick, ed., *Avoiding Inadvertent War* (Lyndon B. Johnson School of Public Affairs, University of Texas at Austin, 1983), pp. 39, 43.

[9] Michael D. Cohen, James G. March, and Johan P. Olsen, "A Garbage Can Model of Organizational Choice," reprinted in James G. March, *Decisions and Organizations* (Oxford, U.K.: Basil Blackwell, 1988), pp. 296–297.

participates and what opportunities for influence exist? Such questions raise the possibility that the growth of redundancy may reflect biased interests or a capricious confluence of events, rather than a purely rational decision to use duplication and overlap to enhance reliability.

What are the likely effects of increased redundancy? According to the normal accidents theory, adding redundant parts tends to increase the complexity and opaqueness of the system, thereby increasing the probability of hidden interactions and common-mode failures.[10] Studies of accidents in the nuclear power industry have in particular emphasized the ironic possibility that actions taken specifically to improve safety can actually *cause* serious accidents. Two extreme examples of this phenomenon best illustrate the point.

The first example is the October 1966 near-meltdown accident at the Fermi demonstration reactor near Monroe, Michigan. This accident was caused by an emergency safety device, a piece of a zirconium plate, which had been installed to protect the steel cones on the floor of the reactor. When installing the special plates, the plant's technical director believed he "was being super-cautious to do so, but with the accidents that were happening around the world with reactors, it wouldn't hurt to be too careful."[11] He was wrong. The attachments to the side of the reactor were weak, and one piece of zirconium plate broke off, blocked a pipe, and stopped the flow of coolants into the reactor core. To make matters worse, this safety device had been installed at the last stage of the construction of the reactor and was therefore *not* on the final "as built" set of blueprints. The power plant operators during the accident, and officials investigating the incident later, could not therefore figure out what was blocking the flow of coolants.[12]

The second example of counterproductive safety improvements is the Chernobyl nuclear power plant accident in April 1986. The Chernobyl reactor, like other reactors, had emergency diesel generators to provide electric power to the plant if the main source, the reactor itself, was shut down in an accident. These backup diesel generators required thirty seconds to start up, however, and the plant officials decided that this was too long of an interruption of power to the pumps circulating coolant water through the reactor. A decision was therefore made to add a third redundant power source by tapping into the spare energy from the power plant turbines, as they slowed down in an emergency, to keep electric power going to the pumps until the diesel generators kicked in. At the start of a

[10] See Charles Perrow, *Normal Accidents: Living with High-Risk Technologies* (New York: Basic Books, 1984).

[11] John G. Fuller, *We Almost Lost Detroit* (New York: Reader's Digest Press, 1975), p. 102.

[12] For a discussion of the October 1966 Fermi accident in Monroe, Michigan, see *Ibid.*, and Perrow, *Normal Accidents*, pp. 50–54.

test of the system on April 26, 1986, the operators deliberately disconnected a number of the reactor's automatic shutdown devices in order to be able to run repeated tests of the backup power source. During the test, however, the heat within the reactor began to rise precipitously as the coolants began to boil, and manual efforts to shut down the reactor proved counterproductive. Within seconds, the metal container around the graphite blocks and then the concrete shield on top of the reactor blew up in a disastrous explosion. A test of a safety system thus produced the worst nuclear power plant accident in history.[13]

A number of less dramatic examples from the nuclear power industry also exist. One safety "improvement" can interfere with another, as when the thermal insulation on pipes prevents adequate inspection for cracks. Careful screening of individuals allowed to enter nuclear power plants, an obviously legitimate security measure in an age of terrorism, can also reduce reactor safety if it delays the entry of needed personnel during a nuclear accident. Special metal restraints are often connected to pipes in the plant to prevent nearby equipment from being damaged by the whipping motion if a pipe rupture occurs; these metal restraints can, however, put extra strain on the pipes making a serious rupture more likely.[14]

In short, normal accidents theory focuses attention on the political and biased causes of redundancy and its potential unintended consequences. High reliability theory, in contrast, views redundancy as a rational response to inevitable human and organizational imperfections, a response which can be extremely effective. Which perspective leads to a better understanding of the behavior of organizations managing hazardous technologies?

## BACKGROUND: REDESIGNING NUCLEAR OPERATIONS

The bomber operations of the Strategic Air Command were radically altered in the late 1950s and early 1960s in apparent response to increases in the Soviet nuclear threat. The Distant Early Warning line (DEW line) radars had provided what was believed to be adequate warning of two to six hours in the event of a surprise Soviet bomber attack in the mid-1950s. A second line of radars, the Mid-Canada Line, provided confirmation and

---

[13] The description of the accident is based on Victor G. Snell, "Introduction: The Cause of the Chernobyl Accident," in David R. Marples, *The Social Impact of the Chernobyl Disaster* (New York: St. Martins Press, 1988). Also see Gregori Medvedev, *The Truth About Chernobyl* (New York: Basic Books, 1991); and Bennett Ramberg, "Learning From Chernobyl," *Foreign Affairs* 65, no. 2 (Winter 1986/87): 304–328.

[14] On these and other examples see Elizabeth Nichols and Aaron Wildavsky, "Does Adding Safety Devices Increase Safety in Nuclear Power Plants?" in Aaron Wildavsky, *Searching for Safety* (New Brunswick, N.J.: Transaction Books, 1988), pp. 126–131.

further details of any incoming attack.[15] When the Soviet Union began to deploy its first ICBMs, however, that warning capability vanished. New U.S. warning systems and new bomber force operational procedures were deemed necessary to maintain the ability of the bomber force to survive a Soviet first strike. The U.S. capability to retaliate under any circumstances, which was the foundation of nuclear deterrence policy, could not be ensured unless something was done to counter the effect of Soviet nuclear-armed missiles. Three major changes were soon forthcoming.

## Building BMEWS

First, within a month of the October 1957 Sputnik launch, the U.S. Air Force developed a plan for an early deployment of Ballistic Missile Early Warning system (BMEWS) radars, and Congress quickly provided initial funds in an emergency supplement to the Defense Department's FY 1958 appropriations bill.[16] Three advanced radars at Clear (Alaska), Thule (Greenland), and Fylingdales (England) became operational in stages between 1960 and 1963, and were designed to provide as much overlapping coverage as possible so that if one radar was not working for whatever reason, another could compensate for the failure.[17] This missile warning system, once fully deployed and operational, provided approximately fifteen minutes of warning of a Soviet ICBM attack.[18]

After the Sputnik launch, there was widespread support for building the BMEWS system within the United States public and Congress. As John

[15] Department of Defense Appropriations for 1960, Hearings before the Subcommittee of the Committee of Appropriations, House of Representatives, 86th Congress, 2d sess., part 1, p. 862. On the evolution of U.S. warning capabilities, see Bruce G. Blair, *Strategic Command and Control: Redefining the Nuclear Threat* (Washington. D.C.: Brookings Institution, 1985); Paul Bracken, *The Command and Control of Nuclear Forces* (New Haven, Conn.: Yale University Press, 1983); Joseph T. Jockel, *No Boundary Upstairs: Canada, the United States, and the Origins of North American Air Defense, 1945–1958* (Vancouver: University of British Columbia Press, 1987); and Thomas W. Ray, *A History of the DEW Line, 1946–1964*, Air Defense Command Historical Study no. 3, K410.041-31, Air Force Historical Research Center (henceforth AFHRC), Maxwell Air Force Base, Ala.

[16] Richard F. McMullen, *Air Defense and National Policy, 1958–1964*, ADC Historical Study 26, pp. 1–3, K410.041-26, AFHRC.

[17] In 1968, the radar at Clear, Alaska, was the only site capable of covering 11 percent of Soviet ICBMs, but "with the Clear site and either Thule or Fylingdales the entire threat should be detected by BMEWs." Major General J. B. Knapp, Memo for Record on BMEWS Monitor Procedures, in History of the Strategic Air Command, January–June 1968, vol. 8, exhibit 1, AFHRC.

[18] See Blair, *Strategic Command and Control*, pp. 104–105.

Toomay has noted, "to spend a billion dollars for missile warning was something new in the world, but there were few dissenters."[19] Given the consensus over the Soviet threat, there was almost no political controversy involved in building the overlapping system of BMEWS radars displayed in figure 4.1 below.

### Authorizing Positive Control Launch

The second important change, however, was more controversial: creating procedures by which the Strategic Air Command could launch its bomber force in the event of a warning that an attack on the United States was imminent or under way. Before March 1958, the commander in chief of the Strategic Air Command (CINCSAC) was not authorized launch the alert bomber force under any circumstances, unless direct orders to do so had been issued by higher political and military leaders.[20] With concerns mounting about the vulnerability of the bomber force to a Soviet missile attack, the Air Force quickly developed a new operational concept, the Positive Control Launch (PCL) or "fail-safe" procedure. Under this concept, the SAC commander could independently order U.S. bomber crews to take off and fly toward the Soviet Union on prearranged routes, if he received a warning that a Soviet attack was imminent or under way. After the aircraft reached a position known as the "Positive Control Turn-Around Point" (PCTAP), a position outside Soviet territory, the bomber crews were to orbit as long as possible and then return to their base, *unless* they receive further orders (the "go-code") to execute the attack. The brief "go codes" were to be transmitted through a special Strategic Air Command HF radio network appropriately known as Short Order.[21] The system was designed to "fail-safe": if there was a false warning or if communications were somehow cut off, SAC pilots were *not* authorized to continue

[19] John C. Toomay, "Warning and Assessment Sensors," in Ashton B. Carter, John Steinbruner, and Charles A. Zraket, eds., *Managing Nuclear Operations* (Washington, D.C.: Brookings Institution, 1987), p. 296.

[20] CSAFM-72-58, Memorandum by the Chief of Staff, U.S. Air Force for the JCS on Launching of the Strategic Air Command Alert Force, March 10, 1958, Enclosure to JCS 1899/393, CCS 381 U.S. (May 23, 1946) (Section 94), Records of the Joint Chiefs of Staff 1958, Records Group 218, Modern Military Branch, National Archives, Washington, D.C. (hereinafter JCS followed by records year).

[21] The Short Order network was the primary communication system for the SAC bomber force once airborne. It was supplemented by the Green Pine system, a set of radio transmitters scattered across northern Canada and Alaska. See Blair, *Strategic Command and Control*, pp. 103–104; SAC Message to AIG 667/DO/DM, March 27, 1968, Subject: BMEWS Monitor, in SAC Historical Study 112, January–June 1968, vol. 8, exhibit 2, AFHRC.

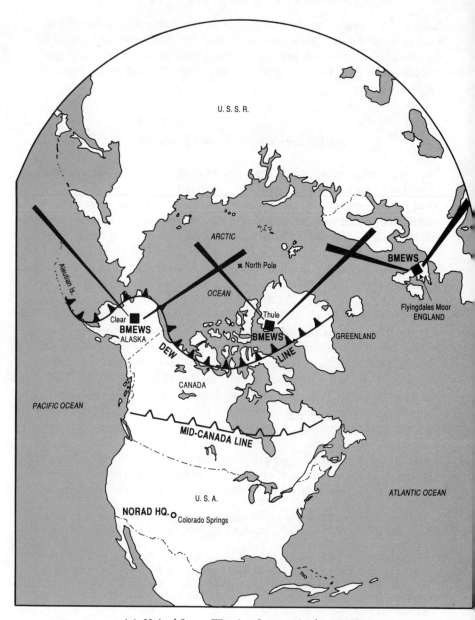

4.1 United States Warning Systems in the 1960s

into Soviet airspace.[22] SAC bomber and tanker crews practiced these "fail-safe" procedures in a number of mock exercises and in early 1958, two questions had to be answered: were such procedures safe enough to be put into operational practice and, and if so, who should have the authority to order such a bomber launch?

How were these decisions made? Previous analyses have simply assumed that the final outcome—the adoption of the fail-safe system in which CINCSAC was authorized to launch the bomber force under positive control rules—was a reasonable response to the problem of ambiguous warning.[23] This viewpoint may ultimately be correct, but a more detailed examination of the process by which the decision was made also highlights the degree to which the air force attempted to manipulate the information that was used by higher authorities to make decisions about the new fail-safe system.

In May 1958, General Thomas White, the chief of staff of the air force, attempted to withhold important information concerning a serious safety problem that had been discovered in the fail-safe system from civilian authorities. In response to a request from the deputy secretary of defense for an estimate of "probable Soviet reaction" to a positive control launch of SAC bomber force, a committee of war planning and intelligence officers working for the Joint Chiefs of Staff drafted the following note to be sent to Secretary of Defense Neil McElroy:

> We do not think there will be any Soviet reaction to the launching of the alert force under the "Positive Control" concept because it will not be detected as such. *For ten years we have been conducting exercises of similar nature and the only time we have ever had a Soviet reaction was when our airplanes inadvertently penetrated the Soviet early warning net.*[24]

General White objected to this note, however, and recommended instead that a much less alarming statement be given to McElroy:

> If the declaration of a Defense Emergency resulted from actual Soviet hostile action short of general war, obviously the Soviets already would be in a high state of war alert and readiness, and the launching of the SAC Alert Force

---

[22] This safety system was entirely dependent upon SAC crews following prescribed procedures, since there were no coded locking devices on the gravity bombs. The crews were not authorized, however, to activate the weapons' final mechanical arming switches until after the Go Code had been received. Atomic Energy Commission, Proposed Changes to Certain Weapons Safety Rules, AEC 25/153, August 12, 1961, FOIA.

[23] See, for example, the discussion of the creation of the "institutional system of checks and balances" in Bracken, *Command and Control of Nuclear Forces*, p. 22.

[24] Report by the Joint Strategic Plans Committee to the Joint Chiefs of Staff on "Positive Control" Presentation to the NSC, JCS 1899/402, May 1, 1958, pp. 2619–2620 (emphasis added), CCS 381—U.S. (May 23, 1946), (sec. 97), JCS 1958.

under the "Fail-Safe" concept would be anticipated by the USSR. . . . In periods of relatively low tension between the United States and the Sino-Soviet Bloc . . . as a precautionary measure the Soviet might launch their long-range bombers under a Soviet "Fail-Safe" concept. *However, the failure of SAC bombers to penetrate the Soviet outer radar screen would confirm to the Soviets in a short time, and before hostile U.S. intent could be concluded from other indications, that the SAC operation was not intended to initiate hostilities.*[25]

The chief of staff of the U.S. Army strongly opposed this effort to present civilian authorities with information suggesting that an accidental penetration of the USSR by SAC bombers had not occurred in the past and was not possible in the future. He insisted that White's proposed statement "cannot be supported by intelligence" and argued that the secretary of defense should instead be told that "it must be recognized that in certain circumstances the Soviets might initiate general war through miscalculation as a result of a 'Fail Safe' operation."[26] White tried again, however, and suggested that rather than directly reporting on previous inadvertent bomber penetrations of Soviet radar nets, a more ambiguous and comforting statement be sent to the McElroy:

> It should be noted that for over ten years SAC has conducted numerous large-scale alert exercises and maneuvers using numbers of aircraft and routes comparable to those to be employed in "Fail-Safe." *During this period there have been no indications that the Soviets have reacted to these exercises in a manner to heighten the danger to national security.*[27]

The details of the final debate within the meeting room of the Joint Chiefs are not known. It appears, however, that a General White backed down: the original committee statement, acknowledging that SAC planes had accidently crossed into Soviet warning zones during exercises in the past, was eventually approved and sent to the secretary of defense.[28] Civilian authorities approved of the decision to give positive control launch authority to the SAC commander, but only after they were reassured that the new SAC positive control system "guarantees this will not happen [again]."[29]

[25] Memorandum by the Chief of Staff, U.S. Air Force, for the JCS on Fail Safe Presentation to the NSC, CSAFM 136-58, May 6, 1958, pp. 1–2 (emphasis added).

[26] Army Flimsy, Fail-Safe Presentation to NSC, May 7, 1958, p. 1, CCS 381, U.S. (May 23, 1946), sec. 98, JCS 1958. There was no intelligence available suggesting that the Soviet bomber force had procedures similar to the fail-safe system in place. See Joint Chiefs of Staff, Decision on JCS 1899/402, enclosure C, CCS 381, U.S. (May 23, 1946), sec. 97, JCS 1958.

[27] Memorandum by the Chief of Staff, U.S. Air Force to the JCS on "Fail-Safe" Presentation to the NSC, CSAFM 141-58, May 9, 1958, p. 1 (emphasis added).

[28] Twining Memorandum for the Secretary of Defense, May 13, 1958, p. 1, CCS 381, U.S. (May 23, 1946), JCS 1958.

[29] *Ibid.*

## Creating the Airborne Alert

The third major change in SAC operations in the late 1950s was even more radical and was therefore even more controversial: placing nuclear-armed B-52 bombers on a constant airborne alert. In September 1958, SAC started to test its capability to maintain a small portion of the bomber force on continual airborne alert missions, through a special ninety-day SAC B-52 exercise called Head Start.[30] General Thomas Power, the SAC commander, immediately began to lobby civilian and military leaders in Washington for the authority and money to make this exercise mission a permanent peacetime operation. From SAC's perspective, there were at least four major arguments for instituting this new airborne alert plan. First, until the BMEWS system was fully operational, SAC bombers would be vulnerable on the ground, and airborne alert therefore offered a way of ensuring that at least some nuclear retaliatory capability would be available even under complete surprise attack conditions. This was the rationale most often presented in the public appeals on behalf of the airborne alert proposal. As Power testified to Congress: "I feel strongly that we must get on with this airborne alert to carry us over this period. We must impress Mr. Khrushchev that we have it, and that he cannot strike this country with impunity. I think the minute he thinks he can strike this country with impunity, we will 'get it' in the next 60 seconds."[31] Second, Power argued in classified documents that such an obvious show of military might would also enhance the general U.S. political position in the cold war: airborne alert would "serve to lower Soviet confidence and at the same time increase the confidence of the Free World in the military power backing its position."[32] Third, even if only a small-scale peacetime operation was approved, it could be quickly expanded to include a larger portion of SAC's force in any crisis with the Soviet Union. This expanded alert option was the operation that was later implemented during the Cuban missile crisis (see chapter 2). Fourth, the airborne bombers flying outside Soviet airspace would be closer to their targets and hence would give SAC a significant military advantage if war began. While the importance of this objective was usually only hinted at—for example, by using Head Start as the code

---

[30] J. C. Hopkins and Sheldon A. Goldberg, *The Development of the Strategic Air Command 1946–1986* (Omaha, Nebr.: HQ Strategic Air Command, 1986), p. 74. Also see Henry Narducci, *Strategic Air Command and the Alert Program* (Omaha, Neb.: HQ Strategic Air Command, 1988), pp. 5–7.

[31] *Department of Defense Appropriations for 1960*, Hearings before the Subcommittee of the Committee on Appropriations, House of Representatives, 86th Congress, 1st sess., part 2, p. 381.

[32] Memorandum, CINCSAC to JCS, June 23, 1960, Subject: Establishment of an Airborne Alert, CCS 3340 (June 23, 1960), JCS 1960.

name for the airborne alert operation[33]—it should not be surprising that a military commander would desire this wartime advantage.[34]

General Power vigorously campaigned for an airborne alert throughout 1959 and 1960, repeatedly testifying to Congress about its feasibility and desirability, which eventually provoked President Eisenhower to rebuke him publicly for his "parochial viewpoint."[35] Eisenhower was unwilling to grant Power's request for the authority and necessary appropriations to maintain about thirty B-52s on constant airborne alert, but eventually did approve a series of smaller-scale airborne alert indoctrination exercises as long as a set of specific operational safety and political requirements were met. B-52 flights during the exercises could "not approach or fly toward Soviet territory or the territory of Communist China."[36] One particular weapon—the B-28 thermonuclear gravity bomb, for which safety problems had been identified—could not be flown on the exercises "until present restrictions are modified or rescinded."[37] Ottawa's approval for any necessary overflights of Canada had to be obtained, and no publicity was to be given to the exercise. Finally, civilian oversight of the operation was to be strict: the secretary of defense had to be informed of any significant

[33] Down Field was another suggestive code-name used for a subsequent SAC airborne alert bomber exercise during this period. Higher authorities occasionally objected to the use of such nicknames and forced U.S. military commands to adopt less emotive terms for public relations purposes. For example, the name of the SAC low-level bomber training flight exercise program was changed form Oil Burner to Olive Branch and NORAD's 1960 Sky Burst exercise, which simulated a nuclear attack on the U.S., was renamed Sky Shield. See Dennis Casey and Bud Baker, *Fuel Aloft: A Brief History of Aerial Refueling* (March AFB, Calif.: 15th Air Force History Office, 1991), p. 34; Lindsay T. Peacock, *Strategic Air Command* (London: Arms and Armour Press, 1988), p. 73; and AF IN message 10592, February 11, 1960, CCS 5310, (December 24, 1959), JCS 1959.

[34] For a rare direct discussion of this wartime advantage of airborne alert operations, see Walt W. Rostow, Memorandum for the President, Subject: SAC Airborne Alert Program, May 21, 1966, National Security File, Memorandums for the President, W. W. Rostow, vol. 3, no. 38, LBJ Library.

[35] On February 3, 1960, Eisenhower responded to a press conference question on Power's call for an airborne alert as follows: "There are too many of these generals (that) have all sorts of ideas. . . . And I have been long enough in the military service that I assure you that I cannot be particularly disturbed because everybody with a parochial viewpoint all over the place comes along and takes (it) and says the bosses know nothing about it." As quoted in Claude Witze, "Can an Airborne Alert Prevent a Space-Age Pearl Harbor?" *Air Force* 43, no. 3 (March 1960): 35.

[36] Unless otherwise noted, all information in the paragraph is from the following document: Memorandum Deputy Secretary of Defense to the Chairman, JCS, Subject: Strategic Air Command Exercises, July 21, 1959, enclosure to JCS 2019/402, CCS 3340 (June 8, 1959), Sec. 1, JCS 1959.

[37] *Ibid.* This may have been a reference to the belated discovery that the Mark 28 weapon was not "one-point safe" in its original design. See Chuck Hansen, *U.S. Nuclear Weapons: The Secret History* (Arlington, Tex.: Aerofax, 1988), p. 151, and Steve Fetter, "Stockpile Confidence under a Nuclear Test Ban," *International Security* 12, no. 3 (Winter 1987/88): 137–138.

changes to flight routes used in the airborne alert and summaries of the ongoing exercises were to be included once a month in Eisenhower's personal briefing book.[38]

These so-called airborne alert indoctrination exercises permitted SAC to achieve most of its operational objectives. Although the number of aircraft involved in the operation (approximately twelve) was considerably smaller than CINCSAC's original request for thirty airborne bombers, the exercises were timed so that at least some B-52s were always airborne, and nuclear weapons were permitted to be carried on the flights, enabling these bombers to retaliate against the Soviet Union if a surprise attack on the U.S. occurred.[39] In January 1961, as the Kennedy administration came into office, SAC publicly announced that a regular peacetime airborne alert program was in place with armed B-52s in the air at all times.[40] In August 1961, the new secretary of defense, Robert McNamara, reviewed and officially approved the routes of the SAC airborne alert operation, now known as Chrome Dome: every day, a total of twelve B-52s, armed with thermonuclear gravity bombs, were launched on twenty-four-hour sorties along a Northern Route circumnavigating the North American continent, and along a Southern Route crossing the Atlantic to orbit over the Mediterranean Sea.[41] A new alert bomber was scheduled to be in the air prior to the landing of each B-52 terminating its mission.

General Power's intensive lobbying effort clearly had succeeded.[42] It is important to note, however, that there was ostensible agreement between CINCSAC and the air force chief of staff that airborne alert was an emer-

[38] The 1959 exercise approval memorandum only required that "any significant changes in flight routes" be "submitted to the Secretary of Defense for his information." Memorandum Deputy Secretary of Defense to the Chairman, JCS, Subject: Strategic Air Command Exercises, July 21, 1959. By 1960, however, civilian *approval* of significant changes in routes was apparently required. See Deputy Secretary of Defense Memorandum for the Chairman, JCS, April 13, 1960, Subject: Route Change for the 4134th Strategic Wing, Enclosure to JCS 2019/486, April 14, 1960, CCS 3340, (June 8, 1959), sec. 2, JCS 1959.

[39] See *Department of Defense Appropriations for 1960*, Hearings before the Subcommittee of the Committee on Appropriations, U.S. House of Representatives, 86th Congress, 1st sess., part 1, pp. 863–864.

[40] Hopkins and Goldberg, *Development of The Strategic Air Command*, p. 98.

[41] McNamara memorandum for the Secretary of the Air Force, August 10, 1961, and Burchinal memorandum for the Director of the Joint Staff, August 16, 1961, both in CCS 4615 (April 3, 1961) section 2, JCS 1961; and History of the 4170th Strategic Wing, 1-30 November 1962, K-WG-4170-HI, p. 26, AFHRC. Some of these routes were changed in 1962 when limited overflights of Canada were approved. See History of the 8th Air Force, July–December 1962, vol. 2, exhibit 49, K-520.01, AFHRC; and History of the 379th Bombardment Wing, April–June 1964, K-WG-379-HI, AFHRC, p. 13.

[42] Power later wrote, with apparent pride, that "my statements (on airborne alert) created considerable discussion and controversy, and the then Secretary of Defense, Thomas S. Gates, told me later that this matter caused him more trouble than anything else he had encountered during his tenure in office." Thomas S. Power, *Design for Survival* (New York: Coward-McCann, 1964), p. 162.

gency operation, a temporary necessity due to the lack of adequate missile warning available at the time. In February 1959, for example, Power informed Congress that "I do not want to keep an airborne alert from here on out into the future": "The minute any responsible person in this country says, 'I will guarantee you warning of this number of minutes,' I would drop the airborne alert and tailor it to a ground alert, because it is an easier way to live."[43] General White was in apparent agreement: "The actual airborne alert, of course, would be an interim measure that could be used, if necessary, until such time as we are assured of adequate warning against surprise ballistic missile attack."[44]

## REDUNDANCY AND THE THULE MONITOR

A potential command and control problem with the new system was, however, quickly identified: if communications between the Strategic Air Command and the BMEWS stations suddenly were cut off, it would be impossible for the SAC commander (CINCSAC) to know whether the NORAD communication systems had simply failed or whether a BMEWS radar had been destroyed in the first wave of a massive Soviet attack. This information was deemed vital, however, since a precursor attack on the BMEWS radar was considered to be a very likely contingency in a war. As General Power testified to Congress: "I like to tell the commander at Thule that he will probably be one of the first ones to go if we get into a war, but that there is one thing I would like to know from him, and that is when he went. This might be very vital intelligence."[45]

Contact with the Thule site was especially vulnerable to disruption. The communications between that BMEWS site and NORAD were maintained, when the radar began operating in September 1960, by a single 1,950 mile-long underwater cable from Greenland to Newfoundland, and from there by a commercial microwave radio-relay system transmitting across Canada and the United States to NORAD Headquarters in Colorado Springs. From Colorado Springs, the information would then be passed back to SAC Headquarters in Omaha, Nebraska.[46] This single

[43] *Department of Defense Appropriations for 1960*, Hearings before the Subcommittee of the Committee on Appropriations, House of Representatives, 86th Congress, 1st sess., part 2, p. 380.

[44] *Department of Defense Appropriations for 1962*, Hearings before the Subcommittee of the Committee on Appropriations, U.S. Senate, 87th Congress, 1st sess., p. 297.

[45] *Department of Defense Appropriations for 1960*, Hearings before the Subcommittee of the Committee on Appropriations, House of Representatives, 86th Congress, 1st sess., part 2, p. 373.

[46] ADC Historical Study no. 32, *History of BMEWs, 1957–1964* (extract declassified by HQ Air Force Space Command, July 1989), pp. 15–16.

communications link was not, moreover, very reliable. The submarine cable, running under North Atlantic fishing grounds, was particularly vulnerable to disruption through accidents or sabotage and, indeed, was severed at least twice during late 1961.[47] Reliance on this underwater cable for such critical communications was clearly undesirable.

To provide redundant communications and intelligence on whether the Thule BMEWS had been attacked or had only suffered a temporary communications blackout, the air force instituted three additional programs in 1961. First, in early 1961, Secretary McNamara, at the request of General Power, authorized the placement of primitive ground-based nuclear bomb alarm sensors—small signaling devices mounted on telephone poles near air bases, which were automatically triggered by the thermal flash of a nuclear explosion—at the Clear and Thule BMEWS radar sites.[48] The first of these bomb alarm sensors became operational in late 1961, and, by 1966, a complete system of ninety-nine sites was connected to a set of warning display consoles at the Pentagon's National Military Command Center (NMCC), SAC Headquarters, NORAD Headquarters, and a number of other critical U.S. command and control centers. This bomb alarm system was, unfortunately, totally dependent upon commercial telegraph and telephone lines.[49] Recognizing the possibility of cutoffs in communication, the system designers constructed the console display boards so that NORAD and most of the other command posts could differentiate between a nuclear blast report and a communications failure: a red light would flash if there was a nuclear detonation; a yellow light meant that communications had malfunctioned; and a green light signaled that the bomb alarms were working and reporting that no weapons had gone off in the area in question.[50]

The second program to increase the reliability of the warning system was the construction of an alternative communications route for the BMEWS

[47] Robert Kipp, Chief, Office of History, Air Force Space Command, letter to author, March 22, 1988.

[48] *Department of Defense Appropriations for 1962*, Hearings before the Subcommittee of the Committee on Appropriations, House of Representatives, 87th Congress, 1st sess., part 2, p. 969, and *Department of Defense Appropriations for 1961*, Hearings before the Subcommittee of the Committee on Appropriations, House of Representatives, 86th Congress, 2d sess., part 4, p. 363.

[49] Each detector was connected to a Western Union telegraph office and then, through Western Union, Bell telephone, and railroad communications to the command posts. See *Department of Defense Appropriations for 1974*, Hearings before a Subcommittee of the Committee of Appropriations, House of Representatives, 93rd Congress, 1st sess., part 7, p. 1057.

[50] The best declassified description of the bomb alarm system is C. E. Fritz, "Some Problems of Warning and Communication Revealed by the Northeast U.S. Power Failure of 9–10 November 1965," Institute for Defense Analyses Report R-142, April 1968, FOIA, pp. 27–29, 105–107.

radar reports. A high powered tropospheric-scatter facility (named Dew Drop) was built at Thule to bounce radio signals off the troposphere to a receiving station on Baffin Island. These communications would then be retransmitted via another tropospheric-scatter radio to Labrador, and again then sent by commercial circuits to Colorado Springs. This back-up route was fully operational in September 1961, a year after the Thule BMEWS and the main submarine cable network began operations.[51]

These two new redundant command and control systems, however, still had a number of flaws. Not only were critical parts of both systems dependent on commercial power and communications lines, but in addition, the BMEWS sites remained highly vulnerable to a conventional attack or sabotage. The electric power to the Thule radar, for example, was carried on above-ground poles from generators on nearby ships,[52] and a Soviet conventional attack or sabotage against the radar would not necessarily be recognized as such by the new network of nuclear detection devices and alternative communication systems. This was a serious concern for U.S. defense planners: Soviet BADGER bombers were estimated to be able to attack targets in Greenland and Alaska on two-way missions and U.S. military exercises explicitly postulated that Soviet sabotage attacks would be launched against U.S. bases in the Arctic.[53]

From the Strategic Air Command's perspective, it was also highly undesirable to rely upon *NORAD systems for the survivability of SAC's bomber force*. SAC wanted communications systems that were independent, not only in the technical sense of not having common-mode failures, but also in the bureaucratic sense of not belonging to another command organization. SAC officers responded to the challenge and creatively devised an alternative autonomous warning and communications system based on the existing airborne alert. In August 1961, the command therefore altered its airborne alert routes: the Northern bomber route was modified so that one of the B-52s on airborne alert missions over Greenland would become a BMEWS monitor, orbiting along a three-hundred-mile route above the Thule radar site until another replacement bomber took its place.[54] This airborne B-52 was to maintain hourly HF radio, radar, or visual contact with the Thule BMEWS site and, in the event that equipment failure caused a bomber sortie to be aborted or delayed, SAC orders stated that the Thule

51 *History of BMEWS, 1957–1964* (declassified extract), pp. 15–16.

52 Bracken, *Command and Control of Nuclear Forces*, p. 186.

53 See Robert McNamara, Draft Memorandum for the President, Subject: Recommended FY 1967–71 Strategic Offensive and Defensive Forces, November 1, 1965, p. 8, FOIA; and Trusted Agent Instructions for Exercise High Heels, CCS 3510 (May 3, 1961), JCS 1961.

54 DJSM-926-61, Memorandum for the Secretary of Defense, SAC Airborne Alert Indoctrination Program, August 8, 1961, CCS 4615 (April 3, 1961), JCS 1961. A map of the BMEWS monitor orbit in 1964 is in History of the 379th Bombardment Wing, April–June 1964, exhibit 17, K-WG-379-HI, AFHRC.

BMEWS would be monitored by the KC-135 (tanker) aircraft used to support the Chrome Dome mission.[55] With this operational innovation, the Strategic Air Command created its own twenty-four-hour-a-day warning system. In the event that the communications with Thule went dead, SAC Headquarters could contact the airborne B-52 through the special SAC Short Order radio network. The Thule monitor B-52 could then report directly to SAC on whether it had witnessed a nuclear detonation at the radar site, signaling that a major Soviet attack had begun, or whether the available information indicated that the Thule BMEWS had merely suffered a temporary communications blackout.

The existence of this special B-52 bomber mission was highly classified in 1961. Indeed, it is not known whether civilian authorities were fully cognizant of the program. It is important to note here that SAC viewed this change in the airborne alert system as only a "minor modification" of the previously approved program. The secretary of defense was simply informed of the new mission and route change in a routine manner; he did *not* need be asked to *approve* it.[56] As a result, there was no civilian review of the new monitor operation in the Pentagon and, in fact, it is not entirely certain that Secretary McNamara was even aware that a change in airborne alert routes had been implemented by the Strategic Air Command.[57]

### Scenarios and Reliability

For those in the know, this classified operation was therefore thought to be a very useful redundant safety measure. The new B-52 monitor operations was considered by SAC to provide an important backup means of clarifying what otherwise could be a highly ambiguous warning of attack. Combined with the other warning and communications systems connecting the Thule base to U.S. military commands, the monitor plane could enable SAC

[55] SAC DOOPOP/1630/14 May 1962, in SAC Historical Study 91, History of HQ SAC, January–June 1962, vol. 3, p. 2, K416.01-91, AFHRC and 8AF message, exhibit 50, History of the 8th Air Force, July–December 1962, vol. 2 (declassified June 19, 1990) K520.01, AFHRC.

[56] DJSM-926-61, Memorandum for the Secretary of Defense, SAC Airborne Alert Indoctrination Program, August 8, 1961, CCS 4615, (April 3, 1961), JCS 1961.

[57] The one paragraph memorandum informing McNamara of the "minor modification to Airborne Alert Routes" was dated August 8, 1961. McNamara's official approval of the FY 1962 alert program and routes was issued on August 10. It does not mention the Thule monitor mission and refers only to the memoranda and plans for the alert sent to him earlier for review. It is therefore possible that the August 8 memorandum on the Thule monitor mission was effectively ignored, since it may have arrived too late to have been relevant to McNamara's decisions on this matter. See Secretary of Defense Memorandum from the Secretary of the Air Force, August 10, 1961, CCS 4615 (April 3, 1961), sec. 2, JCS 1961.

officers to differentiate between a false warning and a real attack under what was believed to be all plausible contingencies.

A conservative military planner will attempt to anticipate every conceivable way in which his forces could be attacked, and the SAC and NORAD warning systems appeared to be an ingenious solution to the problem of how to distinguish real warning from false warning under any conceivable scenario. Table 4.1 displays how the redundant set of communications and warning systems was designed to work. Under normal peacetime circumstances, the bomber simply provided redundant confirmation that the BMEWS system was up and operating as planned (see scenario 1). The additional capability of the B-52 monitor aircraft provided the critical capability to distinguish between a communication failure and a Soviet conventional attack or sabotage at the Thule base (compare scenario 3 with scenario 4). A report from the B-52 that a mushroom cloud had appeared over Thule also could provide independent confirmation of any bomb alarm report of a nuclear attack on the base (see scenarios 2 and 6). This was considered to be a particularly important warning function, because the early BMEWS system had been designed to provide warning of a massive missile attack and did *not* have a reliable capability to pick up one or two Soviet ICBMs, had they been launched in a precursor surprise attack.[58] In addition, the U.S. Air Force had concerns in 1961 that the Soviet Union might utilize submarines with nuclear-armed ballistic missiles or cruise missiles or use ICBMs launched on a depressed trajectory in a surprise attack to avoid warning by the BMEWS system.[59] Another possible scenario was a Soviet conventional attack—utilizing, for example, long-range bombers, saboteurs, or submarines against the base at Thule and saboteurs against the Short Order radio transmitters or other communication links from the B-52 back to SAC headquarters—in an effort to blind U.S. warning systems just before launching a nuclear attack (see

[58] In 1960, Herbert York, the Pentagon's Director of Defense Research and Engineering, testified to Congress: "The BMEWS system is not very good against one missile ever, and especially in the early days of the system it is even less good against one than its ultimate capability. . . . Therefore, it is really best considered as a system for detecting a raid rather than one marauder." *Department of Defense Appropriations for 1961*, Hearings before the Subcommittee of the Committee on Appropriations, House of Representatives, 86th Congress, 2d sess., part 6, p. 38. According to air force testimony to Congress in 1960, "if they [the Soviets] were to shoot one or two, a small number, the research and development type of shooting or testing or what not, that might very well not trigger these things off. What we would really say would be these things [the BMEWS radars] will give us a sure indication of a big attack but not necessarily one or two." *Department of Defense Appropriations for 1961*, Hearings before the Subcommittee of the Committee on Appropriations, House of Representatives, 86th Congress, 2d sess., part 5, p. 612.

[59] See, for example, *Ibid.*, p. 607, and *Department of Defense Appropriations for 1961*, Hearings before the Subcommittee of the Committee on Appropriations, House of Representatives, 86th Congress, 2d sess., part 4, p. 365.

TABLE 4.1
The Thule Warning System: Failures and Attack Scenarios

| | |
|---|---|
| Scenario 1: Normal Peacetime | Scenario 5: Precursor Conventional Attack on Thule and B-52 Monitor |
| BMEWS: No missile attack | |
| Bomb alarm: Green, no detonation | BMEWS: Dead |
| B-52 monitor: Thule operating | Bomb alarm: Yellow, dead |
| | B-52 monitor: Dead |
| Scenario 2: Massive ICBM Attack | |
| BMEWS: Attack coming, dead[a] | Scenario 6: Surprise Nuclear Attack on Thule[c] |
| Bomb alarm: Red, detonation | |
| B-52 monitor: Thule attacked | BMEWS: Dead |
| | Bomb alarm: Red, detonation |
| Scenario 3: Communications Failure | B-52 monitor: Thule attacked |
| BMEWS: Dead | |
| Bomb alarm: Yellow, dead | Scenario 7: Surprise Barrage Attack on Thule Area |
| B-52 monitor: Thule operating | |
| | BMEWS: Dead |
| Scenario 4: Precursor Conventional Attack[b] on Thule | Bomb alarm: Red, detonation |
| | B-52 monitor: Dead |
| BMEWS: Dead | |
| Bomb alarm: Yellow, dead | |
| B-52 monitor: Thule attacked | |

Note: In each scenario the warning sensors work as designed.

[a] Dead means that all communications are cut off between the warning sensor and NORAD/sac.

[b] Conventional attacks could be by aircraft, submarines, or sabotage.

[c] A surprise attack, designed to destroy Thule without providing BMEWs warning, could use SLBMs, submarine launched cruise missiles, depressed trajectory ICBMs, or a small enough number of ICBMs that they might not be picked up by the BMEWs radar.

scenario 5).[60] In this case, the inability to contact the B-52 would provide confirming information on the attack. Finally, if the Soviet Union used a barrage attack of submarine-launched missiles and/or depressed trajectory ICBMs to blanket the area (see scenario 7), destroying both Thule and the B-52 monitor, the bomb alarm system would report the detonation and SAC's inability to contact the B-52 would provide an important confirmation that a major nuclear attack had indeed occurred at Thule.[61]

[60] As Joint Chiefs of Staff exercises demonstrate, U.S. war planners anticipated that Soviet sabotage attacks might be launched against U.S. bases in the arctic just prior to a major attack on the United States. See "Instructions for Exercise High Heels," CCS 3510 (May 3, 1961), Section 1C, JCS 1961.

[61] The B-52 monitor flew back and forth along a predetermined three-hundred-mile-long route passing over Thule. (See History of the 379th Bombardment Wing, April–June 1964, exhibit 17, K-WG-379-HI, AFHRC.) The number of weapons needed for a barrage attack against the base and the aircraft would depend critically on how much Soviet intelligence

## The November 1961 Incident

The utility of the new B-52 BMEWS monitor operation was demonstrated within three months after the flights were initiated. On the night of November 24, 1961, all of SAC's special communications links with the BMEWS radars and NORAD Headquarters suddenly went dead. The SAC duty officers in the Omaha command post attempted to contact NORAD by commercial phone circuits, but they too were not operating.[62] The bomb alarm devices, unfortunately, had not yet been installed at Thule, so they could be of absolutely no assistance to SAC.[63] General Power was immediately awakened by command post duty officers. "I could not take any chances," Power later recalled, since "there could be only one of two reasons for that [communications cutoff]—enemy action or a communications failure."[64] He therefore ordered an emergency alert to be sounded at SAC bases across the United States.

B-52 bomber crews rushed to their planes, started the engines, and taxied to the runways in preparation for a Positive Control Launch. Power specified that no bombers were to take off without further orders and, fortunately, within minutes he was able to establish contact with the B-52 that was orbiting on the airborne alert monitor route near Thule. This bomber's crew established radio contact with the BMEWS station and confirmed that no attack had taken place. Power therefore decided not to order the bombers into the air. According to all available accounts, the brief alert ended without further incidents. Twelve minutes after the BMEWS display lights went dead, Power ordered the bombers to taxi back to the peacetime positions and resume their regular alert posture.[65]

---

knew about the aircraft's location at the time of attack. If only the general route was known, for example, an attack of approximately fifteen to twenty SS-9 ICBMs would be necessary to have a high probability of destroying the aircraft. (This assumes a lethal radius of an SS-9 against an aircraft flying at thirty thousand feet was approximately nine miles. See Blair, *Strategic Command and Control*, pp. 160–161.) If a "base-watcher," a KGB or military intelligence operative in the Thule area, was able to report on when the B-52 passed overhead, however, a much smaller missile force could be used to barrage the base and the aircraft. This was *not* a remote possibility since the Soviet Union did use "base-watchers" to monitor the activities on U.S. Air Force installations and the B-52 above Thule was clearly visible from the ground. (See Stephen M. Meyer, "Soviet Nuclear Operations," in Carter et al., eds., *Managing Nuclear Operations*, p. 488, fn. 41; and "Eskimos Voice Concern," *New York Times*, January 25, 1968, p. 2.)

[62] Memorandum for Air Vice Marshal Lister, 24 November 1961, BMEWs Communications Incident, U.S. Air Force Space Command, FOIA.

[63] SAC Message 131727 November 68 to CSAF, SAC History FY 1969, vol. 10, exhibit 31, K416.01-116, AFHRC.

[64] Power, *Design for Survival*, p. 157.

[65] For accounts of the event see *Ibid.*, p. 157; "Suddenly, at 4:52 A.M.," *Newsweek*, April 16, 1962, pp. 27–28; Richard Fryklund, "Four Minute Nightmare," *The Sunday Star* (Washington, D.C.), April 1, 1962, p. 1; and Jerry T. Baulch, "Faulty Alert Never Reached Top

The cause of the communications problem was soon discovered. Although *redundant* telegraph and telephone communications links between SAC and NORAD (and therefore to the BMEWS system) had been established, they were not *independent*. Despite all assurances to the contrary, all of the lines between SAC and NORAD had been run through a single relay station near Colorado Springs. An overheated motor there had cut all communications to SAC. This serious design error in the national warning system was soon fixed to prevent similar incidents.[66]

The SAC B-52 monitor operation thus proved itself to be an important alternative source of information about the status of the Thule radar. In this sense, the B-52 mission appeared to be a highly successful operational innovation. Simply by altering its airborne B-52 routes, the Strategic Air Command believed it had significantly improved nuclear safety and reliability, adding an independent and redundant element to the national warning system.

## HIDDEN COMMON-MODE FAILURES

Normal accidents theory would lead one to suspect that because this additional communications system would increase the interactive complexity of the whole U.S. warning system, it might also inadvertently *reduce* its reliability. Did this happen? And if so, why did the U.S. maintain the airborne alert and the Thule B-52 monitor system for so long?

An examination of U.S. government's decision-making process concerning SAC's airborne alert operations during the mid-1960s provides a revealing glimpse into the politics involved in maintaining or changing military operations once they become part of the standard operations of a powerful organization. For almost seven years, a B-52 sortie was sent every day to orbit above Thule. No apparent problems occurred during these operations and there was therefore no apparent need to review the program. Indeed, in the absence of any obvious political or military reason to reexamine any aspect of the entire B-52 airborne alert operation, detailed civilian oversight was permitted to deteriorate, and the required annual presidential authorization for B-52 alert flights became *pro forma* over time.[67]

---

Command," *Washington Post*, April 4, 1962, p. A6. It is noteworthy that none of these accounts mentions that the B-52 involved in the incident was on a airborne alert mission specifically designed to provide warning in this particular contingency.

[66] Memorandum to Air Vice Marshal Lister, 24 November 1961, and "Suddenly, at 4:52 A.M.," p. 28.

[67] An interesting indication of this deterioration in civilian oversight can be seen in the way in which the airborne alert routes were reviewed. The 1966 Department of Defense memorandum to President Johnson requesting approval of the program did not bother to include a map

A debate about the need for airborne alert, however, did emerge inside the U.S. government in 1966. A serious bomber accident played a central role in this decision-making process. On January 17, 1966, a B-52 and a KC-135 tanker collided during an airborne alert refueling mission near Palomares, Spain. The bomber exploded in mid-air and four hydrogen bombs fell to the earth. Seven crew members were killed, the conventional explosive materials from two of the bombs went off on ground impact, spreading considerable radioactive material on Spanish soil. One hydrogen bomb was lost at sea for almost three months.[68]

Secretary of Defense McNamara had become convinced that SAC's airborne alert program was no longer necessary for U.S. national security, and in February 1966, taking advantage of the increased attention placed on nuclear weapons safety after the Palomares incident, he proposed the complete elimination of the airborne alert program. McNamara raised three major arguments in favor of ending the operation. First, the BMEWS system was now fully operational and had been improved with the addition of over-the-horizon radars. Bombers on ground alert at bases in the United States could therefore be launched with sufficient confidence so as to make airborne alerts unnecessary. Second, the U.S. bomber force was no longer as significant a part of U.S. retaliatory capability, as it had been in 1961: airborne bombers, he told Congress, "provide us only a small capability, and it has become particularly small in relation to our huge and growing missile force." Third, eliminating daily airborne alert operations could save over $123 million from the Pentagon budget.[69]

---

of the routes to be used, but instead simply noted that route charts had been previously submitted to President Kennedy in May 1962. SAC's operational routes had, however, changed significantly since May 1962, since the "round-robin" B-52 flights, circumventing the North American continent, were no longer in use. Fortuitously, the military adviser attached to the White House could not find the 1962 maps in the files, reported that they had apparently been sent to the archives, and requested that a new set be sent over from the Pentagon. The map sent more accurately reflected the airborne alert routes actually being used in 1966, but nevertheless failed to display accurately the BMEWs monitor operation (see figure 4.5). See: Cyrus Vance memorandum for the President, Strategic Air Command Airborne Alert Indoctrination Program for FY 1967, May 16, 1966; R. C. Bowman memorandum for Mr. Rostow, May 20, 1966; and attached map, all located in National Security Files, Memos to the President, Walt Rostow, vol. 7, box 8, LBJ Library. The 1962 "round-robin" route is described in History of the 4170th Strategic Wing, December 1–32, 1962., p. 23, K-WG-4170-HI, AFHRC.

[68] Department of Defense, *Narrative Summaries of Accidents involving U.S. Nuclear Weapons* (released May 15, 1981), p. 29. For more details see Flora Lewis, *One of Our H-bombs Is Missing* (New York: McGraw Hill, 1967), and John May, *The Greenpeace Book of the Nuclear Age* (New York: Pantheon, 1989), pp. 148–154.

[69] See *Department of Defense Appropriations for 1967*, Hearings before a Subcommittee of the Committee on Appropriations, House of Representatives, 89th Congress, 2d sess., p. 121, and the unsigned discussion memorandum entitled "B-52 Airborne Alert," dated November 11, 1965, National Security Files, Agency File, DOD, FY 1967 Budget Book, box 17, LBJ Library. The $123 million estimate comes from Walt Rostow, Memorandum for the

The Joint Chiefs of Staff and the Strategic Air Command strongly objected to the elimination of the program, however, and questioned McNamara's analysis. They argued that, at a minimum, a small number of daily B-52 flights was needed to provide SAC with realistic training exercises, and supporters of the airborne alert also informed President Lyndon Johnson, who maintained the authority to make the final decision, that the airborne alert flights would "put a certain number of aircraft closer to target with more accurate delivery capability than the missile force . . . (and would) also further reduce the possibility of a surprise disarming attack against the United States."[70] Eventually, a compromise between McNamara and the Joint Chiefs was reached, and SAC was authorized by the secretary of defense to continue only "whatever airborne alert was consistent with the regular (bomber crew) training program and would not require additional funds."[71] President Johnson then approved the curtailed program in June 1966, permitting SAC to maintain a significantly smaller force of only four nuclear-armed bombers on airborne alert each day.[72]

As part of this reduced alert training program, however, apparently *without the awareness of high-level civilian authorities*, the Strategic Air Command continued to maintain a nuclear-armed B-52 above the Thule radar despite the risk of an accident highlighted by the Palomares crash. The available evidence suggests that this was a decision made within the Strategic Air Command and that civilian officials in the Pentagon and White House were not considered to have the need to know about such operational details. All of the available documents concerning the decision to cut back on the size of the alert operation in 1966, for example, fail to mention the Thule monitor mission in any manner. An even more compelling piece of evidence is that Carl Walske, the assistant to the secretary of defense for atomic energy, who was directly responsible for the Pentagon review of nuclear safety after the Palomares accident, was reportedly never informed that a small number of the B-52s now permitted to continue on airborne alert "training missions" would be flying over Thule, armed with

President, Subject: Rationale for Reduction in Airborne Alert, June 8, 1966, National Security Files, Memos to the President, Walt Rostow, vol. 5, box 8, LBJ Library.

[70] Walt Rostow Memorandum from the President, Subject: SAC Airborne Alert Program for FY 1967, May 21, 1966, National Security Files, Memos to the President, Walt Rostow, vol. 3, box 7, no. 38, LBJ Library. Although the memorandum is from the national security adviser, this view accurately reflects the SAC and JCS position.

[71] *Department of Defense Appropriations for 1967*, Hearings before a Subcommittee of the Committee on Appropriations House of Representatives, 89th Congress, 2d sess., p. 121. Also see pp. 521–522.

[72] President Johnson was informed on June 8, 1966, that "the JCS were willing to cut the program from 12 to 6 B-52 airborne alert sorties per day. Secretary McNamara was calling to cut out the airborne alert completely now. Four sorties per day was the compromise." Walt Rostow, Memorandum for the President, June 8, 1966, National Security Files, Memos to the President, Walt Rostow, vol. 5, box 8, LBJ Library.

thermonuclear weapons, on a BMEWS monitor mission.[73] Although not all the evidence on the subject is available, it appears that senior civilian authorities in Washington were completely unaware of the Thule B-52 monitor mission in the late 1960s.

## The Thule Accident

On January 21, 1968, the bizarre bomber accident occurred. The B-52 was on a routine monitor mission when a fire broke out in the lower crew compartment. The pilot prepared for an emergency landing at Thule, but then ordered an immediate evacuation of the plane when dense smoke filled the cabin and all electrical power went out. There was no time for the B-52 or the Thule command post to contact SAC Headquarters before the evacuation of the plane.[74] The pilotless B-52 passed directly over the Thule base, turned 180 degrees, and then crashed into the ice approximately seven miles away (see figure 4.2).

The plane was carrying four B-28 thermonuclear gravity bombs when it crashed.[75] The conventional high explosive materials on all four weapons detonated on impact, spreading radioactive plutonium across the ice. There was, however, no nuclear explosion. The weapons had been designed so that they would not create a nuclear detonation when subjected to the pressure and heat of a crash. Fortunately, this important safety feature worked.

The accident at Thule caused a significant domestic political crisis in Denmark. Ironically, the crash occurred on the day before parliamentary elections, and the Social Democratic government there was severely embarrassed by the revelation that SAC was flying nuclear-armed aircraft above the Danish territory of Greenland.[76] The B-52 crash also raised wide-

[73] Carl Walske, interview with author, April 3, 1989. It is also worth noting that none of the declassified reports on the Thule accident given to President Johnson mention the monitor mission.

[74] The fire broke out when the B-52 was approximately eighty miles outside of Thule, and the pilot contacted Thule approach control to request emergency landing authority. Thule was able to pass on that information to the control towers at Sondrestrom and Goose Bay, but the actual crash of the B-52 was not immediately reported to Goose Bay. The existence of a problem with the B-52 was not passed on immediately, and the available evidence indicates that SAC Headquarters first learned of the whole incident *after* the crash from the Thule Deputy Base Commander. See Transcripts of Thule communications January 21, 1968, and "Altitude, Time, Distance and Profile" chart in USAF Incident/Accident Report File, January 25, 1968, FOIA and USAF Nuclear Safety, vol. 675, part 2, special edition on Project Crested Ice, FOIA. p. 13.

[75] USAF Incident/Accident Report File, Tab S, Weight and Balance Clearance Form, FOIA.

[76] See Alvin Shuster, "Danish Socialists Beaten in Election; Krag Will Resign," *New York Times*, January 24, 1968, p. 1.

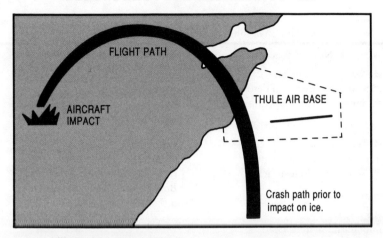

4.2  Thule Accident Map (USAF Nuclear Safety, [January–March 1970] vol. 65, part 2, p. 2, FOIA.)

spread fears about the environmental and health effects of the radiation dispersal, concerns that continued for over twenty years.[77] Yet, the most dangerous aspect of the incident—an increased risk of an accidental war through a false warning—was never discussed in either the newspaper accounts after the crash or in the classified Air Force postmortem reports. The following reexamination of the accident suggests, however, that there were at least three different ways in which the crash of the B-52 on the Thule monitor mission could have inadvertently produced confirmed, but false, warnings that a Soviet attack had been launched. These common-mode false warning scenarios are presented in table 4.2 below.

### Communication Failures

First, consider the possibility that the B-52 had crashed directly into the Thule communications center or had otherwise cut off all communication lines from the base back to NORAD Headquarters. The information provided to SAC and NORAD under this scenario would have been identical to the expected signals warning that a Soviet conventional attack or sabotage was taking place at Thule. (Compare scenario 8 with scenario 5 in table 4.2.) In this scenario, not only would the BMEWS blackout and the loss of the B-52 provide an ambiguous warning, but in addition, if all communications were cut off from Thule, the bomb alarm consoles at command posts in the United States, *if functioning properly*, would also display that information, confirming the possibility that a *conventional* attack had taken place at Thule.

[77] See May, *Greenpeace Book of the Nuclear Age*, pp. 162–168.

## TABLE 4.2
### The Thule Warning System: Common-Mode Failures

Scenario 1: Normal Peacetime

BMEWS: No missile attack
Bomb Alarm: Green, no detonation
B-52 monitor: Thule operating

Scenario 2: Massive ICBM Attack

BMEWS: Attack coming, Dead[a]
Bomb alarm: Red, detonation
B-52 monitor: Thule attacked

Scenario 3: Communications Failure

BMEWS: Dead
Bomb alarm: Yellow, dead
B-52 monitor: Thule operating

Scenario 4: Precursor Conventional
Attack[b] against Thule

BMEWS: Dead
Bomb alarm: Yellow, dead
B-52 monitor: Thule attacked

**Scenario 5: Precursor Conventional
Attack on Thule and B-52 Monitor**

**BMEWS: Dead**
**Bomb alarm: Yellow, dead**
**B-52 monitor: Dead**

Scenario 6: Surprise Nuclear
Attack on Thule[c]

BMEWS: Dead
Bomb alarm: Red, detonation
B-52 monitor: Thule attacked

*Scenario 7: Surprise Barrage
Attack on Thule Area*

*BMEWS: Dead*
*Bomb alarm: Red, detonation*
*B-52 monitor: Dead*

**Scenario 8: B-52 Crash with
Communication Cut-Off**

**BMEWS: Dead**
**Bomb alarm: Yellow, dead**
**B-52 monitor: Dead**

*Scenario 9: B-52 Crash with
Communication Cut-Off and
Faulty Bomb Alarm Report*

*BMEWS: Dead*
*Bomb alarm: Red, detonation*
*B-52 monitor: Dead*

*Scenario 10: B-52 Crash with
Nuclear Detonation*

*BMEWS: Dead*
*Bomb alarm: Red, detonation*
*B-52 monitor: Dead*

*Note:* In each scenario, except number 9, the warning sensors work as designed.
[a] Dead = all communications are cut off between warning sensor and NORAD/SAC.
[b] Conventional attacks could be by aircraft, submarines, or sabotage.
[c] A surprise attack, designed to destroy Thule without providing BMEWS warning, could use SLBMs, submarine launched cruise missiles, depressed trajectory ICBMs, or a small enough number of ICBMs that they might not be picked up by the BMEWS radar.

Second, it is also possible that the bomb alarm system might *not* function properly. (Compare scenario 9 with scenario 7 in table 4.2.) The bomb alarm system was not very reliable and, if communication with the sensors at Thule was cut off, it is possible that the system might report that a nuclear explosion had taken place.

This may appear to be a rather farfetched scenario, but in fact such serious failures did occasionally take place in the bomb alarm system. Indeed, such "false positive" reports had occurred less than three years before the Thule accident, during the November 1965 Northeast power failure. When commercial power went out throughout the Northeastern states, the bomb alarm display at the Office of Emergency Planning command center outside of Washington correctly reported that communications had been cut off from the bomb alarm sensors at Thule and twenty-one other sites. Unfortunately, it also reported that *nuclear weapons had just detonated* near Salt Lake City, Utah, and Charlotte, North Carolina. This mixture of yellow lights (communication failures) and red lights (nuclear detonations) was obviously alarming and the OEP Command Center went onto full alert during the power blackout. According to a declassified investigation, "it was not learned until several days after the power failure that the two reds (nuclear detonation reports) were false indications caused by a peculiarity in the circuitry of the particular Bomb Alarm Console."[78] Such a dramatic failure of the bomb alarm system was frightening enough when it occurred during the November 1965 blackout; it would have been far more alarming had it occurred as a result of a B-52 crash at Thule.

### Accidental Nuclear Detonations

Third, consider the worst case: what if the Thule B-52 accident had produced a nuclear detonation? If this had occurred, the crash would have created a *common-mode* failure of the U.S. warning system suggesting that a nuclear barrage attack on Thule had taken place. The bomb alarm system at Thule, *if it worked properly* in this scenario, would provide accurate indications that a nuclear weapon had detonated. Such a bomb alarm report was the expected first warning that a Soviet attack was under way. The communications blackout from the Thule BMEWS radar and the apparent hostile destruction of the B-52 monitor would then provide falsely "independent" confirmation that a barrage Soviet attack on the Thule area had occurred as a precursor to a strike on the United States. (Compare scenario 10 with scenario 7 in table 4.2.)

This is a particularly serious and frightening scenario. But, how likely was an accidental detonation during the Thule crash? A brief excursion into the highly classified subject of weapons design and safety procedures is necessary here. Unfortunately, insufficient information exists to produce an accurate quantitative estimate of the probability of a denotation of a B-28 bomb in circumstances such as the Thule accident. The following review of the available evidence about the weapons design features and

---

[78] Fritz, "Some Problems of Warning and Communication," p. 106.

procedural mechanisms used to prevent accidental detonations in the 1960s nevertheless points to several reasons for concern.

The B-28 bombs had been designed, tested, and certified at the time of deployment as "one-point safe." This means that the weapon's conventional high explosives and fissile core were carefully designed so the likelihood of even a low-yield nuclear detonation, caused by the accidental detonation of the conventional explosives at any one point in the system, was *believed* to be less than one in a million.[79] In addition, the weapon's electrical system and arming and fuzing mechanisms were *believed* at the time to have minimized the likelihood that "abnormal environments" (such as fire, explosions, bullets, or lightning) could accidentally trigger the electrical signals to detonate the bomb.

Neither of these beliefs, however, should be considered automatically valid. In retrospect, for example, it is by no means certain that one-point safety was accurately measured in the early 1960s. Moreover, even if this design goal was met, it would not necessarily prevent a nuclear detonation if, in an accident, the weapon's high explosives went off simultaneously at more than one point around the weapon's fissile core.[80] It is also important to recognize that significant improvements in the electrical fuzing and triggering systems of U.S. nuclear weapons occurred in the late 1970s, and the bombs that crashed at Thule would *not* meet the current standards for adequate safety.[81] One cannot therefore be completely confident with such older weapons that a nuclear detonation could not have occurred as the

[79] For valuable discussions of such nuclear weapons safety features, see Sidney D. Drell, John S. Foster, and Charles H. Townes, *Nuclear Weapons Safety*, Report of the Panel on Nuclear Weapons Safety, Committee on Armed Services, House of Representatives, 101st Congress, 2d sess.; Gerald W. Johnson, "Safety, Security, and Control of Nuclear Weapons," in Barry M. Blechman, ed., *Technology and the Limitation of International Conflict* (Washington, D.C.: School for Advanced International Studies, Foreign Policy Institute, 1989), pp. 137–150; Shaun Gregory, *The Hidden Costs of Deterrence* (London: Brassey's, 1990), pp. 14–20; and Donald R. Cotter, "Peacetime Operations," in Carter et al., eds., *Managing Nuclear Operations*, pp. 42–46.

[80] According to Sidney Drell: "It was a major conclusion of our study that 'unintended nuclear detonations present a greater risk than previously estimated for some of the warheads in the stockpile.' . . . We now appreciate—and underground tests have confirmed—how inadequate, and in some cases misleading, were the earlier two-dimensional calculations [of one-point safety]. For example, we were wrong in assumptions about the location of the most sensitive point in the weapon at which a one-point detonation of the high explosive could initiate a nuclear yield. We also know very little about the risk of multi-point insults—i.e. incidence of fragments nearly simultaneously—causing a nuclear detonation." Sidney D. Drell, Testimony on Nuclear Weapons Testing before the Defense Nuclear Facilities Panel of the House Armed Services Committee, March 31, 1992, p. 2.

[81] For example, the early B-28 bombs were not designed according to the modern "strong-link weak-link" principles and did not contain Mechanical Safe and Arm Devices (MSADs), which prevent accidental electrical charges from reaching the weapon's detonator. For descriptions of such systems see *Nuclear Weapons Safety*, pp. 25–26; and Aaron Latkin and

result of an unanticipated accident, such as the fuzing together of wires that could close the circuits of the bomb's electrical triggering mechanisms during a crash or fire. Concerns about these kinds of risks with B-28 bombs were in fact strong enough by the late 1970s, that the weapons were retro-fitted with new enhanced nuclear detonation safety systems, to reduce the likelihood of such an accidental detonation.[82]

One additional mechanical safety device existed. Thermonuclear gravity bombs also contained one or more "environmental sensing devices" (ESD). These are typically mechanical switches inside the weapon itself that are designed to close, completing the final firing circuit to detonator, only when subjected to the environmental forces produced by the planned method of delivery: for example, "close-to-zero gravity accelerations (that is, free fall), changes in barometric pressure, and deceleration caused by deployment of a parachute to slow the bomb's descent."[83] Such ESD devices made it much more difficult for a terrorist group to use any stolen nuclear weapon, as well as reducing the likelihood of a nuclear detonation if there was an accident on board a bomber.

Complete reliance on environmental sensing devices for nuclear safety, however, was obviously inadequate: they could be automatically activated in any accident—such as a deliberate or inadvertent jettisoning of a weapon, or any midair collision with a refueling tanker, or a structural failure of the aircraft—in which bombs were knocked free and fell to the earth. Because such accidents *did* occur, the system had to be designed so that additional *procedural* steps—bomber crew member actions to "pre-arm" the weapon—were also necessary to produce a detonation.[84] Two electrical switches—the "readiness switch" on the pilot's control panel and "inflight control" switch in the navigator's compartment—had to be turned to "prearm" the weapons on board (that is to close a number of the bombs' electrical circuits to permit an authorized detonation.)[85]

---

Peter Van Blarigan, "MSAD-A Unique High Energy Detonator," Proceedings of the Eighth International Pyrotechnics Seminar (Chicago: IIT Research Institute, 1982).

[82] *Energy and Water Development Appropriations for 1982*, Hearings before a Subcommittee of the Committee on Appropriations, 97th Congress, 1st sess., part 7, p. 179.

[83] Cotter, "Peacetime Operations," p. 43.

[84] A declassified 1973 Sandia National Laboratory report states that there were twenty-four incidents between 1950 and 1968 in which nuclear weapons were jettisoned or inadvertently released off U.S. military aircraft. See "Report on the Safety Criteria for Plutonium-Bearing Nuclear Weapons," Sandia National Laboratory, January 23, 1973, p. 6. I would like to thank Chuck Hansen for providing me with a copy of this document.

[85] This information is from: Joint Chiefs of Staff Memorandum for the Secretary of Defense, JCSM-539-62, July 23, 1962, Proposed Safety Rules for B-47, B-52/MK-28 FI Weapons Systems, p. 2, FOIA; Atomic Energy Commission AEC 25/125, April 4, 1961, Proposed Air Force Safety Rules, p. 5, FOIA; and Chief of Staff, Strategic Air Command, Memorandum on Congressional Inquiry, July 25, 1964, Subject: B-47 incident at Forbes Air

This step was considered dangerous, since if a bomber had an accident with "prearmed" nuclear bombs on board, the risk of a nuclear detonation would be significantly greater. The weapons were therefore to be "prearmed" only *after* the bomber crew had received emergency war orders (the Go Code) to attack the Soviet Union and even then, only when the bomber was about fifteen minutes away from entering enemy territory (the H-Hour Control Line).[86] A third crew member, the Electronic Warfare Officer, was then responsible for activating yet another device, the Special Weapons Manual Lock Handle, located in his area of the aircraft.[87] Each of these three devices were supposed to be wired in the proper position and have a safety seal placed over it.[88] Only after this complex set of actions was taken would the bombs be "prearmed" and ready for release. At that point, just one final step was necessary to deliver the weapon on target: crewmen had to turn a final "weapons release" switch.[89] The system appeared to be safe. Given the numerous actions that were required to arm and release a weapon, it was considered unimaginable that bomber crew members would inadvertently take all the steps, even in the confusion and tension of a smoke-filled bomber during a serious fire.

## The Dead Man's Switch

At first glance, this mixture of mechanical devices and procedural restraints may appear to be a foolproof system to prevent accidental nuclear detonations. Further investigation, however, suggests that three ways in which the system could have failed existed. Each of them would appear to be quite unlikely to occur. But were they significantly less likely than many of the other bizarre accidents, described earlier in this book, which actually did happen?

First, just as there was some risk of a fire or crash fusing the wires in the bomb's internal electrical system, there was also some danger that the circuits of more than one arming switch on the aircraft could be tripped

Force Base, in Joint Committee on Atomic Energy General Subject Files (classified series), JCAE 8085, box 1, Records of the Joint Committees of Congress, Record Group 128. I would like to thank Chuck Hansen for bringing this last document to my attention.

[86] Atomic Energy Commission, Proposed Changes to Certain Weapons Safety Rules, AEC 25/153, August 12, 1961, pp. 1–5, FOIA.

[87] JCSM-539–62, p. 13. This was called a "manual lock handle" since the crew member was required to pull on a handle on board the aircraft, but the final unlock and release mechanisms appear to have been electrical devices on the bomb rack. See Atomic Energy Commission, Proposed Changes to Certain Weapons Safety Rules, AEC 25/153, August 12, 1961, p. 13.

[88] JCSM-539-62, pp. 12–13.

[89] A number of such switches existed in various locations in the aircraft. *Ibid.*, p. 19.

through an electrical fire or other form of accident. Multiple shorts of this sort in aircraft electrical systems have occasionally caused accidents in commercial airlines. In September 1981, for example, a commercial plane in Iowa had an accident when a fire behind the coffee maker apparently fused a number of wires together, circumventing the existing circuit breakers. According to the National Transportation Safety Board's report in the accident: "Most of the pilot's instruments failed; the pilot's instrument lights went out; the computer for the left engine fuel control became inoperative; and control of several other systems was lost."[90] Although insufficient evidence is available to assess the likelihood of such a bizarre accident with a B-52's electrical arming system, there is little reason to expect that military aircraft are *totally* immune to the problem.

Even if a serious fire inadvertently armed the weapons on board, wouldn't the environmental sensing devices prevent an accidental detonation? In most accidents, the answer would be yes. If, in a fire, the bombs on board were both armed *and dropped*, however, the environmental sensing devices would permit a detonation. Unfortunately, this seemingly bizarre scenario was not as unlikely as it first appears.

To understand why, one has to recognize that preventing accidents under all conceivable peacetime circumstances was *not* the Strategic Air Command's only objective. SAC also had to ensure that the weapons would go off under all conceivable wartime circumstances. What if hostile fire from a Soviet interceptor aircraft or surface-to-air missile killed the crew? Under such circumstances, the crew would not be able to turn the final set of switches necessary to drop the bombs on board. The B-52's "Special Weapons Emergency Separation System" (SWESS) was designed to solve the problem.

SWESS, a highly classified program in the 1960s, was called the Dead Man's Switch by SAC bomber crews. According to Joint Chiefs of Staff documents that were declassified at the author's request, the SWESS system on B-52 bombers provided "a means for *an automatic release of prearmed weapons over enemy territory* in the event the aircraft and/or crew becomes incapacitated during a combat mission."[91] The system worked as follows. Once the Go Code was received and the nuclear weapons on board were prearmed and readied for release (according to the procedures outlined above), then the bomber crew was supposed to turn two electrical

[90] National Transportation Safety Board, Safety Recommendation A-81-93, August 26, 1981. Also see Perrow, *Normal Accidents*, pp. 134–135.

[91] JCSM-539-62, p. 14 (emphasis added). Also see Atomic Energy Commission, Proposed Safety Rules for B-47 and B-52 Aircraft, AEC 25/110, August 1, 1962, FOIA, p. 5. These safety rules were still in effect in 1968, which indicates that the SWESS system was still used at the time of the Thule crash. Roger M. Anders (Department of Energy historian), letter to author, November 10, 1992.

SWESS switches on both the pilot and navigator control panels to their "armed" position. After the SWESS was armed, if the bomber crew was disabled by a Soviet surface-to-air missile during an attack, the SWESS system would automatically release the bombs on board "if the aircraft falls below a preset altitude of *[deleted]* feet."[92] Under such conditions, the environmental sensing devices would then trigger a detonation. The B-52s nuclear bombs would thus not be "wasted" even though the bomber crew had been killed in action.[93]

This Special Weapons Emergency Separation System was, in essence, a *deliberately* built-in way to get around the final bomb release mechanisms that required the activities of crew members. The existence of SWESS therefore points to a particularly ironic possibility. Had a fire on board the Thule monitor B-52 accidently closed the electrical circuits prearming the weapons *and* activating the SWESS during the 1968 accident, the gravity bombs on board would have been dropped and detonated, as the pilotless plane drifted over the Thule base. Once again, inadequate information is available on the design of the electrical systems of B-52s to provide an estimate of how unlikely such a bizarre scenario really was during airborne alerts in the 1960s.

### Accidents and Unauthorized Actions

Second, it is also possible that a nuclear weapon that had been accidentally armed in a fire on board a B-52 could then be accidently dropped or inadvertently jettisoned. Nuclear bombs have been inadvertently dropped in at least four SAC bomber accidents. In two earlier airborne B-52 accidents—the midair breakup of a bomber near Goldsboro, North Carolina (January 1961), and a collision with a tanker near Palomares, Spain (January 1966)—the nuclear bombs on board were knocked loose, though fortunately, they were not armed at the time.[94] Inadvertent jettison-

---

[92] Atomic Energy Commission Proposed Safety Rules for B-47 and B-52 Aircraft, AEC 25/110, August 1, 1962, FOIA, p. 5. To prevent premature release of the B-52's bombs, "the SWESS is operated only on a high-level strike mission," p. 18.

[93] The existence of SWESS clearly had profound effects on the ability to discriminate between military and urban targets in the U.S. war plan, though it is not clear that the issue was recognized by U.S. civilian authorities at the time. SWESS was, in some ways, similar to the widely discussed idea in the 1980s of using "salvage-fusing" in U.S. ICBM warheads as a way of overcoming Soviet ballistic missile defenses. Salvage-fusing was a potential counter-measure technique by which the nuclear warhead would automatically detonate when it was hit by a defensive interceptor. See *Ballistic Missile Defense Technologies*, Office of Technology Assessment, 1985, pp. 171, 325.

[94] Department of Defense Narrative Summary of Accidents Involving U.S. Nuclear Weapons 1950–1980, pp. 21, 29.

ing of weapons also occurred at least twice in other SAC bombers: in March 1958, a B-47 "accidentally jettisoned" an unarmed nuclear weapon "because of a malfunction of the plane's bomb lock system" 6.5 miles east of Florence, South Carolina; and in May 1957, a B-36 bomber was descending for a landing at Kirtland Air Force Base (near Albuquerque, New Mexico) when the "the weapon dropped from the bomb bay taking the bomb bay doors with it."[95] Given the existence of these accidents, one cannot maintain that it was impossible for a similar phenomenon to have occurred over Thule.

Third, at least some risk existed that a bomber crew member could arm the weapons through deliberate, though unauthorized, actions. If a B-52 crashed or broke up in the air with *armed* weapons on board, the likelihood of a detonation would be extremely high. The possibility that a SAC officer might deliberately try to arm the nuclear weapons on board a bomber, however, would seem almost impossible, were it not for the fact that such an incident actually happened. In January 1963, a B-47 bomber crew on ground alert at Forbes Air Force Base in Kansas sounded a Seven High (suspected sabotage) alarm: someone had broken the seals, removed the safety wires, and turned on *both* the navigator's control switch and the pilot's readiness switch. According to a report of the subsequent investigation, the pilot broke down under pressure:

[He] voluntarily interrupted an OSI [Office of Special Investigations] interview of the navigator and stated he wished "to make a clean breast of it." In a signed sworn statement he admitted moving the navigator's switch while "tampering" with it. He then panicked, realizing that a "Seven High" must be reported. In order "to make it appear more of a Seven High," he then moved the switch in the pilot's compartment, and reported a suspected act of sabotage.[96]

It is likely that this serious a violation of discipline and safety in the Strategic Air Command was an extraordinarily rare event. It must be stressed, however, that very little information has been released on the safety record of SAC crews in this regard. We simply do not know precisely how unusual the kind of bizarre behavior exhibited by the pilot at Forbes Air Force Base really was.

[95] "Previous Atom Accidents," *New York Times*, January 23, 1968, p. 12, and Department of Defense Narrative Summary of Accidents Involving U.S. Nuclear Weapons 1950–1980, pp. 13, 8.

[96] Chief of Staff, Strategic Air Command, Memorandum on Congressional Inquiry, July 25, 1964, Subject: B-47 incident at Forbes Air Force Base, p. 1, in Joint Committee on Atomic Energy General Subject Files (classified series), JCAE 8085, box 1, Records of the Joint Committees of Congress, Record Group 128.

*Fear and Security*

In conclusion, none of the accidental detonation scenarios outlined above should be considered likely. Yet none of them should be considered impossible. Moreover, officers at SAC seem to have been aware of the dangers, which is exactly why so much care had been put into the design of the weapon's arming and release system. In the light of what is known now, General Hunziker's confident statement after the Thule accident—"There was, of course, no nuclear explosion since the design of the weapons precluded any nuclear reaction"[97]—may be seen as something other than simply good public relations. From the perspective of normal accidents theory, this appears more like a man whistling past the graveyard.

## WARNING AND RESPONSE

How dangerous would a common-mode false warning have been if it had occurred because of a BMEWS monitor bomber accident? It is impossible, fortunately, to know with certainty how key personnel at NORAD, SAC, or in Washington would have perceived and reacted to such an event. As is the case with most counterfactuals, reasonable people can easily disagree over the probability of various outcomes.

Despite the inevitable uncertainties involved, it is important that the potential dangers of such false warnings neither be exaggerated nor ignored. On the one hand, if one of the common-mode failures had occurred in peacetime, in my view, it is improbable that decision makers would issue immediate orders to retaliate despite receiving a strong set of indicators of a Soviet attack. Under routine peacetime conditions, civilian and military authorities alike would likely be skeptical since they would not be anticipating an attack and because other U.S. radar warning systems would, *if working properly*, be reporting that no hostile Soviet military action was imminent or under way elsewhere.[98]

On the other hand, there are a number of reasons to believe that the probability of a rash reaction to a false report that Thule had been attacked was not negligible in the late 1960s. Consider the following possibilities. First, what if one of these false warning scenarios had occurred in the middle of a military crisis? Under such conditions, the risk of a precipitous

[97] Richard O. Hunziker, "Foreword," to *Project Crested Ice*, p. 1.

[98] The United States did not have an operational early warning satellite system to provide accurate and redundant warning of Soviet missile launches when the Thule B-52 crash occurred in 1968. The infrared satellite early warning system started initial operational capability in 1971. See Toomay, "Warning and Assessment Sensors," p. 311, and Blair, *Strategic Command and Control*, p. 141.

American response would be significantly magnified. Not only would political and military officials be less skeptical about the possibility of an attack, but other sensors might also be reporting that Soviet alerting preparations for war had begun. Civilian and military authorities' inherent skepticism about a surprise bolt out of the blue might then be overcome by the shock of what would incorrectly appear to be redundant and independent warnings that an attack had begun.

Second, what if the immediate U.S. military reactions to this accident produced another accident or incident? The structure of the military alert system means that nuclear command and control accidents are not fully independent of one another: one accident or false warning incident can lead to a second one, thus falsely confirming that an attack has begun. For example, if a SAC Positive Control Launch was ordered because of a mysterious detonation at Thule, the risk of a subsequent bomber crash and an accidental detonation on a SAC base would increase. Similarly, if NORAD issued a Defense Emergency alert declaration, other U.S. military commands would immediately alert their forces, and many peacetime safety precautions would no longer be followed, again increasing the risk of a subsequent accident.[99] The history of other false warning incidents suggests that the probability of some sort of military reaction to a Thule accident, under the false warning scenarios outlined above, would be extremely high. Recall the November 1961 incident in which General Power claimed to have come "close" to launching the bombers when communications with NORAD were cut off.[100] With the various types of additional warning information available in these scenarios—apparent confirmations that Thule had been destroyed and that the B-52 monitor was not functioning—the likelihood of a fail-safe bomber launch would have been much higher.

Information from declassified U.S. military exercises from this period further reenforces these concerns. For example, during Exercise Green Rock, held in July 1961, senior military and civilian authorities simulated a crisis starting in the Middle East and terminating when U.S. nuclear "retaliation" was to be ordered based upon military reports that two nuclear detonations had occurred (one on Okinawa and one in the vicinity of New York) and that a BMEWS warning of missile attacks had been issued.[101]

---

[99] The safety rules governing U.S. nuclear weapons operations in the 1960s contained an exclusion clause, which stated that "these safety rules are mandatory for use until a Defense Emergency or comparable state of readiness is declared by the commander of a designated or specified command." JCS 1899/667, August 17, 1961, "SAC Reaction to BMEWs Alarm," p. 4205, CCS 6820 (March 18, 1961), JCS 1961.

[100] Power, *Design for Survival*, p. 156.

[101] Exercise Green Rock, Situation Background, July 27, 1961, CCS 3510 (May 16, 1961), section 2, JCS 1961.

Although actions in such an exercise or simulation may not accurately reflect how individuals and organizations would respond in similar real world conditions, the psychological biases and mental shortcuts inherent in human and organizational decision-making would encourage such repetitive behavior. All individuals have cognitive limitations that force them to assimilate new information within the context of their previous expectations.[102] In this particular case, since SAC and NORAD had not recognized the potential for a common-mode failure in the complex warning system at Thule, warning and control officers at the two commands were trained to expect that disruptions in communications and nuclear detonation reports would signal that a Soviet attack on the United States was under way. After having experienced numerous simulated Soviet attacks in U.S. military exercises, it would have taken an officer of exceptional flexibility and imagination to recognize one of the scenarios listed above as a false warning. Similarly, since the commands' alerting procedures were also based on the same standard scenarios as the exercises, there would be a natural organizational proclivity to repeat the operations practiced in such exercises.

### Misleading Maps and Blueprints

One final, and perhaps most disturbing, piece of evidence can be brought to bear on this question. What would senior authorities in Washington think if they were informed that a Soviet nuclear attack on Thule had just occurred? Could they have recognized that a U.S. bomber accident was the cause? Unfortunately, if there was an inaccurate emergency report that Thule had just been attacked, it would have been extremely difficult for senior civilian authorities to guess what had really happened there, given their lack of awareness of the details of the airborne alert operation.

It is very revealing to note here that the specific map of the airborne alert routes, which had been forwarded to and approved by President Johnson in May 1966 (see figure 4.3) did *not* show the Thule BMEWS monitor mission route over the base.[103] Just as the safety engineers investigating the

---

[102] On the variety of cognitive biases that influence human judgment, see Daniel Kahneman, Paul Slovic, and Amos Tversky, eds., *Judgment under Uncertainty: Heuristics and Biases* (Cambridge, U.K.: Cambridge University Press, 1982). For an important application of these ideas to crisis decision-making see Robert Jervis, "Psychological Aspects of Crisis Stability," in Jervis, *The Meaning of the Nuclear Revolution* (Ithaca, N.Y.: Cornell University Press, 1989), pp. 136–173.

[103] Insufficient declassified information exists to provide a definitive explanation for why the Thule Monitor mission did not appear in both this officially approved map and in the list of SAC alert route assignments attached to the map. The most likely possibility is as follows. There is some evidence suggesting that after the January 1966 Palomares accident, SAC may

Fermi reactor accident in 1966 could not identify the broken safety device because it had never been added to the "as is" blueprints of the plant, the misleading White House airborne alert map would have given officials there no clue that there had been a SAC nuclear-armed B-52 flying directly above the radar. Had any of the common-mode failures described above occurred at this time, it would therefore have taken an extraordinary amount of imagination to have figured out that the real cause was a U.S. bomber accident, not a Soviet attack. The Thule monitor aircraft thus added redundancy, but it also inadvertently made the national warning system more complex and opaque.

## Reactions to the Accident

Robert McNamara's immediate reaction to the Thule accident was to order SAC to terminate its policy of carrying nuclear weapons aboard the airborne alert bombers. McNamara was in his final days in office and was no longer willing to make further compromises with the JCS and SAC concerning this issue. Within a day, nuclear weapons were taken off all the B-52s on airborne alert, although SAC continued to fly the missions with unarmed bombers.[104]

As discussed earlier, McNamara had wanted to cancel the entire airborne alert program in 1966 and, unfortunately, no declassified documentary evidence exists on why he permitted the airborne alert to continue even without nuclear weapons on board after the second B-52 crash within two years. It is worth noting, however, that in highly politicized debates over military policy, gaining supporters for your arguments can sometimes damage your case. In this instance, the Soviet reaction to the Thule accident—issuing an official protest claiming that the growth of ballistic missile arsenals had made such hazardous flights "senseless"—appears to

---

have temporarily used KC-135 tanker aircraft, instead of B-52 bombers, for the BMEWS monitor mission, as it later did after the Thule crash. If this was the case, SAC would not have felt obligated to show the Thule monitor mission on the B-52 airborne alert maps sent to the White House for approval in May 1966. B-52s were placed back onto the Thule monitor mission in October 1966. (See SAC message 091803Z September 66, in History of the Second Air Force, July–December 1966, vol. 1, supporting document 81, K.432.01, AFHRC.) A new map showing the resulting change in airborne alert bomber routes, however, was apparently not submitted to the White House that year. The maps that accompanied the next year's annual request for White House approval of SAC's airborne alert have not yet been declassified. (See LBJ Library Mandatory Review Submission List, case number 92-263.)

[104] Memorandum for The Record, January 24, 1968, Marshall B. Garth, Deputy Director for Operations, National Military Command Center, Mandatory declassification review No. 88-108, LBJ Library, and John W. Finney, "U.S. Bars H-Bombs in Airborne Alert," New York Times, February 29, 1968, p. 1.

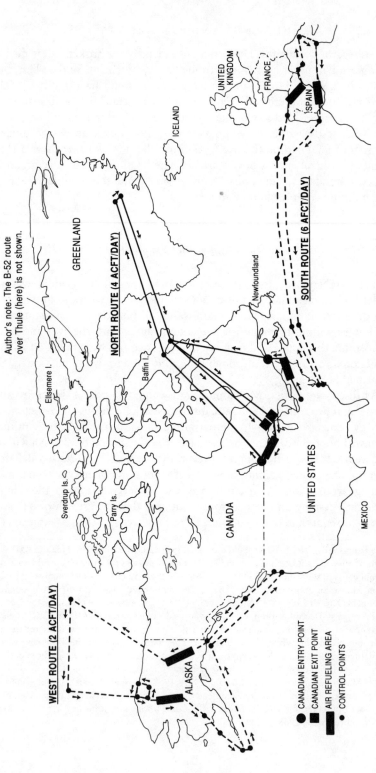

4.3 The White House Airborne Alert Map (Cyrus Vance, memo to the president, May 16, 1966. National Security Files, Memos to the President, Walt Rostow, vol. 7, box 8, LBJ Library.)

have contributed to a hesitation in the office of the secretary of defense to terminate the program immediately. In a public response to the Soviet protest, the State Department entered the debate, claiming that "world tensions make necessary" a continued B-52 airborne alert "against the threat posed by Soviet nuclear forces."[105] According to a contemporary press report, "some high-ranking officials in the Pentagon were privately inclined to concur with the substantive arguments the Soviet note made": "although there is considerable sentiment within the Pentagon for canceling the flights, there is also some reluctance to take the step at this time and thus seem to acquiesce in a Soviet suggestion." Moreover, the Air Force and SAC protested the decision to take nuclear weapons off the flights, arguing that the value of "such training is greatly degraded by the lack of realism."[106] Given these conflicting forces, it is not surprising that instead of immediately canceling the operation, a decision was made to conduct a Pentagon study to determine whether airborne alert operations were still necessary.

The peacetime B-52 airborne alert was finally terminated in July 1968 and was replaced by a plan called SEAGA (for Selective Employment of Air and Ground Alert), whereby bombers kept on day-to-day runway alert could be placed on airborne alert immediately in a crisis.[107] Although the full range of studies and analyses that produced these changes are not declassified, a number of internal SAC documents pertaining to the issue are available. They provide further insights into the organizational processes and politics involved in the decision.

SAC was highly reluctant to end either the airborne alert or the specific Thule monitor operation despite the B-52 accident. General Joseph Nazzaro, the SAC commander, therefore continued to argue through April 1968 that flying nuclear weapons on airborne alert training flights was necessary both as a deterrent to the Soviet Union and as a means of "giving the B-52 crews training under combat conditions with real nuclear weapons."[108] This rationale was no longer compelling to civilian authorities after having experienced the diplomatic repercussions of two B-52

---

[105] Quoted in Finney, "U.S. Reviews Need for H-Bomb Alert," p. 6.

[106] *Ibid*; Finney, "U.S. Bars H-Bombs in Airborne Alert," p. 12.

[107] *Authorization for Military Procurement, Research and Development, Fiscal Year 1970, and Reserve Strength*, Hearings before the Committee on Armed Services, U.S. Senate, 91st Congress, 1st sess., part 1, p. 928. Also see Narducci, *Strategic Air Command and the Alert Program*, p. 6.

[108] Dudman, "B-52 H-Bomb Flights Expected," p. 1. After the Thule accident, flying B-52s with nuclear weapons onboard was politically controversial. Nazzaro artfully dodged the question of whether SEAGA airborne alert aircraft would be armed with nuclear weapons in congressional testimony. See *Status of U.S. Strategic Power*, Hearings before the Preparedness Investigative Subcommittee, Senate Armed Services Committee, 90th Congress, 2d sess., p. 237.

accidents over allied nations' territory within two years.[109] SAC therefore had to settle for maintaining the SEAGA plan to reinstate an airborne alert in a future crisis if the JCS or civilian leaders ordered them to do so.

The termination of the B-52 monitor mission apparently was a more autonomous decision. Although the command could no longer fly missions with nuclear weapons on board after Thule, it nonetheless continued to maintain *unarmed* B-52s above Thule until May 1968.[110] At that date, SAC substituted a continuous orbit of a KC-135 tanker aircraft over the BMEWS site at Clear, Alaska, for the B-52 Thule monitor mission.[111] This new peacetime BMEWS monitor mission was finally terminated in December 1968, almost a year after the Thule bomber crash.[112]

Why was the BMEWS monitor operation finally canceled? Five important points are worth mentioning. First, despite SAC's continual insistence throughout the mid-1960s that airborne alert was needed because warning of a Soviet attack was not assured, the command's *internal* analysis of the BMEWS monitor mission argued after the Thule accident that, on the contrary, such warning was likely. In November 1968, for example, the SAC commander explicitly noted that "circumstances have changed considerably since we first instituted the monitor mission in 1961:"

> At that time, there was only one BMEWS site (Thule), there was no bomb alarm at the site, and a confidence factor for the rearward communications to the CONUS had yet to be determined. . . . Today, with three BMEWS Sites fully operational, with multiple well-tested lines of communication from each site, (and) the bomb alarm installed at Thule and Clear and the 440L system, (the) need for constant surveillance of a single BMEWS site is less critical. For this reason, and in consideration of the other heavy commitments being levied against the KC-135 fleet and crewforce, I intend to discontinue the full time airborne BMEWS monitor.[113]

Second, it is likely that an alternative mission for the force—the "other heavy commitments" is a reference to SAC involvement in the war in

---

[109] Civilian officials grew increasingly exasperated with the Strategic Air Command after these accidents. For example, in one press report, an unidentified civilian official "recalls that Ambassador Angier Biddle Duke found it necessary to go for a swim in the ocean at Palomares to assure the Spaniards that there was no danger and says, 'Next time we ought to make the whole SAC command go swimming.'" Dudman, "B-52 H-bomb Flights Expected," p. 10.

[110] Message SAC to AIG 667/DO/DM, March 27, 1968, in SAC Historical Study 112, January–June 1968, vol.8, exhibit 2, AFHRC.

[111] *Ibid.*

[112] Message CINCSAC to CSAF, November, 12, 1968, in SAC History FY 1969, vol. 10, Exhibit 31, K416.01-116, AFHRC.

[113] *Ibid.*

Vietnam in 1968—made it easier for the organization to accept the termination of the BMEWS monitor mission.[114] This "consideration" by CINCSAC may be viewed simply as a competing requirement, and a more important one in terms of national security, for the use of his limited military forces. Given that the monitor mission only required the use of five SAC tanker aircraft, however, this explicit reference to the forces' "other heavy commitments" may be better seen as part of an organization's reluctant rationalization for ending the BMEWS monitor flights.[115]

Third, it is noteworthy that SAC did not acknowledge, even in its internal records, that the Thule accident had been a major instigating force behind the policy review leading to the cancellation of the monitor operation. Instead, its memorandum for the record on the issue simply stated that "changes in the Soviet ICBM threat" had prompted a review of the need to continue the mission.[116] Given the timing of this review, coming immediately after the Thule accident, this purely "strategic" explanation for its existence is extremely unlikely.

Fourth, although the available documents do not address the fact that nuclear weapons were no longer permitted on the monitor flights, this restriction would have severely diminished the attractiveness of the BMEWS B-52 monitor mission from SAC's perspective. The Strategic Air Command's central mission is to deter aggression by being able to destroy the large array of targets inside the Soviet Union that are identified as requirements in the Single Integrated Operations Plan (SIOP). Having those four thermonuclear weapons on a bomber orbiting above Thule added a few extra points to the damage expectancy charts of SAC war plan. SAC's termination of the alternative KC-135 tanker monitor program within seven months of its initiation is a sign of the degree to which even this marginal increase in SIOP effectiveness produced by the Thule bomber monitor was considered important in Omaha.

Fifth, and finally, it is important to recognize that the suspension of peacetime BMEWS monitor missions in December 1968 did *not* eliminate the possibility of another common-mode failure accident occurring at a BMEWS site in a future crisis. In fact, the risk of similar problems continued under the SAC airborne alert system: KC-135 BMEWS monitor flights were scheduled over the Clear and Thule radars at higher DEFCON alert

---

[114] The SAC official history makes a similar point with respect to the termination of airborne alert: "The advent of a responsive and survivable ICBM force *permitted the bombers to perform more time sensitive duties.*" Narducci, *Strategic Air Command and the Alert Program*, p. 16 (emphasis added).

[115] Message SAC to AIG 667/DO/DM, March 27, 1968, in SAC Historical Study 112, January–June 1968, vol.8, exhibit 2, AFHRC.

[116] Memorandum for the Record, Subject: BMEWS Monitor Procedure Briefing, April 1, 1968, in History of SAC, January–June 1968, vol. 8, exhibit 1, AFHRC.

levels[117]; and nuclear-armed B-52s would have been flying above Thule if the new SEAGA airborne alert was ordered into operation by the JCS or civilian authorities in a crisis.[118] There is no firm evidence in the available records on the degree to which civilian authorities in the Pentagon or White House reviewed these new alert plans or whether they were fully aware of the dangers involved in such future crisis operations.

## CONCLUSIONS: THE POLITICS OF MEMORY

What should one learn from this history of airborne alert and the 1968 Thule B-52 accident? Given the deep and continuing uncertainty concerning the probability of the occurrence of the various scenarios outlined above, it is understandable that different independent analysts could derive different lessons from the experience. What is disturbing is to look at the evidence on how little the Strategic Air Command learned from the experience at all; and, indeed, how creatively it reconstructed the events after this and other accidents.

### Origins Revisited

Why were U.S. nuclear-armed B-52s maintained on day-to-day airborne alert? The traditional explanation is simple: SAC kept a portion of the bomber force in the air at all times because inadequate warning capabilities existed to ensure that ground alert B-52s could be launched and escape destruction in the event of a surprise Soviet ICBM attack. A redundant triad of invulnerable U.S. bombers, ICBMs, and SLBMs was considered necessary for reliable deterrence, and airborne alert was the solution to the problem of vulnerable bomber bases. A closer look at the decision-making process involved in the airborne alert operation reveals, however, a strong set of parochial interests behind the scenes and a more complex set of shifting public rationales. The Strategic Air Command originally empha-

[117] History of the 6th Strategic Wing, October–December 1969, p. 2, and SAC message to AIG 667, March 1, 1968.

[118] The available record is unclear on either why or when the B-52 airborne alert routes began to include flights in the Thule area again. The 1968 route maps sent to the White House do not show routes near Thule (though it should be noted that tanker aircraft were scheduled to fly the monitor mission there). Internal SAC airborne alert maps from 1971, however, clearly show B-52s being refueled near Thule. It is possible, therefore, that the bomber routes were moved to that area to permit refueling by the tankers involved in the monitor mission. See Paul H. Nitze, Memorandum for the President, Subject: Strategic Air Command Airborne Alert Program for FY 1969, Attachment (SEAGA routes), National Security Files, Agency Files, Department of Defense, vol. 6, box 13, LBJ Library; and Giant Lance, option 1 map, Strategic Air Command FY 1972 History, p. 174, FOIA.

sized the lack of adequate warning and communications from Thule and CINCSAC even stated he would terminate the peacetime airborne alert once better capabilities were established. The political arguments against canceling the alert after the Soviet Union publicly demanded its termination became salient in the aftermath of the Thule accident. Finally, in the later years, SAC and the air force placed great emphasis on the need for realistic training missions, which they claimed could not be done without nuclear weapons onboard airborne alert B-52s.

It is certainly not unusual for any given policy to serve multiple objectives, but the shifting emphasis among these goals, and the speed with which SAC acknowledged that U.S. warning and communications systems had improved after the Thule accident, suggests that something more central to SAC's identity than these multiple objectives was also being served by this dangerous military operation. Airborne alert was a solution looking for a problem to justify its existence: if ICBM warning problems were no longer compelling, then the need for realistic SAC training would have to do. Indeed, from an organizational perspective, SAC could hardly be expected not to favor the adoption of a major peacetime operation that would significantly increase the size and power of the command and improve the morale of its members. Although such parochial SAC interests were never mentioned directly in congressional testimony or the official classified reports on airborne alert, an analyst can sense the weight of SAC's devotion to flight, what Morton Halperin calls the air force's "organizational essence," between the lines. As Halperin colloquially puts it, "sitting in silos just cannot be compared to flying bombers."[119] This ingrained belief in the importance and uniqueness of the strategic bomber colored the air force's judgment concerning specific operational practices. The candid comments by SAC B-52 crew members about the personal and organizational desirability of airborne alert, quoted in this chapter's epigram, may therefore say more about the origins of SAC's airborne alert than the public justifications and official rationales.[120] To stretch Halperin's comment a bit further: sitting on runway alert just doesn't compare to flying realistic B-52 airborne training missions with nuclear weapons onboard.

One might expect to find less organizational pressure within SAC for maintaining the BMEWS monitor mission, since the number of aircraft involved in the operation was so small. Yet even in this case, the interest in maintaining flying training missions apparently encouraged SAC to continue the operation long after the original justification, the untested communications from Thule, was overcome. SAC's sudden discovery, after the

[119] Morton H. Halperin, *Bureaucratic Politics and Foreign Policy* (Washington, D.C.: Brookings Institution, 1974), p. 30.
[120] The crew member statements are from Narducci, *Strategic Air Command and the Alert Program*, p. 6.

B-52 accident, that the monitor missions were no longer needed because of improvements in NORAD communications is an important indication that these flights too were a useful solution that had been searching for a problem to justify its existence. After the accident and repeal of SAC's authority to fly nuclear-armed alert, no acceptable alternative problems were available. The solution had to be terminated.

### Consequences and Lessons

The list of potential common-mode false warning scenarios presented earlier in this chapter is strong, though admittedly hypothetical, evidence in support of the normal accidents theory. Adding a redundant warning sensor, the Thule B-52 monitor, may have solved the Thule BMEWS black-out problem, but by increasing the complexity and opaqueness of the overall system, the operation inadvertently increased the probability of a different type of false warning accident. The likelihood of such simultaneous or common-mode failures leading to an accidental war was, in my view, relatively low. It was, however, by no means negligible. And regardless of how one assesses the likelihood of these dangers, it is disturbing that the central organization involved in the accident appears to have actively avoided consideration of the possibility of a common-mode false warning problem even *after* the accident.

The Strategic Air Command's reaction to the Thule B-52 crash indicates that, while it was concerned about minimizing the possibility of another bomber crash producing a nuclear weapons accident, it never focused on the possibility of a false warning produced by a nuclear detonation or an aircraft crash cutting off communications to the BMEWS site. The command continued to fly unarmed tanker aircraft as monitors over the BMEWS radars, argued for a return to nuclear-armed airborne alert training, and planned to fly nuclear-armed B-52s near the Thule BMEWS in future crises. There is no evidence in any of the available SAC documents that anyone in the command recognized that there might be even a remote possibility of a normal accident occurring because of this operation.

Given this failure of imagination, it is not surprising that SAC alert plans continued to permit the dangerous repetition of the Thule accident to occur for an extended period of time after 1968. SAC's 1969 airborne alert operations plan specifically required that SAC forces maintain an "on-the-shelf capability" to monitor the BMEWS sites.[121] The 1971 airborne alert maps clearly show plans for B-52 bomber and KC-135 tanker refueling

[121] Headquarters Eighth Air Force, Eighth Air Force Supplement to SAC Operations Order 23-70, Giant Lance, 1 July 1969, Appendix 7, Annex B, BMEWS surveillance, K520.01 (declassified by the AFHRC, October 12, 1990).

operations above the Thule radar site.[122] The bomber alert routes in place in 1973 continued to schedule such missions over the Thule area.[123] Indeed, the declassified record does not show when, or even whether, the plans for such operations in crises were eventually ended.

### Accidents Waiting to Disappear

Finally, the history of the Thule incident leads to a very pessimistic understanding of the Strategic Air Command's ability to learn from its own operational experience on the subject of accidents. The problem was *not* a result of an inability to innovate due to a mindless following of routines. SAC was certainly able to adjust Chrome Dome bomber routes to maximize wartime targeting objectives and creatively invented the Thule monitor mission to provide an extra warning system, controlled completely by SAC. Instead, the command's inability to imagine a common-mode failure at Thule reflects a deeper organizational blind spot: a severe inhibition against an acknowledgment of the risk of serious accidents with the airborne alert force.

This blind spot can perhaps be best seen in the way in which SAC minimized the influence of the Thule crash in its internal justifications for ending the monitor mission. It was easier to provide a strategic rationale ("changes in the Soviet ICBM threat") for conducting a policy review of the operation in February 1968, than to acknowledge that the Thule crash made such a review necessary. It was easier to discover that BMEWS communications were now reliable, rather than to acknowledge that an accident had raised questions about the safety of the monitor operation. And it is more than curious that the SAC memorandums outlining the rationale for ending the monitor mission fail to mention the Thule crash at all.

This inhibition fits into a longer-term pattern, stretching from the origins of the alert program to official histories written twenty-five years later. In 1961, after a B-52 bomber broke apart in midair, the National Bureau of Standards and the Air Force Directorate of Flight Safety concluded that small fatigue cracks were developing in B-52 wings and recommended immediate corrective actions for the whole SAC fleet. The Strategic Air Command overruled this recommendation, however, insisting that severe air turbulence had caused the crash. Only after two more B-52 crashes occurred for identical reasons in 1963 did the command finally agree to the wing modification program to fix this B-52 structural deficiency.[124]

---

[122] Giant Lance, option 1 map, Strategic Air Command FY 1972 History, p. 174, FOIA.

[123] History of the Eighth Air Force, 1 July 1974–30 June 1975, vol. 1, p. 166, K-520.01, AFHRC.

[124] Memorandum from Luther H. Hodges to President John F. Kennedy, October 29,

The depth of SAC's reluctance to acknowledge such problems is further underscored by what appears to be the complete disappearance of a number of B-52 airborne alert accidents from the command's organizational memory. The accidents were reported to Congress in 1961 and the details of the bomber crashes have been declassified: In October 1959, a B-52 collided with a KC-135 during a refueling operation south of Louisville, Kentucky, and crashed with two nuclear weapons onboard; in January 1961, an airborne alert B-52 broke apart in midair and its two hydrogen bombs landed in farmland near Goldsboro, North Carolina; in March 1961, a B-52 with two weapons onboard crashed near Yuba City, California, after it ran out of fuel and failed to rendezvous with a tanker in time.[125] These specific accidents nevertheless vanished from the Strategic Air Command's 1988 official history of its alert program: "Until 1966, the history of SAC's alert operation *had been without incident*. This untarnished image changed on 17 January 1966 when a B-52 on a training mission collided with a KC-135 tanker during refueling operations near the coast of Spain. Both aircraft crashed near the Spanish town of Palomares."[126]

The normal accidents perspective leads to a deeply pessimistic belief about the ability of large organizations and regulating agencies to predict when safety systems will fail and serious accidents occur. Hindsight, it is often said, produces 20/20 vision, but the ability to see potential safety problems before they emerge is severely limited. As Perrow explains:

> Every time we pry open the lid of damaged systems (Bhopal, Three Mile Island, Chernobyl, Challenger etc.) we find an incredible array of precursurial errors. Aghast, we repeat on each occasion, "This was an accident that was waiting to happen." . . . [Yet], in the absence of an accident, investigatory agencies often find what they were looking for: that everything is in order and an accident is virtually impossible. This was pronounced a year before Chernobyl, a week or so before the Sandoz chemical spill into the Rhine, moments before the Challenger explosion, and so on.[127]

---

1963, pp. 2–3, National Security Files, Department of Defense, July–November 1963, box 274, JFK Library, Boston, Mass. For a description of B-52 accidents in this period, see Milton Leitenberg, "Accidents of Nuclear Weapons Systems," *SIPRI Yearbook 1977* (Cambridge, Mass.: MIT Press, 1977), pp. 52–85, and "5 Men Lost as B-52 Burns over Utah," *New York Times*, January 21, 1961, p. 16.

[125] See *Department of Defense Appropriations for 1962*, Hearings before the Subcommittee of the Committee on Appropriations, House of Representatives, 87th Congress, 1st session, part 2, p. 844, and *Department of Defense Narrative Summaries of Accidents Involving U.S. Nuclear Weapons*, pp. 19, 21–22. An additional B-52 crashed with nuclear weapons onboard near Cumberland, Maryland, in January 1964, though the plane was apparently on a tactical ferry operation and not on an airborne alert mission, p. 24.

[126] Narducci, *Strategic Air Command and the Alert Program*, p. 15 (emphasis added).

[127] Charles Perrow, "Accidents in High Risk Systems," *Technology Studies* 1, no. 1 (forthcoming): manuscript p. 12.

This investigation into the causes and results of the 1968 Thule bomber accident leads to an even more pessimistic conclusion. The Strategic Air Command's B-52 BMEWS monitor operation was a normal accident waiting to happen. But even after the bomber crashed into the ice, the danger of common-mode failures and further escalation was not seen, and the risk of similar airborne alert accidents in the future was minimized by the Strategic Air Command. Twenty years later, some B-52 bomber accidents were even lost in the organization's histories. Even hindsight is not always so clear.

# Learning by Trial and Terror

When there's a launch, one of our sensors sees it. . . . It
is automatically processed and automatically appears
on a display. And when that happens, I go to all the
centers in Cheyenne Mountain to determine where that
missile is going. . . . And it is a foolproof assessment.

*(General James V. Hartinger*
*Commander in Chief, North American*
*Aerospace Defense Command*
*NBC News, July 8, 1983)*

IMAGINE that you are on a Boeing 767 that has just taken off from Los
Angeles International Airport. Look out the window. It is a surprisingly
clear morning: there isn't a cloud in the sky, and the Pacific is a wondrous
shade of blue. At seventeen hundred feet, the roar of the jet engines suddenly vanishes. An eerie silence fills the cabin as the plane pitches forward
and dives toward the earth. Only sixty seconds later, the longest minute
you have known, you hear the engines start up again. The plane has
dropped eleven hundred feet, but quickly levels off some six hundred feet
above the waves. As the plane begins to climb again, the pilot comes on the
intercom and announces that the crew had made an error, but that he has
fixed the problem. Don't worry: there is nothing wrong with the aircraft.
The flight can continue.

The landing in Cincinnati is uneventful. The cabin is a mess, and your
nerves are frayed, but no one has been injured. A Delta representative meets
the plane at the gate and announces that the crew has been temporarily
relieved of flight duty. Another crew will take you on to New York. The
newspapers soon report that National Transportation Safety Board investigators believe that the pilot, while reaching for a fuel control switch,
accidently flipped the two switches that shut down both engines. He has
been temporarily suspended, pending the results of further investigation.

## ORGANIZATIONAL LEARNING AND HIGH RELIABILITY

This is a true story. The pilot of Delta Flight 810 did accidently flip two
switches, turning off both engines, during the plane's ascent from LAX on

June 30, 1987.[1] Should this experience make the passengers on board feel more safe or less safe when flying in the future? The answer is by no means clear. On the one hand, most passengers naturally would be frightened by the shock of the near-accident. On the other hand, perhaps one should be reassured because Delta suspended the pilot and could adjust their training programs and standard operating procedures to prevent a repetition of the mistake.

An optimistic perspective on organizational learning would lead to the second reaction: serious errors can be an important source of future safety improvements. As Bo Hedberg has observed, "learning is typically triggered by problems."[2] Much of the literature on organizational behavior points to this possibility. "Most change in organizations," James March has argued, is the result of "relatively stable, routine processes that relate organizations to their environment": "Action can be seen as stemming from past learning. The underlying process is one in which an organization is conditioned through trial and error to repeat behavior that has been successful in the past and to avoid behavior that has been unsuccessful. The model is one of experiential learning."[3]

Such trial and error learning is typically seen as being cybernetic in nature, substandard performances producing incremental changes in organizational procedures over time. Under this model, militaries will change their rules of engagement when existing rules result in tactical failures; corporations will gradually adjust their production methods and product lines when costs soar or profits fall below expectations; airlines will alter their training and flying procedures when common operator errors are identified. Organizational effectiveness will eventually improve. As John Steinbruner has noted: "Learning occurs in the sense that there is a systematic change in the pattern of activity in the organization. Over time, those programs and standard operating procedures persist that are successful in the limited sense which is pertinent; unsuccessful ones drop out."[4]

---

[1] See Ronald L. Soble, "Boeing Can't Explain How Delta Pilot Made Error," *Los Angeles Times*, July 3, 1987, p. II-1, and Richard Witkin, "Inadvertent Engine Shutoff Prompts F.A.A. Order on Boeing 767s," *New York Times*, July 3, 1987, p. 14.

[2] Bo Hedberg, "How Organizations Learn and Unlearn," in Paul C. Nystrom and William H. Starbuck, eds., *Handbook of Organizational Design*, vol. 1 (Oxford, U.K.: Oxford University Press, 1981), p. 16. For additional reviews of the literature on organizational learning, see Barbara Levitt and James G. March, "Organizational Learning," in W. Richard Scott and Judith Blake, eds., *Annual Review of Sociology*, vol. 14 (Palo Alto, Calif.: Annual Reviews, 1988), pp. 319–340; George P. Huber, "Organizational Learning: The Contributing Processes and the Literatures," *Organization Science* 2, no. 1 (February 1991): 88–115; and Chris Argyris and Donald A. Schon, *Organizational Learning: A Theory of Action Perspective* (Reading, Mass.: Addison-Wesley, 1978).

[3] James G. March, "Footnotes to Organizational Change," in James G. March, *Decisions and Organizations* (Oxford, U.K.: Basil Blackwell, 1988), pp. 169–170.

[4] John D. Steinbruner, *The Cybernetic Theory of Decision* (Princeton, N.J.: Princeton University Press, 1974), pp. 78–79 (emphasis deleted).

This perspective should lead to *increased* confidence after an aircraft accident or near-accident. Indeed, the high reliability organization theorists maintain that such trial-and-error learning is an essential component of efforts to create and maintain adequate safety with hazardous technologies. "Relative safety is not static," Aaron Wildavsky insists, "but is rather a dynamic product of learning from error over time."[5] Joseph Marone and Edward Woodhouse similarly conclude that "learning from previous errors has been an important component of the system for averting catastrophe" with such technologies as toxic chemicals, nuclear power, and recombinant DNA research.[6] From this perspective, even such environmental disasters as the 1986 Chernobyl accident are seen as having at least one positive result. "By providing new information about accidents," Marone and Woodhouse note, "Chernobyl should lead to further improvements in heretofore underemphasized aspects of reactor safety."[7] Finally, the group of Berkeley scholars studying flight and deck safety in U.S. Navy aircraft carrier operations have also argued that "many of the organizational strategies we observed were designed in response to previous serious accidents."[8]

Effective organizations often attempt to supplement this reactive process of learning from experience with more "offensive" efforts to anticipate the future: conducting analytic studies to identify better procedures and products, imitating the behavior of more successful competitors, and performing simulations and experiments when direct experience is lacking.[9] Such strategies are especially important for organizations operating hazardous technologies because a single major accident could produce widespread societal destruction. "Analysis and search come before as well as after errors" in high reliability organizations, according to Todd La Porte and Paula Consolini, since "learning from trial and error in operating their central production systems, while certainly likely, does not recommend itself as a confident or preferred method of system improvement."[10] Wood-

---

[5] Aaron Wildavsky, *Searching for Safety* (New Brunswick, N.J.: Transaction, 1988), p. 30.

[6] Joseph G. Marone and Edward J. Woodhouse, *Averting Catastrophe: Strategies for Regulating Risky Technologies* (Berkeley: University of California Press, 1986), p. 9.

[7] Joseph G. Marone and Edward J. Woodhouse, *The Demise of Nuclear Energy?* (New Haven, Conn.: Yale University Press, 1989), p. 100.

[8] Gene I. Rochlin, "Informal Organizational Networking as a Crisis-Avoidance Strategy: US Naval Flight Operations as a Case Study," *Industrial Crisis Quarterly* 3, no. 2 (1989): 164. Also see Gene I. Rochlin, Todd R. La Porte, and Karlene H. Roberts, "The Self-Designing High-Reliability Organization: Aircraft Carrier Flight Operations at Sea," *Naval War College Review* (Autumn 1987): 79, 83.

[9] See James G. March, Lee S. Sproull, and Michal Tamuz, "Learning from Samples of One or Fewer," *Organization Science* 2, no. 1 (February 1991): 1–13, and Hedberg, "How Organizations Learn and Unlearn," pp. 3–24.

[10] Todd R. La Porte and Paula M. Consolini, "Working in Practice but Not in Theory:

house has called such active search processes part of a "sophisticated trial and error" strategy in which an organization "expects error, carefully monitors initial trials, and prepares for error correction."[11] High reliability theorists have found this type of learning strategy to be important in such systems as multireactor nuclear power plants, where "vicarious" learning (improvements in one reactor because of failures in its neighbor) appears to take place,[12] and U.S. aircraft carriers, where "the Navy monitors even the slightest touches to attenuate concerns about major accidents."[13] Thus, high reliability organizations can learn from neighbors and from close calls, as well as from their own failures.

In summary, the high reliability school argues that trial-and-error learning, supplemented by an active search for improvements, can eventually lead to improved safety even in operations involving hazardous technologies. This learning capability is essential to their argument. Without organizational learning, trials will not produce insights; errors will not produce solutions.

### Constraints on Learning

Normal accidents theory, however, offers a much more pessimistic perspective on organizational learning by focusing attention on four persistent difficulties confronting complex organizations attempting to learn from experience. First, the real world often provides highly ambiguous feedback for organizations. What happened and why it happened is not always clear and it is therefore always necessary for scholars to ask, according James March and Johan Olsen, "What are the incentives that might lead a particular person, or a part of an organization, to select one interpretation rather than another?"[14] In such situations of high ambiguity, even well-meaning organizational leaders may display a tendency to learn only the lessons that

---

Theoretical Challenges of 'High Reliability Organizations'," *Journal of Public Administration Research and Theory* 1, no.1 (January 1991): 29, 19.

[11] Edward J. Woodhouse, "Sophisticated Trial and Error in Decision Making about Risk," in Michael E. Kraft and Norman J. Vig, eds., *Technology and Politics* (Durham, N.C.: Duke University Press, 1988), p. 217.

[12] Wildavsky, *Searching for Safety*, p. 32, citing Alvin M. Weinberg, "Nuclear Safety and Public Acceptance," *Nuclear News* (October 1982): 54–58. On vicarious learning also see Edward Bowman and Howard Kunreuther, "Post-Bhopal Behavior at a Chemical Company," *Journal of Management Studies* 25, no. 4 (July 1988): 387–402, and Huber, "Organizational Learning," pp. 96–97.

[13] Karlene H. Roberts, "New Challenges in Organizational Research: High Reliability Organizations," *Industrial Crisis Quarterly* 3, no. 2 (1989): 114.

[14] James G. March and Johan P. Olsen, "The Uncertainty of the Past: Organizational Learning Under Ambiguity" in March, *Decisions and Organizations*, p. 350.

confirm their preconceptions, attribute success to their own actions, and fit into their longstanding sense of mission.

Second, the normal accidents theory highlights how organizational learning often takes place in extremely political environments in which efforts to determine the cause of accidents are not designed to promote learning, but rather to protect the interests of the most powerful actors. Human errors and organizational failures are not simply internal data points to be used to improve organizational performance. They are also political events for which credit and blame must be assigned. The organizations managing dangerous technologies should therefore not be treated as value-neutral, truth-seeking bodies. Instead, as Lee Clarke puts it, "They are often very active parties, pursuing their own interests and shaping both the form and the context of controversies over what constitutes acceptable risk."[15]

The politicalization of interpretations concerning the causes of accidents also inevitably occurs *within* complex organizations. The power and self-interest of organizational leaders explains why internal investigations of industrial accidents often find that they were caused by "operator errors" and were rarely the result of mistaken design or faulty decisions by the senior management. Changing procedures is time-consuming; buying safer equipment is expensive; accepting responsibility for faulty designs is embarrassing. It is often simply easier, as Charles Perrow puts it, to "blame the victim" rather than the leaders of the organization.[16] Although this is a widespread phenomenon, hierarchical and tradition-bound military organizations may be particularly prone to blame individuals for errors rather than finding fault with the entire organization's structures or procedures.[17]

In such politicized situations, organizational learning would be expected to be highly biased, effectively limited in the types of lessons which can be accepted. The history of the investigations into the causes of the April 1989 explosion aboard the USS *Iowa*, which killed forty-seven sailors, is a recent illustration of the point. The official U.S. Navy investigation ruled that the cause of the massive explosion in the turret of one of the ship's sixteen-inch guns was sabotage, "most probably committed" by one of the victims, a

[15] Lee Clarke, *Acceptable Risk? Making Decisions in a Toxic Environment* (Berkeley: University of California Press, 1989), p. 84. Also see S. Prakash Sethi, "Inhuman Errors and Industrial Crises," *Columbia Journal of World Business* 22, no. 1 (Spring 1987): 101–110. On the general tendency of military organizations to avoid evaluations by outsiders, see Stephen Van Evera, "Causes of War" (Ph.D. dissertation, University of California, Berkeley, 1984).

[16] Charles Perrow, *Normal Accidents: Living with High-Risk Technologies* (New York: Basic Books, 1984); and Perrow, "The Organizational Context of Human Factors Engineering," *Administrative Science Quarterly* 28, no. 4 (December 1983): 521–541.

[17] This is a central theme of Elliot A. Cohen and John Gooch, *Military Misfortunes: The Anatomy of Failure in War* (New York: The Free Press, 1990).

sailor reportedly despondent over the end of a homosexual affair. Operations on the *Iowa*, and on other battleships with sixteen-inch guns, therefore continued as they had before the accident.[18] Two years later, the navy finally recanted, under the pressure of a $40 million law suit from the victim's family and an independent laboratory report, which demonstrated that the sailors could have accidently set off the blast by loading too many gunpowder bags into the gun turret.[19]

The third impediment to effective trial-and-error learning concerns reporting. Even when leaders are unbiased and the environment provides relatively clear "objective" feedback, it will still be difficult for organizations to assess their performance accurately if the information they receive from field operators is inaccurate or incomplete. Yet, faulty reporting should be expected if it is not in the interests of operators to acknowledge the existence of accidents or near-accidents. Commercial airplane pilots, as has been noted, consistently underreported the number of near-miss collisions until the FAA installed automatic recording devices in air traffic control centers.[20] In one extreme case, two Delta L-1011 pilots whose aircraft strayed sixty miles off course and came within a hundred feet of a Continental Boeing 747 suggested that the incident be covered up. A nearby air force jet happened to record the radio communications between the two jumbo jets. "Nobody knows about it except us, you idiots," a Delta pilot reportedly said. "I have passengers pounding on the door, and crying, and they saw the whole thing out the windows," one of the Continental pilots replied.[21] Under such conditions, when individual cover-ups block the basic learning process, trials and errors can occur without producing the slightest change in organizational behavior.

The fourth constraint on organizational learning is secrecy: both in the sense of the compartmentalization within complex organizations and with respect to the disincentives to share information between organizations. Restrictions on the spread of knowledge within an organization is a common tool to prevent secrets from being disseminated outside the organization, but this can also severely limit its ability to learn and implement

[18] The secretary of the navy finally ordered all older U.S. battleships to stop firing their big guns in May 1990, over a year after the incident, after a special independent study, ordered by Congress, raised doubts about the navy's investigation. See "An Honorable if Tragic Discharge," *U.S. News and World Report*, June 4, 1990, p. 13.

[19] John Lancaster, "Iowa Sailor is Exonerated in Blast," *Washington Post*, October 18, 1991, p. 1, and Eric Schmitt, "Suicide is Ruled Out in Battleship Blast," *New York Times*, October 17, 1991, p. 1.

[20] Michal Tamuz, "The Impact of Computer Surveillance on Air Safety Reporting," *Columbia Journal of World Business* 22, no. 1 (Spring 1987): 69–77.

[21] The quotes are paraphrases of the radio communications as provided in Richard Witkin, "Pilot in Near Collision over Ocean Suggested Incident Be Kept Secret," *New York Times*, July 11, 1987, p. 1.

lessons from historical experience. Indeed, one part of the organization may not know what other parts are doing, much less what they have learned from trials and errors. As David Mares and Walter Powell have observed, "Many organizational failures to learn are in fact failures of internal communication and influence": "Solutions to most organizational problems are known somewhere in the organization."[22] Secrecy between organizations is commonly used to protect production methods or procedural innovations in highly competitive industries, but it has the obvious (indeed intended) effect of limiting vicarious learning. An organization in such an environment may attempt to learn from its own errors, but will try to ensure that its competitors go through the same costly trials.[23]

## Nuclear Learning

Scholars from the high reliability and normal accidents camps thus hold quite different views on the ability of complex organizations to learn from errors. The two schools of thought should therefore lead to contrasting predictions about the capability of U.S. nuclear command-and-control organizations to learn from their mistakes. High reliability organization theorists would expect to find significant signs of effective organizational learning taking place in a set of military commands that has operated nuclear forces for over forty years without a single accidental detonation. Normal accident theorists, in contrast, would anticipate discovering far less evidence of organizational learning from past errors: at best, one might find highly restricted and biased learning; at worst, there should be telltale signs of organizational cover-ups.

Which is more compelling, the optimistic or pessimistic perspective on organizational learning? This chapter will evaluate the relative strength of the two theories by examining both the organizational lessons learned from nuclear crises and those derived from peacetime false warning incidents. How well have the organizations that manage U.S. nuclear weapons operations adapted their procedures and operations after close calls to accidental war?

The next section analyzes the impact of the Cuban missile crisis on subsequent U.S. nuclear alert operations through a case study of the October 1973 DEFCON 3 (Defense Condition 3) alert, ordered at the conclusion of the Arab-Israeli war. How safe was the American nuclear alert?

[22] David R. Mares and Walter W. Powell, "Cooperative Security Regimes," in Robert L. Kahn and Meyer N. Zald, eds., *Organizations and Nation-States: New Perspectives on Conflict and Cooperation* (San Francisco: Jossey-Bass, 1990), p. 87.

[23] See Charles Perrow, "Accidents in High Risk Systems," *Technology Studies* 1, no. 1 (forthcoming).

What lessons, if any, did the nuclear command organizations learn from the close calls that occurred during the Cuban missile crisis? Did other accidents or near-accidents in the 1960s produce changes in alert plans and activities? Were procedures adjusted so that the same errors would not be repeated in the next trial? Or did similar safety problems emerge in October 1973 as had occurred in the past?

What lessons the U.S. nuclear command organizations learned from peacetime false warning incidents is the subject of the following section of the chapter. To address this issue, the chapter will examine the available evidence concerning a series of incidents that occurred at the North American Aerospace Defense Command (NORAD) in the late 1970s and early 1980s. What caused these false warnings and how dangerous were they? What did the nuclear command organizations learn from the failures? How was the U.S. nuclear command and control system changed to prevent a repetition of these false warning incidents?

Organizational learning about nuclear safety is both a critically important and a deeply understudied subject. It is critical because learning from past failures can significantly reduce the likelihood of accidental nuclear war in the future. If the high reliability theorists are right, near-accidents in the past are likely to have produced incremental adjustments in organizational practices that have reduced the risks we live with today. If normal accidents theory is correct, then serious errors are likely to continue to exist within the system and could reappear under other, less fortunate, circumstances in the future.

This specific subject has not, however, been studied by either organization theorists or international relations specialists. Organization theorists have typically focused on more transparent, and therefore more easily studied, arenas of potential organizational learning such as universities and corporations. International relations scholars interested in learning have focused almost exclusively on how and why government *leaders* have altered their goals in international politics, and not on whether government *organizations* have gradually learned to improve their practices and procedures through trial and error.[24] Indeed, such incremental learning has been generally assumed to be relatively easy and is therefore seen as a relatively common phenomenon: it is not complex learning, but is rather merely "adaptation" or even just "tinkering with tactics."[25]

The evidence presented in the following case studies challenges that

---

[24] See George W. Breslauer and Philip E. Tetlock, eds., *Learning in U.S. and Soviet Foreign Policy* (Boulder, Colo.: Westview Press, 1991), and Joseph S. Nye, "Nuclear Learning and U.S.–Soviet Security Regimes," *International Organization* 41, no. 3 (Summer 1987): 371–402.

[25] Ernst Haas, "Collective Learning," and Philip E. Tetlock, "Learning in U.S. and Soviet Foreign Policy," both in Breslauer and Tetlock, eds., *Learning in U.S. and Soviet Foreign Policy*, pp. 72–80, 28.

notion and leads to a much more pessimistic conclusion about the likelihood of trial-and-error learning in this area. Despite the experience of serious command-and-control failures, the organizations involved did not take all the necessary, nor often even the most obvious steps, to prevent a reoccurrence of the problems. Organizational learning was severely constrained.

This history will therefore suggest that normal accidents theory is the more powerful tool for understanding the risks and reliability of U.S. nuclear command-and-control operations. Trials have occurred and the ultimate steps of escalation were avoided. That is the good news. But the bad news is that organizational learning from these experiences has been severely limited. This does not bode well for the safety of future nuclear operations. When analyzing close calls to accidental nuclear war, it is important to remember that all is *not* well that ends well.

## THE OCTOBER 1973 DEFCON 3 ALERT

To what degree have nuclear alert operations been made more safe because of errors experienced in the past? The question is very difficult to answer because the United States has so rarely placed its nuclear forces on a higher alert status. Since the Cuban missile crisis in October 1962, there has only been one instance in which U.S. global nuclear forces have been brought to a DEFCON 3 status in a crisis: the October 1973 alert ordered in response to a Soviet threat to send troops to Egypt at the conclusion of the Yom Kippur War.

The purpose of this section is to examine the nuclear alert actions that were implemented in October 1973 and explore what U.S. military organizations learned from the experience of October 1962 and subsequent peacetime accidents. What lessons were drawn from past trials and errors? Although significant portions of the records from 1973 remain classified, enough information has been released to provide at least a preliminary assessment of the management of this military alert operation.

### The Decision and the Nuclear Alert

The causes and consequences of this brief crisis have been more thoroughly analyzed elsewhere, and a brief summary of the political events will be sufficient to provide the context for the nuclear alert decision.[26] The Arab-

[26] For more thorough accounts of the October 1973 crisis, see Richard K. Betts, *Nuclear Blackmail and Nuclear Balance* (Washington, D.C.: Brookings Institution, 1987), pp. 123–

Israeli war in the Middle East appeared to be over on October 24, 1973, with all belligerents accepting the U.N. sponsored cease-fire in place. Fighting between the trapped Egyptian Third Army and surrounding Israeli forces in the Sinai desert broke out again that afternoon, however, and later that evening U.S. policymakers received ambiguous, but nonetheless ominous, signals that the Soviet Union might be preparing to intervene militarily. U.S. intelligence reports suggested that a number of Soviet airborne divisions had been placed on a heightened state of alert readiness, the Soviet airlift fleet appeared to be preparing for a major operation, and an airborne forces command post had been set up. These reports were underscored that night by a message from Leonid Brezhnev to Richard Nixon stating that the Soviet Union was considering unilateral steps to ensure that Israel ceased its attacks on the Egyptian forces.

In response, a high-ranking group of American officials (Secretary of State Henry Kissinger, Secretary of Defense James Schlesinger, Chairman of the Joint Chiefs Thomas Moorer, CIA chief William Colby, White House Chief of Staff Alexander Haig, Deputy Assistant to the President for National Security Affairs Brent Scowcroft, and Kissinger's military aide, Commander Jonathan Howe) met in the White House situation room. President Nixon, who was suffering from severe depression, and possibly drinking heavily in response to the growing Watergate crisis, stayed upstairs and did not participate in the meeting. Late that night, Kissinger and Schlesinger decided that it was necessary to warn the Soviets against sending forces to the Middle East and to order a global DEFCON 3 alert. The purpose of the alert was less military than diplomatic in nature: U.S. officials did not anticipate using nuclear weapons, but did believe that it was necessary to provide, in Kissinger's words, "some noticeable action that conveyed our determination to resist unilateral moves."[27]

The DEFCON 3 alert orders were sent out immediately through the Pentagon's National Military Command Center (NMCC), and throughout the globe a number of visible actions involving U.S. nuclear forces were quickly implemented. At Strategic Air Command bases across the United States, additional SAC nuclear-armed bombers were generated and placed on advanced ground alert, additional KC-135 tankers were alerted and at

---

129; Barry M. Blechman and Douglas M. Hart, "The Political Utility of Nuclear Weapons: The 1973 Middle East Crisis," *International Security* 7, no. 1 (Summer 1982): 132–156; McGeorge Bundy, *Danger and Survival: Choices about the Bomb in the First Fifty Years* (New York: Random House, 1988), pp. 518–525; Raymond L. Garthoff, *Detente and Confrontation: American-Soviet Relations from Nixon to Reagan* (Washington, D.C.: Brookings Institution, 1985), pp. 368–385; Henry Kissinger, *Years of Upheaval* (Boston: Little, Brown, 1982), pp. 545–613; and Scott D. Sagan, "Nuclear Alerts and Crisis Management," *International Security* 9, no. 4 (Spring 1985): 122–128.
[27] Kissinger, *Years of Upheaval*, p. 587.

least some were dispersed, the readiness of ICBM launch crews was slightly enhanced, advance teams were sent to secondary bases to prepare for bomber dispersal, and SAC command-and-control aircraft were placed on an advanced alert posture on their assigned runways.[28] In the Pacific, seventy-one SAC B-52s, which had been stationed on Guam for Vietnam War contingencies, were returned immediately to the continental United States.[29] In the Atlantic and the Mediterranean, an increased number of U.S. ballistic missile submarines also were placed on full alert status: for example, the submarines based at Holy Loch, Scotland, and Rota, Spain, were surged from port.[30] The Air Defense Command immediately placed all operationally ready interceptor aircraft, apparently including those equipped with nuclear-armed air-to-air missiles, on maximum five-minute alert status, but did not disperse the interceptor force to alternative bases.[31] Finally, the United States European Command also was placed on a *modified* DEFCON 3 ("Military Vigilance"), although the available record does not state whether European based U.S. nuclear forces were alerted under this condition.[32]

[28] The description of SAC operations is based on the following sources: Sagan, "Nuclear Alerts and Crisis Management," pp. 125–126; Bruce G. Blair, "Alerting in Crisis and Conventional War," in Ashton B. Carter, John D. Steinbruner, and Charles A. Zraket, eds., *Managing Nuclear Operations* (Washington, D.C.: Brookings Institution, 1987), pp. 84–93; 95th Strategic Wing Chronology of Middle East Related Action, K-WG-95-SU-RE, Air Force Historical Research Center, Maxwell Air Force Base, Ala. (hereafter AFHRC); 28th Bombardment Wing (Heavy), Chronology: Alert in Connection with Mid-East Operations 24–26 October, 1973, K-WG-28-SU-RE, AFHRC; 416th Bomb Wing, Chronology of Middle East Related Actions, 25–26 October 1973, K-WG-416-SU-RE, AFHRC; and History of 449th Bombardment Wing (Heavy), October–December 1973, vol. 2, Chronology of Middle East Related Action, K-WG-449-HI, AFHRC.

[29] Chief of Naval Operations Briefing Notes, October 29, 1973, Operational Archives, Naval Historical Center, Washington, D.C. A number of officials had earlier wanted to redeploy the B-52 bombers from Guam, where they were no longer needed given the deescalation of the Vietnam War, but concerns about sending the wrong signal to the North Vietnamese had prohibited the move. The DEFCON 3 alert provided a convenient excuse. This interpretation is supported by the fact that on October 29, three days *after* the brief crisis was over, sixteen additional B-52s were transferred from Guam.

[30] *Command History, Submarine Squadron Fourteen*, 1973, p. 1 (declassified, National Security Archives), and Blair, "Alerting in Crisis and Conventional War," p. 89.

[31] Message CINCNORAD to JCS, Subject: Alert Actions, 07/2000Z November 1973, in History of CONAD/ADC, 1 January 1973–30 June 1973, vol. 2, document 68, K410.011, AFHRC. Nuclear air-to-air missiles were removed from Air National Guard units in 1974, but remained with regular U.S. Air Force units until the mid-1980s. See Peter D. Feaver, *Guarding the Guardians: Civilian Control of Nuclear Weapons in the United States* (Ithaca, N.Y.: Cornell University Press, 1992), pp. 214–215, and Chuck Hansen, *U.S. Nuclear Weapons: The Secret History* (Arlington, Tex.: Aerofax, 1988), p. 177.

[32] Message, USCINCEUR to CINCUSAFE, 260731 October 1973 (declassified, National Security Archives, Washington, D.C.). The EUCOM DEFCON 3 alert had to be severely

The Soviet government most likely learned about the alert immediately through their global intelligence gathering network.[33] This had been expected by the American decision makers and, indeed, had been essential to their strategy of underlining U.S. opposition to Soviet intervention with "some noticeable action."[34] Kissinger had expected the alert to be a secret only with respect to the American press and public.[35] By the next afternoon, the Soviets agreed to send only seventy "observers" rather than a sizable military force to Egypt. The U.S. DEFCON 3 alert was terminated soon thereafter.

How should one assess the diplomatic consequences of this nuclear alert operation? In retrospect, it is impossible to provide a definitive answer to the question of whether the DEFCON 3 alert achieved its political objective: there is simply insufficient evidence available on Soviet intentions in issuing the threat to intervene in Egypt, which started the alert crisis. The Soviet Union may have seriously intended to send troops especially if the United States had reacted passively to their threat. It is also possible, however, that the main Moscow objective was to shock the United States into putting pressure on the Israelis to stop military operations against the Egyptian army. If the former is true, then the U.S. nuclear alert may have served an important diplomatic objective; if the latter is true, then the U.S. alert may simply not have been necessary. Any judgment on this matter remains speculative given current lack of access to Kremlin records.

## Nuclear Safety in October 1973

How dangerous was the October 1973 alert? What were the risks of a serious nuclear weapons accident occurring during the brief crisis? To what

---

modified in practice since full implementation of many Military Vigilance measures required NATO participation, and the October 1973 alert was a unilateral U.S. action.

[33] A U.S. European Command communications security (COMSEC) group, for example, monitored open (unclassified) communications during the alert to determine what Soviet signals intelligence units in Europe would be able to learn immediately during the crisis. This unit not only picked up the general DEFCON 3 orders, but even the specific numbers of submarines alerted and sent to sea on October 25. Headquarters United States European Command, *COMSEC Assessment during the October 1973 Mid-East Conflict*, pp. D1–D2, National Security Archives. I would like to thank Desmond Ball and Robert Glasser for bringing this document to my attention.

[34] According to Kissinger, "we all agreed that any increase would have to go to at least DEFCON III before the Soviets would notice it." Kissinger, *Years of Upheaval*, p. 588.

[35] Although Kissinger naively believed that an alert operation of that magnitude could be kept secret, other U.S. decision makers knew otherwise but chose not to tell Kissinger, fearing that the information might reduce his willingness to support an alert. See Sagan, "Nuclear Alerts and Crisis Management," p. 128, fn. 84.

degree did the U.S. nuclear command organizations learn from the Cuban missile crisis?

Previous studies of the events of October 1973 have assumed that, in contrast to October 1962, the risk of a serious accident during the brief Middle East crisis was remote. John Steinbruner, for example, has argued that "there is every indication that in its strategic dimensions the Middle East crisis played itself out in a far milder fashion than did the Cuban missile crisis."[36] This view appears to be supported by the lack of even a single report of a serious nuclear weapon or command-and-control incident in the currently available declassified documents.

Indeed, it is noteworthy that the only safety incident reported in the air force documents from October 1973 was a very minor one. On October 25, mechanics fixing the Klaxon horn system at the local softball field at Kinchloe Air Force Base in Michigan accidentally activated the whole base alarm system. When the Klaxon sounded in the bomber alert facility, B-52 crews rushed to their aircraft, started the engines, and prepared for a launch. The duty officer in the base command post, having not received orders to sound the Klaxon and launch the B-52s, however, immediately recognized that the alarm was false. He therefore recalled the bomber crews and returned them to regular DEFCON 3 status.[37] Although the event is indicative of the kind of bizarre and unpredictable interactions that can produce a normal accident in a complex and tightly coupled system, in this case there was sufficient time for the command post officer to intervene and the incident was quickly resolved.

### Learning from the Past?

How does one explain this very impressive record of safety during the October 1973 alert? The high reliability organization theory points to an important possibility: organizational learning from previous errors. To what degree does the documentary evidence support this theory?

A thorough testing of the proposition would require the declassification of much more information concerning decision-making during the crisis than is currently available. There are, after all, numerous reasons why an organization might alter its procedures (such as changes in its goals, in the pool of its members, or in its available technology), and one would need to demonstrate a direct connection between Cuban crisis incidents or subsequent nuclear accidents and the 1973 alert operation in order to prove that

[36] John Steinbruner, "An Assessment of Nuclear Crises," in Franklyn Griffiths and John C. Polanyi, eds., *The Dangers of Nuclear War* (Toronto: University of Toronto Press, 1979), p. 43.

[37] Unclassified excerpt, *SAC Middle East Chronology*, p. 12, TS-HOA-74-250, AFHRC.

trial-and-error learning had occurred. Despite such uncertainties, a high reliability theorist could make at least a plausible case for the nuclear learning thesis by pointing to three dangerous alert activities that took place in October 1962, but that were *not* repeated during the 1973 crisis.

The first example concerns dispersal operations of the Strategic Air Command's bomber force. During the initial Cuban DEFCON 3 operation, SAC dispersed 183 B-47 bombers to thirty-three military bases and civilian airfields, an action that reduced their vulnerability to Soviet attack, but also heightened the risk of a crash and nuclear weapons accident. In contrast, no large-scale B-52 dispersal took place in 1973. With the exception of a minor rotation of FB-111 bombers to alternative bases, the only bombers that were apparently launched in the 1973 alert were the B-52s that were returned to SAC's continental U.S. bases from Guam.[38] In 1968, SAC had constructed a new dispersal plan for the B-52s to replace the operation of the retired B-47 aircraft; so the lack of a bomber dispersal in October 1973 was clearly not due to the failure to maintain such an option.[39] A more plausible explanation is that SAC and the Pentagon learned about inherent safety risks involved with flying nuclear-armed B-52 bombers from the experience of the Cuban crisis and the series of bomber accidents in the 1960s, and therefore changed procedures concerning when and how to disperse aircraft in future crises. Important evidence of the existence of such enhanced awareness of safety issues is the fact that in the few cases in which bombers were dispersed in October 1973, "the weapons were taken off and taken to the dispersal bases by other means," according to the air force.[40] A second likely case of learning is the decision *not* to implement an airborne alert, despite the probability that such an operation would have presented the Soviets with the clearest signal of "some noticeable action" to convey U.S. resolve. Again, plans for such an option still existed: as shown in chapter 4, the Strategic Air Com-

---

[38] JCS Readiness Changes, October 29, 1973, Chief of Naval Operations Briefing Notes, Center for Naval History, Washington Ship Yard, Washington, D.C.; 380th Bombardment Wing, Chronology of Middle-East Related Activity, October 13–27, 1973, K-WG-380-SU-RE, AFHRC.

[39] J. C. Hopkins and Sheldon A. Goldberg, *The Development of the Strategic Air Command, 1946–1986* (Offutt AFB, Neb.: Strategic Air Command Headquarters, 1986), p. 154.

[40] *Department of Defense Authorization for Appropriations for Fiscal Year 1980*, Hearings before the Committee on Armed Services, U.S. Senate, 96th Congress, 1st sess., p. 3518. Two pieces of confirming evidence exist. First, although B-52s from Guam were placed on alert at Ellsworth AFB in South Dakota, the wing history reports that weapons uploading took considerable time and in one case "work (was) delayed waiting for a machinist to drill a hole required to safety wire a weapons system safety switch." Second, the F-111s that were dispersed did not assume an immediate SIOP alert posture. Chronology of the 28th Bombardment Wing (Heavy), ex. 2, p. 5, K-WG-SU-RE, October 24–26, 1973, AFHRC; 380th Bombardment Wing, Chronology of Middle-East Related Activity, p. 2.

mand had maintained a crisis B-52 airborne alert plan, code-named Giant Lance, after the peacetime alert was terminated following the Thule accident in 1968. Units of the command in fact independently made initial preparations to implement this airborne alert operation if ordered to do so during the 1973 crisis.[41] But no such orders were issued. Although political considerations or technical factors may have contributed to this restraint,[42] it is certainly possible that the decision at least in part reflected an increased understanding of the hazards of such operations following the B-52 accidents in 1966 and 1968.

A third, more speculative, example is the decision of the U.S. Air Defense Command (ADC) to alert its nuclear armed interceptors in 1973, but *not* to disperse them to alternate bases. As was shown in chapter 2, a number of safety problems had emerged when ADC interceptors were dispersed in October 1962. Plans for interceptor dispersal at DEFCON 3 still existed in 1973, but according to the command's history of the October alert "dispersal was considered and rejected."[43] Given the numerous command-and-control problems that were experienced during the Cuban dispersal, nuclear learning is once again a plausible explanation for this decision. Indeed, the Air Defense Command's postmortem on the Cuban crisis had acknowledged that many safety problems occurred during the emergency aircraft dispersal, and therefore recommended that ADC interceptors be stationed at the larger set of dispersal bases on a permanent basis.[44] Such a permanent dispersed stationing posture had not been adopted during the 1960s, a period of severe cutbacks in the Air Defense Command budget, and the ADC leadership may therefore have been very reluctant to order a dangerous dispersal of nuclear armed aircraft in anything less than an extremely severe crisis, most likely at DEFCON 2.

Such high-level decisions and changes in alert procedures may be positive signs of improved safety in nuclear alert operations by October 1973. Chapters 2 and 3 presented a lengthy record of serious lapses in nuclear command and control during the Cuban crisis. In contrast, in John Steinbruner's view, "The [October 1973] U.S. alert was limited to what it was

[41] Fifteenth Air Force, Middle East Chronology, 18 October–6 November 1973, exhibit 4, (hereinafter 15AF Middle East Chronology followed by declassified exhibit number) K-670.052–2, AFHRC.

[42] According to one source, a high percentage of the SAC tanker force was operating in the mid-Atlantic in support of the armament airlift to Israel. If this report is accurate, such operations may have limited the U.S. capability to maintain an airborne alert. See Marvin Kalb and Bernard Kalb, *Kissinger* (London: Hutchinson and Co., 1974), p. 491.

[43] Message CINCONAD to JCS, Subject: Alert Actions, 07/2000Z November 1973, in History of CONAD/ADC 1 January 1973–30 June 1973, vol. 2, document 68, K-410.011, AFHRC.

[44] USAF Historical Division, *The Air Force Response to the Cuban Crisis*, FOIA (declassified with deletions), p. 25.

intended to be—a formal change in status meant to support diplomatic action."[45]

## Repeated Risks in 1973

These arguments suggest that considerable organizational learning concerning safety during nuclear alert operations *may* have taken place between the Cuban crisis and the Middle East crisis eleven years later. A more detailed examination of the alert operations that took place during the October 1973 alert, however, leads to a more pessimistic assessment. New declassified evidence reveals that a series of accident-prone nuclear alert activities were in fact initiated in October 1973, despite the fact that the dangers involved had been demonstrated during the Cuban crisis. The majority of these hazardous military operations were not fully implemented in October 1973, but this was primarily because the alert lasted for only approximately thirty-six hours. The fact that such operations were begun, even during a crisis that senior military officers believed was not about to lead to nuclear conflict, is nonetheless indicative of the degree to which standard operating procedures, which had not been changed since the October 1962 crisis, still governed nuclear alert actions. These operations are therefore a serious sign of a failure of organizational learning within the U.S. nuclear command system.

Three important examples exist. First, as was discussed in chapter 2, a number of nuclear safety and false warning problems developed in 1962 when the Strategic Air Command took operational control over and then alerted ICBMs in early deployment or maintenance status and at the U.S. ballistic missile testing facilities. At Malmstrom Air Force Base in Montana, the regular peacetime "two-man rule" safety procedures were apparently *not* followed when the first Minuteman ICBMs were rapidly placed on alert in the confusion of the crisis. At Vandenberg Air Force Base in California, a potential false warning incident occurred when SAC placed nuclear warheads on nine of the ten ICBMS in the testing facilities and then launched the tenth one, on a previously scheduled test, on the night of October 26, 1962.

SAC initiated similar or identical dangerous emergency ICBM operations in October 1973. Throughout the command, ICBMs that were under repair or maintenance were immediately rushed onto alert at DEFCON 3.[46] Preparations to arm and alert the test missile complexes at Vandenberg

[45] Steinbruner, "An Assessment of Nuclear Crises," pp. 45, 43. Also see Blair, "Alerting in Crisis and Conventional War," pp. 118–119.

[46] SAC message 26/2024Z Subject: Status of L CAP Sorties, 341st Strategic Missile Wing, Chronology of Operations during the Mid-East Crisis, 24–26 October 1973, exhibit 23, K-WG-341-SU-RE, AFHRC; and Blair, "Alerting in Crisis and Conventional War," p. 88.

Air Force Base were begun at DEFCON 3 in October 1973, just as had occurred in October 1962. The SAC orders called for nuclear warheads to be mated with the Vandenberg test missiles as soon as qualified launch crews, maintenance teams, and the warheads themselves were all in place at the base, but the missile technicians who were ordered to deploy to Vandenberg were in mid-flight when the alert was terminated.[47] Had the DEFCON 3 alert continued for a longer period of time, this accident-prone operation would have been completed and the type of false warning incident that occurred at Vandenberg in 1962 could have been repeated in 1973.[48] Indeed, there is no evidence that SAC ever recognized the potential for false warnings that can occur if ICBMs at missile test sites are armed with nuclear warheads, and such activities may therefore still be in the DEFCON alert plans today.[49]

The second example of incomplete organizational learning concerns the use of emergency warning systems during crisis alerts. As was noted in chapter 3, a series of false warning incidents occurred in October 1962 when the Moorestown, Laredo, and Thomasville radars were turned toward Cuba and organized into a jerry-rigged missile warning network. These incidents, however, were not reported in the classified history of the operation. Indeed, the warning system managers at the Moorestown and Thomasville sites recommended that their radars be utilized in the future for emergency SLBM (submarine launched ballistic missile) detection.[50]

In the late 1960s and early 1970s, the United States did in fact utilize these sites as part of the national SLBM warning network, and continued

[47] SAC message 25/1436Z October 1973, Subject: RV mating at Vandenberg, in 15AF Middle East Chronology, exhibit 10, declassified extract, 15th Air Force Middle East Chronology, K 670.052.2, 18 October–6 November 1973, AFHRC; 91st Strategic Missile Wing Chronology During the Middle East Crisis, p. 6, FOIA; and Chronology of the 92d Bombardment Wing (Heavy) in relation to the Mid-East Crisis, (19 October–6 November 1973) K-WG-92-SU-RE, AFHRC, pp. 5–6.

[48] No test missiles were launched from Vandenberg between October 5 and October 29, 1973. It is likely that none were scheduled during the brief crisis, though it is impossible to know for sure since the historians there "do not have a data base which would allow us to determine if any launches were delayed because of an alert." William McCorvey, Freedom of Information Manager, Western Space and Missile Center, letter to author, November 15, 1990.

[49] Current alert plans are classified, and it is therefore not possible to determine whether such activities are still planned. Declassified documents show, however, that SAC exercises in the late 1970s continued to practice arming the test missiles at Vandenberg. See Exercise Nifty Nuggets 78 Critiques, in History of SAC, January–December 1978, K.416.01-173, exhibit 50, AFHRC.

[50] Headquarters 9th Aerospace Division, Memorandum for the Record, Subject Falling Leaves, January 11, 1963, pp. 7, 10–11. Cuban Missile Crisis Collection, National Security Archives, Washington, D.C.

their use after the initial deployment of a satellite warning system covering the Atlantic Ocean area in 1972.[51] Redundant radar systems were still necessary for confirmation of an attack and because the first generation of early warning satellites was, according to Defense Department testimony to Congress, "susceptible to temporary solar induced outages . . . (and) not entirely free of false alarms."[52] The Moorestown tracker was *not* used in daily warning operations in late 1973, however, having been shut down largely for environmental reasons. Instead, it was in a permanent standby mode, to be placed into the warning network only if a higher DEFCON alert was ordered in a crisis.[53]

This is precisely what happened on October 24, 1973. When the Air Defense Command went up to DEFCON 3, the Moorestown radar was recalled from standby status and placed into the operational warning network.[54] This alert activity was designed to increase the likelihood of receiving *genuine* warning of an SLBM attack, but since the Moorestown radar was not part of the constantly tested operational network, the likelihood of a *false* warning, caused by some unanticipated problem emerging in the complex system, would also be increased. History did not, fortunately, provide a good test of this proposition since the Moorestown radar was placed in the warning network for less than twelve hours during the brief 1973 crisis.[55] It is certainly possible that air force leaders understood the risks involved with this emergency operation, and chose to implement it anyway. This is unlikely, however, since there is no evidence that senior air force or NORAD authorities were even aware that there had been false warning incidents during the Cuban crisis due to Moorestown operation.[56]

[51] See Bruce G. Blair, *Strategic Command and Control: Redefining the Nuclear Threat* (Washington, D.C.: Brookings Institution, 1985), pp. 140–142, and *Minutes of Proceedings and Evidence of the Standing Committee on External Affairs and National Defense*, Canadian House of Commons, March 2, 1973, 29th Parliament, 1st sess., 2:10.

[52] *Fiscal Year 1975 Authorization for Military Procurement, Research and Development, and Active Duty, Selected Research and Civilian Personnel Strengths*, Hearings before the Committee on Armed Services, U.S. Senate, 93rd Congress, 2d sess., part 1, p. 75.

[53] *Ibid.*

[54] Message CINCNORAD to JCS, Subject: Alert Actions, 07/2000Z November 1973, in History of CONAD/ADC, 1 January 1973–30 June 1973, vol. 2, document 68, K410.011, AFHRC.

[55] *Ibid.*

[56] NORAD also had not learned by 1973 the obvious lesson from the Cuban crisis that it should have procedures in place to cope with the possibility that Canadian forces would be ordered by their government *not* to go on alert with U.S. forces in this joint command. The Canadian officers at NORAD were therefore put in an awkward position, given that they were needed to complete their job for the alert to function as planned. After the October 1973 alert, however, NORAD changed its procedures, making official arrangements for U.S. officers to replace Canadian officers should this problem be repeated in the future. See *Minutes of*

The third example of an organizational learning failure concerns the management of U.S. reconnaissance operations at higher DEFCONs. As was demonstrated in chapter 3, one of the most serious accidents during the Cuban crisis was the inadvertent U-2 overflight of Soviet territory on October 27, 1962. U-2s flying reconnaissance missions on the periphery of the Soviet Union had caused incidents prior to the Cuban crisis, but no one apparently considered the possibility that a provocative accidental overflight might occur during such a tense confrontation. When the incident occurred, however, the blame was placed on the individual U-2 pilot, and not on the U.S. reconnaissance system, which permitted flights at the periphery of the Soviet Union to continue during crises. The secretary of defense did order that the U-2 flights near the USSR be suspended temporarily, but only after the dangerous incident on October 27 brought the risk to his attention.

A thorough examination of the nuclear alert problems that occurred during the 1962 crisis would have highlighted this issue and produced improved procedures to review such reconnaissance activities at higher DEFCONs. There is, however, no evidence that such organizational learning took place. Indeed, the available documents concerning U.S. reconnaissance operations during the October 1973 alert suggests exactly the opposite. SAC electronic intelligence reconnaissance flights near the Soviet periphery, for example, continued on their regular schedules after the DEFCON 3 alert was declared.[57] The U.S. Cobra Ball reconnaissance aircraft, flying from Alaska to the edge of Soviet airspace to record information on Soviet missile tests, also continued their missions on a schedule uninterrupted by the brief crisis.[58] Although the Joint Reconnaissance Center at the Pentagon had responsibility for managing dangerous reconnaissance operations, no procedural mechanism had been set in place to suspend or even rapidly review such missions in crises. Because of this learning failure, in October 1973, to use Kennedy's description of the unfortunate U-2 pilot in 1962, there were many sons-of-bitches who didn't get the word.

*Proceedings and Evidence of the Standing Committee on External Affairs and National Defence*, House of Commons, Issue no. 14, April 22, 1975, 1st sess., Thirtieth Parliament, 14:8, and Brian Cuthbertson, *Canadian Military Independence in the Age of the Superpowers* (Toronto: Fithenry and Whiteside, 1977), pp. 62–63.

[57] See the Elint Interception Report, dated 26/0725Z October 1973, in 15 AF Middle East Chronology, exhibit 32.

[58] History of Detachment 1, 6th Strategic Wing, October 1973, FOIA. For a description of Cobra Ball reconnaissance operations see Jeffrey Richelson, *American Espionage and the Soviet Target* (New York: William Morrow and Co., 1987), pp. 215–217.

## Learning and Ambiguity

It would be extremely surprising to find *no* evidence of trial-and-error learning in U.S. nuclear operations, and this brief case study has indeed identified a number of procedural changes that may have been made in response to earlier command system problems. In contrast to the October 1962 alert, SAC nuclear weapons were no longer flown on board aircraft during bomber dispersal operations, and neither a SAC airborne alert nor an ADC interceptor aircraft dispersal was ordered at DEFCON 3 in October 1973. These examples of possible trial-and-error learning from the 1973 alert are by no means unique. The U.S. Air Force, for example, instituted the "two-man rule," whereby two individuals must be involved in all operations involving nuclear weapons, after an air force mechanic at a U.S. base in England threatened to commit suicide by firing a pistol into the nuclear weapons under his individual custody in 1958.[59] Similarly, all nuclear weapons were taken off U.S. National Guard air defense interceptors in 1974 after a pilot and a weapons system officer at a base near Spokane, Washington, were suspended for drug use and trafficking.[60] Such signs of nuclear learning are the positive side of the safety and reliability ledger.

The negative side of the ledger is, however, equally impressive. A series of very dangerous activities were repeated during the October 1973 alert, despite the fact that potential problems with these operations were actually experienced during the nuclear alert in 1962. A significant degree of organizational learning may have taken place, but the process was incomplete in scope, limited in substance, and biased in interpretation.

In the final analysis, when assessing these nuclear alert operations of October 1973, it is difficult to ignore a central paradox. The organizations involved both learned a great deal and learned very little from the earlier crisis. The U.S. Air Force clearly did study the October 1962 operations in great detail and did adjust plans and procedures in response. But a number of the very serious failure modes that occurred during the Cuban crisis remained hidden afterward. The risks of accidents or near-accidents were therefore discounted and most of the lessons learned pointed solely to how the United States could increase its ability to fight a nuclear war through special alert operations. A number of innovative operations first implemented during the Cuban crisis were fully ingrained into procedures to be

[59] See Jack Raymond, "U.S. Tightens Screening Rules for Handlers of Atom Bombs," *New York Times*, November 29, 1962, pp. 1, 19; and "The Man Who Went Mad with an Atomic Bomb," *The Daily Express* (London), p. 1.

[60] Bill Morlin, "Spokane Incident Led to Removal of Guard's Nukes," *The Spokane Spokesman-Review*, October 23, 1988, p. 1.

implemented at DEFCON 3: missile silos under repair were alerted for possible launch activities, nuclear warheads were to be placed on the Vandenberg test missiles, and even the marginally effective radar at Moorestown was brought onto alert. Emergency actions that were *believed* to have been successful, to have added even a few points to the nuclear war DE (Damage Expectancy) charts at SAC during the Cuban crisis, were repeated in October 1973.

Such biases in nuclear learning may be disturbing, but should not be surprising from the perspective of a normal accidents theorist. After all, SAC had simply not recognized the potential for false warning problems in the emergency ICBM operations at Vandenberg in October 1962, and no thorough civilian review of the alert procedures had taken place. SAC also could be expected to continue to alert the ICBMs under maintenance or in early deployment status, since the safety violations that took place at Malmstrom Air Force Base in 1962 were never reported to higher authorities. It also would be surprising if NORAD did *not* alert the Moorestown radar; after all, the after-action reports for the secret Falling Leaves operation were glowing, and the serious false warning incidents to which it contributed during the Cuban crisis were never reported in the Air Force's crisis operations studies. Finally, it should be noted that, although the Alaskan U-2 incident was well known, reducing the risks of accidental overflights in a crisis would have been organizationally difficult, adding complications to existing plans and reducing the autonomy of individual military commands. It appears to have been easier to trust that a serious pilot error, which SAC believed had caused the 1962 U-2 incident, would not occur again in future crises.

The U.S. military commands appear to have been, to use March and Olsen's term, "intendedly adaptive."[61] Yet, operational errors that are not recognized by anyone inside the organization cannot lead to learning within the organization. Errors that are recognized by individuals involved in the operations, but are nonetheless never reported up the chain of command, are unlikely to produce adaptive responses. Near-accidents that are caused by faulty designs or unsafe practices, but which are explained away as "operator errors" are unlikely to produce organizational learning.

In short, the 1962 nuclear alert was interpreted as a successful example of deterrence in action and many of the command-and-control failures and near-accidents that appeared on the brink were effectively ignored. A trial occurred. Errors were revealed. But very inadequate organizational learning took place.

[61] March and Olsen, "The Uncertainty of the Past," p. 349.

## NORAD'S 1979 AND 1980 FALSE WARNINGS

The size and complexity of the United States' missile warning system increased tremendously throughout the 1970s as new threats emerged and new strategic programs and organizational procedures were developed to counter them. The continual maintenance of Soviet nuclear-armed submarines off the U.S. coasts and Moscow's deployment of increasingly accurate ICBMs in the 1970s, in particular, presented a significantly heightened threat to U.S. land-based retaliatory forces. In response, the North American Aerospace Command deployed a set of major new warning sensors during the decade. In the 1960s, the three BMEWS radar sites in Greenland, Alaska, and Great Britain provided the United States' only reliable tactical missile warning capability; by the end of the 1970s infrared sensors on satellites, the PARCs (perimeter acquisition radar attack characterization system) radar in North Dakota, and both old radars (FSS-7 and FPS-85s) and phased-array PAVE PAWS (precision acquisition of vehicle entry new phased-array warning system) radars for detecting SLBM launches, were in operation.[62] Enormous investments in computer and communication equipment for NORAD's Cheyenne Mountain complex were also necessary to provide prompt warning, while at the same time distinguishing between an attack on the United States and the multiple daily events—such as Soviet missile tests, space launches, solar flares, decaying satellites, or forest fires—that can resemble a missile attack for the NORAD sensors. By the end of the decade, Cheyenne Mountain had what NORAD's commander in chief called "the largest computer system in the world," some eighty-seven different computers assessing data from the global warning sensors and continuously passing such assessments to other military command centers.[63] Finally, more rapid warning and response procedures were also developed within NORAD and the Strategic Air Command in order to ensure that SAC bombers could be launched in time to escape destruction from closely based Soviet submarines and to present the president with a more credible *option* of launching the vulnerable ICBM force on tactical warning of an attack.[64] For example, strategic

[62] The most thorough descriptions of the evolution of the U.S. national warning systems are Blair, *Strategic Command and Control*, pp. 140–147, 212–240, and John C. Toomay, "Warning and Assessment Sensors," in Carter et al., eds., *Managing Nuclear Operations*, pp. 282–321.

[63] Transcript, NBC-TV interview with General James V. Hartinger, July 8, 1983, p. 3.

[64] According to the 1977 congressional testimony of Lt. Gen. Alton D. Slay, air force deputy chief of staff for research and development: "Our options today are these. We can launch ICBMs on unequivocal warning. We can launch on first NUDET (nuclear detonation) on sovereign soil, or we can ride out the attack." *Fiscal Year 1978 Authorization for Military Procurement, Research and Development, and Active Duty, Selected Reserve, and Civilian*

bombers on bases near the U.S. coasts could be placed on heightened day-to-day alert postures and, in direct contrast to the 1960s when missile warning data from the BMEWS radars had to pass through NORAD before reaching SAC headquarters, by April 1979 all missile launch warning information from U.S. satellites and the East Coast PAVE PAWS radar was fed directly to the SAC command post, the National Military Command Center at the Pentagon, and the Alternative National Military Command Center, permitting more rapid reaction measures to be taken if necessary.[65] These links are shown in figure 5.1 below.

A high reliability theorist might not be troubled by these developments. From a normal accidents perspective, however, these developments suggest that the U.S. nuclear warning system may have undergone a transformation in the 1970s making it increasingly similar to the high-technology industries that have suffered catastrophic accidents. The addition of new redundant sensors and communications capabilities, grafted onto the old framework of existing military commands, points to a major increase in *interactive complexity*, and the perceived requirement for very rapid response to warning suggests that the nuclear command system has become much more *tightly coupled*.

Have these developments made the modern U.S. nuclear command system more prone or less prone to experience serious accidents? There has been, fortunately, no Soviet-American military crisis resulting in a major nuclear alert since October 1973, and therefore the U.S. system has not been tested under the most stressful of conditions. In November 1979 and June 1980, however, there was a series of false warning incidents at NORAD headquarters. The following case study of these false warning incidents is an attempt to understand the reliability of the U.S. warning system.

It must be reemphasized at the start that the mere existence of incident or a near-accident does *not* provide strong evidence against the high reliability theory, since the theory assumes that components will fail and that close calls will therefore occur. That is precisely why redundancy is considered necessary. Even highly redundant systems can eventually have accidents, however, if individual failure modes are not eliminated when they are identified over time. That is precisely why organizational learning is con-

---

*Personnel Strengths*, Hearings before the Committee on Armed Services, U.S. Senate, 95th Congress, 1st sess., part 10, p. 6851. There is an important difference, of course, between maintaining an *option* and having the *intent* to use that option.

[65] *Recent False Alerts from the Nations Missile Attack Warning System*, Report of Senator Gary Hart and Senator Barry Goldwater to the Committee on Armed Services (hereinafter, *Hart and Goldwater Report*), U.S. Senate, 96th Congress, 2d sess., October 9, 1980, p. 3. The PAVE PAWS East (Otis Air Force Base, Mass.) became operational in April 1979 and the PAVE PAWS West (at Beale Air Force Base, Calif.) established initial operations in August 1980.

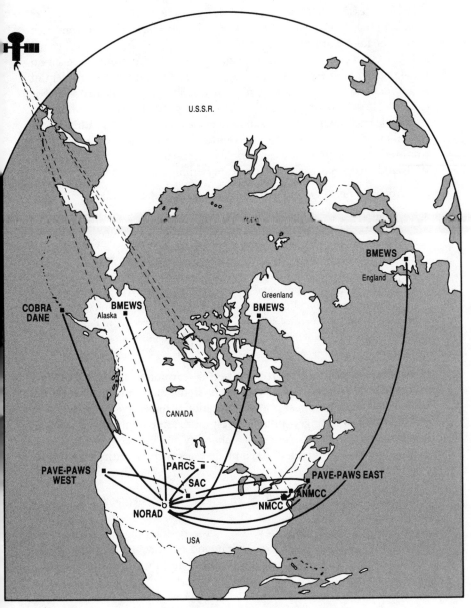

5.1 The NORAD Missile Warning System

sidered necessary. The key issue under consideration here is therefore whether the U.S. nuclear command organizations have learned from such peacetime false warning incidents.

Even critics of current U.S. strategic policy have commonly focused on the dangers of superpower crises and have assumed that the problem of *peacetime* control over routine nuclear operations has been solved. For example, Bruce Blair and John Steinbruner argue that Russian and American nuclear command organizations have experienced a "gradual accumulation of adaptations and concomitant weeding out of unsuccessful routines" in peacetime. Organizational learning over many years of routine trials and errors has produced a safe peacetime establishment:

> The organization must operate strategic forces safely; that is, in a manner that reliably prevents the accidental or unauthorized explosion of even a single weapon. It is questionable that either organization could survive the political repercussions of any major failure of this function, and fortunately both have grasped the imperative. They have evolved sophisticated weapon design principles and operational procedures to preserve effective control with widespread dispersal of weapons and have benefitted in that regard from accumulating experience and the process of error correction it allows. On the essential point the record of accomplishment has been perfect to date, a fact that reflects the strong priority given to maintaining strict peacetime control.[66]

To what degree has such trial-and-error learning actually occurred in peacetime operations of U.S. warning systems and strategic forces? To what extent have political and organizational impediments to learning exerted an even stronger influence despite the apparent interests of the organizations to increase peacetime reliability and safety? A detailed look at the events of 1979 and 1980 can help answer these critical questions.

## The November 1979 "Exercise Tape" Incident

At 8:50 A.M., on November 9, 1979, the operational duty officers at NORAD—as well as in the SAC command post, at the Pentagon's National Military Command Center (NMCC), and the Alternate National Military Command Center (ANMCC) at Fort Richie, Maryland—were suddenly confronted with a realistic display of a Soviet nuclear attack apparently designed to decapitate the U.S. command system and destroy U.S. nuclear forces: a large number of Soviet missiles appeared to have been launched, both SLBMs and ICBMs, in a full-scale attack on the United

---

[66] Bruce G. Blair and John D. Steinbruner, "The Effects of Warning on Strategic Stability," *Brookings Occasional Papers* (Washington, D.C.: Brookings Institution, 1991), pp. 23, 3–4.

States.[67] A threat assessment conference, bringing in more senior officers at the command posts, was immediately instituted. During this conference, the U.S. command system and military forces took preliminary steps to prepare for an attack. For example, NORAD alerted its entire air defense interceptor force, and at least ten interceptor aircraft, albeit with only conventional air-to-air missiles on board, were actually launched during the incident.[68] In addition, it was later revealed that the president's special "doomsday plane," the National Emergency Airborne Command Post (NEACP, pronounced "kneecap") was launched as well.[69] (The president, however, was not aboard the plane and, indeed, was not even notified of the incident during the night.) Finally, FAA air traffic controllers were instructed at some locations to order commercial aircraft in their area of responsibility to prepare to land immediately.[70] For a few frightening minutes, the U.S. military got ready for nuclear war.

The threat assessment conference continued for approximately six minutes, at which point it was terminated by the NORAD commander. What enabled a confident assessment that the United States was not actually under attack? According to government spokesmen after the incident, the key factor was the ability of NORAD, and the other command posts, to establish direct contact with the warning sensors (the satellites and PAVE PAWS radars) and determine whether they were in fact reporting indications of a Soviet attack as suggested by the computer displays. Redundancy worked: direct contact with the sensors shown in figure 5.1 indicated that they were in operation, and that they had *no* indication that an attack was under way, suggesting to the officers involved that the warning information on their display screens was in fact a false warning. "All commands had unanimously and correctly identified and confirmed the data as false in less than six minutes," the State Department reported to U.S. allies.[71]

[67] These descriptions of the November 1979 incident are based on the following sources: Richard Thaxton, "Nuclear False Alarm Gives a Grim Warning," *The Observer* (London) March 2, 1980, p. 12; "U.S. Full Alert by Error," *Sunday Times* (London), November 11, 1979, p. 1; A. O. Sulzberger Jr., "Error Alerts U.S. Forces to a False Missile Attack," *New York Times*, November 10, 1979, p. 30; Richard Halloran, "U.S. Aides Recount Moments of False Missile Alert," *New York Times*, December 16, 1979, p. 25; and *Failures of the North American Aerospace Defense Command's (NORAD) Attack Warning System*, Hearings before a Subcommittee of the Committee on Government Operations, House of Representatives, 97th Congress, 1st sess., pp. 122–123, 136.

[68] For somewhat conflicting accounts see "Strategic Nuclear Missile Risks Disputed," *Washington Post*, August 14, 1982, p. A2; Halloran, "U.S. Aides Recount Moments of False Missile Alert" and "False Alarm on Attack Sends Fighters into Sky," *New York Times*, November 10, 1979, p. 21.

[69] Thaxton, "Nuclear False Alarm," p. 12.

[70] "U.S. Full Alert By Error," p. 1.

[71] State Department message to U.S. mission to NATO, November 28, 1979, FOIA, p. 1 (hereafter State Department Message November 28, 1979).

The initial U.S. military response actions were therefore immediately terminated.

At no time during the brief incident were the president or the secretary of defense even contacted. The event nevertheless created a significant amount of public concern within the United States about accidental war. It even prompted a letter, four days after the incident, from Soviet Premier Leonid Brezhnev to President Jimmy Carter in which Brezhnev, according to the State Department summary "not too subtly implied that the U.S.'s procedures for controlling its forces were somewhat lacking."[72] Finally, the incident also prompted a set of investigations within NORAD to determine what went wrong.

What caused the false warning incident on November 9? NORAD and Pentagon spokesmen informed the press soon after the event that a simple operator's error—the mistaken insertion of an "exercise or training tape" simulating an attack into the live warning system—was at fault.[73] "I defined the November 9 incident a 100-percent personnel error," General James Hartinger, the NORAD commander, informed a congressional investigation: "inadvertently, an exercise tape was inserted into the operational computer system in Cheyenne Mountain."[74]

An optimistic perspective of organizational learning would lead an analyst to anticipate that significant changes in organizational procedures would take place after such an obvious failure. Hartinger, indeed, told the press that "as a result of that incident, we took steps that *guarantee* that it could never recur."[75] Two specific changes were made. First, as Hartinger told Congress, "to strengthen credibility in the eyes of the public and to preclude such human error in the future, we implemented stringent test procedures and rules."[76] Second, a completely off-site computer testing facility costing $16 million was constructed near Cheyenne Mountain reducing the need for software "test tapes" to be stored near or used on the live computer again.[77]

An outside investigation of the computer system involved in the incident (the 427M) by the General Accounting Office (GAO) was apparently satisfied by these changes. The optimistic final GAO report on the NORAD

[72] *Ibid.*

[73] Halloran, "U.S. Aides Recount Moments of False Missile Alert."

[74] *Failures of the North American Aerospace Defense Command's (NORAD) Attack Warning System*, pp. 116, 130–131.

[75] "Nuclear War by Accident—Is It Impossible?" *U.S. News and World Report*, December 19, 1983, p. 27 (emphasis added).

[76] *Failures of the North American Aerospace Defense Command's (NORAD) Attack Warning System*, p. 123.

[77] General Accounting Office, Report to the Chairman, Committee on Government Operations, House of Representatives, *NORAD's Missile Warning System: What Went Wrong?* MASAD-81-30, May 15, 1981, p. 13.

operational improvements therefore concluded: "The implementation of this off-site test facility allows software development and testing, especially stress testing of software, to be performed outside the on-line missile warning system. Since testing is no longer performed on the live 427M system, *this type of false alert should not recur.*"[78]

### The June 1980 Computer Chip Incident

A *different type* of false alert, however, did occur within less than a year. At approximately 2:25 A.M. (EDT) on June 3, 1980, the portion of the warning displays that reported the NORAD missile data at the SAC command post and the National Military Command Center suddenly indicated that a major SLBM and ICBM attack had been launched against the United States. As had occurred in November 1979, a threat assessment conference was immediately initiated and U.S. military commands prepared for retaliation in case the warning was genuine. Indeed, at air force bases across the country, SAC B-52 and FB-111 bomber crews ran to their alert aircraft and started the engines. Minuteman Launch Control officers in their underground bunkers were informed to be ready for launch orders. This time, the president's command-and-control aircraft was not scrambled. In Hawaii, however, the Pacific Command's Airborne Command Post (codenamed Blue Eagle) was immediately launched to protect it from the initial missile attack.[79]

What caused the incident to end without further escalation? Again as in the November 1979 incident, the Threat Assessment Conference was terminated by the NMCC after direct contact with the warning sensors, which showed that they were operating and giving no confirmation of incoming missiles. In addition, at NORAD itself, the warning displays indicated that no attack was under way, and the officers at Cheyenne Mountain had no idea of why the SAC and NMCC displays reported otherwise. Despite the confusion caused by the contradictory evidence presented on the display screens, air force personnel indicated to a congressional investigation after the event that three central facts led them to conclude within minutes that this was a false warning: "(1) there was no indication from the sensors of any detection of missiles; (2) the indication on the display that was received from NORAD did not follow any logical

---

[78] *NORAD's Missile Warning System: What Went Wrong?* p. 13 (emphasis added).

[79] See *Hart and Goldwater Report*, p. 6; Richard Burt, "False Nuclear Alarms Spur Urgent Effort to Find Flaws," *New York Times*, June 13, 1979, p. A16; Richard Halloran, "Computer Error Falsely Indicates A Soviet Attack," *New York Times*, June 6, 1980, p. 14; and William J. Perry, "Measures to Reduce the Risk of Nuclear War," *Orbis* 27, no. 4 (Winter 1984): 1030–1031.

pattern or sequence of events that would be expected from a missile launch; and (3) the different command posts were receiving significantly different indications."[80]

Three days later, while NORAD was investigating what had caused the false warning display, SAC and the NMCC once more received indications of a massive ICBM launch. A Missile Display Conference was begun and SAC bombers were again alerted. Again, when direct contract with the warning sensors failed to confirm indications of an attack, NORAD announced its assessment that there was no attack and the conference was terminated, officially ending the incident.[81]

What had cause these false warnings? Again, NORAD and Pentagon spokesmen quickly explained what happened to the press and to Congress. The failure of a 64 cent computer chip and the use of a faulty message design at NORAD were the root causes of the June 1980 incident. NORAD procedures required that a message be sent continuously to other command posts indicating that communications circuits were functioning properly and informing them of any missile launches against the United States. Under normal circumstances, this routine peacetime message indicated that there were 000 ICBMs and 000 SLBMs detected on the way to the United States. On June 3, a computer chip in the multiplexer, the device that takes the information from NORAD's computer and formats it for transmission to other command posts, repeatedly issued a spurious signal, akin to a typographical error in a telegram. According to a congressional report on the incident, "The effect of the failure of this particular integrated circuit was to fill some of those zeros with the number 2 and to do it on a random basis both as to which command post received the data and to which fields of data had the 2's in them."[82] In other words, the display screen messages indicated something along the following bizarre pattern: first 002 missiles, then 000, then 200 missiles, then 2000 missiles were reported to have been launched at the United States.

These incidents caused a flurry of press reports, numerous congressional investigations, and an in-depth review of NORAD's computer system to prevent another reoccurrence. Four major improvements in the national warning and response system were eventually implemented in reaction to the June 1980 false warnings. First, NORAD added a computer program that automatically reviews the messages transmitted to other command posts to check whether they correspond with the inputs to the message system. Second, a special display was added to the NORAD command post that reports on what information is being transmitted to SAC and the

[80] Hart and Goldwater Report, p. 6.
[81] Ibid., p. 7.
[82] Ibid., p. 7.

NMCC. (In contrast, during the June incidents, NORAD could *not* monitor what messages were actually being sent out.) Third, the format of NORAD peacetime messages was altered to reduce the likelihood of electronic failures. Prior to the computer chip incident, the routine message showing that the NORAD system was operational also indicated that 000 missiles had been launched. This message was put into an entirely different format after June 1980 and now simply indicates the status of the communications system. Finally, SAC alert procedures were altered to reduce the reactions to false warnings. According to a congressional report on NORAD warning problems, prior to the June 1980 incident, the SAC "duty officer was instructed to alert the bomber and tanker ground force upon any indication of missile attack," but, after the incident, "under *most conditions*, he is instructed to compare warning data being received directly from the warning systems with that being received from NORAD (before alerting the forces)."[83] (The phrase "under most conditions" most likely refers to a change in procedures under a higher DEFCON alert status and therefore may again reflect how a crisis can increase the risk of accidents, in this case by loosening the criteria under which the SAC duty officer is supposed to alert the forces.)

These changes in NORAD's computer software and organizational procedures were subjected to the test of time. In the three years after the fixes were made, according to General Hartinger, over 150 million messages were sent over the new communications system without a single error. "I think that is the type of performance you should expect from NORAD."[84]

## Sources of Reliability

It is difficult to know what overall lessons should be drawn from such incidents, since they represent both a *failure* of the command system to prevent false warnings of attack and a *success* of the command system to avoid premature nuclear retaliation. Virtually all previous assessments of the 1979 and 1980 incidents have, quite understandably, emphasized the many factors that contributed to the final success. First, redundant warning sensors exist, so that if one system fails, others can compensate. Second, the U.S. warning system utilizes two different types of missile detection technology: the satellites pick up the infrared plumes of missiles as they are launched from the earth, and the radars later track the missiles and warheads as they move through space. This use of "dual phenomenology" reduces the likelihood of a common-mode failure, of one unexpected phenomenon spoofing *both* types of systems: for example, a gas pipeline

[83] All of these changes are reported in *ibid.*, p. 8 (emphasis added).
[84] Transcript, NBC-TV interview with General James V. Hartinger, July 8, 1983, p. 5.

might look like a missile launch to the satellites and a piece of space debris might look like a warhead to the radars, but a single physical phenomenon is unlikely to fool both systems. Finally, there is always a "man in the loop:" indeed, properly speaking there are many men and women in the loop, and they, not the computers, interpret the data and have to issue the orders to retaliate.

These characteristics of the U.S. warning system led even an organizational pessimist like Charles Perrow to believe that the 1979 and 1980 incidents demonstrate that the "the early warning system appears to be moderately complex and coupled, but not disastrously so." According to Perrow:

> There is much to fear from accidents with nuclear weapons such as dropping them or an accidental launch, but with regard to firing them after a false warning we reach a surprising conclusion, one which I was not prepared for: because of the safety systems involved in a launch-on-warning scenario, it is *virtually impossible* for well-intended actions to bring about an accidental attack (malevolence or derangement is something else).[85]

## What Could Have Gone Wrong?

These safety features undoubtedly enhance the reliability of the U.S. national warning system. Yet, there is an important gap between an accidental war being "unlikely" and being "virtually impossible." In this sense, it is important to balance the knowledge that the November 1979 and June 1980 incidents were successfully managed with an exploration of the ways in which the results could have been much worse. Four unlikely, though plausible, pathways can be identified by which these false warning incidents could have led to a different, more tragic, ending.

First, it is possible that independent failures of components could occur simultaneously. Imagine, for example, what would happen if either of these false warning incidents had occurred simultaneously with a Soviet multiple missile test or military exercise. Under such conditions, U.S. warning system operators checking with the sensors, could receive false confirming evidence that a hostile attack had begun. This would be especially dangerous if the U.S. warning sensors falsely identified the missile test launches as threatening the United States, a serious error that has actually occurred on more than one occasion.[86] Similar risks could also be produced

[85] Perrow, *Normal Accidents*, pp. 291, 257 (emphasis added).
[86] On March 15, 1980, "four SS-N-6 SLBMs were launched from the Kuril Islands as part of Soviet troop training. One of the launches generated an unusual threat fan." *Hart and Goldwater Report*, p. 5. In June 1982, press accounts stated that the Soviet Union had

if an independent event, such as a decaying satellite, produced false indications of a missile attack in one set of warning sensors during an "exercise tape" or "computer chip" incident.[87] It is also possible that a gas pipeline fire could be misidentified or even "blind" the infrared satellites, as reportedly happened in October 1975.[88] Finally, imagine that the 1979 "exercise tape" incident and 1980 "computer chip" incident occurred simultaneously.

Under each of these scenarios, the warning of the missile strike would be ambiguous: there would most likely still be some evidence suggesting that an attack was not under way. If a fire or a decaying satellite spoofed one sensor during an incident, the other sensor still would be reporting accurately. The false warnings could be inconsistent: for example, the inserted training tape might report that a thousand missiles were launched, while the real missile test launch might be only four ICBMs.[89] If a training tape and computer chip problem occurred simultaneously, the NORAD and SAC command post operators would still be receiving direct information from the warning sensors that an attack was not under way. At the same time, however, in each of these scenarios, there would be at least some confirming evidence that an attack was under way and decision makers would have to weigh the contradictory evidence in a matter of minutes. Would they believe the false warnings of an attack or the accurate information that no attack was under way?

Second, it is possible that false warning incidents can produce their own falsely confirming evidence. For example, had a Positive Control Launch (PCL) of the SAC bombers occurred, either by accident or deliberately, during either of these incidents (recall that NORAD interceptors, the NEACP, and the Pacific Command's airborne command post were launched), there would be an increased risk of a bomber crash. Although weapons' design and added safety features were meant to reduce the risk of an accidental detonation under such conditions, the danger was not negligible when the 1979 and 1980 false warning incidents occurred.[90] An acci-

---

simultaneously launched two SS-11s, an SS-20, an SLBM, two anti-ballistic missiles, and an antisatellite weapon, reportedly alarming U.S. warning system operators. See "Soviet Stage Integrated Test of Weapons," *Aviation Week and Space Technology*, June 28, 1982, pp. 20–21. The danger of such a false warning incident was reduced when the U.S. and the Soviet Union agreed in 1988 to provide advanced notification of all ballistic missile test launches.

[87] For example, on October 3, 1979 "an SLBM radar (Mt. Hebo) picked up a low orbit rocket body that was close to decay and generated a false launch and impact report." *Hart and Goldwater Report*, p. 5.

[88] Curtis Peebles, *Guardians: Strategic Reconnaissance Satellites* (Novato, Calif.: Presidio Press, 1987), p. 319.

[89] Perrow addresses this issue in *Normal Accidents*, p. 289.

[90] In 1990, for example, it was discovered that the nuclear-tipped short range attack missiles (SRAMs) carried on the SAC bomber force had been inadequately designed and

dental nuclear detonation, especially if it occurred at a major Strategic Air Command base, could be misinterpreted in the tense minutes at the NORAD command post as a confirmation that a Soviet attack had in fact been launched. Third, there is some possibility, though the probability may be low, that individual duty officers in warning centers would misread or misunderstand the redundant warning information on the display consoles, and therefore report that confirmations of an attack existed when in fact none was present. As far as I know, such a serious operator error has never taken place at NORAD. At the tactical level it did happen, however, when the duty officer on board the USS *Vincennes*, in July 1988, misread the ship's accurate warning displays showing that a plane was *ascending* overhead, and misreported that the unknown aircraft (an Iran Air Airbus) was *descending* in a hostile pattern against the ship. In this incident, key *Vincennes'* command post personnel became so convinced that an attack was imminent that they apparently blocked out all information that disconfirmed that the plane was hostile. The Airbus was shot down; all passengers were killed.[91] Had the NORAD officers experienced that kind of "scenario fulfillment" during the false warning incidents of 1979 and 1980, the risk of further escalation would have been significantly greater.

Fourth, the likelihood of a rash reaction by individual operators or higher authorities would be greater if such a serious false warning incident had occurred during a period of severe political tensions or during a crisis. Rather than interpreting the warning indicators with inherent skepticism, as occurred in 1979 and 1980, military and political authorities at such times would be more inclined to believe such ambiguous warnings. Imagine that either of these incidents had occurred at the height of the Cuban missile crisis or during the October 1973 alert. The reported instances of high-level Soviet alarms over U.S. military exercises in the tense early years of the Reagan administration may also illuminate this danger. Reports exist, for example, suggesting that Soviet authorities seriously feared that the November 1983 Able Archer military exercise in Europe was a cover

---

tested for nuclear safety. Concerns about potential plutonium dispersal and accidental detonations therefore caused the Defense Department to remove the SRAMs from all SAC alert bombers. See R. Jeffery Smith, "Grounding Urged for A-Missiles," *Washington Post*, May 24, 1990, p. 1, and R. Jeffery Smith, "Design Changes Urged for Nuclear Weapons Safety," *Washington Post*, December 9, 1990, p. A4.

[91] On the USS *Vincennes* incident, see Scott D. Sagan, "Rules of Engagement," *Security Studies* 1, no. 1 (Autumn 1991): 91–101; and "Formal Investigation into the Circumstances Surrounding the Downing of Iran Air Flight 655 of 3 July 1988," Department of Defense (sanitized declassified report). A similar incident occurred on October 2, 1992, when U.S. naval officers fired two Sea Sparrow missiles against a Turkish destroyer during an exercise. See Barton Gellman, "Saratoga Missile Firing Seen as Accident," *Washington Post*, December 2, 1992, p. 1.

for a genuine NATO attack.[92] Other sources state that a partial military alert was ordered by a low-level officer in the Soviet Far Eastern Army in August 1984 after President Reagan made a "joke" about "outlawing" Russia and beginning "bombing in five minutes."[93] Finally, imagine that a false warning incident had occurred during the tense atmosphere of the 1991 coup attempt in Moscow. Which set of warning data, the false attack warnings or the accurate disconfirming information, would Soviet or American officials have believed?

It is obviously impossible to answer such questions with confidence. Nor is it possible, at least with currently declassified information, to estimate the likelihood of each of these problems occurring. The important point to note here is that the NORAD system was and is not so well designed that an accidental war stemming from a false warning is impossible. Unanticipated dangers can and do occur. This is why it is imperative that high reliability organizations adjust their procedures and structures to avoid repeating mistakes. Thus we return once more to the issue of organizational learning.

## Organizational Learning Revisited

To what degree did organizational learning take place as a result of these highly publicized events? At first glance, it certainly appears that considerable learning inside NORAD took place as the result of these and earlier false warning incidents. Once a specific problem was identified after each incident, money was spent for new testing and communication systems and procedural changes were quickly implemented. All this suggests that an optimistic assessment may well be warranted: trials produced errors; but errors produced organizational improvements.

The following reexamination of the 1979 and 1980 incidents, however, reveals a number of significant gaps in NORAD's learning process. In response to public disclosure of false warning events, air force officials quickly began to circle the wagons. Important details about what happened were not reported and the incidents were incorrectly blamed on operator errors or simple computer chip failures, instead of reflecting more serious problems with the way portions of the command system had been designed. Under such conditions, learning would be highly biased. From a normal accidents perspective, unfortunately, such behavior is a predictable organizational response to painful or embarrassing errors. Three hidden

[92] See Christopher Andrew and Oleg Gordievsky, KGB: The Inside Story (New York: HarperCollins 1990), pp. 599–600; and Gordon Brook-Shepherd, The Storm Birds (New York: Weidenfeld and Nicolson, 1989), pp. 329–330.

[93] Howard Kurtz, "Reagan Bombing Joke is Said to Cause Partial Soviet Alert," Washington Post, October 12, 1984, p. 10.

aspects of the false warning incidents support this contention that NORAD's learning process was seriously flawed.

### Human Error or Incomprehensible Interactions?

First, it is necessary to reexamine the basic cause of the November 1979 incident. As has been discussed, the official NORAD explanation was that the false warning was "a 100-percent personnel error": "inadvertently, an exercise scenario tape was inserted into the operational computer system in Cheyenne Mountain."[94] A normal accidents theorist would immediately suspect that "operator's error" was too simple an explanation for such a complex organizational failure.

Indeed, recently declassified internal NORAD documents and congressional investigations point to a more bewildering set of *organizational failures* behind the November 9 incident, problems that are more consistent with the patterns of normal accidents witnessed in nuclear power plants and other high-technology industries. In November 1979, NORAD was in the process of deploying an upgraded, integrated computer system (the 427M system) in Cheyenne Mountain to improve the reliability of the NORAD warning system. During its prolonged deployment phase, portions of the 427M computer system required software development and testing on the on-line NORAD missile warning network, since there was no other computer system available for such purposes.

There was in fact no simple operator's error, placing the "wrong tape" into the system, on November 9, 1979. Instead, the ongoing software test information, a simulation of a major Soviet missile attack, was *inexplicably* transferred onto the regular warning display at Cheyenne Mountain and simultaneously sent to SAC, the Pentagon, and Fort Richie.[95] Indeed, after the event, NORAD was *not* even able to determine the exact process by which the false attack information appeared on the operational warning displays. This was clearly acknowledged only in the command's internal investigation of the incident, which stated: *"The precise mode of failure of the Message Generator/Recorder on 9 November could not be replicated."*[96]

It is important to note the strong similarity between the *real* cause of the November 1979 incident and the Moorestown BMEWS radar incident,

[94] Failures of the North American Aerospace Defense Command's (NORAD) Attack Warning System, pp. 116, 130–131.

[95] According to the testimony of Milton J. Socolar, comptroller general of the General Accounting Office, "the NORAD computer system, failing to recognize test data being used for software development, generated inappropriate warning of a massive Soviet missile attack." Ibid., p. 4.

[96] Lt. General James V. Hartinger, letter to General Lew Allen, March 14, 1980 (emphasis added) FOIA.

which occurred during the Cuban missile crisis. As was discussed in chapter 3, a serious false warning occurred on October 28, 1962, as the result of a software test, simulating a missile attack from Cuba, which was being tested in the on-line Moorestown computer system during the crisis. By a bizarre coincidence, a satellite apparently passed over the horizon just as the simulation was appearing on the warning display screen. The warning system operators "became confused" and reported that a missile had been launched from Cuba and was about to detonate in Florida.

This 1962 incident should have served as a permanent and effective reminder of the danger of running simulation tapes on the computers that are operating active warning screens. Someone at NORAD had apparently independently identified the risks of software testing on on-line computers in 1974, according to NORAD documents, but a request for a special computer to provide "an isolated means to continued development testing" was denied "because of lack of funds."[97] The danger was treated as hypothetical; the risk was considered to be acceptably low. Had the 1962 incident been retained in the organization's memory, it would have been raised in the discussions of funding, and the arguments for a separate off-line computer for software testing might have been more effective.[98] At a minimum, NORAD would have warned the command post officers that a simulation of an attack could inadvertently appear on their screens. There is, however, no evidence of such actions.

This fact should be disturbing, but not surprising. As noted in chapter 3, the October 1962 software testing incident had never been reported even in the classified reports of air force warning operations after the Cuban crisis. All information on the problem was buried in the command post logs and the memories of the individuals involved in the incident. These officers may have passed along stories about this, and other, incidents to their successors, but over time such informal mechanisms of organizational memory fade. Better organizational reporting procedures and a more complete learning process might therefore have prevented or at least ameliorated the consequences of the November 1979 incident.[99]

[97] NORAD message to ASD C³I, 202115Z, December 1979, pp. 2–3 (emphasis added), FOIA.

[98] Although there is no indication in the declassified NORAD and air force documents that the Moorestown incident had anything to do with the request for an off-line computer for software testing, the author has not had access to all relevant documents. The possibility cannot therefore be entirely ruled out.

[99] It is worth noting here that, even if simple case of mistaken tape insertion had occurred in 1979, the incident would still demonstrate limited learning at NORAD since such an error had already in fact be experienced in the past. In February 1971, a warning system operator was supposed to place a test message into the Emergency Action Notification System that informs radio and television stations that a military emergency was declared and that they should immediately cease broadcasting. The test message was located on a hook in the

## Interceptor Launches and Faulty Message Design

The second reason for a pessimistic conclusion about NORAD's ability to learn from its mistakes stems from a reinvestigation of the interceptor aircraft launches that occurred during the November 1979 incident. There was a puzzle in the public reports of this event. Why were some, but not all, NORAD controlled air defense interceptors launched during the brief false warning episode? The answer is not what was reported at the time.

Launching aircraft because of a false warning is not an activity that is taken lightly by U.S. military commands. For example, the commander of the Strategic Air Command has held the authority to launch the alert bomber force under "fail-safe" rules since 1958. Yet, at least according to the public record on this matter, he has never used this authority during a false warning incident. During the November 9 incident, however, a number of NORAD interceptor aircraft were launched. This represents, therefore, a serious case of U.S. military reaction to a false warning, albeit a reaction that was both defensive and recallable in nature.

Why were these aircraft launched during the "exercise tape" incident? According to Defense Department press briefings after the incident, the following ten NORAD fighter interceptor aircraft were launched before the false warning alert was called off six minutes after it began: two F-106s from Kingsley Field Oregon, two F-106s from K. I. Sawyer Air Force Base in Michigan, and six F-101s from the Royal Canadian Air Force Base at Comox, British Columbia.[100] NORAD officials stated after the incident that these interceptor launches "were normal," suggesting that alert plans called for such scrambling of aircraft within six minutes under such warning conditions.[101] In fact, U.S. allies were explicitly told (in what was at the time a document classified as "secret") that "all command levels demonstrated entirely proper responsibility in handling the [warning] data" and that the air defense interceptors were launched "because of an alert prior to that time [when the data was confirmed as false]."[102]

These statements were inaccurate. They appear to be the organization's

---

command post right next to the real message (which contained an authenticating code word), but the operator inadvertently inserted the wrong taped message. Moreover, when he tried to fix the error by sending out a message canceling the emergency alert, he forgot to include the proper cancel message code word and so that message was ignored. See Hank Buchard, "A-Warning Proves a Blunder," *Washington Post*, February 21, 1971, p. 1; and Paul L. Montgomery, "'Nuclear Alert' Proves False," *New York Times*, February 21, 1971, p. 1.

[100] "False Alarm on Attack Sends Fighters into Sky," and Sulzberger, "Error Alerts U.S. Forces."

[101] See *Failures of the North American Defense Command's (NORAD) Attack Warning System*, p. 116.

[102] State Department Message, November 28, 1979, pp. 2–3.

effort to reassure outsiders and do not reflect the more alarming reality reported in the internal NORAD investigation reports. Although the critical documents have been only partially declassified (under the Freedom of Information Act), this material reveals that a serious set of communication and message formatting errors were the root cause of the interceptor launch. In addition, these documents demonstrate that at least two additional air defense fighters from an undisclosed air base in Alaska were also scrambled into the air during the incident, a fact that was not publicly released to the press in 1979.[103]

In each case in which U.S. interceptors were launched, improper procedures or communications failures were involved. NORAD orders called for all aircraft to be *prepared* for possible launch when the alert was sounded on November 9. At the 23rd NORAD Regional Command Center in Duluth, the weapons director in the command post simply "misunderstood the Senior Director's instructions" and ordered an immediate launch instead of just increasing the status of runway alert, and two local F-106s "became airborne before the error was corrected."[104] In Alaska, at least two aircraft were also scrambled after the initial warning because, according to the sanitized NORAD documents, the operations officer in charge "did not hear the *[deleted]* announcement."[105]

The cause of launching of the two interceptors at Kingsley Field in Oregon represents the most serious and most easily preventable communications design error. Considerable attention has been given in some hazardous industries, most notably in commercial airlines, to create what Earl Wiener has called "error-resilient coding of information."[106] Pilots, for example, are trained to repeat key words in verbal orders (e.g., "do *not*, repeat *not*") to avoid potential miscommunications. Standard terminology is invented to prevent the use of ambiguous phrases. For example, the standard phrase for takeoff acceleration, "maximum power," was created in the 1950s after a C-124 pilot gave the emergency command "takeoff power" to the flight engineer because the aircraft was too low in its final

[103] This, and the following paragraph, are based on Air Defense Command Director of Operations memorandum to President, Operations Review Board, November 14, 1979, FOIA (hereinafter DOO memorandum), and Air Defense Command, Director of Command and Control Systems memorandum to President, Operations Review Board, November 16, 1979, FOIA (hereafter DOC memorandum).

[104] DOC memorandum, p. 2, and DOO memorandum, p. 1.

[105] DOC memorandum, p. 1. Full details on the incident in Alaska are not available, since the Alaskan NORAD Region Command Post, apparently following routine procedures, has unfortunately destroyed the relevant command post logs. William Hanable, Deputy Chief Historian, HQ 11th Air Force, letter to author, November 1, 1990.

[106] Earl L. Wiener, "Fallible Humans and Vulnerable Systems: Lessons Learned from Aviation," in John A. Wise and Anthony Debons, eds., *Information Systems: Failure Analysis* (Berlin: Springer-Verlag, 1987), p. 178.

landing approach. The flight engineer understood the command to be "take off power" and therefore turned off the engines, causing the plane to crash short of the runway.[107]

An example from fiction can illustrate the point even more dramatically. In the 1963 novel *The Bedford Incident*, a U.S. destroyer captain accidently fires a nuclear depth charge when his orders in the ship's control post are misunderstood:

> "I'm not going to shoot first, Commodore. But if he fires a torpedo at me, then . . ." His voice rose up above the pinging of the sonar and the range-calling of the plotter. ". . . then I'll fire one!"
>
> "Fire one!" Ensign Ralston's voice echoed in a high pitch of excitement.[108]

This type of problem needs to be avoided in the preparation of preformatted warning alert or execution messages: prudent planners should anticipate the possibility that portions of the message might be lost in communication and therefore should carefully design execution and alert messages so that they do not resemble each other. Orders to *prepare* for possible future military actions must be carefully designed so that receiving units can distinguish between *execute* and *alert* orders even if they are only partially communicated. Phrases such as "initiate attack preparations," "execute war plan changes," or "get ready to launch missiles" should therefore be avoided in order to prevent units from believing they should "attack," "execute war plan," or "launch missiles" if parts of the message are cut off in communication.

It was precisely this type of error that caused the launch of the two U.S. interceptor aircraft at Kingsley Field on November 9, 1979. According to the NORAD investigation report: "The order *[deleted]* was only partially understood. . . . only the word *[deleted]* was heard so the alert aircraft became airborne."[109] Although the specific terminology used remains classified, the nature of the problem—an improperly designed order message—is quite clear.

This type of communications design error would be disturbing enough if it only occurred once. Evidence that organizational learning was limited at NORAD, however, can be seen in the fact that the June 1980 incident was caused by a very similar problem in the design of the NORAD missile warning message to SAC and the NMCC. The poorly formatted message system for the interceptor aircraft was in fact altered after the November 1979 incident to prevent a repetition of the accidental launch problem.[110]

---

[107] *Ibid.*, p. 174.
[108] Mark Rascovich, *The Bedford Incident* (New York: Athenaeum, 1963), p. 307.
[109] DOC memorandum, p. 3.
[110] Message JCS (J-3) to RUWRNLB, CINCNORAD, 300114Z November 79, FOIA.

Yet this serious error, discovered during the 1979 incident, did *not* lead to a review of the rest of the NORAD message system for similar problems. Had such a review taken place, it is unlikely that the on-line message that the communications between NORAD and SAC were functioning would have been formatted so that it routinely reported that 000 missiles had been launched at the United States. This was an accident-prone message just waiting for a typo.

The fact that no U.S. interceptors were launched during the June 1980 incidents suggests that the design changes of the messages from NORAD to the alert interceptor bases were successful. Yet while the messages to these bases may have been fixed, the tactical warning message from NORAD to SAC clearly was not. Trial-and-error learning existed, but was quite incomplete. One part of the NORAD command did not learn from the mistakes of another.

### Airborne Command Post Activities

The real cause of the interceptor launch was not the only command-and-control system problem that was not acknowledged after the incidents in 1979 and 1980. The third sign of inadequate organizational learning concerns the launch of airborne command posts during both incidents. Why was the National Emergency Airborne Command Post (NEACP) launched during the 1979 incident, and why was the Pacific Command's airborne command post launched during the 1980 false warning?

The precise chain of events leading to the launch of the NEACP in November 1979 has not been declassified. The reassuring descriptions of the false warning incident provided to allied governments in secret State Department messages—that "all command levels demonstrated entirely proper responsibility in handling the data"[111]—would, however, lead one to think that the president's plane was appropriately launched because the alert was not called off until after the aircraft was scheduled to scramble in a real emergency. Close examination of the evidence suggests that this is highly unlikely. Under normal procedures, it took nine minutes to start the engines and launch the aircraft.[112] It only took NORAD six minutes, however, to determine that the warning of a missile attack was false information. This strongly suggests that the NEACP took off *after* the warning was declared false by NORAD. It thus appears likely that some sort of communications error caused the president's emergency plane to be

[111] State Department Message 280022Z November 1979, p. 2 (declassified under the FOIA).

[112] The nine-minute estimate is from 1972 Defense Department testimony cited in Blair, *Strategic Command and Control*, p. 149.

launched in November 1979. This assessment was shared by Department of Defense civilians, who apparently were not kept fully informed of the NEACP incident. "My guess is that when the 'kneecap' took off it was due to a mistake," one official "close to the investigation" told the press soon after the incident.[113]

Did this "mistake" produce a system-wide review of the communications and procedures for the launch of the network of U.S. airborne nuclear war command posts? There is no evidence that any such review took place. The point is significant because a similar mistake appears to have been committed during the June 1980 incident as well. Although the public was again quickly reassured afterward that NORAD officers had been certain from the start that the warnings of attack were false, declassified documents paint a more alarming picture. The speed by which events unfolded and the atmosphere of confusion that existed in the various U.S. command posts can be seen in table 5.1.

Indeed, although NORAD is shown to have determined that the warning was false within seven minutes, Blue Eagle, the Pacific Command's Airborne Command Post, was launched *after* NORAD had determined that the warning was false and had therefore issued its "no" output.[114] Although Defense Department officials stated after the incident that "in accordance with standard procedures . . . command and control aircraft were brought to a higher state of readiness" during the incident, the timing of this launch strongly suggests that a communications failure of some sort preceded the aircraft launch in the Pacific.[115]

This was confirmed by the congressional investigation of the mysterious June 3 events:

The NMCC Duty Officer convened a threat assessment conference as a way of terminating the incident and insuring that all parties knew that there were no

---

[113] Thaxton, "Nuclear False Alarm," p. 12. The author requested, under the Freedom of Information Act, that the air force declassify any internal reports explaining why the NEACP was launched on November 9, 1979. In response, the air force "partially declassified" a four-page memorandum entitled "NEACP in Response to the Missile Threat Assessment Conference, 9 November 1979." Everything in the document except the address, the memorandum title and subject, and the closing signature was blanked out.

[114] In addition, a declassified NORAD document mysteriously states that officers at the Commander of the Atlantic Command's (CINCLANT) control post "incorrectly reported SLBM [submarine launched ballistic missile] indications" during the incident. NORAD Assistant Deputy Chief of Staff for Operations, "Talking Paper on June 3/6 False Indications," July 21, 1980, FOIA, p. 2. The cause and consequences of this false report apparently cannot be determined, however, since the CINCLANT command post logs are routinely destroyed after three years. Kendell Pease, Public Affairs Officer, U.S. Atlantic Command, letter to author, December 19, 1990.

[115] George C. Wilson, "Computer Errs, Warns of Soviet Attack on U.S.," *Washington Post*, June 6, 1980, p. 5.

**TABLE 5.1**
The June 3, 1980, False Warning Incident

| | |
|---|---|
| (05:21) | First "nonthreat" missiles appear on the warning display at the NMCC.<br>—Display clears within seconds |
| (05:25) | Two SLBMs appear on SAC warning display<br>—Eighteen seconds later two hundred SLBMs appear on SAC display<br>—SAC Fast Klaxon Alert sounded |
| (05:28) | NORAD announces "All Clear"<br>—No indications on NORAD displays<br>—No reports by direct connected DSP/PAVE PAWS data at SAC<br>—No reports by any direct connected sensors at NORAD<br>—No NORAD alarm levels generated<br>—No NORAD alert aircraft notified |
| (05:29) | SAC directs Alert Posture 5 (shut down engines, remain in aircraft) |
| (05:28–05:43) | SAC and NMCC displays intermittently show ICBM and SLBM launches |
| (05:39) | NMCC convenes Missile Display Conference |
| (05:40) | NORAD assesses information as false |
| (05:49) | NMCC convenes Threat Assessment Conference<br>—CINCPAC Airborne Command Post prepared for launch |
| (05:53) | "CINCLANT incorrectly reports SLBM indications" |
| (05:54) | NORAD "No" output |
| (05:56) | CINCPAC Airborne Command Post launched |
| (05:57) | NMCC terminates Threat Assessment Conference |

Sources: NORAD Assistant DCS/Operations "Talking Paper on 3/6 June False Indications," 21 July, 1980 (FOIA); *Recent False Alerts from the Nation's Missile Attack Warning System*, Report of Senator Gary Hart and Senator Barry Goldwater to the Committee on Armed Services, U.S. Senate, 96th Congress, 2d sess., 9 Oct. 1980, pp. 5–7; and U.S. CINCPAC Command History 1980, p. 201, FOIA.

threatening activities. As part of the normal activities associated with a threat assessment conference, the airborne command post of the Pacific Command prepared for takeoff as a survivability measure. After a brief period, the Commander of NORAD confirmed that there was no threat. But as part of the ongoing reaction of the threat assessment conference, the Pacific Command airborne command post took off *after* this.[116]

[116] *Hart and Goldwater Report*, p. 6 (emphasis added). The declassified NORAD "Talking Paper" on the incident suggests that the CINCPAC command post was launched "when

This timing strongly suggests that there was a serious communications or command-and-control failure during the incident. This admittedly speculative explanation is certainly more plausible than the alternative: that it was "standard procedures" to launch the Blue Eagle command post aircraft *after* NORAD announced that no attack was under way. The event therefore appears to provide further support for a pessimistic assessment about organizational learning in the nuclear command system: the kinds of communications problems that caused the mistaken launch of the NEACP in November 1979 were apparently not fixed before the June 1980 incident.[117]

## CONCLUSIONS: CONSTRAINTS ON LEARNING

The history of the October 1973 alert and the November 1979 and June 1980 false warning incidents leads to a quite pessimistic understanding of ability of the organizations that manage U.S. nuclear operations to learn from their trials and errors. Although the study of past mistakes was found to produce some safety improvements in alert procedures and warning systems, as the high reliability theory would predict, the learning process was *severely* constrained by the types of problems predicted by the normal accidents theory. Errors did not produce learning in many cases.

Faulty reporting by field-level operators was found to inhibit learning by senior authorities, increasing the probability that such close calls would be repeated: the 1962 NORAD "training tape" incident was not included in the Operation Falling Leaves after-action reports and the Minuteman ICBM safety problems that occurred at Malmstrom Air Force Base in Montana were not reported by missile system operators, located quite literally in the field. The common tendency to assign blame for accidents on operator errors, and thereby protect the interests of those who designed the system and the leaders of the organization, was also found to increase the likelihood of repeated mistakes. The stray U-2 incident in 1962 did not

the conference was convened," prior to the declaration from NORAD that there was no attack under way. The declassified CINCPAC Command History states, however, that "the aircraft was airborne in 7 minutes" after the conference was started, which confirms the *Hart and Goldwater Report*'s contention that the launch occurred after NORAD's declaration. NORAD Assistant Deputy Chief of Staff for Operations, "Talking Paper on June 3/6 False Indications," July 21, 1980, FOIA; U.S. CINCPAC Command History 1980, FOIA, p. 201.

[117] This apparent error within the U.S. nuclear command system in 1980 may never be fully explained. The best source on the cause of the problem would be the command post logs of the Pacific Command. That command, like the Atlantic Command, however, routinely destroys all their command post "watch logs" and other operations logs after three years. Lawson W. Magruder, Executive Assistant to the Deputy USCINCPAC/Chief of Staff, letter to author, August 24, 1990.

therefore produce a reexamination of crisis reconnaissance rules, and the November 1979 incident did not produce a thorough search for potential failure modes that remained in the system.

The negative effects of compartmentalization of knowledge also played an important role here. One command, or even subgroups within an organization, failed to learn from the mistakes of others. Airborne command post communications and procedures were not apparently reviewed by one command if another's aircraft was launched by accident. The message formats from NORAD to its interceptor bases were fixed, but the warning message format to SAC was not.

## The Guise of Safety

It would be tempting to treat this failure of organizational learning as a necessary result of the central ambiguity of the incidents examined in this study. After all, military organizations are by no means unique in having problems learning from events that can plausibly be interpreted as either a success, because no disaster occurred, or as a failure, because there was a close call to catastrophe. "The most obvious learning problem with near-histories," James March, Lee Sproull, and Michel Tamuz have argued, "arises from the necessary ambiguity of their interpretation": "Every time a pilot avoids a collision, the event provides evidence both for the threat and for its irrelevance. It is not clear whether the learning should emphasize how close the organization came to disaster, thus the reality of danger in the guise of safety, or the fact that disaster was avoided, thus the reality of safety in the guise of danger."[118]

This basic ambiguity of interpretation may be unavoidable, but it need not lead to persistent biases in organizational learning. What is striking about the nuclear command organizations studied in this chapter is how consistently they have emphasized only one interpretation of command-and-control near-accidents. Civilian leaders and the general public might be frightened by the events, but to the organizations involved the incidents represented "the reality of safety in the guise of danger." This central bias in interpretation greatly inhibited organizational learning by discouraging more thorough investigations, more accurate reporting, deeper imagination, and greater sharing of information.

When one considers how controversial nuclear weapons operations are in the wider U.S. political debate, it is understandable that the organizations involved in such incidents would emphasize the strength of their forces and the reliability of their procedures in their presentations to Con-

---

[118] James G. March, Lee S. Sproull, and Michal Tamuz, "Learning from Samples of One or Fewer," *Organization Science* 2, no. 1 (February 1991): 10.

gress and their public relations efforts. The failures of organizational learning outlined in this chapter, however, suggest that such displays of confidence have been internalized. What is perhaps most disturbing, is the degree to which a set of internal organizational myths appears to have developed over time: that false warning problems have been solved; that there is no chance of an unauthorized use of a nuclear weapon; that nuclear alerts are not dangerous; and that public fears about accidental nuclear war are therefore deeply misguided.

Mary Douglas, the British anthropologist, has written that "institutions create shadowed places in which nothing can be seen and no questions asked."[119] For the U.S. military, the problem of accidental nuclear war exists in such a shadowed place. For example, only 13 percent of the nation's senior officers, according to a 1984 Gallup poll, were concerned "a great deal" or even "a fair amount" about the possibility of accidental nuclear war.[120] General Robert Herres, the NORAD commander in 1986, insisted that "our systems are absolutely reliable and accurate."[121] In February 1991, former Air Force Chief of Staff General Lawrence Welch went even further, stating that the "possibility of a launch of an ICBM without the president's authorization is as close to zero as anything I can imagine."[122] Over time, the organizations have come to believe their own myths: the system is, as General James Hartinger put it, "foolproof."[123]

## Back to LAX

The evidence presented in this and the preceding chapters suggests that the U.S. nuclear command-and-control system is by no means foolproof. Reasonable people may well disagree about precisely how serious these nuclear alert and false warning incidents were. That is always the case with near-accidents and counterfactual history. But such close calls should not have been repeated, and the world is less safe than it would be if the organizational inhibitions to learning from errors were less persistent.

Consider the Delta Airlines near-accident that began this chapter. The degree of confidence one should feel after such an incident should depend upon how well the organizations involved learned from the mistake. If Delta had been permitted to blame the incident on the pilot's error, and to

---

[119] Mary Douglas, *How Institutions Think* (Syracuse, N.Y.: Syracuse University Press, 1986), p. 69. I would like to thank Lynn Eden for pointing out this source to me.

[120] *Newsweek*, July 9, 1984, p. 37.

[121] Robert T. Herres, "Preface," in John Borowski, ed., *Avoiding War in the Nuclear Age* (Boulder, Colo.: Westview Press, 1986), p. xiii.

[122] As quoted in David C. Morrison, "Loose Soviet Nukes: A Mountain or a Molehill?" *Arms Control Today*, April 1991, p. 16.

[123] Interview with General James V. Hartinger, NBC-TV transcript, July 8, 1983, p. 3.

tell customers that he has been suspended, so it won't happen again, one should not have felt reassured. Indeed, as long as the cockpit switches that shut down the engines were located next to the fuel control switch, the possibility of another pilot repeating the same error would remain unacceptably high.

The likelihood of trial-and-error learning is increased when independent investigations gather information, when other interested parties offer interpretations, and when distribution of information concerning accidents is encouraged.[124] Fortunately in the case of Delta Flight 810, the Federal Aviation Administration investigated the incident and ordered that the cockpits of all 767s, not just Delta's aircraft, must undergo an emergency modification program. A safety guard was placed over the two switches, reducing the likelihood that a future "operator error" would inadvertently turn off both engines.[125]

Trials and errors occur. But, learning from them is not an automatic process. Unfortunately, the evidence suggests that the U.S. nuclear command organizations are primed to repeat serious errors in future trials.

[124] Perrow, "Accidents in High Risk Systems," pp. 26–33.

[125] See Soble, "Boeing Can't Explain How Delta Pilot Made Error," p. 1, and Witkin, "Inadvertent Engine Shutoff Prompts F.A.A. Order on Boeing 767s," p. 14.

_____ CHAPTER 6 _____

# The Limits of Safety

The dangerous accidents lie in the system, not
in the components.

*(Charles Perrow)*

WHEN I BEGAN working on this book, I believed that the likelihood of a
serious nuclear weapons accident occurring in the United States was extraordinarily remote. The safety record of U.S. nuclear forces, or at least
the record available to the public at that time, pointed to what appeared to
be a major success story. Nuclear bombs have been inadvertently dropped
from aircraft; but the weapons involved had, according to the Department
of Defense, "redundant safety features to *insure* that a nuclear explosion
does not occur as the result of an accident."[1] In a number of cases, warning
sensors have reported false indications that the United States was under
nuclear attack, but the existence of redundant warning systems, which
reported that no attack was under way, and the "man in the loop" solved
the problem. As the Defense Department reported to Congress after a
series of false warning incidents in 1980: "We have highly trained and
experienced personnel in charge of all phases of the warning process, and
*there is no chance* that any irreversible actions would be taken based on
ambiguous computer information."[2] Individual military officers certainly
have become mentally unstable; but psychological testing under the military's Personnel Reliability Program (PRP) and the "two-man rule" system
(under which two people are required to be involved in all nuclear weapons
operations) are designed to ensure that no unstable individual could ever
gain control of a U.S. nuclear weapon. "These procedures have served us
well, and *they are respected and observed*," General Russell Dougherty, the
former Commander of the Strategic Air Command, reassured us.[3] We have
been told that there have been minor safety problems in the past, but that
the system has learned how to deal with them over time.

[1] *Narrative Summaries of Accidents involving U.S. Nuclear Weapons, 1950–1980* (Department of Defense Press Release, May 1981), p. ii (emphasis added).

[2] Department of Defense, *Annual Report for FY 1982*, p. 121 (emphasis added).

[3] Russell E. Dougherty, "The Psychological Climate of Nuclear Command," in Ashton B.
Carter, John Steinbruner, and Charles A. Zraket, eds., *Managing Nuclear Operations* (Washington, D.C.: Brookings Institution, 1987), p. 415 (emphasis added).

The hidden history of U.S. nuclear weapons safety problems belies such confident assessments. During the 1962 Cuban missile crisis, as was shown in chapter 2 and chapter 3, numerous dangerous incidents with nuclear weapons and command-and-control systems occurred, despite all the efforts of senior authorities to prevent them. The historical evidence has also demonstrated the inadequacy of a strategy for nuclear safety that attempted to ensure reliability by simply adding more and more redundant parts to the system. As was shown in the analyses of the Falling Leaves radar system during the Cuban crisis in chapter 3 and the 1968 Thule B-52 accident in chapter 4, adding redundant safety devices can cause accidents by making the system more complex and opaque; and human operators and organizations can often "work around" redundant safety features, if the devices do not serve their immediate interests. Finally, the analysis in chapter 5 of the October 1973 nuclear alert and the North American Aerospace Defense (NORAD) Command's false warning incidents in 1979 and 1980, showed that trial and error learning often did not occur even after serious safety problems emerged in the U.S. nuclear weapons command-and-control system. When I began this book, the public record on nuclear weapons safety led me to expect that the high reliability school of organization theorists would provide the strongest set of intellectual tools for explaining this apparent success story. Indeed, I hoped that the history of U.S. nuclear weapons operations might become an important model for better management of other hazardous technologies. The evidence presented in this book has reluctantly led me to the opposite view: the experience of persistent safety problems in the U.S. nuclear arsenal should serve as a warning.

When I began this book, I also believed (like many political scientists and historians) that nuclear weapons tend to be a stabilizing force in the dangerous realm of international politics. According to the logic of deterrence theory, nuclear weapons, precisely because they make war so clearly catastrophic, make war less likely. I did not think that a serious accident, or even an accidental nuclear war, was impossible; for almost nothing is truly impossible when complex human beings, complex organizations, and complex machines interact. But I did believe that the possibility was so remote that we did not have to rethink fundamentally the role of nuclear deterrence in our national security policy. The evidence presented in this book, however, has also challenged that reassuring view about the stabilizing effects of nuclear weapons.

This concluding chapter has three objectives. First, it presents the implications of this study for our understanding of other modern organizations that attempt to manage hazardous technology. What should we learn from our experience with nuclear command-and-control systems about the risk of serious accidents in other such complex organizations? Second, it examines the implications of the study for understanding the role of nuclear weapons in international relations. Are nuclear weapons stabilizing, and, if so, how will they influence international security in the post–Cold War world? Third, and finally, it will present some general recommendations for changing U.S. nuclear weapons policies. What steps could be taken to reduce the dangers of nuclear weapons accidents?

## IMPLICATIONS FOR ORGANIZATION THEORY

In chapter 1, two contrasting perspectives on safety in complex organizations—high reliability theory and normal accidents theory—were presented in considerable detail. Which theoretical perspective proved to be most helpful in understanding the history of nuclear weapons safety? Which theory won the test?

Although the high reliability perspective did lead to a number of useful insights into the problem of nuclear weapons command and control, the historical evidence provides much stronger support for the ideas developed by Charles Perrow in *Normal Accidents* and by other authors writing within that intellectual tradition. The importance of this finding is increased when one recalls that this was a "tough test" for normal accidents theory: the apparent excellent safety record, the importance with which political leaders viewed nuclear weapons safety, and the strict discipline and socialization present in professional military organizations, all led to a logical expectation that U.S. nuclear weapons operations would be exceptionally safe.

The research for this book, however, identified a long series of close calls with U.S. nuclear weapons systems: serious accidents or near-accidents that could have led to catastrophes had they occurred in somewhat different, but nonetheless plausible, circumstances. While this evidence supports the normal accidents perspective, it leads to an even more pessimistic vision of the limits of organizational safety than existed in Perrow's book. Why? Four important additions to our understanding of the causes of accidents in high technology systems are suggested by the history of U.S. nuclear weapons operations.

### The Dark Side of Discipline

The first issue concerns the effects of strong "organizational culture" on safety. As was discussed in chapter 1, the high reliability theorists and the normal accidents theorists agree on one important point: a strong organizational culture—in the form of intense socialization, strict discipline, and isolation from the problems of broader society—can encourage safety with hazardous technologies. These cultural characteristics are fostered in what has been called "a total institution": any organization in which "a large number of like-situated individuals, cut off from wider society for an appreciable period of time, together lead an enclosed, formally administered round of life."[4] The work of the Berkeley high reliability project on U.S. Navy aircraft carriers, for example, stresses the importance of group cohesion, intense training, prolonged socialization, and strict discipline on improved safety of flight operations. Aircraft carriers are indeed "the most total of total institutions": "the fact that organizational members cannot walk away, and cannot quit, affords the organization greater control through socialization."[5] Where Perrow parts company with the Berkeley scholars on this subject, is not over the effects of such cultural characteristics on safety, but rather over whether it is possible and desirable to run other hazardous organizations along such a strict "military" model:

> Since risky systems are run by organizations, the degree of *organizational control over members* is probably an important factor [enhancing safety]. . . . The navy has virtually complete control over the personnel, isolates them from civilian society when they are on sea duty for months at a time, can control every aspect of their behavior, has the means to exercise extensive surveillance over that behavior, can drill them endlessly since there is often not much else for the 6,000 men living under two pitching runways to do anyway, and can make it very plain that their very life is at risk. Were we able to run our nuclear plants this way they might do better, but hopefully we are not prepared to have all risky systems exist as total societies separated from normal civilian affairs.[6]

Such extreme discipline and intense socialization may indeed reduce such common dangers as carelessness, poor training, and drug abuse among individuals operating hazardous technologies. The history of U.S. nuclear weapons command-and-control problems, however, points to a set

---

[4] Erving Goffman, *Asylums: Essays on the Social Situation of Mental Patients and Other Inmates* (New York: Doubleday, 1961), p. xiii. Goffman's main focus is on mental institutions—especially St. Elizabeth's Hospital in Washington, D.C.—but his analysis includes prisons, orphanages, concentration camps, monasteries, and military bases.

[5] Karlene H. Roberts, "Some Characteristics of One Type of High Reliability Organization," *Organization Science* 1, no. 2 (May 1990): 173. Also see Karlene H. Roberts, Denise M. Rousseau, and Todd R. La Porte, "The Culture of High Reliability: Quantitative and Qualitative Assessment aboard Nuclear-Powered Aircraft Carriers" (unpublished manuscript); and Karl E. Weick, "Organizational Culture as a Source of High Reliability," *California Management Review* 39, no. 2 (Winter 1987): 124.

[6] Charles Perrow, "Accidents in High Risk Systems," *Technology Studies* 1, no. 1 (forthcoming): manuscript p. 22. Also see Charles Perrow, *Normal Accidents: Living with High Risk Technologies* (New York: Basic Books, 1984), p. 173.

of severe, but often hidden, side effects, which can significantly *increase* the risk of serious accidents. In any "total institution" (whether it is a military command or a mental hospital) the official goal of the organization (to protect society, for example, or to serve patients) coexists with a set of more parochial, self-serving organizational objectives (to promote and protect itself).[7] Because this is the case, strong "organizational control over members" can be used not only to promote the official goal of the organization, but also more narrow self-interests. This can encourage excessive loyalty and secrecy, disdain for outside expertise, and in some cases even cover-ups of safety problems, in order to protect the reputation of the institution.

Extreme manifestations of such tendencies may well be rare when it comes to nuclear weapons safety in the highly professionalized military organizations of the United States. But they are clearly not totally absent. The apparent misrepresentation of safety violations by the officers and crews at Malmstrom Air Force Base during the Cuban crisis (chapter 2), the failure to report the false warnings in the NORAD Falling Leaves warning radars (chapter 3), and, perhaps most dramatically, General Thomas White's effort to hide the fact that U.S. military aircraft had accidentally penetrated the USSR's warning net from President Eisenhower (chapter 4), all appear to be serious cases in point.

In addition, it must not be forgotten that ordinary men, confronted with such extraordinary demands, can react in counterproductive ways. The Strategic Air Command prided itself on the strict discipline and professionalism expected of SAC officers controlling nuclear weapons: "We demand absolute conformity and near perfection from them in certain aspects of their jobs," General Bruce Holloway, the SAC commander, noted in 1971.[8] The pressures of such an organizational culture, however, clearly backfired in the case of the B-47 pilot at Forbes Air Force Base in January 1963, as was discussed in chapter 4. When the pilot inadvertently flipped on the weapons control switch, one of two switches necessary to arm the thermonuclear bombs on board the aircraft, his fear of reprimand overcame his concern for nuclear safety. He therefore deliberately turned the other switch, to arm the weapons on board, in order to create a more plausible cover story, that a saboteur had somehow sneaked into the aircraft.

---

[7] It is ironic that the Berkeley high reliability theorists explicitly cite Goffman on socialization in total institutions, since he so clearly understood this negative side of such organizations. "Whatever else these institutions do, one of their central effects is to sustain the self-conception of the professional staff employed there. Inmates and lower staff are involved in a vast supportive action—an elaborate dramatized tribute—that has the effect, if not the purpose, of affirming that a medical-like service is in progress here and that the psychiatric staff is providing it. Something about the weakness of this claim is suggested by the industry required to support it." Goffman, *Asylums*, pp. 385–386.

[8] As quoted in Russell E. Dougherty, "The Psychological Climate of Nuclear Command," in Carter et al., eds., *Managing Nuclear Operations*, p. 425.

I strongly suspect that this particular type of behavior has been extremely rare within the Strategic Air Command and other U.S. military commands with control over nuclear weapons. I find it very hard to believe, however, that this one declassified case is the only one of its kind that has occurred over the first forty-seven years of the nuclear age.[9] The extreme discipline and conformity demanded of ordinary individuals can create an "underlife" inside a total institution: hidden forms of behavior, in which men and women follow their own unique voices, against the interests and beyond the grasp of the organization and its leaders.[10] No amount of military socialization, psychological testing, or personnel surveillance is likely to guarantee the mental stability of each and every individual who holds responsibilities for the management of U.S. nuclear weapons.

## Conflicting Interests

The second reason to be pessimistic about the ability of complex organizations to manage hazardous technologies concerns the inevitable existence of conflicting organizational priorities. The evidence in this book has highlighted how difficult it is to improve safety with hazardous technologies, even when leaders place a very high priority upon maintaining such safety. While Perrow is right to note that safety is often significantly reduced when leaders do not have strong incentives to improve safety ("elites do not ride on Liberian tankers"), analysts must be very careful *not* to assume the opposite. The process by which leadership priorities are transformed into organizational behavior is inevitably problematic in large, highly complex organizations. As the "garbage can model" reminds us, ambiguous preferences and conflicting interests often coexist in a state of uneasy tension, and leaders may pay only arbitrary attention to the critical details of deciding among trade-offs.[11]

---

[9] While I do not know of other cases in which officers deliberately armed nuclear weapons, the difficulty in assuring mental stability among nuclear weapons personnel is best seen in the following list of incidents, which occurred within one year of each other at Washington's Bangor Submarine Base. In January 1989, a Marine who was certified as stable by the Personnel Reliability Program (PRP), shot himself in the head with his M-16 in the guard tower. He had earlier told friends that he was the reincarnation of a soldier killed in Vietnam, but they had not reported this. In July 1989, a fire-control technician on a submarine was arrested for the murder by suffocation of an elderly couple in their home. In August 1989, a commander heading a reserve unit was arrested for stabbing a man and a woman to death. In January 1990, a submarine fire-control technician shot and killed two fellow crew members. On these incidents see, Herbert L. Abrams, "Human Reliability and Safety in the Handling of Nuclear Weapons," *Science and Global Security* 2, no. 4 (1991): 325–349.

[10] See Goffman, *Asylums*, pp. 171–320.

[11] Michael D. Cohen, James G. March, and Johan P. Olsen, "A Garbage Can Model of

Some of the dangerous events that occurred during the Cuban missile crisis are less surprising when viewed from this organizational perspective. President Kennedy may well have been, as Robert Kennedy later put it, "committed to doing everything possible to lessen . . . the chance of mistake, miscalculation, or misunderstanding."[12] But he also wanted to display political determination and maximize military preparedness. He also had other priorities—the economy, alliance management, the upcoming elections—to attend to.

It would be highly misleading, however, to view most of the dangerous nuclear operations that occurred during the crisis as the result of a conscious trade-off by President Kennedy between conflicting values. Most of the critical decisions influencing the risk of accidental war were made by lower-ranking officials, without the involvement or full awareness of political authorities in Washington. The priority of officers at Vandenberg Air Force Base—to keep up with their missile test schedule—produced the ICBM launch on the night of October 26 (chapter 2). The priorities of the Falling Leaves radar operators and the NORAD command post officers— to demonstrate how well the Cuban Missile Early Warning system had worked—apparently led these men to fail to report the false warnings that occurred during the crisis in the official after-action reports (chapter 3). The priority of General Truman Landon—to be ready for nuclear war if necessary—resulted in the potentially provocative increases in the number of nuclear-armed aircraft on alert in Europe (chapter 2). These were not the products of mindless individuals following organizational routines. They reflected the priorities of important actors, but not those of the president.

### Constraints on Learning

Third, although normal accidents theory usefully focuses attention on the ways in which organizational learning can be constrained by the lack of incentives for change and biased interpretations about the causes of accidents, the evidence here suggests that the difficulties involved with organizational learning with hazardous technologies may be even more severe than has been previously recognized. The problems of learning from past safety incidents, witnessed in both the Strategic Air Command and the North American Aerospace Defense Command, were not the result of their senior leaders lacking an interest in learning to improve safety. Such inter-

Organizational Choice," in James G. March, *Decisions and Organizations* (Oxford, UK: Basil Blackwell, 1988), pp. 294–334.
[12] Robert F. Kennedy, *Thirteen Days* (New York: W. W. Norton, 1969), p. 127.

ests existed and were often expressed. Nor was the failure to learn caused by a basic lack of innovative capability within the organization. When it came to weapons procurement, war planning, or emergency crisis operations, innovation came quickly. The root of the problem was more political in nature: strong disincentives existed against exposing serious failures. This influenced the reporting of near-accidents by operators, the beliefs of organizational historians about what is acceptable to record, and the public interpretation of events by senior authorities.

Learning was also constrained by the inherent difficulties involved in keeping two sets of records (one for outsiders and one for insiders) straight in one's organizational memory. Anthropologists talk about "back-stage behavior" and "front-stage behavior," highlighting how important it is for the scholar to get behind the social mask of the subject.[13] That is certainly also important in any effort to understand the activities of a modern, complex organization. I would emphasize, however, how often the front-stage behavior can influence the back-stage behavior, in ways that are neither intended nor fully understood by the actors themselves. It is not surprising that the military commands that are responsible for controlling nuclear forces would create a veil of safety to manage their image in front of the president, the Congress, and the public. What is surprising is that the degree to which this veil also influenced their internal perceptions, their recording and use of history, and their ability to learn from past mistakes.

The persistence of this phenomenon is striking. After the January 1961 crash of a B-52 bomber, SAC insisted that severe air turbulence, and not structural fatigue cracks in the wings, was the problem and refused to fix the B-52 fleet (chapter 4). Despite the series of serious false warnings that emerged in the Falling Leaves warning system during the Cuban crisis, Air Defense Command officers declared that the radars "satisfactorily" performed their mission, commended the operators for "superior performance," and recommended (successfully) that the Moorestown radar be used again in future crises (chapter 3 and chapter 5). After the January 1968 Thule bomber crash, SAC could not admit, even in its internal documents, that the accident had anything to do with the termination of the BMEWS monitor mission (chapter 4). A number of B-52 bombers accidents even mysteriously disappeared from SAC's 1988 history of the command's alert operations (chapter 4).

Organizations are often viewed as being able to learn only through the slow, incremental process of trial and error. The history presented here, however, is not just a further piece of evidence showing how difficult it is for

---

[13] For example, see Gerald D. Berreman, *Behind Many Masks* (Ithaca, N.Y.: Society for Applied Anthropology, 1962).

large organizations to learn from success.[14] These cases show something more disturbing: the resourcefulness with which committed individuals and organizations can turn the experience of failure into the memory of success.[15]

## The Measure of Safety

A fourth set of lessons for the study of organizational safety is suggested by the insights of the "institutional" school in sociology. In 1949, Philip Selznick published his seminal study of the Tennessee Valley Authority, which warned his readers that "the important point about organizations is that, though they are tools, each nonetheless has a life of its own."[16] Organizations have their stated goals, but they are also strongly influenced by powerful individuals, both inside and outside the organization, who try to shape their goals and manipulate their behavior. More recent writers in the institutionalist tradition have focused on the pressures that run in the other direction, emphasizing how outside observers and actors are also influenced by powerful organizations through the information they provide, the criteria they set for evaluation, the assumptions they spread, and the expectations they raise.[17]

This points to a disturbing problem. Scholars are part of that outside environment and are thus also influenced, in ways in which we are usually unaware, by the organization. Unless this is more fully recognized, scholars and the public alike will too uncritically accept the self-image of the powerful organizations that manage hazardous technologies in our society.

A certain skepticism about the organizations we observe and an awareness of the subtle influences that they have on us is therefore warranted. The severe difficulties involved here can perhaps be best seen in the high reliability theorists' home court: the study of U.S. naval aircraft carrier operations. Are U.S. aircraft carriers really, as has been repeatedly claimed, a model of a high reliability organization? The available records do clearly show that there have been impressive decreases in the number of aircraft

---

[14] See Graham T. Allison, *Essence of Decision* (Boston: Little, Brown, 1971), p. 85, and Barry R. Posen, *The Sources of Military Doctrine* (Ithaca, N.Y.: Cornell University Press, 1984), p. 57.

[15] For related insights in what may only appear to be a very different context, see Leon Festinger, Henry W. Rieken, and Stanley Schachter, *When Prophecy Fails* (New York: Harper and Row, 1964).

[16] Philip Selznick, *TVA and the Grassroots* (Berkeley: University of California Press, 1949), p. 10.

[17] See Walter W. Powell and Paul J. DiMaggio, eds., *The New Institutionalism in Organizational Analysis* (Chicago: University of Chicago Press, 1991).

accidents on the flight decks of U.S. carriers over the past decade.[18] A more skeptical approach would be concerned, however, with that fact that the records here are entirely generated and maintained by the navy itself. A more skeptical approach would be concerned about whether the number of aircraft accidents is the appropriate measure of safety and reliability on aircraft carriers. (An obvious alternative would be to examine whether the nuclear weapons on board carriers have been handled in a safe and secure manner.)[19] Finally, a more skeptical inquiry would be concerned about the possibility that improvements in carrier flight safety in peacetime exercises, which is in fact what is being touted as a sign of high reliability, might lead to *decreased* safety in real crisis or wartime operations. After all, to the degree that fewer risks are taken in peacetime exercises, it is possible that the safety improvements are real in one sense, but quite artificial in another: they may result in safer exercises, but in less safe operations in any real military contingency.

In short, the final lesson for organizational theorists is a simple reminder, which applies to all other organizations that attempt to manage hazardous technologies, as well as the U.S. nuclear arsenal. Things may not be as they seem. One should never assume that the machine does not need to be fixed, simply because one has been told that it "ain't broke."

## IMPLICATIONS FOR DETERRENCE THEORY

After Hiroshima and Nagasaki, there was relatively little debate about the central *physical* effects of nuclear weapons. That is not surprising. The atomic destruction of those two cities was so devastating that political authorities could not ignore that a revolution in military technology had occurred. It may have taken some time for some military officers, who had to justify existing weapons systems, to accept the bomb's awesome

[18] See the evidence discussed in Karlene H. Roberts, "Managing High Reliability Organizations," *California Management Review* 32, no. 4 (Summer 1990): 102–103, and Rosario Rausa, "To Fly Safely," *U.S. Naval Institute Proceedings* 112, no. 8 (August 1986): 69–73.

[19] The declassified data are very incomplete on this issue, but what exists paints a less than perfect picture of this "high reliability organization." In 1986, portions of three U.S. Navy reports were released to the American Friends Service Committee as evidence in a law suit. These documents outline a total of 381 navy nuclear weapon accidents and incidents from 1965 to 1977. About one third of these were aboard U.S. aircraft carriers, including one accident in 1965 in which an A-4E aircraft carrying a B-43 nuclear bomb was accidently dropped off the deck of a carrier and sank to the bottom of the Sea of Japan. Moreover, there did *not* appear to be a trend toward improved nuclear weapons safety over time in the navy records, a significant piece of evidence cutting against the belief in organizational learning. See Summary of Navy Nuclear Weapons Accidents and Incidents, American Friends Service Committee, Philadelphia, 1986.

power.[20] American political leaders, however, quickly understood that these were weapons of unprecedented destructive power.

What is more surprising is the absence of a continued debate about the *political* effects of nuclear weapons on international politics. Among both political scientists and historians who study this issue, a near-consensus seems to exist: a long and distinguished list of scholars argue that nuclear weapons have been a moderating force in international relations. There is a shorter, but still impressive, list of scholars who argue that since nuclear weapons added an element of stability to the superpower rivalry during the Cold War, the spread of nuclear weapons to further countries may not be such a bad thing in the future. At a very basic level, the ideas and evidence presented in this book challenge both of these beliefs about the stabilizing effects of nuclear weapons.

### The Effects of Nuclear Weapons

The logic of nuclear deterrence theory suggests that nuclear weapons were a force for stability in the Cold War, precisely because they made the consequences of war so horrible. This has been called "the crystal ball effect" of nuclear weapons. Imagine that Kaiser William II of Germany or Tzar Nicholas I of Russia had held a crystal ball that enabled them to see the future during the July 1914 crisis. If they had been able to see the world of 1918, with their empires shattered, millions of their countrymen killed, and their governments overthrown, wouldn't they have acted far more cautiously?[21]

Among historians, John Lewis Gaddis has perhaps best expressed the belief "that the statesmen of the post-1945 superpowers have, compared to their predecessors, been exceedingly cautious in risking war with one another":

> In order to see this point, one need only run down the list of crises in Soviet-American relations since the end of World War II: Iran, 1946; Greece, 1947; Berlin and Czechoslovakia, 1948; Korea, 1950; the East Berlin riots, 1953; the Hungarian uprising, 1956; Berlin again, 1958–59; the U-2 incident,

[20] As late as 1949, the director of the U.S. Navy's Ordnance Branch told a congressional committee that "you could stand in the open at one end of the north-south runway at the Washington National Airport, with no more protection than the clothes you now have on, and have an atomic bomb explode at the other end of the runway without serious injury to you." As quoted in Robert Frank Futrell, *Ideas, Concepts, Doctrine: A History of Basic Thinking in the United States Air Force, 1907–1964* (Maxwell AFB, Ala.: Air University, 1971), p. 122.

[21] See Albert Carnesale et al., *Living with Nuclear Weapons* (Cambridge, Mass.: Harvard University Press, 1983), p. 44.

1960; Berlin again, 1961; the Cuban missile crisis, 1962; Czechoslovakia again, 1968; the Yom Kippur war, 1973; Afghanistan, 1979; Poland, 1981; the Korean airliner incident, 1983—one need only to run down this list to see how many occasions there have been in relations between Washington and Moscow that in almost any other age, and among almost any other antagonists, would sooner or later have produced war.[22]

"It seems inescapable," Gaddis concludes, "that what has really made the difference in inducing this unaccustomed caution has been the workings of the nuclear deterrent."[23]

Many political scientists hold almost identical views. They differ from Gaddis only in their greater willingness to predict the future, rather than just explain the past. Nuclear weapons have never been used in any war since 1945, and, as long as states have sufficient forces to guarantee massive retaliation, numerous political scientists have argued that this nuclear peace can be maintained into the indefinite future.[24]

The writings of Kenneth Waltz are the most clear and confident expressions of this faith in the deterrent power of nuclear weapons. "Nuclear weapons have been given a bad name," Waltz maintains:

Because catastrophic outcomes of nuclear exchanges are easy to imagine, leaders of states will shrink in horror from initiating them. . . . Never since the Treaty of Westphalia in 1648, which conventionally marks the beginning of modern history, have great powers enjoyed a longer period of peace than we have known since the Second World War. One can scarcely believe that the

---

[22] John Lewis Gaddis, "The Long Peace: Elements of Stability in the Postwar International System," *International Security* 10, no. 4 (Spring 1986): 121 (emphasis added). For similar views among historians see: Michael Howard, *The Causes of War* (Cambridge, Mass.: Harvard University Press, 1983), p. 22; and McGeorge Bundy, *Danger and Survival: Choices About the Bomb in the First Fifty Years* (New York: Random House, 1988), pp. 593–594.

[23] Gaddis, "The Long Peace," p. 121.

[24] Robert Jervis, for example, argues: "The most obvious reason why the pattern [of successful nuclear deterrence] is not likely to change is perhaps also the most important one. The costs of a major, but still limited, nuclear war would be greater than those ever experienced; the costs of an all-out war are simply unimaginable. . . . With the penalty of blundering into war so great, even bold or foolish decision-makers behave cautiously." Robert Jervis, *The Illogic of American Nuclear Strategy* (Ithaca, N.Y.: Cornell University Press, 1984), p. 155. For similar views among political scientists see: Michael Mandelbaum, *The Nuclear Question: The United States and Nuclear Weapons, 1946–1976* (Cambridge, U.K.: Cambridge University Press, 1979), pp. 217–223; Stephen Van Evera, "Primed for Peace: Europe After the Cold War," *International Security* 15, no. 3 (Winter 1990/91): 12; John J. Mearsheimer, "Back to the Future: Instability in Europe After the Cold War," *International Security* 15, no. 1 (Summer 1990): 28; and Robert J. Art, "A Defensible Defense: America's Grand Strategy After the Cold War," *International Security* 15, no. 4 (Spring 1991): 21–23.

presence of nuclear weapons does not greatly help to explain this happy condition.[25]

Waltz's confident prediction seems to follow inexorably from this logic: in a nuclear world, "a nation will be deterred from attacking even if it believes that there is only a possibility that its adversary will retaliate;" therefore "the probability of major war among states having nuclear weapons approaches zero."[26]

The underlying assumption that unites so many historians and political scientists on this issue is the belief that wars begin only when political leaders determine that war is in the interest of the state.[27] These scholars are all following Clausewitz's famous maxim: "War is a continuation of policy by other means." War is seen as a rational tool, controlled and used by statesmen, to achieve important ends. Wars do not begin by accident.

## The Dangerous Side Effects of Nuclear Weapons

This book has obviously not discovered the existence of an unknown accidental nuclear war. It has uncovered a series of accidents and near-accidents and has presented some plausible scenarios under which these events could have led to further escalation. Even here, however, reasonable readers can disagree over the probability that any one of the incidents would have escalated to an accidental war. But at a minimum, the theories and evidence presented here should raise serious doubts about the central assumption that a nuclear war could not occur unless political leaders decided it was in their state's interests. In light of the evidence presented here, the belief that nuclear deterrence can prevent nuclear war under all circumstances should be seen as exactly that: a belief, not a fact.

In prenuclear history, "accidental" wars—wars that were caused by unauthorized actions of military officers, false warnings that an attack was imminent, or technical failures of weapons systems—were admittedly rare. "It is difficult," as Geoffrey Blainey writes, "to find a war which on investi-

[25] Kenneth N. Waltz, "Nuclear Myths and Political Realities," *American Political Science Review* 84, no. 3 (September 1990): quotes from pp. 731, 734, and 744.

[26] Kenneth N. Waltz, "The Origins of War in Neorealist Theory," in Robert I. Rotberg and Theodore K. Rabb, eds., *The Origin and Prevention of Major Wars* (Cambridge, U.K.: Cambridge University Press, 1988), pp. 50–51.

[27] Even scholars who do not emphasize the stabilizing effects of nuclear weapons nevertheless hold this central Clausewitzian perspective. John Mueller, for example, maintains that "wars are not begun out of casual caprice or idle fancy, but because one country or another decides that it can profit from (and not simply win) the war—the combination of risk, gain, and costs appears preferable to peace." John Mueller, "The Essential Irrelevance of Nuclear Weapons: Stability in the Postwar World," *International Security* 13, no. 2 (Fall 1988): 68–69.

gation fits this description."[28] It is indeed difficult, but it is not impossible. The Japanese invasion of Manchuria in 1931, for example, was clearly an unauthorized attack, initiated by Japanese Kwantung Army officers against the wishes of the government in Tokyo.[29] The French and Indian War in North America (1754–1763) was at least sparked by a false warning, which was sent to London in April 1754 by the colonial governor of Massachusetts, that the French had invaded Maine.[30] The Battle of Wounded Knee on December 29, 1890, was caused by the following events, which occurred during a U.S. Army search of a Sioux village: "Nervous troopers fingered their carbine triggers. One seized a deaf man and grasped his rifle. It went off. The chanting priest threw a handful of dust into the air. A knot of Indians dropped their rifles and leveled Winchester repeaters at a rank of soldiers. Both sides fired at once, and the fight that neither side intended or expected burst upon them."[31]

In an important sense, however, prenuclear history is a very poor guide in this matter. Not only should one worry more about rare events when nuclear weapons are involved; but the nuclear weapons arsenals we have created appear to have themselves increased the likelihood of accidental war. In the past there was usually a considerable amount of time, often days or weeks, between a statesman's receipt of warning that war was on the horizon, the final decisions to go to war, and the actual use of force.

[28] Geoffrey Blainey, *The Causes of War* (New York: Free Press, 1973), p. 141. This is also a central theme in Marc Trachtenberg, *Strategy and History* (Princeton, N.J.: Princeton University Press, 1991), pp. 47–99; and Evan Luard, *War in International Society* (New Haven, Conn.: Yale University Press, 1987), pp. 229–233.

[29] See Seki Hiroharu, "The Manchurian Incident, 1931," and Shimada Toshihiko, "The Extension of Hostilities, 1931–1932," both in James William Morley, ed., *Japan Erupts: The London Naval Conference and the Manchurian Incident, 1928–1932* (New York: Columbia University Press, 1984), pp. 139–230, 241–335; and W. G. Beasley, *Japanese Imperialism* (Oxford, U.K.: Clarendon Press, 1987), pp. 175–197. Concerning this example, Blainey argues that "nevertheless the war, while not intended by the Japanese government, was fully intended by the Japanese Kwangtung army; and the army by its defiance had become in effect the Japanese government in Manchuria." Blainey, *The Causes of War*, p. 144. By arguing that whoever makes a decision to begin a war is "in effect" the government, Blainey defines away the possibility of an unauthorized attack.

[30] See Patrice Higgonet, "The Origins of the Seven Years' War," *Journal of Modern History* 40, no. 1 (March 1968): 59. For a contrary view, however, see T. R. Clayton, "The Duke of Newcastle, The Earl Of Halifax, and the American Origins of the Seven Years War," *The Historical Journal* 24, no. 3 (1981): 571–603.

[31] Robert M. Utley, *The Indian Frontier of the American West, 1846–1890* (Albuquerque: University of New Mexico Press, 1984), p. 256. Some Army officers claimed that the dirt throwing was a prearranged Indian signal to begin fighting, but most witnesses rejected that assumption. See Richard E. Jensen, R. Eli Paul, and John E. Carter, *Eyewitnesses at Wounded Knee* (Lincoln: University of Nebraska Press, 1991), p. 118. For more details, see Robert M. Utley, *The Last Days of the Sioux* (New Haven, Conn.: Yale University Press, 1963), pp. 200–230. I would like to thank Stephen Van Evera for suggesting this example.

Military mobilization took time, time that could be used to review decisions, correct mistakes, and send new orders if necessary to the field.[32] It is the constant readiness of modern nuclear forces—especially the ability of modern missiles to launch on a moment's notice (and their lack of ability to return)—which underscores the tight coupling inherent in current arsenals.

Thus, normal accidents theory pessimism and deterrence theory optimism may both be correct. Nuclear weapons may well have made *deliberate* war less likely, but, the complex and tightly coupled nuclear arsenal we have constructed has simultaneously made *accidental* war more likely. Therefore, even if one accepts the possibility that nuclear weapons (or more precisely secure second-strike forces) greatly reduce the likelihood that a major war would be in a state's interests, this does not mean that war is impossible. The long history of "near accidents" with U.S. nuclear weapons suggests indeed that the structural characteristics that have led to serious accidents in other hazardous high-technology systems— interactive complexity and tight coupling—have had the same pernicious effect in nuclear arsenals. There has never been an accidental detonation. There has never been the final step of escalation. But that may just be a matter of time.

Given the evidence presented in this book, the burden of proof should shift. The history presented here suggests that nuclear weapons have been far less safe than has been previously recognized. At a minimum, the attraction some feel for nuclear weapons as an ultimate deterrent must be tempered by a much greater awareness of the risk of accidents. And those who predict that nuclear weapons can be managed safely indefinitely into the future should have to prove their case and not simply refer back to a perfect safety record that never really existed.

### The Spread of Nuclear Weapons

A smaller, but prominent, group of scholars have taken the argument about the stabilizing effects of nuclear weapons to its logical extreme: nuclear arsenals, not only significantly reduced the risk of Soviet-American armed conflict during the Cold War, but these weapons could also reduce the likelihood of war if spread through many regional settings. Kenneth Waltz, once again, serves as the best example of this position:

> Nuclear weapons, responsibly used, make wars hard to start. Nations that have nuclear weapons have strong incentives to use them responsibly. These

[32] See Thomas C. Schelling, *Arms and Influence* (New Haven, Conn.: Yale University Press, 1966) p. 20.

statements hold true for small as for big nuclear powers. Because they do, the measured spread of nuclear weapons is more to be welcomed than feared.[33]

Others limit their support for proliferation to specific regions of the world. Stephen Van Evera, for example, makes an argument, similar to Waltz's position, with respect to Europe:

> The nuclear revolution makes conquest among great powers virtually impossible. A victor now must destroy almost all of an opponent's nuclear arsenal— an enormous task requiring massive technical and material superiority. As a result, even lesser powers can now stand alone against states with far greater resources, as they never could before. . . . The possibility of nuclear proliferation should thus be seen as a net benefit to peace in Europe.[34]

Both Waltz and Van Evera, to their credit, do recognize that nuclear proliferation, at least in theory, does pose some increased risk of nuclear weapons accidents and accidental war. Both maintain, however, that such dangers are temporary and can be easily fixed. Waltz insists, for example, that "hiding nuclear weapons and keeping them under control are tasks for which the ingenuity of numerous states is adequate":

> All nuclear countries must live through a time when their forces are crudely designed. All countries have so far been able to control them. . . . Why should we expect new nuclear states to experience greater difficulties than the old ones were able to cope with?[35]

Van Evera limits his enthusiasm to states that are large and rich enough to be able to duplicate the apparent U.S. experience with nuclear safety. "If Germany decides to become a nuclear power, the United States should not resist," he argues. The Germans have "the resources needed to develop an invulnerable deterrent *secure from accident* and terrorism."[36]

---

[33] Kenneth N. Waltz, *The Spread of Nuclear Weapons: More May Be Better*, Adelphi Paper 171 (London: International Institute for Strategic Studies, 1981), p. 30. Bruce Bueno de Mesquita similarly argues that "the logic of deterrence indicates that beyond some point, each addition of a nuclear capability diminishes the threat of nuclear war, and does so at an increasing rate. . . . Such logic shows clearly and compellingly that retarding nuclear proliferation can be extremely dangerous, not only to America's interests, but to world peace as well." Bruce Bueno de Mesquita, "Nuclear Peace Through Selective Nuclear Proliferation," (manuscript, Stanford University), p. 30. Also see: Bruce Bueno de Mesquita and William H. Riker, "An Assessment of the Merits of Selective Nuclear Proliferation," *Journal of Conflict Resolution* 26, no. 2 (June 1982): 283–306; John J. Weltman, "Nuclear Devolution and World Order," *World Politics* 32, no. 2 (January 1980): 169–193; and Bruce Berkowitz, "Proliferation, Deterrence, and the Likelihood of War," *Journal of Conflict Resolution* 29, no. 1 (March 1985): 112–136.

[34] Van Evera, "Primed For Peace," pp. 13–14.

[35] Waltz, *The Spread of Nuclear Weapons*, p. 16.

[36] Van Evera, "Primed for Peace," p. 54 (emphasis added). Van Evera does acknowledge

## Proliferation and Accidents

This book challenges these ideas on two key grounds. First, the U.S. and the former USSR did not easily control their nuclear forces and, indeed, there are strong reasons to believe that many bugs in the command-and-control systems of those countries still remain. The superpowers had many more close calls than previously recognized, and these close calls continued to occur long after the early years when "forces were crudely designed." Why then should we expect new nuclear states to have fewer difficulties than the old ones experienced?

In this light, nuclear proliferation appears to be more dangerous than Waltz and Van Evera recognize. Existing nuclear powers have "coped" with the problem only in the narrow sense that accidental detonations and accidental war have thus far been avoided. They have not, however, made nuclear arsenals that are "secure from accident."

Second, there are compelling reasons to predict that many would-be nuclear proliferators will develop arsenals that are considerably *less* safe than those of current nuclear powers. First, some emergent nuclear powers, including former republics of the Soviet Union, may not be able to afford even a modicum of mechanical safety devices and modern warning sensors and will therefore be more prone to accidents and false warnings. Moreover, although all countries may start with crude nuclear arsenals, some may be significantly more crude than others. This clearly was the case with the Iraqi nuclear weapons program, as United Nations' inspectors discovered soon after the 1991 Persian Gulf War:

> The inspectors found out one other thing about the Iraqi bomb—it is highly unstable. The design calls for cramming so much weapon-grade uranium into the core, they say, that the bomb would inevitably be on the verge of going off—even while sitting on the workbench. "It could go off if a rifle bullet hit it," one inspector says, adding: "I wouldn't want to be around if it fell off the edge of this desk."[37]

Second, the military services in many of these states are more powerful, relative to civilian leaders, than is the case in the United States. In states

that "Europe is more dangerous with 20 or 25 fingers on the nuclear trigger than with a handful, because the additional states might be unable to secure any nuclear forces that they build." John Mearsheimer, who has also recommended German acquisition of nuclear weapons, similarly argues against the widespread proliferation of nuclear weapons since it "could increase the likelihood that nuclear weapons could be fired due to accident, unauthorized use, terrorist seizure, or irrational decision-making." Mearsheimer, "Back to the Future," p. 38.

[37] Gary Milhollin, "Building Saddam Hussein's Bomb," *New York Times Magazine*, March 8, 1992, p. 32.

with a less professionalized pattern of civil-military relations, organizational learning is likely to be even more constrained by biased analyses, compartmentalization of information, and incentives to protect the autonomy and reputation of military organizations.[38] Thus, even if one accepted Waltz's argument that all nuclear countries live through a period of risk, that period may be considerably longer for nuclear powers in the developing world.

Third, many emerging nuclear powers will be developing their nuclear forces to counter pressing security threats. Under such circumstances, the governments will feel strong pressures to keep their new nuclear arsenals on a high state of alert readiness. This will ensure that these arsenals, even if they are less complex than the existing superpower array of forces and command systems, will nevertheless have the other structural characteristic (tight coupling) that will make them accident prone.[39]

In short, the nuclear weapons safety problem is like walking on thin ice. The fact that system has not caved in so far, does not mean than it will not in the future. One should hope that fewer heavily armed states step forward.

## IMPROVING NUCLEAR WEAPONS SAFETY

Normal accidents theory suggests that serious accidents with hazardous technologies are inevitable, in the long run, in any organization that displays high degrees of both interactive complexity and tight coupling. The historical evidence presented in this book has provided strong support for this theory. Although there has never been an accidental nuclear detonation, there have been numerous close calls with U.S. nuclear weapons in both peacetime and in crises. I have tried to demonstrate, with a number of counterfactual scenarios, that it was less good design than good fortune that prevented many of these incidents from escalating out of control: under other plausible circumstances, these incidents could have had tragic

[38] A counterargument is that professional military officers may be *less* likely to recommend using military force than civilians. Richard Betts's work has shown that this has been the case in the United States since 1945. Betts's work is explicitly limited to the U.S. experience, however, and he also notes that when they recommend using force, professional military officers tend to advise using *decisive* force. Following Betts's logic, it appears likely that a state in which military officers have more power over decisions would be more likely to use nuclear weapons, if it does go to war. See Richard K. Betts, *Soldiers, Statesmen, and Cold War Crises* (Cambridge, Mass.: Harvard University Press, 1977).

[39] If a nuclear power acquires an arsenal largely to enhance its international prestige, it may maintain its forces on a low state of alert, thereby reducing this problem. See Peter D. Feaver, "Command and Control in Emerging Nuclear Nations," *International Security* 17, no. 3 (Winter 1992–1993): 160–187.

endings. The historical evidence has further shown that efforts to improve nuclear weapons safety, by adding redundant safety devices, can be counterproductive and that organizational learning from dangerous incidents in the past has been less than complete.

Thus logic and evidence both lead to a very pessimistic conclusion. The risk of a serious nuclear weapons accident on any given day may be extremely low. In the long run, however, unless something is done to change the current situation, the likelihood of a serious nuclear weapons accident is extremely high. Under some conditions, that accident could lead to an accidental war. So what can be done?

Three basic approaches to a better future exist. First, we could try to manage the problem: following the advice of the high reliability theorists, we could adopt policies and try to reform organizations in order to provide enhanced safety. Second, we could simply abandon the technology. Third, we could change the structure of the organizations that control the technology. With respect to nuclear weapons, the first approach focuses on improving the safety of the nuclear arsenal through better organizational design and management. The second approach calls for complete nuclear disarmament. The third approach requires that radical changes be made in the structure of the U.S. nuclear arsenal. Each option will be discussed in turn.

### High Reliability Efforts

The first option is to continue doing what we have always done: to try to manage the nuclear weapons safety problem though trial-and-error organizational learning, by better organizational culture, training, and exercises, and through the deployment of more and improved redundant safety devices. I certainly do not want to dismiss the value of such activities entirely. In some contexts, they can have a positive impact. Yet, as the analysis of high reliability theory throughout this book has stressed, there are likely to be severe limits to the degree to which such strategies can ever be effective. In addition, there are reasons to believe that such schemes are not likely to be implemented fully. It should also be recognized that such strategies can backfire, producing effects on safety counter to those intended. For all these reasons, a pessimistic appraisal of this approach for improving future nuclear weapons safety is warranted.

### Learning Revisited

It is possible to identify three ways in which organizational learning about nuclear weapons safety could be improved. First, learning could be encouraged through having more vigorous and more *independent* review of nuclear operations and safety. Independent review and monitoring agencies are helpful for all organizations that manage hazardous technology: they provide a forum for devil's advocacy, prevent organizational blind spots from developing, help monitor the implementation of regulations, and reduce the temptation for organizations to be guided by narrow conceptions of self-interest. The military commands that control the U.S. nuclear arsenal, however, are to a great extent *self-monitoring organizations*. When compared to the set of strong regulatory agencies developed to help society control other hazardous technologies, the weakness of independent oversight over safety issues in the U.S. nuclear arsenal is striking. Civilian officials in the Department of Energy and Department of Defense do have considerable power over safety-related design issues in specific nuclear weapons systems, but even here the influence of the military services is extremely strong.[40] With respect to controlling the details of the kinds of military operations that produced many of the safety problems described in this book, however, civilian oversight is minimal. The nuclear alert plans are developed by the military commands themselves; military organizations develop and maintain their own safety records; the military services monitor, to a large extent, their own implementation of nuclear safety regulations. Under such conditions, it is not surprising that full information is not always forthcoming, or that criticism of the organizations will be constrained in investigations of safety problems.[41] The creation of an independent institution, run by civilians with military assistance, to review and monitor critical operational aspects of nuclear safety could help considerably.[42] One should not be optimistic, however, about the likelihood of

[40] At the time of this writing, two interagency groups exist to make detailed decisions on nuclear weapons safety during weapons design process: the Project Officers' Group (POG) and the Nuclear Weapons System Safety Group (NWSSG). As Sidney Drell, John Foster, and Charles Townes diplomatically noted, however, in their special report to Congress in 1990: "Both the POG and the NWSSG are always chaired by the Using Service, and the majority of their members are usually both active duty military officers and civilians who report directly to the military service which is the customer. This structure builds in career conflict-of-interest issues." Sidney D. Drell, John S. Foster, and Charles H. Townes, *Nuclear Weapons Safety*, Report of the Panel on Nuclear Weapons Safety of the Committee on Armed Services, House of Representatives, 101st Congress, 2d sess., p. 18.

[41] For an important example see Tom Burgess, "Cover-up aboard Nuclear Sub Alleged: Encounters with Soviet Vessels Distorted Crewmen Declare," *San Diego Union and Tribune*, August 6, 1989, p. 1.

[42] Such an organization would provide oversight of the existing Department of Defense and Department of Energy weapons inspection units. One possible model would be the Aerospace Safety Advisory Panel (ASAP), which provides an independent means to review and monitor safety issues for the National Aeronautics and Space Administration (NASA). By Congressional statute, ASAP has no more than nine members, of whom up to four may come from NASA. See Diane Vaughan, "Autonomy, Interdependence, and Social Control: NASA and the Space Shuttle *Challenger*," *Administrative Science Quarterly* 35, no. 2 (June 1990): 242–245.

creating such an institution. The history of past efforts to provide strong civilian oversight over other aspects of nuclear operations strongly suggests that military resistance against intrusions into areas of their traditional autonomy and control will be prolonged and severe.[43]

Second, nuclear weapons safety could be greatly improved through extensive *vicarious* learning: Russian and American officials could, for example, share with each other the details of both previous safety problems with nuclear weapons that have occurred and the set of bizarre, unpredictable events that have produced false warning incidents in the past. The objective of such talks would be to supplement simple trial-and-error learning with learning from each others' past mistakes. There are, however, a number of reasons to be quite pessimistic here as well. Even with the end of the Cold War, concerns about the stability of democratic reforms in Russia and fears about the potential for critical design information being passed on to third countries, make it unreasonable to expect that many details about nuclear weapons designs, for example, will be shared. Moreover, the fact that Russia and the United States have not already shared information about even less sensitive operational problems that have been fixed—such as the causes of the 1979 and 1980 NORAD false arming incidents discussed in chapter 5—suggests that something more than national security is at stake here. Strong organizational impediments against such talks exist: the desire to protect the nuclear command organizations from embarrassment makes it unlikely that full and frank disclosure of their past errors will occur.

Third, it would be of great help if more detailed studies of past nuclear weapons and command and control safety problems were conducted. It is almost a cliché for scholarly studies to recommend that more research on the subject be done, but in this case, it is more than justified. The research for this book uncovered what I believe is more than the tip of the iceberg of safety problems in the U.S. nuclear arsenal, but how much more than the tip, I do not know. This has been the product of an independent scholar—armed with useful theories, aided by the Freedom of Information Act, and assisted (sometimes) by cooperative government officials and military officers—but it is by no means the definitive history of nuclear weapons command and control problems. For more effective learning to take place, much more work will need to be done at a classified level inside the government to develop a deeper understanding of the trials and errors experienced in the past. If my theories are right, such research is desperately

---

[43] For example, it took over forty years to develop even a moderate amount of civilian control over the details of the nuclear weapons targeting process. See Scott D. Sagan, *Moving Targets:Nuclear Strategy and National Security* (Princeton, N.J.: Princeton University Press, 1989), pp. 176–186; and Janne E. Nolan, *Guardians of the Arsenal: The Politics of Nuclear Strategy* (New York: Basic Books, 1989), pp. 233–285.

needed. Unfortunately, if my theories are right, the organizations involved in nuclear operations are also highly unlikely to conduct such research.[44]

## Culture and Training Revisited

Following the high reliability theory would also lead to efforts to change the organizational culture of the military commands that control nuclear weapons, and the training that is given to their officers. One key lesson of the historical experience of the Cuban missile crisis was that despite General Thomas Power's admonition to all SAC officers to "use calm judgment" and make "no mistakes," a number of activities nevertheless took place that increased the risk of an accident, as officers pushed vigorously to maximize the readiness of their nuclear forces. This was unfortunate, but it should not have been entirely unexpected. The culture of the Strategic Air Command, after all, strongly emphasized operational safety, but it also emphasized the great necessity to maximize military power for the sake of nuclear deterrence. It was a culture of warriors.[45] SAC officers felt, to a degree that is hard for outsiders to recognize, a deep and personal responsibility for preventing a Soviet nuclear attack. Under such conditions, some tension between the desire for safety and the desire for readiness was inevitable, and the fact that some officers would occasionally "cut corners"—taking risky actions to prepare for the war they hoped to avoid—should not have been surprising.

In the wake of the end of the Cold War, the air force's Strategic Air Command was deactivated, and replaced by a new joint air force–navy organization, the U.S. Strategic Command. If nuclear safety is to be an even higher priority in the post–Cold War world, there is a corresponding need to change organizational culture, a point that is apparently understood by the leaders of the new Strategic Command.[46] In an ideal world, the organi-

[44] To make matters worse, some important data have been destroyed. It appears unlikely, for example, that the full details explaining why, during the June 1980 false warning incident, the Pacific Command's airborne command post was launched or why the Atlantic Command incorrectly reported an indication that SLBMs had been launched, can ever be reconstructed, since both these military commands reported that they have destroyed the command post logs for those critical dates. See chapter 5 for details.

[45] In the late 1980s, General John Chain, the SAC commander, even changed the motto of the Strategic Command from the traditional "Peace is our profession," to "War is our profession; peace is our product." General George Lee Butler, Chain's successor and the first commander of the new Strategic Command, immediately reinstated the traditional motto upon assuming command.

[46] See Lynn Eden, "The Political Preconditions for Very Deep Cuts or Elimination of Nuclear Weapons in the United States and Russia," paper prepared for the Twenty-first Pugwash Workshop on Nuclear Forces, Geneva, Switzerland, June 1992, p. 9.

zation's culture would evolve so that nuclear weapons officers no longer thought of themselves primarily as warriors, but rather primarily as guardians of a highly dangerous technology. Training and education would both emphasize that whenever a trade-off had to be made between readiness and safety—whether in military exercises, transportation of nuclear weapons, or maintenance of weapon systems—individuals should *never* compromise safety even in the slightest in order to increase military readiness.

There are good reasons, however, to suspect that such changes in organizational culture can neither be rapid in implementation nor total in their effects. Changes in organizational culture, for example, are usually the product of prolonged education and gradual personnel turnover. Moreover, a primary mission of the Strategic Command will continue to be the maintenance of nuclear deterrence in the post–Cold War world. Some tension between the goals of nuclear safety and nuclear readiness will be unavoidable. Finally, military officers in the Strategic Command will continue to rotate in and out of different military commands during their careers and will therefore serve in conventional war planning and combat positions, as well as in the Strategic Command. During his career, for example, a bomber pilot would be trained and indoctrinated into the traditional warrior's culture, taking risks when necessary to complete the mission, as a member of the Air Combat Command; yet he would have to be trained never to take risks that can compromise safety when serving as a guardian of the arsenal at Strategic Command. It may be barely possible for the U.S. Air Force to maintain two separate cultures in two separate command organizations; but it is hard to imagine individuals transferring between them without some tensions existing.

It would also be useful to have more training and exercises devoted solely to preventing accidents with nuclear weapons. One could imagine, for example, a military exercise in the post–Cold War world that was devoted to preventing an unauthorized launch of a SLBM or responding to a false warning of a massive nuclear attack. While that is imaginable, it is also highly improbable. Exercises are not just practice sessions for the participants; they are political statements made to inside and outside audiences alike. During the Cold War, for example, U.S. and NATO military exercises underlined our stated policy (which we may or may not have followed) to use nuclear weapons in the event of a major Soviet and Warsaw Pact attack on Western Europe.[47] It may therefore be expecting too much for the U.S. military to conduct extensive exercises in which major nuclear accidents happen; it would cut against the concerted effort to

---

[47] By the end of the Cold War, these exercises reportedly created problems in the NATO alliance, as West Germany and the U.S. disagreed over the targeting of East Germany. See Elizabeth Pond, "War Games Brought NATO Rift into the Open, *Boston Globe*, June 4, 1989, p. 8.

convince the public, and themselves, that such events could not occur.[48] The Defense Department is, after all, responsible for maintaining nuclear deterrence, and therefore has strong disincentives against acknowledging publicly that nuclear weapons are, or have ever been, less than perfectly safe.[49]

## Redundancy Revisited

The final advice, following the logic of high reliability theory, would recommend adding redundant safety devices and warning systems to those that already exist in order to create a more reliable system out of unreliable parts. The degree to which this basic approach to nuclear weapons safety is accepted can be seen in the popularity of proposals to supplement the highly redundant system of Russian and American warning sensors that already exist—multiple radars, infrared satellites, and nuclear detonation detectors—with a fourth type of warning device: small sensors and radio transmitters that could be placed in the other state's missile fields to provide one more check on whether a reported missile launch was real or just a false warning.[50]

[48] U.S. Air Force bomber wings do participate in unpublicized exercises in which nuclear weapons are involved in simulated aircraft accidents, rehearsing the responses to the dispersal of hazardous plutonium. Yet, organizational inhibitions to accepting the possibility of other types of serious nuclear weapons accidents clearly exist. For example, it appears difficult for military forces in the field to accept that an unauthorized seizure of a nuclear weapon could occur. According to an official air force publication: "Recovery planning is the detailed written plan on how to organize and conduct the recovery of special weapons. Department of Defense Manual 5210.41M requires that each unit have a security plan dealing with capture, denial, and recapture. However, *the plans are often shallow, not well organized, hampered in some cases by higher headquarters guidance, and never rehearsed.*" Timothy A. Capron, "Nuclear Weapons Recovery Planning," *USAF Nuclear Surety Journal* 9, no. 2 (1990): 13, (emphasis added) FOIA.

[49] For example, in June 1990 Secretary of Defense Richard Cheney ordered that all Short-Range Attack Missiles (SRAM-A) were to be taken off SAC alert bombers after the directors of U.S. nuclear weapons laboratories told Congress that there was an unacceptable risk of an accident with the weapon. Cheney told the press that "I believe that it is prudent to take this action," but nevertheless felt compelled to add that the weapons had posed "no safety hazard to the public." See R. Jeffrey Smith, "A-Missiles Ordered Off Planes," *Washington Post*, June 9, 1990, p. 1. Also see Melissa Healy, "Cheney Pulls Risky Missiles off Aircraft," *Los Angeles Times*, June 9, 1990, p. 1.

[50] See Frank von Hippel, Roald Sagdeyev, William G. Miller, and Robert S. McNamara, "How to Avoid Accidental Nuclear War," *Bulletin of Atomic Scientists* 46, no. 5 (June 1990): 37, and A. A. Kokoshin, A. V. Menshikov, M. I. Garasev, and M. S. Vinogradov, *Questions of Collaboration between Russia and the USA in the Area of Strategic Defenses* (Moscow: Center of Scientific Research of the Committee of Scientists for Global Security, February 1992), pp. 3–4.

If the normal accidents theory is right, however, there is considerable risk that such warning devices would make the whole system more complex and more opaque, and thereby increase the likelihood of some unforeseen common-mode failure. These devices might help increase the seriousness of false warning incidents, for example, if a single unanticipated event triggered both these devices and another warning system. (Imagine a silo fire in a field triggering both the overhead infrared satellite and the new sensor device.)

The point here is *not* that we should never build backup systems or redundant warning devices. It is that we should not place faith in such efforts. The lesson from this book is that we need to be more conscious of the potential for bizarre, unexpected interactions in complex systems, and therefore be more wary against habitual efforts to improve safety simply by adding more and more redundancy to the system. This is especially true if alternatives are available.

### Complete Nuclear Disarmament

If managing the problem is not likely to prove effective, then the most obvious alternative is to abandon the technology. Complete nuclear disarmament is a policy most often advocated by individuals who are highly pessimistic about the prospects for successful nuclear deterrence; it also, however, has obvious appeal for those who are pessimistic about the ability to maintain reliable nuclear weapons safety.[51] The arguments in favor of this position, and those against it, are exceedingly complex and a whole chapter would be needed to begin to do them justice.[52] This is not the place to enter that debate. Yet since complete disarmament position *appears* to be a natural outcome of any argument stressing that nuclear accidents are inevitable in the long run, I should at least briefly outline the reasons why,

[51] Among the first group are Jonathan Schell, *The Abolition* (New York: Avon, 1984), and Telford B. Taylor, "Go Cold Turkey," *Bulletin of Atomic Scientists* 45, no. 6 (July/August 1989): 26–27. In the second group is Perrow, *Normal Accidents*, pp. 346–347. Although Perrow is optimistic about avoiding accidental wars caused by false warnings, he argues that "there is much to fear from accidents with nuclear weapons such as dropping them or an accidental launch," p. 257.

[52] The best discussions are Charles Glaser, *Analyzing Strategic Nuclear Policy* (Princeton, N.J.: Princeton University Press, 1990), pp. 166–203; James N. Miller, Jr., "Zero and Minimal Nuclear Weapons," in Joseph S. Nye, Jr., Graham T. Allison, and Albert Carnesale, eds., *Fateful Visions: Avoiding Nuclear Catastrophe* (Cambridge, Mass.: Ballinger, 1988), pp. 11–32; Sidney Drell, "Not So Fast," *Bulletin of Atomic Scientists* 45, no. 6 (July/August 1989): 27–29; Lynn Eden, "The End of Nuclear Arms Control," in Regina Cowen Karp, ed., *Security without Nuclear Weapons* (Oxford, U.K.: Oxford University Press, 1992); and Schelling, *Arms and Influence*, pp. 248–259.

despite my pessimism about nuclear safety, I simply do not see complete nuclear disarmament as a feasible option for the foreseeable future.

The arguments are both technical and political. Nuclear weapons are relatively small, and it is difficult to conceive of a way in which any international institution, even if much stronger ones are created in the post–Cold War world, can verify complete disarmament with absolute certainty. If this is the case, sovereign nuclear powers will have strong incentives (even if only because of the inherent uncertainty about whether other states are cheating) to maintain possession of at least some nuclear weapons. Some states, with aggressive ambitions, but currently without nuclear weapons, might even feel greater incentives to acquire them in such a world. In addition, even if political relations between the governments of all nuclear powers improve to the point that they no longer have any *immediate* fears of an enemy attack, *residual* concerns about maintaining deterrence will exist simply because states cannot be certain that friendly governments will remain in power around the world.

Even if there was an international agreement to abolish all existing nuclear weapons, and it was in fact followed, the knowledge of how to build them would remain in the world. In any conventional conflict, states would have very strong incentives to build nuclear weapons, and the first state to get them would have incentives to use them before other states acquired them. It is therefore not even clear whether the likelihood of nuclear war would be increased or decreased if current policies of nuclear deterrence were replaced by complete disarmament.

These are admittedly speculative arguments and, eventually, the international political system may change so fundamentally that good solutions to all such problems can be devised. I certainly hope so, though I am not optimistic on that score. Fortunately, complete disarmament is not the only alternative for producing nuclear safety in the future.

### The Structure of Safety

The logic of the normal accidents argument does *not* necessarily lead to an abolitionist position. It is not the massive destructive power of nuclear weapons that creates the likelihood of an accident. It is the *structure* of the existing nuclear arsenal, an arsenal that displays signs of both high interactive complexity and tight coupling, that produces the risk. If these structural characteristics are the root of the problem, then the root of the solution should be to change the structure of nuclear arsenals.

What would a safer nuclear arsenal look like if it was designed according to the logic of normal accidents theory? The central principle of many recent arms control agreements, to reduce the numbers of weapons, would be deemphasized. Having fewer nuclear weapons could improve safety, since the number of bizarre random events that could produce an unanticipated accident would be reduced, but the key element of a new strategy for safety would be to try to reduce the characteristics of interactive complexity and tight coupling in modern nuclear arsenals.

What distinguishes highly complex high-technology systems is the persistence of unanticipated and often baffling interactions. It should not be surprising, therefore, that it is very difficult to identify the specific dangers, the latent failure modes, that may lie hidden in the current U.S. arsenal. That difficulty is inherent to the problem. Some general principles can nevertheless be applied.

First, as discussed in chapter 1, unanticipated interactions tend to occur in high-technology production systems in which many coordinated actions must take place simultaneously, in which many feed-back loops exist, and in which dangerous components are in close proximity to one another. Apply this concept to the U.S. nuclear weapons system, and a few potential problems can be identified. U.S. military aircraft with nuclear weapons on board should never fly above or near U.S. national warning systems, whether in crises or in peacetime weapons transportation missions. Important components of the U.S. national warning systems should not be co-located with nuclear weapons systems. (For example, the Perimeter Acquisition Radar at Grand Forks, North Dakota, is located on a major nuclear bomber and ICBM base.) Nuclear warheads should never be stored near or at missile testing facilities.[53]

One can also apply this concept to individual nuclear weapons. It is possible, for example, to construct nuclear weapons in which the nuclear materials are kept, in peacetime, entirely separated from their detonation devices. In the post–Cold War world, it is conceivable to return to such simpler and safer weapons designs. For example, Sidney Drell, John Foster, and Charles Townes, in their 1990 congressional report on nuclear weapons safety, recommended research into the designs for such "inherently safe" nuclear warheads in which the plutonium capsules are kept separated from the conventional high explosives.[54]

As was also discussed in chapter 1, tightly coupled systems are distinguished by the inability to recover from individual failures before they

---

[53] According to one press report, the U.S. Navy, Sandia National Laboratories, and Pantex Corporation are developing "tamper-evident seals to help ensure that nuclear weapons have not been reinstalled in denuclearized flight test units." I do not know whether this is an example of imaginative anticipation of a potential accident, or whether it is the result of a weapons incident that has never been publicly reported. See "Industry Observer," *Aviation Week and Space Technology* 136, no. 10 (March 9, 1992): 11.

[54] *Nuclear Weapons Safety*, p. 30.

escalate: no one can figure out what do to, or what they do makes the problem worse, and then disaster strikes. Tightly coupled systems tend to have plans for very rapid reactions. They have time dependent and invariant production processes, little slack, and little opportunity for improvisation once problems occur. Apply this to the nuclear weapons arsenal. Do U.S. ICBMs really require the capability to launch on warning in the post–Cold War world? Should the crews of U.S. nuclear submarines, which are not equipped with electronic PAL locking devices, continue to have the physical capability to launch immediately the SLBMs on board? It is possible to install timers, or other devices that prolong the time necessary for a launch, into U.S. ICBMs and SLBMs. A less complex alternative (and therefore a safer option) would be to remove warheads from the missiles in peacetime. Ultimately, it may be possible to return to the safer nuclear weapons custody system that existed in the late 1940s, in which the U.S. nuclear weapons were stored in special sites under the control of a special civilian agency, to be turned over to the military only at the brink of war.[55] Movement toward such a nonalert nuclear arsenal will take time and would require coordination with other nuclear powers to ensure that activities are mutual and verifiable. The goal, however, is not beyond our reach in the post–Cold War world.

Finally, it is possible to put radio-controlled devices on U.S. missiles that could destroy the missiles in flight, if they were ever launched by accident. It is also possible that the U.S. and Russia will eventually cooperate in building limited ballistic missile defenses to destroy accidental launches.[56] This is not the place to analyze these issues in depth. Each raises a complex set of technical problems, economic costs, and political trade-offs. But clearly such issues need to be considered anew in light of the end of the Cold War. If nuclear warheads are taken off ballistic missiles, however, the need for these other safety mechanisms would be greatly reduced.

The key point is that nuclear weapons are not inherently complex and nuclear arsenals are not inherently tightly coupled. Unfortunately, the weapons and the arsenals we have built, in the name of nuclear deterrence, are. They need not be.

[55] The best analysis of the custodial arrangements for the nuclear weapons stockpile during this period is in Peter Douglas Feaver, *Guarding the Guardians: Civilian Control of Nuclear Weapons in the United States* (Ithaca, N.Y.: Cornell University Press, 1992), pp. 67–148.

[56] On "postlaunch control devices" see Sherman Frankel, "Aborting Unauthorized Launches of Nuclear-armed Ballistic Missiles through Postlaunch Destruction," *Science and Global Security* 2, no. 1 (1990): 1–20. On limited strategic defenses see, Charles L. Glaser, "Nuclear Policy without an Adversary: U.S. Planning for the Post-Soviet Era," *International Security* 16, no. 2 (Spring 1992): 61–74, and Keith B. Payne, *Missile Defense in the 21st Century* (Boulder, Colo.: Westview Press, 1991).

## Operator Error Revisited

A final observation returns to a theme that ran throughout this book: the politics of blame. When a petrochemical plant explodes, a jumbo jet crashes, or an oil tanker runs aground, accident investigators round up the usual suspects: the control room operator, the pilot, or the captain who committed an error. It is extremely misleading, however, to place such a significant emphasis on "operator error" as the cause of most accidents. The safety regulations may have been poorly written, but it is easier for plant management to blame the operator, than to accept responsibility itself for writing incomprehensible rules or having poor review procedures. The cockpit switches may have been poorly designed, but it is cheaper to fire the pilot than it is to redesign the control panel. The captain's task may have required absolute perfection, but the ship's owners want the cargo delivered immediately. "'Operator error' is an easy classification to make," as Perrow puts it in his review of dangerous accidents in mines: "What really is at stake is an inherently dangerous working station where production must keep moving and risk taking is the price of continued employment."[57]

To blame the Strategic Air Command or other military organizations for all of the nuclear weapons safety problems discussed in this book would be a grand-scale version of the same mistake. This is not to ignore that individual operator errors were made. And we should not condone the issuance of misleading reports, the lapses in judgment and imagination, or the loss of discipline, discovered in some of these incidents. Nor should we forget that these organizations have played a major role in creating the military requirements for nuclear deterrence that they then had to meet to maintain the peace for the rest of the nation.

Still, at a fundamental level, it is important to recognize that the military commands controlling U.S. nuclear weapons have been asked to do the impossible. Peter Feaver has used the phrase, the "always/never dilemma" to describe the twin requirements placed on U.S. military commands.[58] Political authorities have demanded, for the sake of deterrence, that the organizations *always* be able and willing to destroy an enormous variety of targets inside the Soviet Union, at a moments notice, under every conceivable circumstance. They have demanded that military commanders *always* be able to execute such attacks at any time of day, 365 days a year. They have demanded that our nuclear forces *always* be effective, regardless of

---

[57] Perrow, *Normal Accidents*, p. 249. Also see E. L. Warren, "Mid-air Collisions: The Accidents, the Systems and the Realpolitik," in Ronald Hurst and Leslie R. Hurst, *Pilot Error: The Human Factors* (New York: Jason Aronson, 1982), pp. 101–118.

[58] Feaver, *Guarding the Guardians*, p. 12.

whether the U.S. struck first or was retaliating after having suffered a catastrophic nuclear attack. And, finally, they demanded that the military, while doing all this, *never* have a serious nuclear weapons accident, *never* have an accidental detonation, and *never* permit the unauthorized use of a weapon to occur.

In retrospect, it should be acknowledged that while the military organizations controlling U.S. nuclear forces during the Cold War performed this task with less success than we knew, they performed with more success than we *should* have reasonably expected. The problems identified in this book were not the product of incompetent organizations. They reflect the inherent limits of organizational safety. Recognition of that simple truth is the first and the most important step toward a safer future.

# Index

Sabotage alarms, 3, 99–100, 153, 189
SAC. *See* Strategic Air Command
Safety rules, 72–73, 82–91; two-man rule, 93–94, 118–19, 219, 223, 250. *See also* Nuclear weapons safety
Safety theory. *See* High reliability theory; Normal accidents theory
SAGE, 125
Salvage-fusing, 188n
Satellites, 6, 131–32, 225
Schecter, Jerrold, 146
Schlesinger, James, 213
Scott, W. Richard, 17
SEAGA, 195–96
Searching for Safety (Wildavsky), 16
Secrecy, 43, 209–10
Secret Intelligence Service (SIS), 146
Selective Employment of Air and Ground Alert (SEAGA), 195–96
Self-destruct mechanisms, 277
Selznick, Philip, 258
Semi-Automatic Ground Environment (SAGE), 125
Senior management. *See* Leadership safety priorities
Short Order network, 163, 173
Short-range tactical nuclear weapons, 10
Simulations, 6, 26, 131, 191–92, 238–39
Single Integrated Operations Plan (SIOP), 59, 72–73, 149, 197
SLBM warning network, 134, 220–21, 225
Socialization, *see* Organizational culture
Software, 6, 130–31, 153, 230–31, 238–39
Soviet Union, 9–10, 66–67, 74, 113–14, 213; B-52 operations response, 165–66, 193, 195; false warning problems, 122, 134n, 140–50 *passim*, 237; intelligence information, 80, 122, 146–50, 215; space program, 118, 134n, 162; U-2 overflights, 135–46 *passim*, 222
Space shuttle, 38
Spain, 63, 178, 188, 202
Special Weapons Emergency Separation System (SWESS), 187–88
Sproull, Lee, 247
Sputnik launch, 118, 162
Standard operating procedures, 23
Stealth fighter, 42–43
Steinbruner, John, 205, 228

Strategic Air Command (SAC), 47, 56–57, 62–77, 91, 154, 213–20, 271–72; bomber accidents, 156–58, 178–93 *passim*, 188, 200–203, 257; communication links, 176–77, 226; culture of reliability, 57, 70, 115; fail-safe system, 163–66, 235, 240; Thule Monitor mission, 65, 172–76, 196–200. *See also* Airborne alert operations
Strategic Command, 271–72
Submarine forces, 63, 214, 255n, 277
Submarine launched ballistic missile (SLBM) warning system, 134, 220–21, 225

Tamuz, Michal, 38, 247
Tennessee Valley Authority, 258
Test launches, 78–80, 117, 127–30, 219–20, 224, 256
Thomasville radar site, 220
Three Mile Island accident, 33
Thule, Greenland: B-52 crash, 156–58, 180–93 *passim*, 200–201, 257; BMEWS station, 119, 162, 170–72; Monitor mission, 65, 172–76, 196–200
Tight coupling, 34–36, 40, 154, 226, 264, 276–77
Time-dependent processes, 34
Training, 24, 56–57, 61, 271–73
Trial-and-error learning, 25–27, 41–43, 205–7. *See also* Organizational learning
Tropospheric-scatter communications, 172
Turkey, 109–11
Two-man rule, 93–94, 118–19, 219, 223, 250

U-2 flight operations, 135–46 *passim*, 222, 246–47
Ukraine, 10
United Kingdom, 63, 111–13, 146
United States Air Forces Europe (USAFE), 104–11
University systems, 35
USS *Iowa*, 208–9
USS *Pueblo*, 137
USS *Vincennes*, 236

Vandenberg Air Force Base, 78–80, 219–20, 224, 256
Van Evera, Stephen, 265–66
Vaughan, Diane, 38